PLACE IN RETURN BOX to remove this checkout from your record.
TO AVOID FINES return on or before date due.

DATE DUE	DATE DUE	DATE DUE
DEC 0 2 2015		

MSU Is An Affirmative Action/Equal Opportunity Institution

c:\circ\datedue.pm3-p.1

The American Judaism of
Mordecai M. Kaplan

REAPPRAISALS IN JEWISH SOCIAL
AND INTELLECTUAL HISTORY

General Editor: Robert M. Seltzer

Martin Buber's Social and Religious Thought:
Alienation and the Quest for Meaning
LAURENCE J. SILBERSTEIN

The American Judaism of Mordecai M. Kaplan
EDITED BY EMANUEL S. GOLDSMITH, MEL SCULT,
AND ROBERT M. SELTZER

The American Judaism of Mordecai M. Kaplan

Edited by
Emanuel S. Goldsmith, Mel Scult,
and Robert M. Seltzer

NEW YORK UNIVERSITY PRESS
NEW YORK & LONDON

To Barbara, Cheryl, and Shirley

Library of Congress Cataloging-in-Publication Data
The American Judism of Mordecai M. Kaplan / edited by Emanuel S.
Goldsmith, Mel Scult, and Robert M. Seltzer.
p. cm. — (Reappraisals in Jewish social and intellectual
history)
Includes bibliographical references.
ISBN 0–8147–3024–8
1. Kaplan, Mordecai Menahem, 1881–1983. 2. Reconstructionist
Judaism. I. Goldsmith, Emanuel S. II. Scult, Mel.
III. Seltzer, Robert M. IV. Series.
BM755.K289A84 1990
296.8′344′092—dc20   90–5953
CIP

New York University Press books are printed on acid-free paper,
and their binding materials are chosen for strength and durability.

Book design by Ken Venezio

7816108

Contents

v

0

Preface

The academic study of Judaica has undergone a remarkable efflorescence in America during the last twenty years. The dream of the pioneers of *Wissenschaft des Judentums* in the early nineteenth century that Judaica would become accepted into the curriculum and research program of great universities has largely come to pass. As the modern study of Jewish history and literature spread east, west, and south of its original German home, the scholarly investigation of Judaica itself became far richer, more varied, and far-reaching. Still encompassing traditional disciplines of philology, literature, theology, biography, and traditional history, the study of the Jewish past and civilizations shows, since the late nineteenth century, the powerful impact of the perspectives and methodologies of the social sciences—sociology, economics, anthropology, and psychology—as well as new trends in social thought and literary criticism. A far more complex map of the Jewish heritage has emerged. Simplistic understandings of what was normative and what was nonconformist have given way to a more objective and more sensitive appreciation of historic Jewish subcultures, of intellectual and social tensions and cycles within the Jewish people, and of dissident and marginal forms of Judaism.

Equally important has been the astonishing and often traumatic history of the Jews since the first appearance of *Wissenschaft des Judentums* (the scholarly reconstruction of the Jewish past). In the 1820s the modern odyssey of the Jewish people and the Jewish tradition had barely commenced—indeed, the modern age (better, the sequence of modern ages) had just begun. More than a century and a half later, the academic study of Judaica includes not only ancient and medieval texts, practices, beliefs, and institutions but the dialectic of two centuries of modern challenges and responses: ideological replies to liberalism, conservatism, anti-Semitism, and socialism; institutional reactions to the pressures of acculturation and assimilation; social reconstruction after the experience of migration, economic dislocation, and attempted genocide; and secular and spiritual reactions to the vast technological and scientific changes occurring since the industrial revolution. The careful study of all these phenomena and more is indispensable for an adequate grasp of contemporary Jewish postures and mentalities. And modern Jewish studies has proven to be of immense value in the comparative study of traditional and modern ethnic and religious groups everywhere on the globe.

This series, *Reappraisals in Jewish Social and Intellectual History*, seeks to contribute to the further growth and clarification of Jewish studies, especially in the early modern and modern periods, through a dedication to two tasks. First, the books included will deal with topics that at one time were high on the agenda of Jewish research and now can be subjected to fresh appraisal in the light of newly discovered data or newly developed explanatory models. There are individuals, events, and movements whose exemplary significance are illuminated through concepts and methodologies developed since the classical presentation or the authoritative treatment of the subject. Second, the series is intended to facilitate the reappraisal of topics in a broad comparative perspective. Works included will articulate the reciprocal influences and parallel developments that clarify the interrelationship of Jewish history and thought and the general context and that further integrate Jewish studies into the contemporary academy.

Some publications in *Reappraisals in Jewish Social and Intellectual History* will be diachronic, tracing development through time; others will be synchronic, cutting across the temporal process to look for new patterns of interrelationship. In common will be a bridging of the gap between highly specialized studies directed primarily to scholars working in the area and popular accounts for the general public through an up-to-date, fresh synthesis for students, teachers, scholars, and laypeople struggling to keep abreast of current knowledge. Some works will be collections of studies by groups of scholars who have met together in a preliminary conference for the initial phases of the development of the theme. Others will be monographs by an individual scholar on a subject of intense interest to him or her for a number of years.

The publication of this volume of essays on Mordecai M. Kaplan, who dominated so much of non-Orthodox American Jewish intellectual life for so many years, is especially appropriate for this series. The authors of these essays have approached Kaplan from many perspectives, asking a wide variety of different questions that add new depth to our knowledge of his personal development and remarkably consistent point of view. Together, these essays constitute a mosaic portrait of a representative twentieth-century figure in American religion who symbolizes (and affected) the transformation of American Jewry in the crucial decades when it came of age as one of the great historic centers of the Jewish diaspora.

ROBERT M. SELTZER

Acknowledgments

The idea for a book evaluating Kaplan's thought and laying the groundwork for a new assessment of his importance emerged from the conference entitled Mordecai M. Kaplan: A Reappraisal, organized by the editors for the Joseph and Ceil Mazer Institute for Research and Advanced Study in Judaica of the Graduate School and University Center of the City University of New York and held on April 9 and 10, 1986. Earlier versions of some of the essays were delivered at that conference, but most were written subsequently for this book.

The Mazer Institute, directed by Robert M. Seltzer, is a constituent of the Center for Jewish Studies of the CUNY Graduate School. The institute sponsors lectures and conferences on various aspects of Jewish history and ideas with the aim of shedding new light on major Jewish figures, issues, and movements. The present volume is part of its publication series.

The editors are grateful to the following individuals for their support of the 1986 conference: Martin Abelove, Frances and Daniel M. Berley, Bess and Roy Berlin, Adele and Samuel Blumenthal, Sidney I. Feiner, Suzette and Harold S. Kushner, Mimi and Charles D. Lieber, Evelyn and Benjamin Wm. Mehlman, and Kay and Jack Wolofsky. In addition, Mr. and Mrs. Wolofsky supported research for the preparation of this book, and the Reconstructionist Press generously granted us permission to quote from the works of Mordecai M. Kaplan.

Contributors

REBECCA TRACHTENBERG ALPERT was born in Brooklyn, New York. She currently serves as director of the adult program of Temple University. She is a former dean of students of the Reconstructionist Rabbinical College. She coauthored *Exploring Judaism: A Reconstructionist Approach* and has lectured and published widely on the subjects of Jewish feminism, medical ethics, and American Jewish history.

The late MEIR BEN-HORIN was a professor of education and chairman of the Division of Education of Dropsie University and served as managing editor of *Jewish Social Studies*. He was coeditor of *Studies and Essays in Honor of Abraham A. Neuman* and *Judaism and the Jewish School*. His publications include *Max Nordau: Philosopher of Human Solidarity*, *Common Faith—Uncommon People*, and many essays on Mordecai Kaplan.

S. DANIEL BRESLAUER is a professor of religion at the University of Kansas. He is the author of *Covenant and Community in Modern Judaism*, *Contemporary Jewish Ethics*, *Modern Jewish Morality*, and *The Ecumenical Perspective and the Modernization of Jewish Religion*. His essays have appeared in *Judaism*, *Conservative Judaism*, and the *Reconstructionist*.

JACK J. COHEN, a retired director of the B'nai B'rith Hillel Foundations in Israel, taught philosophy of religion at the Jewish Theological Seminary, the Hebrew University of Jerusalem, and the David Yellin College of Education in Jerusalem. He also served as rabbi of the Society for the Advancement of Judaism and as director of the Jewish Reconstructionist Foundation. Among his publications are *The Case for Religious Naturalism, Jewish Education in Democratic Society,* and *The Reunion of Isaac and Ishmael.*

WILLIAM CUTTER is a professor of education and modern Hebrew literature at the Hebrew Union College–Jewish Institute of Religion in Los Angeles and was a founding director of the Rhea Hirsch School of Education there. He has authored numerous articles and papers on modern Hebrew writers, literary criticism, and educational theory.

IRA EISENSTEIN is president emeritus of the Reconstructionist Rabbinical College and editor emeritus of *Reconstructionist* magazine. He coedited the *New Haggadah,* the *Sabbath Prayer Book,* and the *High Holiday Prayer Book.*

HARRIET A. FEINER recently retired as a professor of social work at the Wurzweiler School of Social Work of Yeshiva University. She has published articles in *Social Casework, Affilia: The Journal of Women and Social Work,* and *Reconstructionist* magazine and has developed a program of mutual support networks for Reconstructionist congregations in New York City and throughout the country.

EMANUEL S. GOLDSMITH is an associate professor of Yiddish language and literature and Jewish studies at Queens College of the City University of New York, rabbi of Temple Adas-Hadrath Israel in Hyde Park, Massachusetts, and author of *Modern Yiddish Culture: The Story of the Yiddish Language Movement* and *Modern Trends in Jewish Religion.* With Mel Scult, he coedited *Dynamic Judaism: The Essential Writings of Mordecai M. Kaplan.* His articles on Jewish literature and thought have appeared in the *Jewish Book Annual, Judaism, Conservative Judaism, Journal of Reform Judaism, Reconstructionist, Midstream, Forum, Jewish Frontier, Yiddish, Migvan: Studies in Hebrew Literature, Reflections of the Holocaust in Art and Literature,* and *American Journal of Theology and Philosophy.*

WILLIAM E. KAUFMAN is rabbi of Temple Beth El in Fall River, Massachusetts. He is also a visiting lecturer in philosophy at Rhode Island College and the author of *Contemporary Jewish Philosophies* and *Journeys: An Introductory Guide to Jewish Mysticism.*

CAROLE S. KESSNER is a professor of comparative literature and Judaic studies at the State University of New York at Stony Brook and serves as a book review editor for *Reconstructionist* magazine. She has published numerous articles on Jewish literature and on women's studies and is writing a biography of Marie Syrkin.

ALLAN LAZAROFF is rabbi of Congregation Mikveh Israel in Philadelphia. He has taught at Temple University, Boston University, and the University of Toronto. A recipient of National Endowment for the Humanities and Dewey fellowships, he is the author of *The Theology of Abraham Bibago* and of scholarly articles on medieval Jewish philosophy and modern religious thought.

RICHARD LIBOWITZ is rabbi of Congregation Ner Tamid of Delaware County in Springfield, Pennsylvania. He is also a lecturer in theology at Saint Joseph's University and serves as education director of the Anne Frank Institute of Philadelphia. His writings include *Mordecai M. Kaplan and the Development of Reconstructionism, Faith and Freedom: In Honor of Franklin H. Littell*, and *Methodology in the Academic Teaching of the Holocaust.*

SIMON NOVECK is the author of *Milton Steinberg: Portrait of a Rabbi* and the editor of the B'nai B'rith series of volumes on great Jewish personalities and thinkers. He has taught Jewish history and philosophy at Brooklyn College and the Hartford Seminary Foundation and political and social philosophy at the City College of the City of New York. He is currently rabbi of Congregation Mevakshe Derekh of Scarsdale, New York.

HAROLD M. SCHULWEIS is rabbi of Valley Beth Shalom Congregation in Encino, California. He contributes regularly to numerous Jewish journals and is the author of *Evil and Morality of God* and coeditor of *Approaches to the Philosophy of Religion.*

ELIEZER SCHWEID is a professor of modern Jewish thougth at the Hebrew University in Jerusalem. His numerous publications in Hebrew include *A History of Jewish Thought in Modern Times, Judaism and Secular Culture, Democracy and Halakhah,* and *The Cycle of Appointed Times.* His books that have appeared in English incude *The Land of Israel, Israel at the Crossroads,* and *Mysticism and Judaism According to Gershom G. Scholem.*

MEL SCULT is a professor of Jewish thought at Brooklyn College. His essays have appeared in *Judaism, Modern Judaism, American Jewish History,* and the *Reconstructionist.* With Emanuel S. Goldsmith, he is coeditor of *Dynamic Judaism: The Essential Writings of Mordecai M. Kaplan.* He is the author of a forthcoming biography of Kaplan to be published by Wayne State University Press and is editor-in-chief of the *Kaplan Diary* project.

ROBERT M. SELTZER is a professor of history at Hunter College and the Graduate School of The City University of New York, chairman of the Hunter Jewish Social Studies Program, director of the Joseph and Ceil Mazer Institute for Research and Advanced Study in Judaica at the CUNY Graduate School, an editor of the *Encyclopedia of Religion,* and the author of *Jewish People, Jewish Thought* and of studies on eastern European Jewry.

BAILA ROUND SHARGEL is an intellectual and social historian who is currently assistant dean of the Graduate School and coordinator of the summer school program of the Jewish Theological Seminary. Her articles have been published in *Judaism, Conservative Judaism, Shofar, American Jewish History, The Encyclopedia of Jewish-American History and Culture,* and the *Jewish Spectator.* Dr. Shargel is the author of *Practical Dreamer: Israel Friedlaender and the Shaping of American Judaism.*

JACOB J. STAUB is dean of the Reconstructionist Rabbinical College and author of *The Creation of the World According to Gersonides.* He coauthored *Exploring Judaism: A Reconstructionist Approach* and coedited *Creative Jewish Education: A Reconstructionist Perspective.*

Kaplan and Jewish Modernity

Robert M. Seltzer

Does "modernity" designate a distinct and novel stage in the history of Judaism? Mordecai M. Kaplan, the foremost advocate of the intentional modernization of Judaism in twentieth-century America, would certainly concur. Dedicated to the survival of the Jewish people and confident of the abiding value of religion, Kaplan had no doubts concerning the extent of intellectual progress and the degree of social betterment since Copernicus, Newton, and Darwin and since the American and French revolutions. An unremitting sequence of intellectual, political, and social breakthroughs, however, meant that contemporary Jewry faced challenges far beyond any that ancient or medieval Judaism could have anticipated. (In the first essay of this volume, Emanuel S. Goldsmith proposes that Kaplan's thought indicates the durability of the *Haskalah*, the eighteenth- and nineteenth-century Jewish Enlightenment, in the twentieth century as well.) Because Kaplan is the outstanding modernist in the intellectual history of American Judaism, a volume devoted to the context and content of Kaplanism should begin by asking why the hackneyed notion of modernity remains an indispensable key to recent Jewish history.

It was Kaplan, of course, who introduced into Jewish discourse the appellation "civilization" to convey the cultural weight, distinctive style, and historical importance of Judaism. Civilization encapsulated the organic totality of human consciousness and social structure: history, literature, language, folklore, family and group relations, ethical sanctions, esthetic values, spiritual ideals, and so forth. With the hindsight of two hundred years experience with Jewish adjustment to modern conditions, it would seem that the crisis of Jewish civilizational continuity revolves around two crucial elements: the modern relevance of peoplehood and of religion. The dual hallmarks of the modern era in Jewish history are the search for a substitute for the old Jewish legal and social autonomy and a defense of the truthfulness of the Jewish worldview of the Bible and the rabbinic texts in light of modern science and historiography.

Various as were the features of the premodern Jewish polity, from ancient commonwealths to early modern *kehillot*, the *ancien régime* provided Jews (most of the time) with a common address vis-à-vis the gentile powers and with communal institutions that were usually able to enforce cohesion and discipline. The line to modernity was crossed when gentile governments undertook to integrate the Jews into civil society, affording a far greater degree of access to the general economic and social order but, in the process, disassembling the tried-and-tested framework of the Jewish collectivity. The survival of the Jewish people (the preservation of Judaism seems impossible without some corporate structure, as Kaplan reiterated) required reconstruction of communal institutions according to the new limitations and possibilities available since the great modern revolutions: a reorganized *Gemeinde* here, a consistory there, a federation of philanthropies and a conference of presidents of major Jewish organizations elsewhere, a program for legal recognition as a nationality in a multinational empire, or a maximalist renewal as a nation-state through the Zionist movement. The multiplicity of efforts bespeaks a desire to rescue as much coherence as possible for Jewry in each circumstance—and the difficulties of doing so.

The dilemmas posed by modern science to Judaism since the eighteenth century provoked a parallel crisis of a different nature, stemming from novel conceptions of the structure and working of the physical universe allied with epistemologies that, in turn, generated new conceptions of the texture and significance of history and of the psychosocial components of human nature. One modern definition of enlightenment after another (those of Voltaire, Less-ing, Kant, Mill, and so forth) and a series of scientific positivisms alternated with a sequence of Romanticisms and fideisms as modern Jews (and Christians) searched for a dependable foundation for religious faith and ultimate value in the gigantic and seemingly impersonal cosmos depicted by modern science.

Even though Judaism has been tested repeatedly by social and political change and intellectual ferment in the three millennia of its history, and even though the challenges of the last two centuries have been unprecedented in degree and extent, is not the very concept of *modernity* too vague, equivocal, and open-ended to retain its usefulness? Is it not merely a catchall for a mutating sequence of circumstances and issues—a moving target at which Jewish ideologists and theologians valiantly but futilely aim their proposals? Judaism has confronted seven or eight modernities, perhaps more. The modernity to which Jewish intellectuals responded at the end of the nineteenth century with the classical Zionist and Jewish Socialist ideologies was virtually antithetical to the modernity confronted by German Reform Jews and their Jewish critics in the 1830s and 1840s or by American Reform Jews and *their* Jewish critics in the 1870s and 1880s. The "postmodern" Judaism formulated in Europe in the second and third decades of the twentieth century may be linked via the writings of Rosenzweig, Buber, and others to the "postmodern" Judaism that emerged in America by the 1960s and 1970s, but these are quite different concatenations because of the dissimilar possibilities and resonances of their respective times and places. The modernity of the *yishuv* from the 1920s to the 1960s seems increasingly remote, even old-fashioned, in light of the new tone and social dynamics of post-Begin Israel. If we define Kaplan's place in Jewish intellectual history by his enthusiastic appreciation of the benefits of modernity as such, we must ask to which modernity was Kaplan responding?

Kaplan enjoyed a remarkably productive career during his life span of 102 years—one of the longest stretches of intellectual creativity and active involvement in Jewish affairs of any recent Jewish leader. But the heart of his subjective time and place was America from the Progressive Era to the New Deal: the buoyant industrial America of twentieth-century liberalism and pragmatic meliorism, the daring

America of the theoreticians of cultural pluralism, the Sinclair Lewis–influenced America of the anti-Fundamentalist higher criticism of the Bible, and the search by Henry Nelson Wieman and other liberal religionists for a religious humanism based on the insights of social science. With due allowance for the slow gestation of Kaplan's mature position and the long duration of his direct influence, Kaplanism is located most easily in the years from the closing of mass Jewish immigration to America in the mid-1920s to the post–World War II shift in American culture and Jewish orientation toward new preoccupations and styles. The pivot was the publication of *Judaism as a Civilization* in 1934, the first and still the most famous of his books.

Unlike many Jewish religious intellectuals who came to America when they were older, Kaplan did not emigrate after being fully formed by the Old World setting. However, he did retain an intimate rootedness in an observant and ethnically rich Jewishness maintained by large numbers of eastern European immigrants. Born in 1881 in the Lithuanian region of the tsarist Pale of Settlement, Kaplan was brought to America in 1889 and grew up in turn-of-the-century New York City. Young Mordecai's father was a traditional but broad-minded rabbi. He saw that his son was given substantial training in Jewish texts, with the intention that he too would become a rabbi. (Kaplan's early family setting is described in some detail in Carole Kessner's essay in this volume.)

Throughout his life Kaplan retained the basic optimism and self-confidence of so many of the freethinking intellectuals of the late Victorian era. He received a solid secular education at City College of New York and Columbia University, where he studied with an eminent faculty during the heyday of the application of the evolutionary theory to every sort of tradition and social institution. (An extensive discussion of this late-nineteenth-century evolutionary approach appears in Simon Noveck's essay.) Shaped by this milieu, Kaplan's critical rationalism was sociological, empirical, and pragmatic—decidedly not the individualistic, historicist, idealist rationalism of the critically minded German Jews of two generations earlier, nor the militantly materialistic positivism of radical Russian Jewish youth. Kaplan's beliefs are sometimes treated as a fusion of ideas from Matthew Arnold, Émile Durkheim, William James,

John Dewey, and Ahad Ha-Am. Mel Scult, a coeditor of this volume and Kaplan's preeminent biographer, indicates that Kaplan frequently read the works of these and other "obvious" influences on him long after he had formulated his own position and that the origins of his affinity with Durkheim and Dewey lie in the less well-remembered teachers with whom he studied at Columbia University and the books they recommended. Allan Lazaroff, who writes in this volume of the similarities and differences in the approaches to religion of Dewey and Kaplan, notes that "most early twentieth-century reformers were Deweyites before they read Dewey." In a similar vein, Eliezer Schweid, Meir Ben-Horin, and Baila Shargel discuss the extent and limits of Kaplan's indebtedness to the great Zionist essayist Ahad Ha-Am.

Kaplan's Jewish upbringing was so integrally a part of his identity that there was no question of his preparing for rabbinic ordination. He did not throw off the mantle of the congregational rabbi even after becoming an academic administrator and professor. (Mel Scult discloses that Kaplan once confided in his journal an urge to escape the rabbinate by becoming a businessman—but only for a few days.) Gradually formulating his critical standpoint, Kaplan defined his Jewish adversaries as those who adhered to a rigid, bemused Orthodoxy that had not recognized that Jews were living in a temporal, as well as a physical, New World and those who followed a rigid, pompous Reform Judaism that idealized Judaism as a philosophical society, the goal of which was to spread a denationalized but not totally denaturalized ethical monotheism to the world. Kaplan was quite aware of possibilities beyond the pale of Judaism, such as the de-Judaized universalism of his teacher Felix Adler, a former Reform rabbi and founder of the Ethical Culture movement, or early twentieth-century American Catholicism (whose particularistic cohesion and social discipline he rather admired).

The Jewish Theological Seminary of America, under the aegis of Solomon Schechter, Cyrus Adler, and Louis Finkelstein, provided Kaplan with suitable teaching and administrative positions that enabled him to attract congenial students and disciples during the five decades he was principal and then dean of the Teacher's Institute (to 1945) and professor of midrash, homiletics, and philosophies of religion. (He formally retired in 1963.) Unlike the Orthodox *yeshivot*, the Conservative seminary was from its inception committed to the scientific study of a Jewish tradition evolving through history (although Seminary authorities frowned on the critical treatment of the Pentateuch, as Mel Scult points out in his essay on Kaplan and the Bible). Also, the Conservative movement's philosophy placed great emphasis on the unity of the Jewish people and the need to provide a substantial Jewish education for their children. Despite these affinities, there were tensions during Kaplan's tenure at the Seminary. (For example, his ambivalent friendship with his colleague Israel Friedlaender is described by Baila Shargel, and his testy relationship with Cyrus Adler, a long-time president of the Jewish Theological Seminary, is discussed in Richard Libowitz's essay.)

The same Conservative movement that provided him with a hospitable setting for the articulation of his ideas, in the long run rejected Kaplanism as its official left wing. One of the untried paths of Kaplan's life was his turning down the invitation by Stephen Wise in the 1920s to become head of the Jewish Institute of Religion, thus postponing the emergence of a rabbinical seminary shaped by the Kaplanian approach for almost half a century. (Details of Kaplan's toying with resignation from the Jewish Theological Seminary are recounted in Richard Libowitz's essay.) The lively Morningside Heights environment that contained Columbia University and the Union Theological Seminary, as well as Kaplan's series of Manhattan synagogues (Kehilath Jeshurun on East Eighty-sixth Street until 1909, the Jewish Center on West Eighty-sixth Street from 1918 to 1922, and the Society for the Advancement of Judaism two blocks eastward on West Eighty-sixth Street after 1922) provided ample opportunity for him to play the dual role of thinker and doer. From 1935 on, *Reconstructionist* magazine became the means for spreading his ideas to Jewish leaders, including many Reform rabbis, throughout the United States. The much-abused term *ideologist* is still useful to designate a social theorist who does not consider himself *only* a thinker, for, as Karl Marx said of Ludwig Feuerbach, "the philosophers have only interpreted the world, in various ways; the point, however, is to change it."[1] (Baila Shargel and Emanuel Goldsmith both indicate that, unlike many Jewish modernists, Kaplan did not champion pure *Wissenschaft des Judentums* as an end in itself and expressed some irritation with academicians completely immersed in the minutiae of historical analysis.) Kaplan believed that understanding leads to praxis. He was an ideologist also in the sense that praxis had to be underpinned by solid theory. The concern for unity of theory and practice was one of Kaplan's most salient features.

Kaplan's willingness to take a chance on new definitions of Jewishness—to follow where critical, pragmatic reasoning led—resulted in his compulsion to address in the most serious, painstaking fashion an exceptionally wide range of topics and issues. Kaplan directed his attention to theology and philosophy on an exceptionally high level for a rabbi. (The present volume contains critiques of theological and philosophical themes in Kaplan's writings by Eliezer Schweid, Harold M. Schulweis, William E. Kaufman, and Jacob Staub, as well as comparisons of Kaplan's thought with that of noted thinkers of his time by Simon Noveck, Allan Lazaroff, Emanuel S. Goldsmith, and S. Daniel Breslauer.) Kaplan engaged in biblical studies and interpretation and was an accomplished preacher who left a large body of unpublished sermons. (Some of these sermons are discussed in Mel Scult's essay on Kaplan's biblical exegesis. And, as Rebecca Alpert relates, he addressed issues of social justice as one of the most publicly involved pulpit rabbis of his time.) Kaplan produced solid pieces on Jewish ethics. (In 1936 the Jewish Publication Society published Kaplan's translation of Moses Hayyim Luzzatto's *Mesillat Yesharim*; in 1949 he contributed a study on the philosophy of Jewish ethics to Louis Finkelstein's encyclopedic collection, *The Jews: Their History, Culture, and Religion*.) He guided a revision of the liturgy for the Society for the Advancement of Judaism and the Reconstructionist Foundation that provoked more recent efforts by the Reform and Conservative movements. (Kaplan's involvement in the formulation of a new Haggadah and a series of new prayer books and meditative anthologies is discussed by Ira Eisenstein; his views on the role of women in the synagogue are discussed in Carole Kessner's essay.) Kaplan's involvement and influence on American Jewish life was multifaceted: He sought to define a nondenominational American civil religion that was suitable for Jews. He wrote on the nature and future of the Zionist movement (as Jack J. Cohen discusses in his essay). He had considerable impact on an influential circle of Jewish educators (as William Cutter explores). He was a presence in the nascent field of Jewish social work (as Harriet Feiner indicates). He proposed a blueprint for a new global Jewish covenant to clarify Jewry's status as a "transnational" people (described by S. Daniel Breslauer). In addition to all this, Kaplan was a consummate diarist, and his twenty-five handwritten accountant-type journals of daily notes constitute a major chronicle of American Jewish history of his time. In our era of professional specialization, one would long hesitate before writing so extensively on such a plentitude of topics, all of which were on Kaplan's agenda of rethinking fundamentals and clarifying interconnections.

Even more significant is that Kaplan's views on faith and on community complement each other so well. A few comments on his theology and his sociology are in order as prologue to the more extended treatments in this volume.

Kaplan's functionalist emphasis seems to be a radical departure from the classic theological method (he emphasized this disjunction in his book-length critique of Hermann Cohen, *The Purpose and Meaning of Jewish Existence* [1964]). But his appropriation of pragmatism was another instance of the time-honored Jewish practice of using the philosophies of the age to pour new wine into old vessels. What Jewish philosophy had always tended to do (in contrast to the less critical Midrash and Kabbalah) was to render intelligible certain Jewish symbols that seemed to be losing their rational referents—not *all* Jewish symbols, since philosophy remains critical as well as creative. The pragmatism formulated by C. S. Peirce and William James may have enabled Kaplan to render personally applicable to twentieth-century, urban, college-educated American Jews some precious Jewish rubrics, but it was a firm rule of Kaplan's that what was obsolete should be expunged. A prime instance of a notion he could endow with new relevance was his redefinition of salvation as self-fulfillment rather than beatitude. Salvation to him was an enriched, completed life in this world rather than a compensatory, second life in the hereafter. For Kaplan, yearning for salvation was one of the key elements that distinguishes the human from the subhuman and endows human life with meaningfulness. Indeed, the modern confusion in values could be alleviated only with the emergence of a normative science, which he labeled "soterics," which would go beyond sociology and psychology as usually understood. For Kaplan, a humanly authentic concept of salvation was to be based on the rational analysis of realistic human needs and how they could be gratified, on an appreciation of the relations of means to ends ("technics"), and on a scale of spiritual values that was ultimately religious. (Kaplan's "soterics" is explicated at length in Harold M. Schulweis's essay, and his concept of salvation is discussed in many of the other essays in this volume.)

A characteristic of Kaplan's mentality was that he would not allow himself to avoid the difficulties of offering a coherent account of what a Jewish principle meant literally, where another rabbi would have recourse too quickly to symbolic or poetic homilies. No defensive apologetics, no beautiful writing, no casuistic elegance or hints of mythic profundities allowed one to avoid facing facts, especially to ignore what a certain idea plainly meant to *amkha*, to ordinary Jews. A conspicuous instance was Kaplan's lifelong aversion to the concept of miracle as an alleged suspension of a scientific law. Another more controversial example is his blanket rejection of the hallowed notion that the Jews are God's chosen people, which led, as Ira Eisenstein shows, to Kaplan's fierce determination to purge all traces of this formula from the liturgy. (Copies of Kaplan's Reconstructionist *Sabbath Prayer Book* were publicly burned in 1945 in New York City, and a ban was issued against him by some Orthodox rabbis.) For Kaplan, no subtle reinterpretation of the chosenness of the people of Israel erased its taint of superiority; any implication of such superiority was antithetical to the democratic ideal that he steadfastly sought to have recognized in Judaism. The only acceptable substitute was a "vocation" that any people can assume by devoting itself to universal values and ethical nationhood, a thoroughly democratic vocation inasmuch as all nations possess the potential to contribute to the richness of human life on earth.

Kaplan thought he could save the truthfulness of Jewish theology by switching from the metaphysical to the functional—that is, from a theology of spiritual agents to one of spiritual attributes. (Whether Kaplan actually avoided metaphysics so conveniently is

disputed in the essays by William E. Kaufman and Jacob Staub.)
Kaplan's procedure might be called a pragmatic hermeneutics of
religiosity or a functionalist demythologizing—that is, the investigation of the soteric purposes, sometimes subconscious, served by
religious ideas and practices. His hermeneutics was designed as a
method for answering the questions, Which of those purposes maintain their abiding value for modern Jews and How do they promote
self-fulfillment and moral worth?

Certainly the most controversial aspect of Kaplan's theology among
religious Jews of all denominations was his antianthropomorphic,
antisupernaturalistic divinity—attributing divine status only to those
natural forces (which include human nature) that promoted goodness. In a characteristically functionalist inversion, for Kaplan faith
in God was the conviction that the natural order is so constituted
that human beings have the potential to achieve this-worldly salvation. His critique of traditional theology was based, first, on the
principle that every "God-idea" is replete with historical elements.
Because God is "correlative" (a term Kaplan borrowed from Hermann Cohen) to the idea of humanity, the God-idea of an age is
closely tied to a people's self-understanding and its understanding
of the world. Second, considered pragmatically, faith in God stems
not solely from the intellect but also from the more primal level of
the subconscious human drive for meaning. Third, divinity is to be
understood functionally and naturalistically as a "supra-factual,"
"trans-natural" dimension that facilitates a sense of the worthwhileness of life, the urgency of moral responsibility, and the
achievement of ethical reciprocity. In one of Kaplan's often quoted
and infuriatingly problematic formulations, "God is the sum of the
animating, organizing forces and relationships which are forever
making a cosmos out of chaos."[2] Divinity is the supreme integrating
factor—one might say the gravitational force—that enables reality
to produce organic wholes greater than the sum of their parts and
that empowers these organic wholes, in their human manifestations, to fulfill the highest demands of conscience.

The difficulties in relating an immanentist divine actuality to
the unified, commanding divinity of biblical revelation and Jewish
prayer have often been pointed out by Kaplan's theological opponents, especially in relation to the venerable theological problems

of theodicy. How can Kaplan reconcile his assumption that his God is truly monotheistic, considering that there are so many manifestations of evil in the world and so few of salvation? For Kaplan, this is not as burning a problem as it was to Jewish thinkers earlier and later because for him evil was not a positive category but (as in certain other Jewish theologies) the profane waiting to be hallowed. (Kaplan's attitude to evil is discussed in Simon Noveck's essay in juxtaposition with that of Milton Steinberg, who was at the same time one of Kaplan's most sympathetic and severest critics.) Kaplan's remarks on the divine are susceptible to development in a number of directions: Does Kaplan conceive of a limited God that operates as a benign element within a pluralistic reality (like William James's)? Or, does he conceive of a panentheistic God that is the mind for which the universe is the body (like Hartshorne's), an aspect of human interaction (like Wieman's), or an emergent deity who inheres in the unfolding process of cosmic evolution yet transcends it (like Whitehead's)? Kaplan himself never pushed these ideas as a professional philosopher would. But Kaplan was not a professional philosopher. Despite his prosaic style, he was a theological visionary. To call such an unpoetic, perhaps rather leaden author a visionary might seem inappropriate, but it indicates that his image of what Jewish theology should fulfill is perhaps far more important than the specific formulations he articulated.

What may turn out to be the most generative aspect of Kaplan's theology was his pointing the way to a modern Jewish natural philosophy akin to the process theology developed by Charles Hartshorne, John B. Cobb, and Schubert Ogden. (In his essay in this volume, Jacob Staub develops some of the ways in which Kaplan's approach contrasts with process theology.) Kaplan had neither the inclination nor the technical tools to develop a Jewish process theology out of his religious naturalism (or, as he preferred, "transnaturalism"). But his ample suggestions that Jewish values must be grounded not only in the existential angst of pure faith but also in the hard evidence of nature and in a neoclassical form of reason indicate the direction in which a modern (or post-postmodern) Kaplanian Jewish theology should move. Such a theology would be rooted in Maimonidean rationalism and would look to the possible implications of microbiology, communications theory, particle physics, astrocosmology, and other revelations of twentieth-century science.

Even where Kaplan's pragmatic hermeneutics seems excessively matter-of-fact (to be sure, according to the collective temperament of a later generation more tolerant of the mysteriously poetic and less impressed with the often graceless methodology of social science), his ideas are stimulating and generative beyond what he himself said in so many words. Kaplan's prosaic literalism does not result from a lack of a poetical streak, which he kept under lock and key. To be sure, this disposition does shine through occasionally (for example in the original liturgical poetry Ira Eisenstein cites). Kaplan's literalism, a characteristic of the particular American modernity he inhabited, is also related to a certain quality of "principledness," which eastern European Jewish intellectuals of the late nineteenth and early twentieth centuries had, sometimes in excess. That is, that one's principles meant that one could not affirm—especially not utter during worship—that which could not be maintained in one's heart of hearts. Unlike secularist eastern European Jewish intellectuals who were often distinctly uncomfortable with any religious formula or ceremony, Kaplan the rabbi fully appreciated the positive side of religion. Among the reasons why he was religious and they were not was the relative strength of liberal religious thinking in America, in contrast to the reactionary reputation of religion in early twentieth-century eastern Europe. (There may have been differences of temperament between Kaplan and the eastern European agnostics at work as well, rooted in Kaplan's specific relationship with his father and mother.)

It is Kaplan's sociology and his insistence that peoplehood is the primary category of Judaism and certainly not his liberal religiosity that was the main point of contact between him and eastern European ideologists. The closest parallel to Kaplanism among the eastern European spokesmen of Jewish nationalism was not Ahad Ha-Am's cultural Zionism but Simon Dubnow's autonomism. Except for a radically different evaluation of Zionism, Kaplan could be considered the Americanizer of Dubnovism—the ideology of Jewish cultural rights in the Diaspora.[3] For both Kaplan and Dubnow, the sociological and cultural dynamics of Diaspora peoplehood were fundamental. Kaplan was a Zionist (Dubnow was not), but Kaplan was a Diaspora Zionist. Like Dubnow, he was an "affirmer of the *galut*," a believer in the possibility of creative Jewish survival in the diaspora. Kaplan's famous definition of Judaism as "the evolving religious civilization of the Jewish people"[4] accords (except for the crucial word *religious*) with Dubnow's conception of Judaism as the evolving culture of a world Jewish people held together by loyalties, historic values, and a national will-to-survive that enables the Jewish people to devise novel institutions adjusted to every benign geographical and social milieu. To be sure, for Kaplan the term *civilization* had the special edge that Judaism is not merely a religion in the modern Christian sense but a polychromatic whole that includes language and literature, folkways, values, laws, art and music, philanthropy, and activities affirming the centrality of the Land of Israel. As various essays in this volume point out, a Kaplanian "civilization" had in its menu *sancta*, a term popularized by Kaplan to define spiritual symbols such as persons, events, places, writings, and objects that preserve group identity and inspire feelings of veneration but that are said to emerge from the historical experience of a people rather than to be handed down by God in an instant of supernatural revelation.

Dubnow and Kaplan were similar in still other ways: they both detested the mediocrity, materialism, and hypocrisy they perceived, especially among the leaders of their people. Despite their elitism, they were spokesmen for a populist love for the Jewish people in the abstract. What is striking is the parallel of Kaplan's dual concern with communal structure and democratic values and Dubnow's that the strengths of the *kahal* must be fused with the individual autonomy fostered by the Enlightenment. For Dubnow, the synthesis of tradition and *Haskalah* would be a new Jewish polity respecting freedom of thought and religion while safeguarding Jewish identity and ethnicity. Both men sought to formulate a Jewish constitutional order that would be a protective umbrella under which all Jewish groups would be gathered; these various parties and movements were expected to accept unambiguously the liberal freedoms that were the hallmark of modern Western nations and to disavow atavistic claims to infallibility. Kaplan's famous formula that the past had "a vote and not a veto" meant paying heed to precedent but making provision, as the *halakhah* had not formally done before, for deliberate communal enactment. Dubnow expected his revived *kahal* system to regulate Jewish life in the interests of all. Both men disapproved of the atomistic individualism of classical liberalism and accepted as a truth established by sociology the indebtedness of the individual's personhood to the collective of which he or she was a part. (Kaplan's knowledge of social theory was more up-to-date than Dubnow's, which was shaped by few thinkers later than Herbert Spencer.) Both denied the validity of a deracinated cosmopolitanism, used frequently by self-denying Jews as a mask for assimilation. Adamantly rejecting reghettoization, both were comfortable with the notion that Jews in the Diaspora participated in more than one culture, but wanted to rejuvenate the "organic Jewish community" (a favorite phrase of Kaplan's) in modern dress through a reformulated Jewish covenant in order to strengthen the future of the Jewish people.

It is too easy to say that Kaplan and Dubnow were both overly optimistic about the trends they discerned in Jewish life. In the post–World War II era, the ecumenical Jewish infrastructure that Dubnow and Kaplan projected has found only a partial and limited actuality. The value of *kelal Yisrael*, as they espoused it, did resonate to a post-Holocaust generation that witnessed the establishment of the State of Israel, but the national and global mechanisms for ensuring Jewish survival that both sketched have proved to be far from what has been feasible. Nor did Kaplan predict (who could have?) the dramatic shifts within Reform, Conservative, and Orthodox Judaism since the 1940s and especially since the seventies toward greater ethnic feeling in Reform and a resurgence of neotraditionalism down the line.

Neither anticipated exactly how his own ideology would take root. For all its impact, Dubnovism ended up as a delimited ideology of a minuscule *Folkspartei* in a continuum of eastern European Jewish movements that contained far greater movements: the Zionist Organization and the Jewish Workers Bund. In another irony of history, Kaplan's design for an ecumenical organic Jewish community produced a fourth American Jewish denomination with a set of institutions paralleling those of the Reform, Orthodox, and Conservative movements. In Kaplan's role as founder, there are analogies to the lives of Samson Raphael Hirsch, Isaac Mayer Wise, and

Solomon Schechter, none of whom set out to create separate structures for the Jewish people but all of whom ended up by doing so.
That the movement that Kaplan created is valiantly struggling for
its own momentum since his death in 1983 may be inevitable. It is
all the more useful, therefore, to view the life and work of Mordecai
M. Kaplan in a balanced perspective, without hagiography or ful-
mination. The editors hope that the essays in this volume contribute in that spirit to a finer understanding of a remarkable human
being.

Notes

1. Karl Marx, *Theses on Feurbach* (1845), number 11.
2. Mordecai M. Kaplan, *The Meaning of God in Modern Jewish Religion*
   (New York: Reconstructionist Press, 1964), 76.
3. Evyatar Friesel, "Ahad Ha-Amism in American Zionist Thought," in *At
   the Crossroads: Essays on Ahad Ha-Am*, ed. Jacques Kornberg (Albany:
   State University of New York Press, 1983), 139–41. I have dealt with
   Dubnow's theory of autonomism most recently in "Jewish Liberalism
   in Late Tsarist Russia," *Contemporary Jewry* 9, no. 1 (Fall-Winter
   1987–88): 56–61.
4. Mordecai M. Kaplan, *The Religion of Ethical Nationhood* (New York:
   Macmillan, 1970), 4–5.

PART ONE

Contexts

CHAPTER I

Kaplan and the Retrieval
of the *Haskalah*

Emanuel S. Goldsmith

Throughout his long life, Mordecai M. Kaplan devoted his seemingly inexhaustible energy to redefining and reinterpreting Judaism. This activity was born out of an unshakeable faith in the capacity of the Jewish people to reconstruct its historic way of life so as to ensure its survival and the advancement of humanity. Although he is best known for defining Judaism as a civilization, as an evolving civilization, and as an evolving *religious* civilization, Kaplan's most far-reaching definition was that of Judaism as "the ongoing life of a people intent upon keeping alive for the highest conceivable purpose, despite changes in the general climate of opinion."[1] This definition takes into account both the existential dimension (the ongoing life of a people) and the essential dimension (the highest conceivable purpose) of the Jewish phenomenon. It takes into account both peoplehood or nationalism and civilization or culture. Religion is subsumed under the rubric "highest conceivable purpose," since religion is that aspect of human culture or civilization that consciously seeks cognizance of and contact with the transcendent or highest aspects of human experience. In Judaism, the latter are conceived as divinity, deity, or God. Finally, the words "intent upon keeping alive" remind us that, whatever other objectives it may assume, the survival of the Jewish people (*kiyyum ha-umah*) remains a *sine qua non* of Judaism.

In these words one also hears echoes of Kaplan's polemic against attempts to categorize particular ages in the annals of Jewry as "classical," "normative," or "axial." To Kaplan, the designation of any specific period in the history of the Jewish people as preeminent was both an attempt to overemphasize the significance of that period at the expense of others and a denial of the evolutionary character of Judaism. Kaplan took exception, for example, to George Foot Moore's use of the term "normative Judaism" to refer to the Judaism of the first centuries of the Christian era. He pointed out that Moore identified "normative Judaism" with beliefs and practices that were, in fact, standardized subsequent to the rabbinic period. He also felt that Moore ignored the significance of polity and social structure, which formed the framework within which Jewish life functioned. Kaplan preferred the term "traditional Judaism" for the period Moore discussed in his classic study, *Judaism in the First Centuries of the Christian Era*, because an evolving civilization consists of different stages.[2] Each stage differs both in form and content from the one preceding it and the one following it. It may be considered normative only for those who live within it. In any event, Kaplan saw the proto-Judaism of the Bible as more authoritative and hence more "normative" than rabbinic Judaism.[3]

Having said this, however, I must add that Kaplan himself may be justly accused of preferring one age of Jewish history to all others —his own. And Kaplan's age, the age of modern Jewish history, is dominated by the *Haskalah*. As with the Enlightenment, which is both a specific period in European history and the beginning of modern history generally, the *Haskalah* was both a particular phenomenon at a specific period in Jewish history and the beginning of modern Jewish history. It represents a movement within a specific period to which it lent its name and to which it imparted lasting significance, but "its aspirations and anxieties, its debates and methods are still with us in their original form. . . . Though its values have been belittled by subsequent reaction, they appear increasingly meaningful to the survivors of the catastrophes of modern history.[4]

The *Haskalah* phenomenon, the roots of which reach back to the historical explorations into the Jewish past by Azariah de Rossi in the sixteenth century and the critical analysis of the Bible by Baruch Spinoza in the seventeenth, constitutes the very shaking of the foundations of Jewish life. Although a case may be made for the inappropriateness of a term such as *haskalah* (rationalism) for a phenomenon that embraces social reconstruction, religious radicalism, philosophical romanticism, and literary innovation, *Haskalah* as an ideology or movement does involve the application of rational or objective—as opposed to traditional or subjective—criteria to the peoplehood, culture, and religion of Jewry. The *Haskalah* undermined the spiritual and cultural walls that legitimized the dichotomies of tradition and objectivity, faith and truth, loyalty and criticism, religious and secular, eternal and temporal, and universal and particular.

The *Haskalah* was the Jewish version of the European Enlightenment of the eighteenth century, which substituted this-worldliness, rationalism, and universalism for the other-worldliness, authoritarianism, and exclusivism of the medieval world. The Enlightenment has been characterized as "the hinge on which the European nations turned from the Middle Ages to 'modern' times, marking the passage from a supernaturalistic-mythical-authoritative to a naturalistic-scientific-individualistic type of thinking."[5]

In its first, rationalist phase, the Enlightenment held that men should enjoy such rights as freedom of information, freedom of speech, and freedom from arbitrary arrest. Some of its spokesmen also claimed economic liberty as a natural right. The men of the Enlightenment believed that people would have greater dignity and be happier if their social institutions were based on reason and science rather than on tradition. The second phase of the Enlightenment, associated with Rousseau, "insisted that 'reason' must accommodate itself to an inner moral sense, which in turn implied the duty of the individual to sacrifice his personal advantage to the moral welfare of the living community on which he depended. Although this community was the source of his own existence as a moral being, its legitimacy was, in the last resort, dependent on its satisfying the moral and material needs of the individuals who composed it."[6] In sum, the Enlightenment "promoted the cause of freedom more widely, directly, positively than any age before it.

. . . For the first time in history it carried out a concerted attack on the vested interests that opposed the diffusion of knowledge and the free exercise of reason."[7]

Mordecai M. Kaplan viewed the Enlightenment as both the most adventurous reliance upon reason and experience and the most daring revolt against political and religious authoritarianism that mankind had ever known.[8] In *The Greater Judaism in the Making*, he quotes Carl L. Becker's summation of the essential articles of the religion of the Enlightenment: "1) Man is not natively depraved; 2) the end of life itself is the good life on earth instead of the beatific life after death; 3) man is capable of being guided solely by the light of reason and experience, of perfecting the good life on earth; and 4) the first and essential condition of the good life on earth is the freeing of men's minds from the bonds of ignorance and superstition." Kaplan believed that each of these principles had contributed to the radical transformation of the inner and outer conditions of human life, in general, and Jewish life, in particular. In the attempt to survive such transformation, Judaism was experiencing a metamorphosis.[9]

The Jewish Enlightenment, the *Haskalah*, which began as the Jewish wing of the general European Enlightenment, was of crucial moment for modern Jewish history. The *Maskilim*, or advocates of enlightenment, sought through education, religious reform, and communal reorganization to alter the contours of Jewish existence and thus modernize and "Europeanize" the Jewish people. The modern transformation of Jewish society, they hoped, would, in turn, lead to emancipation, integration, and enfranchisement. The *Maskilim* have long been held accountable for paving the road to assimilation and for the ills of modern Jewish life. The truth of the matter is, however, that they were, by and large, loyal and committed Jews who struggled valiantly against overwhelming odds, both within and without the Jewish community, to prove that a synthesis of Judaism with modernity was necessary, desirable, and feasible. "Every thinker," writes John Dewey, "puts some portion of an apparently stable world in peril, and no one can wholly predict what will emerge in its place."[10]

The *Haskalah* was essentially a social and cultural trend with strong political, economic, and religious overtones that effected a significant aesthetic and literary awakening. It embraced rationalism, romanticism, scholarly research (*Wissenschaft*) and the rethinking, reevaluation, reformulation, and reinterpretation of Judaism. It was also a messianic movement inasmuch as it sought to redeem the Jew from alienation and homelessness by encouraging him to become part of the countries of Europe and embrace the culture and mores of the European peoples. The *Maskilim* eventually succeeded in preparing European Jewry for emancipation and citizenship in the countries of Europe. They were responsible for the flowering of Hebrew and Yiddish letters; for the emergence of the modern trends in Jewish religion; for the development of modern Jewish literary and historical research; for the growth of Jewish socialism, nationalism, and Zionism; and, ultimately, for the reestablishment of Jewish sovereignty in the twentieth century. They brought about both a secular and religious revolution in Jewish life and cleared the way for modern Judaism.

The *Haskalah* movement began in the age of Moses Mendelssohn in the last quarter of the eighteenth century. In the 1860s and 1870s, and especially after 1881, the leading advocates of *Haskalah* preferred to be called Socialists, Lovers of Zion, and Zionists. Contrary to popular misconception, however, the *Haskalah* continues to this very day. The leading representatives of the *Haskalah* phenomenon from the eighteenth through the twentieth centuries have as much if not more in common than the various books in the Hebrew Bible have with each other. A representative list of leading *Maskilim* from Moses Mendelssohn to Mordecai Kaplan would have to include Nahman Krochmal, Isaac Baer Levinsohn, Peretz Smolenskin, Yitzkhok Leybush Peretz, Ahad Ha'am, Hayyim Nahman Bialik, Simon Dubnow, Martin Buber, and David Ben-Gurion. Geographically, the *Haskalah* spread from central to eastern Europe, western Europe, America, and Israel.

The *Maskilim* advocated changes in Jewish occupations and economic practices as well as educational and religious reforms in order to "rectify the alleged backwardness of Jewry and eliminate the supposed irrational features of Judaism at that time."[11] They helped make Jews more self-aware and self-critical, attacking both the normal human failings of the Jewish community and the excesses of the *Kabbalah* and Hasidism. They fostered the emergence of a modern Jewish literature (including philosophy and history) in the Hebrew language and, later, in Yiddish as well, which could vie with the traditional religious culture. Manifestly, by supplanting belief with reason and the ideal of the traditional scholar-hero or Hasidic saint with that of the secular moral individual, the *Haskalah* gradually helped render traditional values and concerns extraneous to the modern thinking Jew.[12]

The essence of traditional Judaism as a unique life style and culture style had been that every aspect of life and culture was interpenetrated with religion. According to Yehezkel Kaufmann, "Jewish culture in its entirety was Torah. Jewish learning was the study of Torah. . . . Torah was not simply sacred creativity that occupied a place alongside other cultural values. It was Jewish creativity *in toto*. . . . Other disciplines and sciences, to the extent that they were not forbidden or disaparaged, were considered of no real value; they had their place only if they were of practical use—otherwise they were relegated to insignificance."[13]

The *Haskalah* was the Jewish counterpart of the attempts of the Renaissance and European Enlightenment to limit the domination of life by religion, to put an end to religious coercion, to assign to religion a delimited area of life so that a new secular, humanistic culture and life style could emerge. The intellectuals of the Enlightenment were tired of the conflicts and polemics of religious groupings that considered themselves orthodox, or "right-thinking," as James L. Adams writes. "It [the Enlightenment] wished to dissolve the myths that had sanctioned arbitrariness and pretentiousness. It wished to do away with the beliefs in the gods of the competing absolutes . . . and with belief in supernatural interventions in human affairs. . . . The desire for autonomy is the nerve of the myth of the Enlightenment; and its guide is reason, not calculating, utilitarian reason, but substantial reason—in the human mind and in the cosmos."[14]

The ideal of the *Haskalah*, which it shared with the European Enlightenment, was the confinement of religion to its own sphere. It saw cultural creativity as essentially autonomous and sought to make room in Jewish life for nonreligious values as no less significant than religious values.[15] The *Haskalah* opposed the idea that all spiritual activity belonged to religion and had to be subjugated to it. Yehezkel Kaufmann describes the *Haskalah* in the following way: "The *Maskilim* advocated the study of arts and sciences, native languages, practical trades, and the development of Hebrew poetry and prose. They opposed the forcing of all culture and life into the four ells of *halakhah* or Torah."[16] The significance of the *Haskalah* lies, therefore, not in its advocating the pursuit of the secular arts and sciences in Jewish life alongside religion but in its conferring upon such pursuits a significance equal to that of the sacred pursuit of Torah.

We have become accustomed to view Kaplan's definition of Judaism as a civilization primarily as an attempt to correct the Reform, Orthodox, and Conservative reductions of Judaism to a creedal, legislative, or historical religion. It would be more correct to see it as an attempt to counter the traditionalist assumption that all of Judaism must be subsumed under the concept of religion or Torah, and that Torah in that sense is the only worthy form of Jewish interest. "Paradoxical as it may sound," writes Kaplan, "the spiritual regeneration of the Jewish people demands that religion cease to be its sole preoccupation."[17]

Kaplan's thought represents a highly significant contemporary attempt to deal with the modern redefinition of Torah or Judaism that began with Moses Mendelssohn and subsequent leaders of the *Haskalah*. Mendelssohn drew a distinction between the truths of religion that were universally acknowledged and the divine legislation that had been revealed exclusively to the Jewish people. Naftali Hertz Wesseley spoke of knowledge of the "Torah of Man," or human culture, which must precede knowledge of religion, or the "Torah of God." Peretz Smolenskin redefined Torah as a national culture that could always be adjusted to new historical conditions. Ahad Ha'am spoke of *Torah shebalev*, the "Torah of the heart," as the modern cultural creativity of the Jewish people that gives expression to its national spirit. In these and other related versions, Judaism is redefined as permitting the emergence of a Jewish culture no longer dominated by religion and open to outside influences, while at the same time expressing and encouraging Jewish identity and continuity.

"The traditional Jewish way of life," writes Kaplan, "was predicated on the self-segregated and isolationist status of the Jewish community. That status has become absolutely untenable in the modern world which demands free intercourse and exchange of ideas and experiences, as indispensable to intellectual and moral growth as well as to the general peace."[18] For Kaplan, the cultural implication of Jewish peoplehood in relation to the non-Jewish world involves "the appropriation and integration into Jewish culture of values found in other cultures that are compatible with Judaism, and the translation and interpretation of Jewish cultural creations as a contribution to other cultures."[19] For him it is not separatism but otherness that must become the principle of Jewish life. "Separatism is the antithesis of cooperation and results in an ingrown and clannish remoteness which leads to cultural and spiritual stagnation. Otherness thrives best when accompanied by active cooperation and interaction with neighboring cultures and civilizations, and achieves an individuality which is of universal significance."[20]

In Kaplan's thought, religion is viewed as "the integrating and soul-giving factor"[21] of a civilization, and the term *Torah* is expanded to embrace "whatever knowledge would enable us Jews to retain our individuality as a people, discern our true destiny, and know the means and methods of achieving it."[22] To broaden the concept of Torah it is necessary to realize that Jews have no monopoly on the wisdom of life. On the contrary, "the wisdom which we should display as synonymous with Torah should consist in our learning from the wisdom of all peoples, both ancient and modern, acquired by them in the course of their striving for the fulfillment of human destiny."[23]

Immanuel Kant defined the Enlightenment as "the liberation of man from his self-caused state of minority. Minority is the incapacity of using one's understanding without the direction of another. The state of minority is self-caused when its source lies not in lack of understanding, but in lack of determination and courage to use it without the assistance of another. *Sapere aude*. Dare to use your own understanding! is then the motto of Enlightenment."[24] This statement may be viewed as the quintessential expression and definition of both the Enlightenment and the *Haskalah*.

In his simultaneous reaffirmation of tradition and his repudiation of its dogmatism and intolerance, Kaplan's writings constitute a twentieth-century restatement of the core of the Enlightenment and the *Haskalah*. To him, a man without a tradition is in a far worse situation than a man without a country. "For a man without a country is a man without a present, from the standpoint of citizenship, while a man without a tradition is a man without a past, without a future, and without a present, from the standpoint of being fully human."[25] On the other hand, he writes, "if tradition is to be a means toward our growing up, it has to be partly outgrown. . . . We should feel toward our tradition as we should feel toward our country: My tradition right or wrong: if right, to be kept right; if wrong, to be set right. . . . It is necessary to be rooted in a tradition in order to have not only something to live by, but also something to rebel against."[26] He also states that "to possess inner freedom, the human mind must be able to rouse itself from . . . inertia, to challenge or question the inherent value of any purpose, ideal, belief or standard which we are asked to accept merely because it has back of it the prestige of a long tradition or the weight of numbers."[27]

Contrary to popular impression, the Enlightenment brought about a renewed interest in religion and effected a revival of religious thought. Helmut O. Pape writes that "dissent was thriving in the new, less hierarchical society; religion gained a new and deepening meaning in various strata of society, from philosophical deism and Rousseau's *religion de Genève* to the popular revival movements of Pietism and Methodism."[28] Kant's approach to religion was based on a faith in God derived from the moral element in human nature and freed of the belief in supernatural revelation. The poet Byron spoke of conscience as the "oracle" of God. For Kaplan, God's reality should be experienced through conscience, which is the human functioning of the ontological polarity of independence and interdependence. Conscience operates in individuals and groups as moral responsibility for the effects of our thoughts, feelings, and actions on others.[29]

In Jewish life, the *Maskilim* were the pioneers of new religious outlooks and theologies. The *Maskilim*, like their non-Jewish counterparts, sought to disentangle religion from the excrescences of superstition and credulity. They sought a distilled, purified religion in which the essence of the Jewish faith would be more clearly visible. They spoke of *hāma'or sheba-Torah* (the light of the Torah) and *emunah tserufah* (a purified faith). Of the philosophy of Nahman Krochmal, the father of the *Haskalah* in Galicia, Kaplan writes that "it points the way to a *conception of God that is the product of progressive human experience and knowledge as the basis of Jewish religion.* It thereby frees Jewish religion from commitment to the doctrine of the supernatural origin of the Torah. . . . It *shifts the center of Judaism from dogmas and rituals to the will-to-live of the Jewish People.* . . . It frankly recognizes not only the legitimacy, but also the *necessity, of studying the tradition in the light of so much historical context as it is possible to discover and reconstruct.* This does away at one stroke with the oracular approach to the tradition, particularly the Bible. . . . Krochmal's historical approach, on the other hand, *establishes a rational basis for the modern historical study of the Bible, as well as of the post-Biblical writings.*"[30]

As a result of the Enlightenment, the term *Providence* as a personal noun came into widespread usage, conveying a conception of a God whose sole concern was to care for the happiness of humanity. The providential care of mankind was no longer merely one of God's many functions. It became his *raison d'être.* God was now "that which so governs the total scheme of things as to ensure that it will serve men's—which are also God's—interests. And God's objective is not, primarily, to redeem men, to forgive them, or to mete out justice to them but to secure their final felicity, their ultimate perfection."[31] Nahman Krochmal's concept of God as the element of purpose in a people's culture is an elaboration of this view. Thus, Kaplan's idea of God as the power that makes for salvation is as directly related to the religion of the Enlightenment and the *Haskalah* as to the concepts of Matthew Arnold, William James, John Dewey, Alfred North Whitehead, and Henry Nelson Wieman, with which he is usually associated.

The *Maskilim* enthusiastically reiterated the Enlightenment faith in humanity but utilized that faith to encourage the Jews to transform themselves into a modern people with a modern culture, in which formal religion was no longer all-pervasive. It is too easy to criticize the Enlightenment's views of progress and human perfectibility as naive and simplistic. Such criticism is too facile. As Herbert J. Muller writes, "We should know that except for the gloomiest prophets, men in the past almost always look shortsighted, and their foresight may be overlooked because it has become part of our common sense."[32] The optimism of the Enlightenment was based on the belief that if superstition, bigotry, and tyranny were weakened, human life could be improved.

The men of the Enlightenment believed that groups, like individuals, had a quintessential spirit, a definable character or essence. This essence could be discovered, identified, and defined in simple terms. It was believed to pervade every aspect of national and religious life and to be immune to the ravages of time. "In the twentieth century," writes Frank E. Manuel, "the working out of the Esprit of a religion or culture might become rather sophisticated in the hands of an anthropologist or a sociologist, but the fundamental conception has not changed much since the Enlightenment."[33]

The *Maskilim*, too, began a quest for the quintessence and soul of Judaism—a quest that has continued unabated to this day. If Judaism was more than Torah and if Torah was not all there was to Judaism, what was the unique, particular essence of the Jewish experience? For Mendelssohn, Judaism possessed no special truths but was the bearer of a ritual law divinely revealed to the Jews alone. Krochmal asserted that the basis of Judaism is its faith in the primacy of reason or self-awareness. According to him, as Kaplan explains, "the Jewish people is enabled to avert death through its extraordinary power of self-awareness or reason. When the Jewish people reaches the end of one (historical) cycle, it exists for a time in a state of suspended animation. It later revives, however, and resumes its career, this time on a higher level of existence."[34] Peretz Smolenskin saw the essence of Judaism in national feeling, the Hebrew language, and the hope for national restoration. For Ahad Ha'am, the essence of Judaism was the pursuit of absolute justice. For A. D. Gordon, it was the quest for objective truth.

Kaplan continued this quest for the unique spirit of Judaism. He was indeed the outstanding representative of the ideals of the *Haskalah* in the twentieth century. He saw the essence of Judaism in ethical nationhood, or the limitation of absolute sovereignty and the implementation of moral responsibility in the life of individuals and nations. He believed that civilization was in great danger because both the nuclear powers and the smaller nations behave in their international affairs without a sense of moral responsibility. "The very survival of mankind demands the modification of absolute sovereignty in the direction of ethical nationhood. From the very beginning that has been the purpose and meaning of Jewish existence."[35]

Isaac Baer Levinsohn, the founder of the *Haskalah* movement in Russia at the beginning of the nineteenth century, had taught that "there is no greater sin than that of the man who causes the disappearance of his nation from the world."[36] To him *kiyyum ha-umah*, the survival of the Jewish people, was the greatest of all the commandments. In the middle of the twentieth century, Kaplan reformulated Levinsohn's thought in the following way: "Nothing more tragic can happen than for a people and its civilization to disintegrate and die. To be in any way responsible for this tragedy is to be guilty of snuffing out life in its most human and sacred form."[37] Elsewhere he writes, "We act irresponsibly . . . when we do not belong to some spiritual group that exists for the purpose of fostering moral and spiritual values. And we act irresponsibly when we do not persuade such groups to give primacy to the task of arousing mankind to the imperative need of putting an end to all international and civil wars."[38]

Rational religion encompasses a wide variety of approaches to religious truth, ranging from deism and naturalism to neo-Kantianism and existentialism. In its various forms, rational religion constitutes an outgrowth of the Age of Enlightenment. Such a religion fosters faith in the idea that the voice of universal reason and conscience is the voice of God. The attempt to discover universal elements in religion makes possible a coming to terms with the new insights and challenges of the natural and social sciences and philosophy. Rejection of the goals of the Enlightenment leads to a regression to irrationalism and fanaticism. It is certainly true, as James L. Adams states, that "apart from this effort the religion of the West would be unable to elicit integrating commitment or to find vital points of contact with secularism and with the myths of other religions and cultures. . . . The eighteenth century's demand for the universal is the perennially valid intention of its myth of reason."[39]

The major weakness of rational religion has been the inability to sustain a sense of intimacy and mystery, which may account for its failure to attract wide support. Adams attributes this one-sidedness to the Enlightenment's preference for the neoclassical mood and a rational self-consciousness. "Any natural religion that loses contact with the historical and the concrete substitutes ideas *about* religion for piety."[40] This may indeed be the result of an overriding concern with the Cartesian "clear and distinct ideas" of reason and a failure to appreciate the depth and richness that only poetry and myth can convey.

Kaplan's *transnaturalist* interpretation of Judaism espouses the Enlightenment's loyalty to universal reason but tempers it with the intimacy and mystery that only a wholehearted recognition and embracing of the historical, evolutionary, and civilizational perspectives on Judaism make possible. Kaplan observes that Israel was the first nation to discover the God of history. In his view, "actual revelation of God took place not amid thunder and lightning on Mt. Sinai but in 'the still small voice' of Israel's sense of human history,"[41] which accounts for the incomparable impact the God of Israel has had on the religions of mankind. Nor does Judaism fail to provide an outlet for the mystical leanings of human nature. "The self-identification of the individual Jew with his Jewish people is the source of the mystical element in the Jewish religion. . . . identification with the Jewish people provides Jewish religion with the indispensable dimension of the mystical."[42] History and community are central categories of Kaplan's transnaturalist approach to Judaism. "Jewish identity demands of the individual Jew that he so come to know the Jewish people, its entire history, its civilization, and its destiny as to experience the reality of its God. This God, YHWH, is that aspect of the Jewish people which renders it more than the sum of its individuals, past, present, and future, and gives meaning to all its virtues, sins, successes and failures."[43]

The vicissitudes in the twentieth century of humanity, in general, and of the Jewish people, in particular, tempered Kaplan's espousal of the Enlightenment and the *Haskalah* but did not shatter his faith in their worth. The Enlightenment gave us a dynamic concept of reality and a radical transvaluation of values. With confidence in the human ability to extend the boundaries of scientific knowledge and experience came a respect for reason and hope for progress. Much has happened since the Enlightenment to dampen the human spirit and cast people into despair. Antirationalism and supernaturalism are on the ascent. Many continue to be victims of intellectual and spiritual schizophrenia and to live with compartmentalized minds. The decimation of European Jewry during the Second World War was a particularly painful reminder of the evils that supernaturalist and irrationalist ideologies can engender. Nevertheless, Kaplan believed that reason and hope would regain their power. Faith in automatic progress would be replaced by the realization that progress must be rationally planned and spiritually willed. People would once again strive to see life in this world as significant and worthwhile. That was the kind of future in which he hoped a place would be assured for the Jewish people.[44]

Notes

1. Mordecai M. Kaplan, *The Purpose and Meaning of Jewish Existence* (Philadelphia: Jewish Publication Society of America, 1964), 40. Kaplan's description of Judaism as a civilization may have been influenced by the teachings of the popular American Protestant preacher and thinker David Swing. Toward the end of the nineteenth century, Swing utilized the term *civilization* to characterize Christianity. See William R. Hutchinson, *The Modernist Impulse in American Protestantism* (Cambridge: Harvard University Press, 1976) 58. Kaplan's debt to the American Reform rabbi Bernhard Felsenthal, who drew a distinction between "Judaism" and "Jewish Religion," is well known. See, for example, David Polish, "The Changing and the Constant in the Reform Rabbinate," in *The American Rabbinate, a Century of Continuity in Change: 1883–1983*, ed. Jacob R. Marcus and Abraham J. Peck (Hoboken: KTAV Publishing House, 1985), 194–95, 242–43.
2. George Foot Moore, *Judaism in the First Centuries of the Christian Era*, 3 vols. (Cambridge: Harvard University Press, 1927–30).
3. Mordecai M. Kaplan, *The Greater Judaism in the Making: A Study of the Modern Evolution of Judaism* (New York: Reconstructionist Press, 1960), 515.

4. Helmut O. Pape, "Enlightenment," in *Dictionary of the History of Ideas*, vol. 2 (New York: Charles Scribner's Sons, 1973), 89.
5. Franklin L. Baumer, *Modern European Thought* (New York: Macmillan, 1977), 141.
6. Norman Hampson, *A Cultural History of the Enlightenment* (New York: Harper & Row, 1968), 252.
7. Herbert J. Muller, *Freedom in the Western World* (New York: Harper and Row, 1963), 321f.
8. Kaplan, *Greater Judaism* (New York: Reconstructionist Press, 1960), 183.
9. Ibid., 168f.
10. John Dewey, *Characters and Events*, vol. 1 (New York: Henry Holt, 1929), xi.
11. Robert M. Seltzer, "Enlightenment," in *Contemporary Jewish Religious Thought*, ed. Arthur A. Cohen and Paul Mendes-Flohr (New York: Charles Scribner's Sons, 1987), 171.
12. Cf. David Sorkin, *The Transformation of German Jewry, 1780–1840* (New York: Oxford University Press, 1987) 16; and Kaplan, *Greater Judaism*, 197.
13. Yehezkel Kaufmann, *Golah ve-Nekhar*, vol. 1 (Tel Aviv: Dvir, 1954), 495f.
14. James L. Adams, *The Prophethood of All Believers* (Boston: Beacon Press, 1986), 115.
15. Kaufmann, *Golah ve-Nekhar*, vol. 2, 27.
16. Ibid.
17. Mordecai M. Kaplan, *Judaism as a Civilization* (New York: Macmillan, 1934), 345.
18. Mordecai M. Kaplan, *Judaism without Supernaturalism* (New York: Reconstructionist Press, 1958), 208.
19. Mordecai M. Kaplan, *Questions Jews Ask: Reconstructionist Answers* (New York: Reconstructionist Press, 1956), 33.
20. Kaplan, *Judaism as a Civilization*, 515.
21. Mordecai M. Kaplan, *The Future of the American Jew* (New York: Macmillan, 1948), 36.
22. Kaplan, *Questions Jews Ask*, 383.
23. Mordecai M. Kaplan, *A New Zionism* (New York: Herzl Press, 1959), 156.
24. Quoted in Frank E. Manuel, *The Changing of the Gods* (Hanover, Mass.: University Press of New England, 1983), viii.
25. Kaplan, *Judaism without Supernaturalism*, 207.
26. Mordecai M. Kaplan, *Not So Random Thoughts* (New York: Reconstructionist Press, 1966), 274–76.
27. Kaplan, *Future of the American Jew*, 289.
28. Pape, "Enlightenment," 91.
29. Cf. Mordecai M. Kaplan, "The Evolution of the Idea of God," in *The*

Seventy-fifth Anniversary Volume of the Jewish Quarterly Review, ed. Abraham A. Neuman and Solomon Zeitlin (Philadelphia: Dropsie College, 1967), 345.
30. Kaplan, *Greater Judaism*, 204.
31. John Passmore, *The Perfectibility of Man* (New York: Charles Scribner's Sons, 1970), 210.
32. Muller, *Freedom in the Western World*, 318.
33. Manuel, *Changing of the Gods*, 113.
34. Kaplan, *Greater Judaism*, 202.
35. Mordecai M. Kaplan, *The Religion of Ethical Nationhood* (New York: Macmillan, 1970), 49.
36. Isaac Baer Levinsohn, *Zerubavel*, part 1 (Warsaw: B. Z. Sheynfinkel, 1901), 84; quoted in Meyer Waxman, *A History of Jewish Literature*, vol. 3 (New York: Thomas Yoseloff, 1936), 210.
37. Kaplan, *Future of the American Jew*, 83f.
38. Kaplan, *Purpose and Meaning*, 319.
39. Adams, *Prophethood of All Believers*, 122.
40. Ibid.
41. Mordecai M. Kaplan and Arthur A. Cohen, *If Not Now, When?* (New York: Schocken, 1973), 22.
42. Kaplan, *New Zionism*, 114f.
43. Kaplan, *If Not Now, When?* 68.
44. Cf. Kaplan, *New Zionism*, 50.

CHAPTER 2

The Reconstruction of Jewish Religion Out of Secular Culture*

Eliezer Schweid

As early as the beginning of the nineteenth century several attempts were made to derive the basic concepts of the Jewish religion (faith in God as creator and overseer who reveals himself, instructs his people in his Torah, and designates a messianic reward for his followers) from the elements of secular ethics, society, and culture. Nevertheless, one should not term such attempts the "reconstruction of religion." They are still aimed at replacing (or retreating from) religious Judaism, in its old traditional sense, with the concepts and forms of the new secular culture. The problem is still how to purify secular culture and dull the edges of the conflict between its values and forms and the values and ways of the Jewish religion. In other words, the objective of "liberal" Jewish thought is to prove that the concepts and values of humanistic secular culture are in harmony with the original contents of the Jewish religion—if we remove distortions, confusions, and incorrect interpretations rooted in an earlier cultural level and understand them properly. It is easy to prove, however, that the basic assumptions of secular humanism provide the point of departure for thinkers like Nahman Krochmal

*This essay first appeared in Eliezer Schweid, *Judaism and Secular Culture* (in Hebrew) (Tel Aviv: Ha-Kibbutz ha-Me'uhad, 1981), and was translated for this volume by Emanuel S. Goldsmith.

(the author of *Guide for the Perplexed of Our Time*), Solomon Formstecher, Samuel Hirsch, and Abraham Geiger—the founders of the thought of the Jewish Reform movement.[1] These men investigated, clarified, and interpreted the contents of the Jewish religion in terms of its sources in the Torah according to these assumptions. It is therefore not surprising that they identify religion with a specific set of ethical values and the symbols that embody them, while removing from religion all independent content that might be preferable to the general principles of humanism. The concept of God is the ideal of the unity of human reason. Revelation in its varied meanings is the form of rational self-awareness; Providence is the law of moral existence in human society; worship is expressed essentially in ethics and in the commandments that relate man to God, which are only educational means to strengthen the feelings of human moral obligation.

Nevertheless, this idealist understanding of reality has still not brought about an identification of religion with natural human abilities. The transcendence of God as an absolute spiritual-autonomous being who rules over nature and in so doing reveals himself and issues commandments is upheld in this thought by drawing a sharp distinction between the realm of nature and the realm of spirit. *Nature* is the domain of physical and mechanical causality, while *spirit* is the domain of ethical will operating according to the idea of purpose.[2] Spirit attempts to impose moral unity on nature, and this explains the tension between man's ethical will and his natural physical impulses. In any event, on the basis of the distinction between nature and spirit, the concept of God is still the concept of a supernatural being—the supreme source of both nature and spirit, destined to dominate nature. For humanity, God is both the original idea and the idea of purpose for which it strives. This is an infinite ideal, which dwells within and beyond humanity so that humanistic culture is conceived as guided by a religious ideal. This is a continuation of the early religious character of humanism.

In Jewish thinking, which continued this trend of thought in our century, the tension between the realm of nature and the realm of spirit gradually disappears. The ideal of humanity emerges from the nature of man. The point of departure is, therefore, a secular culture that has managed to assimilate completely the special categories of religious thought, feeling, and behavior.[3] But then an annoy-ing deficiency reveals itself, and the need to overcome this deficiency produces a reconstructive thought that attempts to discover religion anew from the contents of secular humanistic culture (as if to cause it to expunge what appeared to have been completely assimilated). The most developed effort in this direction is the thought of Morde-cai Kaplan.

Kaplan's teaching begins with an enthusiastic affirmation of the achievements of secular culture.[4] He evaluates these achievements in moral terms as manifestations of progress. Modern science ad-vanced the human knowledge of reality. It tore the curtains from illusions, myths, and wishes and revealed facts and the causal con-nections among them. Modern technology provided humanity with practical tools with which to rule nature and to derive what people needed for their well-being. This meant an increase and even a boost in the standard of living for the individual and the masses. Science and technology made possible democracy—the most ethi-cal form of government—to which we attribute the freedom and happiness of most people. In this respect Kaplan continues on the path of the secular thinkers of the nineteenth and early twentieth centuries. The enthusiastic faith in scientific-technological progress and in its chance of reducing human misery may be found in all his writings. Nevertheless, Kaplan does not avoid the questions that arise with progress—questions that now appear most serious, threatening the destruction of the marvelous achievements of sci-ence. Progressive human society seems to be disintegrating morally. There is a need to restrain technological achievements associated with the frightening pollution of the atmosphere. Most impor-tantly, together with progress in satisfying human needs and over-coming suffering, the superpowers have amassed a mighty destruc-tive capability that can at any moment annihilate humanity. This fact, with its positive and negative ramifications, provides the back-ground for Kaplan's renewed struggle with the ideas and values of religion, in general, and of Judaism, in particular.

The enthusiastic positive evaluation of the achievements of sci-ence and technology leads Kaplan to a decisive rejection of religion as crystallized in traditional thought and deed. In an extremely simple—perhaps simplistic—way, he argues that the truth revealed by science with its experimental tools completely denies traditional theology. As scientists we cannot believe in miracles as events directed toward a specific purpose in contrast to the known laws of nature. Nor can we believe in the "revelation" of a truth derived from a source beyond human comprehension and reason. We know with certainty that our destiny depends on nature and on the decisions we make freely in the light of definite consequences of action within nature. As men of science, we know of no force aside from the forces of nature operating in the human environment and in man himself. This being the case, faith in a divinity in the sense of a personality external to nature—omnipotent and dominant throughout the earth—also is denied. Such faith is opposed to scientific truth, which is firm and incontrovertible. This means that we must consider traditional religion and the sources that confirm it as products of the human spirit—that is, exalted products full of useful content but in no way to be considered the word of God. As scientists we may even explain why our ancestors saw reality as they did and why they could not view it in any other way. Thus, we can learn much from what they said without accepting their explanation of the source of their beliefs and practices. To this point we have an extreme and even zealous secularist viewpoint.

Now, however, Kaplan raises the issue of science's inability to deal with ethical questions. Science describes reality. Technology based upon science gives us tools with which to cope with reality but does not give us an answer to the question of our destined purpose as human beings or of our duty to ourselves, to others, and to our natural environment. To the degree that we are free to choose, toward what should we direct our will? In order to respond to this question a spiritual enterprise entirely different from science is necessary. Indeed, it is becoming clearer that without appropriate responses, scientific progress is impossible and the possibility of human existence itself becomes doubtful. Morality is a necessity of human existence. With the increase in human power, there is also an increase in the need to establish ethical norms. The scientific enterprise itself depends on these norms. Whence may we derive them? The posing of such questions causes Kaplan to turn again to religion. It is a fact that religion has answered these questions, and its answers are not contested by science. They are necessary as the foundation of science. Religion was always a power creating values and placing humanity in a framework of purpose and meaning for its existence. Therefore, religion must once again be restored and reconstructed as a spiritual force.

In order to achieve the required reconstruction, Kaplan suggests that a distinction be made between two kinds of spiritual activity —science and wisdom. Science tries to describe reality as it is on the basis of experience. It is analytic, clinging to details and more and more precise definitions in order to exhaust what may be known about the structure and relationships of parts of the world. Such knowledge makes it possible for humanity to be at home in the environment and to create tools with which to control it. But humanity is also in need of the kind of general observation that makes possible self-understanding in the environment. Where did humanity come from, and where it is headed? What is its destiny, and what is its responsibility? This is a generalizing observation that is concerned not only with what is but also with what ought to be. Indeed, a generalizing observation that ascertains the "ought" is wisdom, and wisdom creates religion as a compendium of values and obligatory norms. We are speaking, then, of two distinctive functions of the spirit. These functions are, however, supplementary, and are even based upon one another. Wisdom creates ethical bases for scientific activity; without it, such activity lacks direction and restraint. Science provides wisdom with a factual background, without which wisdom is blind and its ethical will bereft of an opportunity for realization. This is the reason Kaplan believes that wisdom is part of "natural" knowledge. In nature, various forces operate; some are determined and others autonomous. We may discern in nature a clear tendency operating in the direction of more comprehensive and more complex organic unities. This tendency is manifest in a conscious way in the voluntary and social activity of humanity and is indeed the natural source of wisdom.

This conception of the relationship between spirit and nature constitutes the basis of natural theology and may be clearly distinguished from the idealistic theology of the nineteenth century. Idealistic theology posited a directional confrontation between spirit and nature and threatened eventually to "swallow" nature as a category of spirit. Kaplan, on the other hand, does not assume a dialectical confrontation but rather the activity of various forces in the broad, open, and heterogeneous arena of nature as depicted by science. In this way Kaplan is apparently attempting to escape from pantheism, or the identification of God with all of nature, as well as from supernaturalism, or the identification of God as a supernatural force. In Kaplan's thought, God is revealed in nature as one power operating in it—a purposeful, autonomous power creating organisms and crystallizing societies. It is, therefore, not a defined being and certainly not a person in the anthropomorphic sense but a tendency we identify through its activity. The word *God* is only a pictorial or symbolic image for that tendency. We are in need of it in religion in order to place this tendency before humanity as a guiding ideal. From this point of view, religion is a supreme educative instrument. But we must always remember that "personality," which may be influenced by various forms of worship, must not be attributed to God. We can influence God only in the sense of discerning in our ethical will a supreme manifestation of divinity and behaving in agreement with the dictates of this ethical will. When we behave in consonance with this will, God reveals himself in our actions. In any event, our deeds, based on both science and the ethical ideal, determine the destiny of civilization.

It is easy to see that this conception views ethics as the essence of religious teaching. If divinity is the unifying tendency in nature, it manifests itself primarily in organic wholes and afterwards in social harmony or morality. We can say, therefore, that divinity as manifest in human society is the tendency toward the cooperation, mutuality, and love that unites humanity. When we say that God is the source of ethics, or that God commands ethical behavior, we are simply stating in figurative, didactic language the "simple" truth that the ethical tendency is divinity on the level of human nature. In this sense, it is correct to say that God "commands" morality because without morality human society would fall apart and human existence would disintegrate.

It is permissible, then, to define Kaplan's theology as *ethical naturalism*. His theology is essentially secular and does not cross the boundaries of secular thought. God, too, is conceived by him as an element in a secular *Weltanschauung*—as a power among the powers of nature. But in Kaplan's secular view of the world, religion returns and acquires a principal role in his teachings. Secular culture with all its glorious attainments will not survive without faith, that is, the intent of the moral will. If we interpret the fundamentals of the Jewish religion in this way, we will rescue it from the "childish" images of the past and raise it to a level of maturity, so that it will once again direct us on the path of our life.

The discussion thus far has been extremely general. I have dealt with the position of religion—any religion—and of culture—any culture. If there was in it any preference for the Jewish religion, it was because for Kaplan the latter appeared nearer the naturalistic understanding of the God-concept, at least from the point of view of the centrality of ethics. But Kaplan is aware of the demand that religion fulfill its function of shaping a way of life, that is, it must place its stamp on all cultural creativity. From this point of view as well, he sees in Judaism an excellent model. The shaping of a comprehensive way of life is accomplished in Judaism by means of Halakhah—by means of the detailed and defined norms that apply to the Jewish community. There is no such thing as religion or culture in general, only specific religions that operate in the cultures of definite peoples. Judaism is the religion of the Jewish people. It needs to be the religion of Jewry because this people created it and shaped its culture in accordance with it.

This brings us to the nationalist and Zionist dimension in Kaplan's teaching. Here, too, we find an expression of consistent secular naturalism. For its survival and the survival of its culture, the Jewish people (like all other peoples) needs a national basis that is territorial, demographic, economic, social, and political. Judaism is not *only* a religion, and the framework of an ecclesiastical organization is not enough for it. It is a people's culture or, using Kaplan's word, a "civilization."[5] The Jewish religion is an active and formative factor among the totality of natural factors that create Jewish culture. For this purpose Zionism is necessary. To Kaplan, the realization of the Zionist vision constitutes an essential condition for the revival of Judaism. At the same time, he rejects Herzlian Zionism and holds to an approach close to that of Ahad Ha'am. The Jewish people has a structure different from that of other peoples: Its survival in exile stamped it with an ineradicable seal. It is a people scattered in several centers throughout the world. It is not conceivable that the entire people, or even most of it, will be gathered in its own land and state. It will, therefore, remain an international people. Indeed, it would seem that Kaplan sees this not only as an incontestable historical fact but as the fulfillment of a cultural value. If the political and territorial center expresses the ordinary, "normal" basis of the Jewish people, the Diaspora expresses the uniqueness of direct participation in a "universal" reality. Just as Jews as a people have a life apart from others, they also participate directly in the life of other peoples. Kaplan is inclined to interpret this phenomenon in terms of a precious uniqueness and destiny. Kaplan believes that the future of humanity depends on fostering a feeling of international responsibility and cooperation. Just as society exists on the basis of morality in interpersonal relations, humanity cannot exist except on the basis of morality in relationships among peoples. This is not the current situation. In relationships among peoples, there is an ugly egoism and a violent and destructive belligerence. It is clear to everyone, however, that this fact threatens a holocaust today because the large nations possess huge destructive power. Nationalism requires, therefore, an ascent to the level of "ethical nationhood"; and the Jewish people, living as it does on two levels of existence, the national and the international, can represent the need to symbolize and exemplify its realization. If the Jewish people wills it, it can indeed become a "treasured people." The Jewish religion in its modern interpretation should shape the culture of this unique people striving to reach a new level of national life.

The combination of theological-ethical and national considerations serves as the basis of a highly detailed active program. These are its principles: In modern times, the Jewish people must renew the covenant that established the framework of its life. This is the ancient covenant of the patriarchs and of Sinai, which was renewed at historical turning points so that it might acquire new authority and harmonize with new circumstances. Following the crisis of the emancipation, the need has arisen to renew the covenant again, that is, to establish representative organizational frameworks that will unify the people, place a clear national ideal before the people, and lead it to realization. To accomplish this, a superframework is needed for the Jewish community in the State of Israel and for the centers in the Diaspora. A representative leadership must arise. The basis of belonging will be voluntary but will signify the acceptance of clearly defined responsibilities. Whoever wants to enter the framework of the covenant will mark it with a ritual and symbolic ceremony to include the acceptance of the yoke of commandments —commandments concerning public activity on behalf of national survival and commandments concerning the ambiance of daily life. It is clear that the application of this requirement will differ from place to place, and there will be an obvious difference between the obligations of the Jews of Israel and those of the Diaspora. A Jew who lives in the State of Israel has by virtue of his living there already accepted a general obligation toward the Jewish people. He upholds a vital political framework without which the Jewish people cannot survive, and his obligations as a citizen of the state are also his responsibilities to the Jewish community. But Kaplan believes that Israeli Jews must complete their project in two areas: responsibility for the survival of Judaism in the Diaspora (and especially for Jewish education in the Diaspora) and responsibility for the survival of a Jewish way of life in terms of its cultural character. In the State of Israel, too, there is a need for a communal organization in which human relations based on justice and charity are fundamental. In this communal framework Jewish tradition must find expression, although this must be in consonance with the life circumstances of a modern secular society. A Jew who lives in the Diaspora must, first of all, enter a communal framework and accept duties in this framework. To repeat, by means of the framework of the community each individual will participate in a national-religious way of life distinguished by language and traditional symbols. Adherence to the Jewish community will not, of course, deter the Diaspora Jew from the course of his activities as a citizen of his own country. He must be loyal to it and contribute to it as much as he can. Furthermore, he will need to emphasize his identification with national and international ethical objectives. In this, too, he will be expressing an important dimension of his Judaism.

Therefore, the symbols of Jewish tradition, especially the Sabbaths and festivals, occupy an important position in Kaplan's characterization of the Jewish way of life. It is clear that the direction is not that of *Halakhah*, as crystallized in the *Shulhan Arukh*. Kaplan rejects the principle of supernatural revelation. He advocates the autonomy of democratic society. Ancient tradition is for him a source of inspiration. One draws from it and distills from it according to humanistic-secular criteria. Therefore, Kaplan has no difficulty in creating a synthesis among cultural, scientific, technological, and aesthetic activity and the unifying traditional symbols in the Land of Israel and in the Diaspora. A unique consciousness of religious obligation will express itself in a high morality on the level of both personal and national activity.

Mordecai Kaplan's propositions appear to supplement Ahad Ha'am's teachings on the continuity of the Jewish tradition and on the relationship between Eretz Yisrael and the Diaspora. The supplementation rests upon three proposals in addition to those of Ahad Ha'am: community organization; establishment of a representative and obligatory super-national framework; and complete identification of the ethical ideal of prophecy with the idea of God. In this connection, mention should be made of the fact that, in Ahad Ha'am's essays "Moses" and "Of Two Opinions," a conception like this is hinted at, but it was Kaplan who developed it into a naturalistic theology.

Does this supplementation allow Kaplan's teachings to avoid the weaknesses in the teachings of Ahad Ha'am? This question must be examined in a detailed, point-by-point investigation. Let me begin with theological considerations and with the question as to whether there is a basis for the claim that science has "refuted" traditional faith in God as the creator of the world and giver of the Torah. The definiteness in Kaplan's words does indeed reflect a mood typical of a period of great achievements in the sciences and technology. These achievements arouse the expectation and faith that humanity will be able to control its natural abilities for the sake of survival and well-being and overcome its suffering. The tendency to rely on human abilities undercuts the psychological tendency of the believer who relies on God and turns to him in time of trouble. It is not surprising, therefore, that in the daily experience of contemporary people, the immediate experience of God's presence or of being commanded by him is generally missing. But this fact does not constitute a "refutation" of faith in a supernatural God who is creator, commander, and overseer. Again, the experience of evil in nature and society has always raised major questions concerning faith in a commanding and overseeing God. Even if human evil increases greatly because of the powerful means provided for it by modern science and technology, the questions themselves have not changed. These questions place the believer in a difficult situation, but they do not refute faith, which is based on primary human experience realized during the growth of personality within the framework of a religious way of life. As scientists we cannot establish whether this psychological experience is indeed essential to human life. Straightforward and convincing human documents testify that it does occur and that it is different from other psychological experiences. Among other things, Kaplan points to the Holocaust as having completely demolished and voided faith in supernatural Providence. But the fact is that although the Holocaust shook the faith of many, it strengthened the faith of others; and these too are many. In contrast to this, there is validity to the claim that the Holocaust deeply diminished confidence in the moral strength of humanity and in its ability to confront the problems of human existence. Despite this, without claiming that this fact destroyed the principles of Kaplan's faith, we do indeed claim that science itself has no arguments that can deny or affirm faith.[6]

Let us examine Kaplan's positive proposal: the identification of the unifying trend in nature and especially in humanity with divinity. It would appear that Kaplan believed that not only does science not contravene such an identification but actually proves it. But what does such an identification mean? If the tendency to create organic unities is part of nature in the scientific sense, then it is one of several mechanical processes and cannot serve to explain the phenomenon of purposeful ethical will in humanity. Certainly, it can not replace the idea of God without making this idea devoid of meaning. If, in spite of this, we insist that a purposeful, autonomous trend exists in nature creating evermore comprehensive organic unities, such a tendency is beyond the term *nature* as it is scientifically understood. The "wisdom" that Kaplan distinguishes from science and that provides us with a general perspective with which to create obligatory ethical values places humanity beyond nature as defined by science. If, on the basis of that wisdom, we arrive at the belief that there is a purposeful ethical tendency in nature, we have arrived at faith in a supernatural power who intervenes in nature or oversees it. If, on the other hand, we assume the identification of the tendency creating unities in nature with the *idea* of God, this is no more than a manner of speaking, which, from the rhetorical point of view, may influence the imagination of people and therefore deserves to be utilized in education. In Kaplan's early writings, there is sometimes this kind of noticeable pragmatic orientation; but upon examining his principal later writings, we find in them the intuition of someone who believes in a supernatural power that subdues nature for an ethical purpose. This is the basic intuition of biblical prophecy and of the talmudic rabbis, but Kaplan prefers to mask his faith in camouflaging scientific colors in order to make it attractive to those impressed by the importance of science in our time. It is doubtful that he succeeds in responding adequately to the doubts and perplexities that besiege even the scientific person in quest of moral decisions related to his achievements.[7]

Similar observations may be made about the argument that personal and social ethics constitute a condition for the survival of humanity. Is there any sensible person who would deny this claim today? Was there ever a sensible person who denied this even at times when humanity's power of destruction was much less? The trouble is that the fear of destruction that awaits humanity still does not place it under an obligatory moral authority. Therefore, when humanity acts only out of fear and in consonance with the inclination that fortifies its faith in science and technology, it reacts to the danger of destruction by others through amassing even greater means of destruction for the sake of mutual intimidation. Moral authority, to the extent that it appears, is beyond this vicious circle. Moral authority is the active force of autonomous personality. It can indicate the dangers inherent in immoral behavior and the indispensability of morality for human survival. But the autonomous choice of life and the good derive from a prior decision. The positive motivating power for action does not derive from fear but from personality radiating strength of will. In other words, morality

embodies something beyond itself: the "I" that loves, directs, commands, and confers meaning. This loving "I" reveals itself in moral
behavior, but its essence is beyond morality and even the experience of the presence by which it stimulates the "other" is beyond
morality. Therefore, without the transcendent "I," morality has
neither meaning nor obligating power. This is the center of gravity
of religious experience. Man's stance before the divine as a realm
beyond nature is what gives meaning to his separate existence in
nature and gives strength to his particular destiny.[8] Because of this,
the identification of the idea of God with one of the forces of nature
empties the idea of content in order to save its shell. What a believer like H. N. Bialik lost was the certainty of a supernatural
presence in the process of his life. In all his searchings, he circled it
but never reached it. That is why Ahad Ha'am's teaching could not
release him from the awareness of loss, and Kaplan's naturalistic
theology changes nothing in this respect. His theology preserves the
longing for faith and tries with excessive optimism to describe modern man's longing for transcendent faith as if it were faith itself.

Let us turn to the national element in Kaplan's teaching. Two
issues need to be examined: Does Jewish life in the Diaspora have a
future? And can the Jewish people support both the State of Israel
and the Diaspora? Is not the investment of national energy in two
directions at the same time a destructive contradiction? The difference between the proposals of Kaplan and those of Ahad Ha'am in
this area is actually the difference between an overly optimistic
assessment of the power of Zionism and an overly pessimistic assessment. Ahad Ha'am did not believe in the ability of Zionism to
establish a state that would solve the problem of Jewry; therefore,
he sought a solution to this problem in the Diaspora and made do
with a "spiritual center" in Eretz Yisrael. Kaplan believes in Zionism's ability to establish and sustain a state and at the same time
strengthen the Diaspora with stable organic frameworks. For Kaplan,
the two activities support each other. Since the State of Israel is a
fact, we know that Ahad Ha'am's assessment was too pessimistic;
but certain trends in the Jewish people today, both in Israel and the
Diaspora, indicate that Kaplan's positive assessment is exaggerated.
It is, of course, possible to strengthen communal organization in
the Diaspora in the free world and to develop further the network

of Jewish schools and enrich their programs. With these means it may indeed be possible to slow down the pace of assimilation, an aim worthy of great effort. Unfortunately, it does not seem possible to halt the assimilation of the Jewish masses. Among these masses there is a steadily declining interest in these matters. They do not want the strengthening of the Jewish community or an increase in its activities, and even less do they want the strengthening and enrichment of Jewish education. This is the quest of only a small minority with limited means, while the opposing forces, the enticing powers and pressures of an open secular society, are diverse and powerful. It is impossible to withstand such pressures for long.

In the State of Israel, the Jewish people has the strong framework of a majority society capable of activating institutional authority in order to achieve national objectives. This is a decisive advantage. But we must not avoid the fact that the State of Israel is far from having an adequate base and that its Jewish majority is not certain. Without adequate *aliyah*, Israel will not succeed in assuring its Jewish majority and certainly will not succeed in playing a role in strengthening Jewish education in the Diaspora. We must also take into account that the State of Israel is still compelled to deal with serious external and internal problems. For personal reasons, the life of many individuals will be more comfortable in the Diaspora in the free world than in Israel. Under these conditions, can we recognize the equal legitimacy of the Diaspora and develop it while simultaneously strengthening *aliyah* and preventing emigration? While it is impossible to arrive at definite conclusions on such matters, from a logical point of view Kaplan's proposals appear to be an attempt to go in two opposing directions and, unfortunately, seem to be an attempt to erect a framework for Jewish life with very little chance of success. In order to save itself, the Jewish people must invest most of its energy and means in the consolidation of the State of Israel.

Our answer to the question of the advantage of Kaplan's thought over that of Ahad Ha'am is therefore negative. Despite the criticism, however, we must emphasize its important positive contributions: the serious attempt to deal positively with the religious elements as the central elements of Jewish culture; emphasis on the communal framework as the foundation of the Jewish way of life;

stress on the significance of an obligatory institutionalized national framework for the Jewish people and on the exalted ideal of "ethical nationhood" as a vision that we must strive to realize. These are important elements for the revival of Judaism as a complete civilization uniting the best achievements of modern humanism with the ethical and religious values of the Jewish heritage.

Notes

1. On Krochmal, Formstecher, Hirsch, and Geiger in relationship to the Jewish Reform movement, see Eliezer Schweid, *History of Jewish Thought in Modern Times* (in Hebrew) (Jerusalem: Keter, 5738), chaps. 5 and 7.
2. See Julius Gutmann, "Post-Kantian Idealism in Jewish Philosophy of Religion," in his *Philosophies of Judaism* (New York: Holt, Rinehart & Winston, 1963), part 3.
3. An interesting attempt in this direction is found in the writings of the renowned Yiddish publicist Chaim Zhitlovsky. See especially his article "The National Poetic Rebirth of the Jewish Religion," in *The Faith of Secular Jews*, ed. Saul L. Goodman (New York: Ktav, 1976), 151–58.
4. Kaplan was a productive author, and his writings are many. Among his major works are *Judaism as a Civilization* (New York: Macmillan, 1934); *The Future of the American Jew* (New York: Macmillan, 1948); and *The Religion of Ethical Nationhood* (New York: Macmillan, 1970). All of these works display a coherent and consistent thought, and the differences among the works are minor and do not affect the basic elements of his worldview, which excels in consistency and decisiveness.
5. The term *civilization* refers here to sociospiritual culture. In his major work, *Judaism as a Civilization*, Kaplan refers to national homeland, language, and literature and to law and education as constituent elements of a civilization. He does not include the economic and technological basis, that is, the technical aspect, among these elements.
6. For the rest of this argument, see Samuel Hugo Bergman, *Peoples and Paths* (in Hebrew) (Jerusalem: Mosad Bialik, 1967).
7. The reference is to Kaplan's *Judaism as a Civilization*, in which there is a noticeable tendency toward a pragmatic interpretation of faith as a "requirement" of practical value in moral education.
8. This idea is brilliantly developed in the thought of Julius Gutmann. See chapter 7 in Schweid, *Judaism and Secular Culture*.

PART TWO

Stages in a Life

CHAPTER 3

Becoming Centered: Community and Spirituality in the Early Kaplan

Mel Scult

It was in connection with the Jewish Center that Kaplan first formulated the concept of Judaism as a civilization. With eloquence and power he put forth the idea of a new kind of institution that would meet the needs of the emerging Jewish community in America. The Jewish Center movement and the name of Mordecai Kaplan are inextricably connected. He is credited by both his supporters and his critics with formulating the concept of the "Center" and establishing the first concrete example in the Jewish Center in Manhattan.

Kaplan had been thinking in terms of groups, cultures, and civilizations since his graduate days. At Columbia University from 1900 until 1906, he studied the social sciences and particularly sociology, under Professor Franklin Giddings, the first appointee in sociology in the country. Thus, it was natural that Kaplan should think of Judaism sociologically rather than according to a traditional definition of religion. Kaplan's most profound passion was to do everything possible to bring unity to the Jewish people and to help his people to survive. In a series of articles which appeared in 1915 and 1916 in the *Menorah Journal,* he spelled out a general approach to Judaism. In them, he indicated that he saw the essence of Judaism not in a set of beliefs but in the life energy of the Jewish people. This life energy would be expressed in different truths at different times, but the essence of Judaism was not in these truths themselves but in the life-force that gave rise to them. Survival was, therefore, a matter of doing everything possible to nurture and enhance the life-force of the Jewish people. It is in this context that we must understand Kaplan's work at the Jewish Center. In other words, just as he was formulating his concept of Judaism as a civilization, he began his involvement with the Jewish Center.[1] The Center can thus be seen as a concrete embodiment of his philosophy at the time. I shall examine in detail Kaplan's work at the Center to see wherein he failed in the implementation of his philosophy of community.

The Jewish Center was an experiment in social engineering, as Kaplan was fond of saying. At the same time, it was a synagogue where the rabbi ministered to the personal and spiritual needs of his congregants. In exploring his experiences at the Center, I shall also look at Kaplan the rabbi, who was sensitive to spiritual issues and presented Judaism with deep spiritual understanding. When he spoke from the pulpit as a rabbi, he was a somewhat different Kaplan than when he was analyzing the nature of Judaism and the concept of Judaism as a civilization.

We shall see that the Center was an idea whose time had come. Kaplan did indeed formulate the concept of the Center, but he was not alone. The idea was being proposed on many fronts, and he was the idea's originator.

Let me begin by emphasizing that the term *center* can be used in a variety of ways. In 1923 a prominent social worker suggested that the term be used "to include every type of organization which attempts to provide leisure activities for the entire Jewish community or for a part thereof."[2] Such a generic definition would include the settlement houses intended for the immigrant generation, as well as the YM/YWHA and community centers that were not primarily philanthropic in nature. The Jewish community centers established in the 1920s and 1930s were essentially secular institutions, while synagogue-centers—the so-called "pool with a *shul* and a school"—were, of course, religious. The name of Mordecai Kaplan is connected with the secular and religious centers. He is considered by most to be the ideological father of both these kinds of institutions. Such an important contention warrants examination.

In the case of the secular community centers, even strong supporters of Kaplan find it difficult to provide facts on his contribution. In a tribute to Kaplan in the early 1950s, Louis Kraft, a longtime disciple of Kaplan's, begins an essay on Kaplan and the Center movement by saying almost apologetically "that Dr. Kaplan at no time had an official role as a member of any of the governing bodies of [the Jewish Welfare] Board." (This Board is the umbrella organization for Jewish community centers all over the United States.) Kraft briefly discusses Kaplan's concept of the synagogue-center and then goes on at length to show that Kaplan supported the secular community center.[3] There is no doubt that Kaplan believed in the pluralism inherent in the community center and in the commitment to Jewish culture represented by these institutions. But do we really need particular ideological underpinnings in order to explain such developments? The "Y" movement predates Kaplan and probably would have developed extensively after World War I in any event.

In the case of the synagogue-center, I would note that while Kaplan was serious in his commitment to the idea of the synagogue-center, there were a great many other ideas about which he was also serious. It would be a distortion to imagine that Kaplan's devotion to the synagogue-center was the sole expression of his philosophy at this time. His mind was extremely fertile, and he was advocating new projects all the time, many of which were unrelated to the center idea. For a number of reasons that I will explain later, Kaplan did not want to be the center's rabbi. In March of 1918 it appeared he had freed himself from this obligation, and he immediately began to think of other contexts that might express his philosophy. He conceived the idea, for example, of a kind of school that he called a Zionist *beth midrash*. The *beth midrash* was meant to replace the synagogue as the primary mode of Jewish expression. He gathered together about thirty of his supporters and explained to them that the Zionist *beth midrash* would focus on the renascence of the Jewish people, and its primary activity would be study, which was to be construed as religious in nature. Only a month or so after meeting with his supporters, he conceived the idea of what he called a "Society for Jewish Culture." "The very term," he wrote, "would suggest that our movement is analogous to that of ethical culture, thereby perhaps offsetting in time the danger of assimilation which is being furthered by the latter."[4]

In order to gauge Kaplan's significance with respect to the synagogue-center movement, I need to use a concept developed by the philosopher Sidney Hook. In discussing different kinds of significance, Hook draws the distinction between what he calls the "event-making man" and the "eventful man." In *The Hero and History*, Hook deals with the significant individual who turns events in a new and unexpected direction, the primary example being Lenin. After the democratic revolution of the spring of 1917, it was by no means clear that Russia would be headed in the direction of a Communist state. Russia became Communist only because of Lenin and his followers, who brought about a second revolution in October of that year. Lenin is thus an "event-making man" because he makes a unique contribution, and the course of events would have been very different without him. The "eventful man," on the other hand, is one whose significance derives from his being at the right place at the right time. Anyone who was there would have been significant. Harry Truman with respect to the dropping of the atomic bomb could be described as an "eventful man." His decision to use the bomb marks him as one of the most important men in history; yet, anyone who was president at the time probably would have done the same. Truman exercised no unique influence on the course of events because of who he was and what he believed. On the other hand, Lenin changed the course of history in a way that could not have been anticipated and probably would not have happened had he not been a participant.

With respect to the synagogue-center movement, Kaplan was "eventful," not "event making."[5] The Central Jewish Institute, the Institutional Synagogue, and the direction already espoused by some younger New York rabbis led logically to an expanded synagogue, which included an extensive social and recreational program in addition to the traditional educational and religious activities.

The Americanization of the immigrant synagogues proceeded on several levels at the same time. On the Lower East Side of Manhattan, there was Young Israel, where lectures, geared to attract the young and unaffiliated, were given in English. Uptown on the East Side were synagogues such as Kehilath Jeshurun. In 1903 Kaplan, a college-educated, English-speaking rabbi who could more easily relate to the younger generation of American-born Jews than the traditional rabbi, was hired. There were a number of young rabbis who were experimenting with late Friday evening services, English sermons, and decorum not usually associated with the Orthodox *shtiblekh* (one-room synagogues.) Rabbis Henry Morais, Jacob Dolginas, and others conducted services that were thoroughly respectable. The urge for respectability was perhaps the strongest social need Jews had at this point.[6]

One of the projects meant to serve the needs of the second generation was the Central Jewish Institute (CJI). This experiment embodied the idea of combining a whole range of social and recreational activities with a school at the hub. The Institute was more the creation of Samson Benderly, director of the Bureau of Jewish Education; Rabbi Herbert Goldstein; and Isaac Berkson than of Mordecai Kaplan. The CJI was an original American creation. It offered classes for all ages, in addition to choral music, an orchestra, a gymnasium, folk dancing, an employment bureau, and public lectures on a wide range of topics. Kaplan's participation was peripheral. Though he was on the board, he refers to himself as a "stationary director" who did relatively little. He spoke at CJI from time to time and used the opportunity to formulate the principles that gave shape and purpose to the institution. Thus his importance was the articulation of what was occurring, although the institution would have grown and prospered without him.[7]

In synagogue innovation, Herbert Goldstein's programs at the Institutional Synagogue paralleled or perhaps even predated Kaplan's at the Jewish Center. The term *institutional synagogue* derives from a Protestant experiment in the late nineteenth century, called the Institutional Church. The YM/YWCA movement was quite successful, and a number of ministers, particularly in the New York City area, decided that their churches could expand by opening their doors during the week to the community for leisure and recreational activities. Goldstein adopted the idea and advocated it publicly for synagogues as early as 1916.[8]

Goldstein was a student of Kaplan and was influenced by him, even though there were significant disagreements between them.[9] There is, however, no evidence that the idea for the Institutional Synagogue came from Kaplan. While Goldstein was still rabbi at Kehilath Jeshurun and the CJI, of which he was the head, had just opened, he proposed the idea of the Institutional Synagogue.

My plea for the future is the Institutional Synagogue which would embrace the Synagogue, the Talmud Torah and the YMHA movements. . . . If we desire to perpetuate the real Judaism of the past, we must so shape Jewish spiritual activity that it will all find expression in one institution. . . . Instead of a man belonging to three separate institutions, he could pay a little higher membership in the Institutional Synagogue, which would include all the advantages of the three separate institutions.[10]

His motivation is not at all clear, but in April of 1917 Goldstein resigned Kehilath Jeshurun and the CJI. His biographer never explains why he left this large, prosperous East Side congregation and the newly founded Central Jewish Institute for a rather uncertain future. He quickly became involved in two ventures, both of which were Jewish adaptations of Christian modalities. The first was revivalism. Goldstein was a fine preacher and organized large rallies in the Harlem area. He hoped to appeal to the young and disaffected and apparently was quite successful. The meetings were held on Sunday, when even those who worked on the Sabbath could attend. Usually, he was able to pack the Mount Morris Theater, sometimes with over a thousand people. He also invited prominent public figures, such as Nicholas Murray Butler, to attend and to speak.[11]

Goldstein's second venture was the Institutional Synagogue. He made it clear that the synagogue was to be Orthodox, but at the same time "high-class, clean, and American. . . . There will be decorum at all times as well as a dignified reverential spiritual Orthodox service." The 1917 constitution of the Institutional Synagogue commits the corporation to a wide range of activities and concerns. "The objects and purposes of the corporation shall be to promote the religious, civic, moral, social, and physical welfare of the Jewish youth and to maintain a school for the same purpose." Goldstein began his experiment in a brownstone on 116th Street in

Manhattan, where he held regular services plus programs on Friday evening. These events could best be described as an *Oneg Shabbat* with a speaker and refreshments. Goldstein attempted to implement his idea of a combined "Y" and synagogue by having a gymnasium, although his biographer admits that at the beginning the gymnasium consisted of little more than a bare room with a basketball hoop. There were also clubs and music groups; eventually, a pool was added. In the early 1920s, the synagogue had a Benny Leonard Club, devoted to the Jewish boxer who appeared once at the synagogue.[12]

The expanded synagogue-center parallels Kaplan's efforts and is not derived from him. It is easy to see that the synagogue-center was a logical outgrowth of institutions like the YM/YWHA, the Central Jewish Institute, and the Institutional Church. Yet Herbert Goldstein is all but forgotten, and Mordecai Kaplan lives on in the minds of many as the synagogue-center movement's founder. The reason is that, more than anyone else, Kaplan gave eloquent expression to the synagogue-center concept and put it within the context of ultimate concerns. However, Kaplan's contribution, which lies in the realm of ideology, should not be confused with the actual beginnings of synagogue-centers, which resulted from efforts by Kaplan and others.[13]

Insofar as ideology is concerned, we need to remember Kaplan's understanding of religion and of the relationship between religion and community. Kaplan believed that historic religions grew or declined depending on the vitality of their group's life. This is not to say that religion is confined to group expression; obviously, it is not. The spiritual search of the individual is undeniably the center of the quest for meaning, but unless the individual locates himself in some vital group his spiritual creativity will wither and die. Religious life and group life cannot be detached from one another, according to Kaplan. Even the solitary monk lives in a community and lives out the ideals of his community's tradition.

Kaplan was concerned with the "thinness" of contemporary religious life. Traditionally, Jewish life had been bound up with the life of the community as a whole. Religion and life were coextensive. Since the emancipation, religious life had become detached from so many aspects of the individual's life that it had become for many Jews a "sometime" thing. Kaplan believed that Judaism would survive only if Jews have a life together other than just praying together: Community precedes religion and gives rise to it. A thriving community will inevitably crave religious expression to give form and context to its joys and pains.

In other words, for Kaplan it was necessary to understand Judaism as a total civilization and not only as a set of beliefs. Kaplan had been pondering this notion for a long time; and it seemed that in the years 1915–18, everything was falling into place. Just as the synagogue helped to rescue the Jews after the destruction of the Temple in Jerusalem, so the synagogue-center would help to solve the contemporary Jewish problem. The center would help to restore Jewish life because it would embrace all facets of that life.

He summarized his idea by stating that "the Jewish Center, in insisting that Judaism must be lived as a civilization, will endeavor to have us work, play, love, and worship as Jews." He hoped, for example, that his congregants would learn to bring their Judaism into the workplace. It was not a matter of voicing pious platitudes about economic justice but of trying to bring ethical living into agreements to which his followers were a part. Kaplan wanted to emphasize "the need for Jews who exercise power in the dominion of industry and traffic to come together in the name of their faith . . . to see what they can do to ameliorate the evils and to improve the relations between employer and employee."[14]

Judah Magnes was one of those who criticized Kaplan's movement as being too synagogue centered. In January 1921, Magnes wrote to Kaplan, "Your movement is purely synagogal. You seem to leave out of account the large Jewish life and the important Jewish forces, spiritual and material, outside the synagogue."[15] Such a criticism is based on an inadequate understanding of what Kaplan was trying to do. In proposing the notion of Judaism as a living civilization, Kaplan was implying that a Judaism confined to conventional religious expression in the modern sense, that is, intermittent praying and holiday celebrating, will never survive. A people constitutes a community with prayer as one of its many functions, not as its primary function. The synagogue as it had evolved could not serve this goal and, therefore, must be superseded. Kaplan seemed to stand with those who were non- or antisynagogue. He differed from them, however, in that he saw the Jewish community of the future as building on the synagogue and transforming it. The transformation would result in a new kind of institution—the synagogue-center—which would reflect the total life of the community. It was not conceived as a place where rabbis arranged recreational activities to lure Jews to services on Sabbaths and holidays. Kaplan was serious about his notion of a living Judaism as a total civilization and the synagogue-center as the vehicle for this concept.[16]

In dedicating the center's building on Manhattan's West Eighty-sixth Street in 1918, he put forth an ideal that he hoped the synagogue would embody. This ideology would serve as a map to help the congregants to orient themselves and clarify their goals.

The Jewish Center was originally created by a number of prominent Jews who had moved from the Upper East Side of New York City to the West Side. The East Side, including Yorkville, had many Jews and a host of prominent synagogues. The West Side had fewer Jews and virtually no prominent houses of worship. The group consisted of wealthy Ashkenazic Jews who had been successful in the clothing business, were traditional in their understanding of Judaism, and wanted a synagogue that would reflect their new-found status. As Kaplan put it many years later, they wanted a synagogue that would make Judaism fashionable. They wanted to show the world that you could be rich, be an observant Jew, and live on the West Side of Manhattan at the same time. The group turned to Kaplan because he was well known in the New York City area, respected for his work with the *Kehillah* and the Teacher's Institute and for his fine speaking ability. He was young, dynamic, college educated, and spoke English without an accent.

Kaplan was without a congregation at this point and was hard at work at the Teacher's Institute. He also lectured widely and published his thoughts on the nature of Judaism in the *Menorah Journal*. The articles he wrote for this periodical focused on the relationship between religion and social life. He wrote, "I have come to the conclusion that religion derives its vitality from the social activities with which it is bound up. Detached from social life it becomes an empty formalism and a corpse." When the West Side group came to him and asked his help in forming a synagogue, he began to think about the concrete implications of what he was saying. If the key to survival was the social life, then the synagogue as an institution devoted primarily to prayer and study was clearly inadequate. The synagogue had to become something else: "It would not only provide a place to worship for the elders and a school for the children but also an opportunity to all affiliated with it to develop their social life Jewishly."[17]

Although the idea for an expanded synagogue was not well established, it also was not incompatible with a traditional understanding of Judaism. The West Side group had no trouble in accepting Kaplan's ideas for the structure and program of the synagogue. His concept of a synagogue-center was new but not radical. At the same time, Kaplan's general conception of Judaism was already a clear departure from tradition. He rejected the cardinal concept of traditional Judaism that the Torah (Pentateuch) was given to Moses at Mount Sinai and he publicly accepted biblical criticism.[18]

The West Side group was clearly Orthodox. Its head was Joseph H. Cohen, a wealthy clothing manufacturer who was active in Jewish affairs and had been a member of Kehilath Jeshurun when Kaplan was rabbi there. Cohen was traditional in his attitude toward Judaism and was a supporter of Beth Israel Hospital. At this time, Beth Israel was Manhattan's only hospital that respected Orthodox Jewish principles. As one historian put it, "[Beth Israel] . . . exercised a strong hold on thousands of New Yorkers and particularly upon the citizens of its own neighborhood. Built and developed by the Jewish inhabitants of the Lower East Side, it was looked upon not as an institution, but as a place where people could feel at home."[19]

Kaplan wanted the West Side group to understand clearly his general position on Judaism. He made a point of reading Cohen his notes on Genesis that he used for teaching at the Teacher's Institute. These notes indicated Kaplan's acceptance of Darwin's ideas on evolution and biblical criticism. Cohen, for his part, seemed unconcerned with matters of ideology. He was a practical man and only wanted Kaplan's commitment on certain religious forms that he considered crucial. Kaplan, according to his own account, was less concerned about "particulars" (seating, order of the service,

etc.) and so was willing to give in on all the details. He did insist
on support for the revival of Hebrew and for the rebuilding of Zion.
Cohen wanted Kaplan to come out strongly for traditional customs,
which Kaplan found difficult at this point, but he did agree to be
"tactful and circumspect" about his own views.[20]

As in so many other situations, the two parties were talking past
each other and not really hearing the other. Kaplan was satisfied
because he warned the group about his radicalism, but the *bale
batim* (community leaders) cared little for ideology as long as they
got their way on practical matters. They certainly believed they
could control Kaplan if he stepped out of line. They did not take his
growing radicalism seriously, and he did not see their Orthodox
commitments as a problem. Kaplan wanted to see signs of flexibility
and a willingness to try new ideas. There was some slight basis for
this feeling. At one point Cohen expressed interest in "the good
points of Christian Science" and also suggested to Kaplan that "the
Center might hold services in the vernacular during the week." But
in the final analysis Cohen and his followers were Orthodox.[21]

It is at this point that Kaplan wrote in his journal that, though he
was radical in his thought, he was completely Orthodox in his
religious behavior. The statement is true at this time but not later.
In his later years, Kaplan allowed a number of historians to read
the first volume of his journal and to quote from it. They took this
particular statement to be a description of Kaplan's behavior
throughout his life, which it was not. It is evident from the diaries
that the character of Kaplan's religious observance changed significantly as time passed.

The meetings with Joe Cohen and the West Side group were
exhilarating for Kaplan. He was in his early thirties and had a
strong sense of his own mission and the contributions he might
make. The Teacher's Institute kept him busy, but it was a limited
operation. The idea of a new kind of synagogue represented "a
method in religion" and not just another *shul*, Kaplan told the
group one *Shabbos* afternoon. He saw the primary problem of Jewish
life as "how to Judaize or vitalize in a Jewish way a greater fraction
of the Jews' life," and he believed that the synagogue-center was
the way to do it. After one meeting he confided in his journal, "I

find myself at the beginning of a new spiritual enterprise which holds out great promise."[22] Kaplan had such feelings more than once. Throughout his whole life he was spawning new ideas and getting groups together to discuss them, becoming energized by the whole process. It may be that the process was as important to him as the product.

The discussions that began in earnest in the spring of 1915 continued through the summer and fall. Cohen made it clear to Kaplan that he wanted him to take the position of rabbi as soon as the building was completed. Cohen and Kaplan met frequently for lunch at the Waldorf Hotel to discuss their plans for the center. Kaplan noted that the waiters all knew Cohen and made obvious efforts to meet his religious needs so he would not be embarrassed when washing his hands or saying the *Motzi*.

The people who supported Cohen in establishing the Jewish Center were Jewish laymen who had served with him at Beth Israel Hospital. They were either born or grew up in this country and were self-starters who were already well known in their particular careers. Otto Rosalsky, for example, was born and educated in New York City and was appointed to the Court of General Sessions as a judge in 1905. His father was one of the best-known butchers on Allen Street and was respected for his knowledge of Jewish matters. Rosalsky served on the bench for thirty-one years, with very few of his decisions ever being reversed. Kaplan describes him as being rather long winded, with a propensity for summarizing speeches he had given while talking in private to individuals. Rosalsky and Julius Schwartz were the only members of the Center's board who were not in manufacturing. Schwartz, also born in New York City, was a staff member of the *New York Tribune* and later organized the Jewish Biographical Bureau, which published *Who's Who in American Jewry* during these early years.[23]

The other members of the board were all businessmen, whose average age was forty. Almost without exception they had founded their own companies, most of which were in the area of clothing manufacturing. For example, Israel Unterberg, who came to America alone at the age of ten, established his own shirt-manufacturing company at the age of twenty-one. Like most of the other Center directors, he was active in many Jewish organizations. He served as a board director of Montefiore Hospital. Unterberg was a strong supporter of Kaplan and was one of the founders of the Society for the Advancement of Judaism.

The Center's board members were also strong advocates of other religious causes. Most were active in the Rabbi Isaac Elhanan Theology Seminary (RIETS), where they raised money and served in various capacities. The Lamport family, which had four members on the Center's board, was especially important to Dr. Bernard Revel and the growth of RIETS. Nathan Lamport, the *paterfamilias*, had given over $200,000 to RIETS during his lifetime. He was not a Center member; but his sons, Arthur and Samuel C., were both members of the Center's board. Samuel C., who took over the family business, became one of the largest exporters of cotton goods in the United States. He was widely known for his philanthropy and bought over $1,000,000 worth of Liberty Bonds during World War I. His brother, Arthur, went into investment banking and formed his own firm. The Lamports were "star workers" for the Center, as one Center staff member put it, and were in evidence everywhere in all branches of the synagogue.[24]

The Center was constructed in a relatively short period of time. The West Side group and particularly Cohen started talking with Kaplan on a serious basis in the spring of 1915, and by the summer of 1917 the building began to go up. That it was wartime did not seem to retard the process of planning and construction. The Jewish community, including the Center's leaders and members, were involved in raising money for the Jewish communities in Europe, but the Center's supporters seemed to have had enough for all their needs. The men building the Center spared no expense in order to have the kind of building they wanted. They started out with a plan for a four-story structure; by the time the building was finished in 1920, it came to nine stories.

There were a number of problems involved in the project, and Kaplan met continuously with Cohen and the group to work on them. Mixed or family seating was a hotly debated issue at the time. Reform Jews had introduced mixed seating in the middle of the nineteenth century, but this innovation did not become an issue for many until the twentieth. The movement for the emancipation of women was gaining ground, and the matter of seating became emblematic of the differentiation between the more liberal (that is, Conservative) synagogues and the more strictly Orthodox. In one early case, the conflict over seating led to the rabbi leaving the congregation because he wanted separate seating but his congregants wanted mixed. Kaplan, who was a strong supporter of the emancipation of women in general and of women's right to vote in particular, wanted mixed seating. The board on the whole wanted separate seating. The compromise they arrived at was to have separate seating, with the women sitting on the two sides of a large center section but with no curtains or dividers between the two groups, who thus remained in full view of each other. Cohen consulted Rabbi M. Z. Margolis on the matter, "not so much for the purpose of knowing the actual law, but how to be sufficiently within the letter of the law and yet please the members." Part of the compromise also included a stipulation that in all synagogue matters women were to have a vote equal to men's.[25]

Whenever possible the Center's backers arranged a ceremony to celebrate a stage in the completion of the project. This procedure gave them publicity and perhaps was significant in helping them to gain members. It also reflected their belief, certainly influenced by Kaplan's rhetoric, that they were engaged in a venture of heroic proportions. At the ground-breaking ceremony that took place on May 22, 1917, Kaplan told the crowd that this was not just a foundation that was being dug but a "well" that would become "a fountain of new and inexhaustible energy for living the Jewish life." Kaplan lifted the event to a higher plane when he said that those who are building the Center are "the tools of a will not their own and higher than their own to perpetuate the life of the Jewish people."[26] At the ceremony marking the laying of the cornerstone, which took place some two and a half months later, he again emphasized that what was needed was not just another synagogue or a rich man's club with a chapel to outdo the Gentiles. Kaplan harped on his theme that community needs come before religious needs, when he said, "We have established a Jewish Center that shall enable us to live together as Jews, because living together as Jews is an indispensible condition to Jewish religion. Before we can have Judaism we must have Jewishness."[27]

Surprisingly, after all the work he put into the planning between 1915 and 1918, Kaplan did not want to be the Center's rabbi. The reasons for his hesitation tell us much about Kaplan the man and his sense of himself. Objectively, we can see that he was very busy: the Teacher's Institute was growing significantly and was taking more and more of his time. He spoke frequently not only in New York City at Kehilath Jeshurun and the Central Jewish Institute but also in the Midwest. In Chicago, for example, Kaplan addressed a group of rabbis. He also lectured at Menorah societies along the East Coast. Moreover, he wanted time to devote to his writing and scholarship. By 1918 the Kaplan family already consisted of four small girls, which kept Mordecai and Lena sufficiently busy.

But there were other reasons for his ambivalence. Deep down he had contempt for the Center's members and the social class they represented. The constant repetition of his conviction that the Center was not to be a rich man's club represented his private fears that this was precisely what it would become. He was consistently ready to judge the Center's leaders harshly. In talking about the size of the building, for example, he said that it would only serve to make the leaders smug and complacent. He had no illusions about the spiritual depth of the people he was dealing with and referred to them more than once as a "group of typically successful bourgeois type."[28]

The other reason for Kaplan's ambivalence was his sense of himself as a writer and scholar. In 1915 and 1916, Kaplan published a series of articles in the *Menorah Journal*. He enjoyed not only the creative process but also the recognition he received. However, he was only at the beginning of his creative career and still doubted his ability. The choice in taking the position at the Center seemed to be between an unsure future as a writer-scholar, on the one hand, or the more immediately available respect and influence that the position at the Center might bring, on the other hand. In his own words, "I have not much confidence in my literary ability and I am afraid that if I let go of this opportunity of becoming a public factor, I might be a disappointed man in later years."[29] Kaplan had no way of knowing that he would become important both as a writer and as a public figure in the course of his long and productive life.

His ambivalence about the Center is also reflected in his flirtation with the notion that he might leave professional Jewish life altogether. While at Kehilath Jeshurun (1903–09), Kaplan had considered seriously attending law school or selling insurance. In 1917 he investigated the possibility of going into business. Bernard Revel's brother-in-law, a man by the name of Travis, had many different kinds of investments, and Kaplan turned to him for advice and the possibility of some kind of position. Travis suggested that, other than a minor salaried job, the best thing for Kaplan to do was to gather some capital, and Travis would help him set up his own company—possibly in oil, since Travis had holdings in Oklahoma. Kaplan turned to his brother-in-law, Jacob Rubin. He advised Kaplan against making such a commitment because he discovered that Travis had a rather unsavory reputation. Kaplan also found out that Travis wanted to give money to the Seminary for scholarships so that students might study for traditional rabbinical ordination (*hatra'at hora'ah*). Travis hoped to see an Orthodox *rav* at the head of the Seminary and apparently was willing to donate up to $10,000 for that purpose. Kaplan did not know all the details, but he understood that the offer was never accepted.[30]

The Center's board perhaps reluctantly gave in to Kaplan and started searching for another rabbi. They interviewed only one candidate, Kaplan's colleague and distant cousin Hillel Kauvar. Kauvar traveled from Denver and preached at the synagogue and was interviewed by the board. Kauvar ended up having a long and distinguished career in Denver, but he was no match for Kaplan and the board rejected him.[31]

On Sunday evening, April 21, 1918, Judge Rosalsky and Abe Rothstein came again to see Kaplan to offer him the position of rabbi. This time he accepted and was voted in by the congregation the next week. The only problem that remained was the matter of salary. Kaplan the ideologue showed himself the true idealist when he adamantly refused to take any salary at all. The board, for its part, was understandably concerned because of the way this complicated their relationship with Kaplan. They offered him $7,500 a year, a considerable sum for those times. In refusing the salary, Kaplan had a number of considerations in mind. First and foremost, he wanted to be free to express himself in whatever way he chose.

Every rabbi, from that day to this, is caught between his function as a leader of the congregation and the fact that the congregation also pays his salary. It is not easy to bite the hand that feeds you. Moreover, Kaplan seemed to have genuine contempt for the monied classes and did not want to join their ranks. He knew that once his income went up he would be tied into a higher standard of living, which would enslave him. He did, of course, have many expenses. With four young children the decision was not an easy one. His wife Lena seemed to be genuinely supportive of his idealistic stance, which shows her strength of character since she was the one who ran the household and balanced the budget. He recorded his struggle in his journal:

[If I were to take the money] I would become the slave of a higher standard of living or at best save up another fifty thousand dollars in the course of the next ten years. Besides, I am convinced that unless those who are at the helm of Jewish life display something of the spirit of sacrifice that now permeates the nations of the world, the Jewish people have no chance for survival. . . . I pray to God that I be strong enough to resist all temptation to accept a salary from the Center.

Kaplan and the board agreed that his salary should be given to the Teacher's Institute, where it would be used for scholarships.[32]

Following the successful conclusion of Kaplan's negotiations with the board, the Center's bulletin joyously declared that Kaplan had accepted the call to be rabbi. It characterized him "as the thinker and spiritual leader who called the Center idea into being and who helped to bring it to its present stage of development." Kaplan was represented as combining "in himself so completely the authority of the old and the new learning, as well as the social vision and individual power as thinker and leader."[33] It was at this time (the summer of 1918) that Kaplan and his family moved from 120 East Ninety-third Street to 1 West Eighty-ninth Street.

In the midst of all these negotiations, the building was finished (or at least the first four floors), and it was time for another ceremony. Judge Rosalsky presided, with Rabbi M. Z. Margolis offering the opening prayer. In addition to Kaplan, Louis Marshall spoke, as did Mathilde Schechter, who represented the women of the Center. The occasion seemed to bring together many diverse parties within the Jewish community. Kaplan had not yet alienated the Orthodox community and was well known in both Reform and Zionist circles. He clearly had in mind that the Center should serve as a model, when he told the group that "we must create for ourselves the kind of recreational, cultural, and religious opportunities which we shall then have the right to provide for others."[34]

The Center was one of the first American synagogues of a "modern Orthodox" or Conservative type. The reality fell far beneath the vision. Nonetheless, Kaplan was able to create a wide range of activities through an experimental educational program and a synagogue service that was meaningful even though it was not experimental in character. The community never achieved the cohesiveness he had hoped for nor were there changes in the area of ritual. In comparison with traditional synagogues prior to this period, the Center marked a significant step toward a bold and innovative American institution.

There were two educational tracks, an afternoon Hebrew school and a day school. Referring to the afternoon school, which started in 1918 with some forty children, Kaplan described it as being "very small and very expensive." Kaplan's eldest daughter, Judith, attended this school; and Max Kadushin, who later became a noted scholar of rabbinics, was her teacher. As I shall discuss later, it may be that Kadushin's teaching was one of the major causes of the split that led to Kaplan's leaving the Center.[35]

The day school was quite innovative for its time and was one of the projects Kaplan barely had time to begin. He started with a kindergarten in 1918; by the time he left the Center in 1922, the school had three, possibly four grades. Naomi, Kaplan's third daughter, attended the day school from the beginning and has clear memories of it. It was more experimental than the other schools she attended. The students were taught carpentry, tie-dyeing and candle-making and learned arithmetic by using paper money. She remembers that there was much Isadora Duncan–type dancing and a musical program as well. Kaplan himself was not directly involved but brought in people from Columbia University, where John Dewey was holding forth about experimental education. Patti Hill from Teacher's College, the composer who wrote the song "Happy Birthday," came around from time to time. Curiously, the day school continued at the Center for some time but was never instituted at the Society for the Advancement of Judaism. Much later, in 1931, Judith was offered a job at the Center's school, but she turned it down.[36]

The adult-education program included weekly lectures by Kaplan on the Bible and later a *hevra shas*, which met for five hours a week to study Talmud. In the Bible class, Kaplan used the same material he had prepared for his students at the Teacher's Institute. He felt relaxed with these classes and expressed himself freely on the origins of the Jewish people and the development of the biblical text. As he observed, "Now and then there would come to the class someone who was in search of heresy and he would not have to wait long before he got what he had come for. Such a man would then complain to Fischman or Cohen, but the latter would always find some way of drawing his fangs."[37]

Kaplan's openness about his "heresy" indicates that his leaving the Center calls for a more complex explanation than just his heterodox ideology. Students of Kaplan ordinarily assume that the sole reason for his departure was his ideological stance on fundamental religious matters. His ideas certainly constitute part of the story, but there are other factors as well.

In addition to education, the Center provided a wide range of activities in music and the dramatic arts. Kaplan engaged a local drama coach named Amelia Morganroth to supervise the plays and the drama groups. She apparently was well liked by the young people, but they often were more interested in doing vaudeville than plays on biblical themes. Seminary children, such as Eli Ginzberg, participated in these plays, as did Shaw Benderly, the son of Samson Benderly. Kaplan had little patience with the adolescents and referred to the girls as "foolish gigglers" and the boys as "rich boobs." Morganroth functioned in a number of different capacities at the Center. As a teacher of education, she reacted to Kaplan's sermons on a continuous basis. She would attend the Sabbath services and then write him, analyzing the modulation of his voice, his use of gestures, and his general delivery. She reacted to everything—from his pronunciation ("would you" came out as "woodje" and "could you" as "coodje," she tells him), to the quality of his voice ("there really was a smile in your voice"), to a general evaluation of the content ("the subject was a monstrous one and most clearly put before your listeners"). She sometimes quoted to him good lines that she liked, such as "man must primarily live right and then God will take on form according to his way of living and thinking."[38]

Music also played a prominent role at Kaplan's synagogue. This was the era of the great cantors, and the center was not to be outdone. Cantor Pinhas Jassinowsky, with his beautiful high tenor voice, sang each Sabbath and on holidays. Congregational singing was just coming into vogue in the more traditional congregations. In order to help things along, the Center hired a man who sat in the back of the congregation and sang along with the congregants. During the week, there was a choral society and other opportunities for the Center's members to learn the hymns for Sabbath services. The school put a strong emphasis on Zionist songs, and on the occasion of the British mandate (April 1920), Judith Kaplan remembers being on a float constructed by the Jewish Center. "Several thousand men and women formed a parade when the first reports concerning Palestine came . . . and marched through East Broadway and other streets. They sang 'The Star-Spangled Banner,' 'Hatikvah' and 'God Save The King' and were greeted with cheers by spectators."[39]

With all its extra activities, the Center was nonetheless still a synagogue. Although the synagogue could be described as rather Americanized, there was little of the innovative ritual that characterized Kaplan's work at the Society for the Advancement of Judaism. There were no late Friday evening services, but neither did the SAJ participate in this important American innovation. Kaplan always felt that Friday evening should be a family time, so he never held late services. The preaching at the Center was in English with a very limited number of English readings during the services. Honors were not auctioned from the pulpit. From time to time Kaplan did try to innovate, but his efforts were not always successful. For example, in 1919 he experimented with a forum method from the pulpit, but it did not catch on.

Kaplan's greatest strength and special contribution was as a preacher. He had a strong voice, spoke without an accent, and turned a fine phrase. At the Seminary, he had been teaching homiletics since 1910 and became increasingly conscious of the structure

of the sermon and what distinguished a great sermon from a medio-
cre one. Although there was variety in what he did, his themes
usually derived directly from the week's Torah portion. He would
begin with the text but would go far afield into important ethical
and religious issues.

Sermons are not generally thought of as great literature; as a
form of thought and expression they have been held in low esteem.
The essay informs or analyzes whereas the sermon exhorts, although some degree of analysis may be included. In a sense, it is
much easier to exhort than to analyze because the former may
reflect a limited understanding of the way things actually are and
why they are as they are. In evaluating a sermon, listeners must ask
whether the sermon moves them to do, to think, and to believe that
which is necessary for their own best interest and self-fulfillment. A
sermon is like a conversation and should be evaluated as to how
well the speaker makes himself or herself understood.

Kaplan was a great preacher, even though the analytical aspects
of his sermons may have been too sophisticated for many in his
congregation. They were, after all, ordinary people, businessmen
and their wives and children who came to hear him week after
week. As a leader, Kaplan's primary weakness was the inordinate
faith he put in preaching. Perhaps there was too much analysis in
his sermons and too much exhortation in his essays. His true feelings about preaching were thinly disguised when in a sermon in
May 1918, he denied the transcendent significance of preaching.
"Bear in mind," he told his congregation, "that preaching is not a
means to the solution of all difficulties in Jewish life." He went on,
"If it [preaching] can diagnose the evils and at least create a demand for the proper remedy, it is discharging its function."[40] The
question that underlies Kaplan's assertion concerns the matter of
change and the way change is effected. He seems to believe that
people need only to be told the right way and they would do it.
Kaplan himself said that habits change over time as a result of
complex social forces. Habits evolve and are much less subject to
the will than we would like to believe.

Let me emphasize again that Kaplan had a strong impact on
those who heard him. He was a passionate, rousing speaker, and
people could not help but be moved when they listened. They were

lifted up by his rhetoric and by the strength of his feelings. He seemed to make things clearer and to make the listener part of a great adventure. His congregants clearly understood this, and the center's Journal reflects the members' feelings that theirs was a special institution and that they were the vanguard of a new direction in Jewish life.[41]

Kaplan's sermons dealt with issues ranging from theology (God as healer) to religious practice (the nature of public worship), to economic issues (the five-day workweek), to pressing matters of war and peace. The Great War was constantly on everyone's mind, and Kaplan talked about it frequently. From the beginning, Kaplan was a strong supporter of Wilson. The idealism of Woodrow Wilson found a responsive chord in Mordecai Kaplan. When America entered the war in 1917, Kaplan, speaking at the Ninety-second Street Y, encouraged the young men to go willingly to the army when they were drafted. He told his congregation that the war, which had been a clash of nations seeking power, was transformed when Wilson proclaimed the League of Nations and the rule of international justice as the only worthy outcome of the conflict. He compared Wilson to Abraham through the concept of the test or trial. "Ideals are distorted as soon as we attempt to put them into practice," he said. If we continue to believe in them despite the distortion, we might be said to have withstood the trial. President Wilson was undergoing such a test, just as Abraham had. At another point, Kaplan used the image of Jacob wrestling with the angel to comment on Wilson and the League. When the war ended, he tried to draw lessons from the conflict. He emphasized that "the forces of bestiality were always there, ready to break up the coherence of civilization." Unfortunately, "to restore the world to sanity, it is necessary to become mad and irrational." Soldiers are brutalized by war, and there is inevitably a loss of freedom at home. Most importantly, he emphasized, the insanity must not be prolonged.[42]

Kaplan's support for the war and for Wilson flowed from a strong sense of patriotism. His feelings of loyalty and gratitude were characteristic of many of the immigrants and their children. In a sermon he gave a few weeks after the armistice was signed, he said:

Americanism is falsely regarded as demanding the surrender of all group traditions, values, and loyalties. It is thought that being a good Jew prevents one from being a full-time American. The discussion of this question is relevant to the celebration of Hanukah because we commemorate on this festival Judaism's triumph over the melting pot idea.[43]

Parallel to his strong patriotism was his commitment to democracy and the ideals of pluralism. In a sermon preached on November 9, 1918, he said, "Democracy's conception of preeminence is the full development of one's distinctive and individual traits and capacities. It is distinctiveness that makes for distinction."

Kaplan managed to present his Zionism as compatible with American loyalty. His argument reveals how strong was his loyalty to America. His approach was as follows: If we see Wilson as the emancipator of the nations, we must still understand that full emancipation did not come to the Jews until the Balfour Declaration. Kaplan suggested that the anniversary of the declaration should be called *Yom Ha-Ge'ulah*, the day of redemption. "The Jews were slaves before, because a slave is one who accepts from another the purposes which control his conduct," and until the Jews have their own land, they will not be in a position to control their destiny. Thus, the slogan "making the world safe for democracy" really means making the world safe for nationalism. The job "of the Jews is to make nationalism safe for the world. . . . Nationalism misapplied is dynamite but nationalism together with the goal of righteousness and social justice makes Zionism and American loyalty not incompatible."[44]

Kaplan presented a broad definition of Zionism to his congregation. He put forth the notion, which he later called "peoplehood," when he asserted that more than anything else, Zionism reflected the identification of Jews with each other. To the Jew with sympathy and imagination, Kaplan suggested, "nothing Jewish is alien or indifferent." He believed that only the Zionist movement was capable of restoring unity to the Jews, thus ensuring their survival. Zionism was a mode of developing "new standards of fraternity and solidarity" among the Jews. Such solidarity would, however, not be narrow or chauvinistic. He strongly rejected the kind of group pride that sees little value in others. When such chauvinism was backed by force, he believed, it was called imperialism. When it was not, it resulted in "proud self-isolation." Jewish loyalty called for a wider perspective because "of the fealty to the God of Israel who is (also) the God of Humanity."[45]

Was Kaplan softening his Zionism in order to make it more palatable to his congregation? Surely, the recently successful clothing manufacturers who made up the bulk of Kaplan's flock had little interest in *aliyah* for themselves. They could, however, be easily drawn into philanthropic Zionism—that is, into the idea that "we need a homeland for those who suffer but not for ourselves." For his part, Kaplan was not a hard-line political Zionist who despaired of the Diaspora. A journal entry from this period demonstrates that Kaplan's Americanism meant that even in the privacy of his diary he had to turn his Zionist understanding into an aspect of his devotion to the United States. In December 1918, he briefly contemplated settlement in Israel and went to talk with Jacob De Haas, a key figure in the Zionist movement. Feeling guilty about his actions, he wrote in his journal:

Does this [the desire to go to Palestine] mean ingratitude to America? To love America is simply to love myself, for it is only in this blessed country that I could have achieved what I value most in myself. . . . If I will go to Palestine it would be not only for the purpose of helping to interpret my people to itself, but also of interpreting America to her own people. Very few of her own people understand her.[46]

The setting for the newly developing sense of Jewish solidarity as fostered by Zionism was the synagogue or, more precisely, the synagogue-center. Kaplan saw Jewish solidarity—Zionism—as the goal and the synagogue-center as the means. Kaplan's Zionism at this time was perfectly compatible with the needs of his congregation to feel fully loyal. His was a Zionism that envisioned a Jewish community in Palestine that would complement and enhance the Jewish life of communities around the world. He was concerned about the Jewish future but never thought it would be assured by emigration alone. It was, instead, a revitalized Jewish civilization that would become the foundation for a brighter future. A vibrant Jewish community in Palestine or in the United States could only come into being if the core of Jewish civilization—its religion—were made compatible with the modern world.

Kaplan continuously used the pulpit to explore ways of revitalizing Judaism. His understanding of the key theological issues was not identical with the theology he later espoused. At this point, he seems to have had a strong sense of the spiritual as conventionally understood. The synagogue setting perhaps encouraged him to be somewhat less analytical and more traditionally spiritual when he spoke on theological matters. His sermons, at this time, contained none of his later attacks on supernaturalism. He told his congregation: "We have to cultivate a sense of the reality of things spiritual. God should be so real to us that in place of fear and distrust which overcloud our lives, we should be possessed of such peace, poise, and power as to render us free and joyful and give us a sense of dominion." The only way to experience the reality of God was "by having our inner life permeated by 'kedushah' and 'bitahon', inward holiness and faith."[47]

His optimism was present here as in everything he touched. In a rousing sermon about Sinai and the drama of revelation, after contrasting the power made manifest at the mountain with the still, small voice Elijah heard in the wilderness, he declared that "the significant fact about the Jewish Spirit, is that no matter how near extinction it may appear, it is not only imperishable but resurgent. . . . The voice that spoke at Horeb may no longer thunder forth its divine message but it can never be completely silenced."[48]

In his later writing, Kaplan talked frequently about God as the "power that makes for salvation." This formulation has been criticized as being metaphysically muddled and unsatisfying. At this early point, however, his theology is less abstract and in an immanentist mode. In the following example, Kaplan sees human fellowship as a manifestation of the spirit of God. In his words, "God is not merely a transcendent being but the spirit which manifests itself in human fellowship, in the brotherhood of man." Another example comes from Kaplan's speech in the spring of 1918 at the dedication of the Center's building. Again we see another, perhaps more traditionally spiritual side of Kaplan:

It is only that kind of community (i.e. a true and close one) that develops associations, traditions, and memories that go to make up its soul. To mingle one's personality with that soul becomes a natural longing. In such a community one experiences that mystic divine grace which, like radiant sunshine, illumines our lives when joyous and like balm heals them when wounded or sore-stricken. Then all questions about saying this or that become trivial, for the real purpose is attained in having each one feel with the Psalmist: One thing have I asked of the Lord that will I seek after, that I may dwell in the house of the Lord all the days of my life, to behold the graciousness of God.[49]

With such formulations, he could easily have remained within the Orthodox community if he had not attacked it so explicitly later on in 1920. His theology does not really alienate but has a unifying effect. In the sermon just quoted, he affirmed, "There is no justification at the present time for any part of Israel inaugurating changes without the authority of Catholic Israel."[50]

It is in connection with his stand on women and Judaism that we see Kaplan and the dynamics of the congregation in all their complexity. The Center seemed to be reasonably progressive insofar as women were concerned. In the Center's journal, we find statements strongly supporting women's rights but presented in a somewhat defensive manner. For example, there is the following: "We are the last to subscribe to the German idea of *Küche, Kinder*, and *Kirche*. Women must play a significant role in the great social changes that are taking place." Wherever possible women were included in important ceremonies. As part of the dedication of the Center, a *Sefer Torah* was finished by each person writing in a letter. The Center's journal noted proudly that "all the women as well as the men participated in the ceremony."[51]

The Synagogue was Orthodox, so that seating was separate (though equal) and there was never any question of changing the synagogue's rituals to include women. A major question of the day was the matter of women's right to vote. Kaplan advocated the emancipation of women and in his preaching went beyond mere support of the vote, which he took for granted. At the same time, he did not argue for changing any rituals to include women. In the fall of 1918, he took the occasion of the *sidra* "Haye Sarah" to deal with the issue. He prepared the way for his sermon by publishing a question in the Center's journal during that week. "Shall the Emancipation of women be merely a duplication of men?" he asked. On *Shabbos* morning Kaplan pulled no punches, when he said that "Judaism of the *Galut* has said nothing and done nothing to lay claim to any share in the Emancipation of women." The major religions, moreover, always lagged behind when it came to movements for social betterment. He asserted that "the movement to emancipate women was nothing more than the logical extension of democracy."[52]

If Judaism offered no help on the issue of emancipation, Kaplan suggested that we look to the Bible for guidance. He pointed out that there are many strong, holy women in the Bible—including Deborah, Miriam, and, of course, Rebecca. However, if Genesis presented us with the matriarchs, it also presented us with the curse on Eve: "Toward your husband shall be your lust, yet he will rule over you" (Gen. 3:16). It is clear that Kaplan maintained that woman is destined to be redeemed from this curse in the time to come, just as man will be redeemed from his curse. We know this because Genesis tells us that God said, "Let us make humankind in our image, according to our likeness! Let *them* have dominion over the fish of the sea" (Gen. 1.26). The key word here is *veyirdu* (they) —both male and female—shall rule the earth together. The ideal is that men and women were meant to be equal, and the world is a fall from that ideal.

Kaplan used Rebecca as a model. Women must be emancipated not for power but for service. Just as man's essential sinfulness stems from his lust for power, women in the past have sought to gain power through their charms. Women have both benefited and lost because of this—in Kaplan's words, "What if not her desires to entrance man with her charms has caused man to look upon her as his doll and plaything to minister to his wants?" The enslavement of women has resulted from her femininity, "the power of the eternally feminine" as he called it. Now women must be emancipated not for more power but for greater service. Just as Rebecca went the extra measure in her service to Abraham's servant, so must women do the same. It is as if Kaplan was talking about women in the same terms that Jews have always talked about themselves—as the chosen people. The Jews alone are the only ones who have known God, says the prophet, and therefore they have a higher standard to follow. If women were really free they would revolutionize the political sphere by lifting it to a higher level. The chosenness of women, Kaplan believed, made them more humane. In his words, "women will purify politics, make industry more humane, and make justice to the consumer, instead of profits to the producer, the standard of the market." It is not to be an emancipation for power, "neither her own particular power, nor that masculine power which has contributed so much to the destruction of the world." As Hannah so eloquently put it in her hymn of thanksgiving to God, "For not by strength [power] shall man prevail."[53]

Kaplan was often at his most original when he reinterpreted fundamental concepts. At one point he put forth the idea that reverence for the individual because he was made in the image of God was more basic than the concept of "love thy neighbor," because being created in God's image was the biblical way of indicating the absolute value of human life. As Kaplan put it, "The reason it is wrong to take human life is that the human being wears the image of God; therefore, when a human being is slain, something more than that which is merely human is destroyed, the very image of God is shattered." The proper attitude toward our fellow human beings is respect, the same awe and respect "we associate with the idea of God." We revere human life because "it is a spark of that life that animates the universe," Kaplan told his congregation. He believed that acting out of reverence was a higher principle than acting out of love. "It is only after mankind will have acquired the principle of reverence for man that it will be possible to love man as he should be loved, not merely 'as thyself' but as the reflection of the Divine. 'Beloved is man,' said R. Akiba, 'for he was made in the image of God.' "

In the same sermon, Kaplan went on to draw some conclusions based on this notion of reverence and respect. If, for example, we truly respect our children we will not try to "make them replicas of ourselves." It is not only at home that we need to show reverence but also in the marketplace. Genuine concern for the worker is not enough by itself, he said, for it might still lead the misguided to be benevolently despotic toward those whom they control. A real relationship of respect, however, involves "giving the employee a share in the management, since it is only through having a share in the management that he can exercise his right to be responsible. This may be considered poor economics, but it surely is good religion, and religion is not satisfied with prayers. It also means business."[54]

Kaplan was not afraid to hit hard at economic injustice even though it seemed to put him at odds with the Center's members who were successful businessmen. His sentiments with respect to economic questions were made clear in a Passover sermon delivered in 1919. He saw two social systems in moral conflict with each other: one based on competition, and one based on cooperation.

Those who believe in the virtues of competition do so, he said, not because they think it will call forth the best in man but because they profit from the process. He spoke of the "moral bankruptcy of the competitive system" and advocated the minimum wage, health insurance, and the five-day workweek. With such sermons, considering the times, it is not surprising that some of his congregants called Kaplan a Bolshevik. He was never one to shrink from a fight and went so far as to use the term Bolshevik in reference to the prophets, on one occasion speaking from the pulpit of Amos as "the wide-eyed preacher" and "this radical Bolshevist." He did not hesitate to attack the evils of wealth and told his followers that "power and luxury are the very antithesis of the spiritual."[55]

At times Kaplan attempted to be even-handed and critical of the Bolsheviks, but he was not emotionally detached and he identified strongly with the working classes. In a sermon entitled "Democracy versus Bolshevism," he condemned the Bolsheviks as working to abolish the distinctions between man and beast. A few years later, in 1924, he was looking over the text of this sermon and penciled the following remark in the margin, "As I read these lines, I feel ashamed to think that I allowed myself to be bamboozled by the journalists, preachers, and other white collar slaves who were engaged in fighting their masters' battle against Bolshevism." We ought to remember that this was the time of the "red scare" and that many were afraid the Bolshevik revolution would come to America. At the same time that Kaplan was proudly calling the prophets Bolsheviks, others, such as Rabbi Herbert Goldstein, were preaching on "the crime of radicalism."[56]

One practical issue of the period was the five-day workweek. Many unions went on strike demanding that the workweek be reduced and standardized to forty-four hours. Kaplan was one of many observant Jews who supported the five-day week. Sunday blue laws were still very much in force, and observers of the Jewish Sabbath were severely penalized in the workplace. In a rare activist mood, Kaplan arranged for a meeting of leading Jewish manufacturers in order to discuss the issue. Jacob Schiff was scheduled to speak but never came. Magnes and Kaplan addressed the group, and Kaplan was surprised that there was relatively little opposition at the meeting to the idea of a five-day workweek.[57]

With respect to wealth, Kaplan's whole situation was anomalous. The concept of the Center assumed that it would be supported by wealthy people. All the facilities the Center had were impossible to sustain without a large wealthy group in the congregation. In his journal, Kaplan often ridiculed his congregants for their vanity and materialism; yet, he was certainly proud of the Center's nine-story building, which was completed in the summer of 1920. The poor masses of Jews on Manhattan's Lower East Side had neither the time nor the resources to develop their "Judaism as a living civilization." Kaplan, of course, needed his congregants, but he never ceased to regard them with contempt. In his journal he wrote, "the men are busy making money and the women spending it, and they have no taste for the intangible realities which the Center is to further." Throughout his life Kaplan as rabbi always ministered to upper-class Jews but was never comfortable with this situation, and his critics never let him forget it. In 1941 he noted that Professor Louis Ginzberg, a member of the Seminary faculty, attacked him for producing a Judaism only for manufacturers. He did not mind being called names but was concerned that such diatribes would allow people to dismiss his views without really considering them. In his journal, he quoted a statement from George Bernard Shaw that "under the present system clergymen are nothing but chaplains of pirate ships," to which Kaplan replied, "Precisely so; and what ships have a greater need for chaplains."[58]

If we can believe him, there really were some quite vulgar people in the congregation. One particular man on the board who always seemed to find fault with the building as it was going up was arranging for his son's bar mitzvah ceremony. He had planned to have it out of town but William Fischman, a key member of the board and later its president, induced him to have the ceremony at the Center. Sabbath morning came, and he did not show up until the honors of the Torah reading were half-finished. On another occasion, the high holidays came early, and Kaplan and the board were afraid that many people would stay at the shore and not come back. A group of people were vacationing at Far Rockaway and called a meeting to make plans for getting people to come back to the city in time for Rosh Hashanah.[59]

Kaplan's harping on economics took its toll with the congregation, so that when an opening came his opponents jumped to the
attack. There is no doubt that his economic views played a significant role in his leaving the Center, and that the alienation of
members caused by his strong stand on economic questions was
certainly a sufficient if not the necessary condition. In the spring of
1921 when things were coming to a head Joseph Cohen said to
Kaplan, "You wrung our hearts every time you spoke on the industrial question. If you had taken my advice to gather around you a
sort of cabinet you would have refrained from saying and doing
many of the things that should not have been done."[60]

Kaplan's exodus from the Center came in part as a consequence
of his expanding career. No longer was it possible for him to be
identified with traditional Judaism. His views had been evolving
over the previous decade, but it was not until 1920 that he finally
took a clear and irrevocable stand. In 1919 he had brought many of
his colleagues and friends together to form an organization called
the Society for Jewish Renascence. His opening speech to the group
was published in the *Menorah Journal* the following year. The
article, which was entitled "A Program for the Reconstruction of
Judaism," launched a frontal attack on Orthodoxy. Kaplan wrote:

Nothing can be more repugnant to the thinking man of today than the
fundamental doctrine of Orthodoxy, which is that tradition is infallible.
Such infallibility could be believed in, as long as the human mind thought
of God and Revelation in semi-mythological terms. Then it was conceivable
that a quasi human being could hand down laws and histories in articulate
form. . . . The doctrine of infallibility rules out of court all research and
criticism and demands implicit faith in the truth of whatever has come
down from the past. It precludes all conscious development in thought and
practice and deprives Judaism of the power to survive in an environment
that permits of free contact with non-Jewish civilizations.[61]

It is difficult to understand how Kaplan thought he could remain
at the Center after publishing such an article. It is true that he had
been open and above board with the Center's leaders and that at
their retreat in Tannersville, New York, during the summer of 1917
he had explained his philosophy fully. They had also heard him
preach every Sabbath in the synagogue for a number of years. However, the sermons were by no means theologically radical, and in

any case he had never attacked Orthodoxy from the pulpit. Kaplan's article provoked quick and strong reactions. Rabbi Bernard Drachman, a past president of the Union of Orthodox Congregations and a former teacher of Kaplan's at the old Seminary, thought that his views would have been bad enough coming from a representative of radical Reform "but emanating as they do from one who holds a high position on the faculty of a theological Seminary which declares that it stands on the platform of Orthodox Judaism and who is spiritual guide of an Orthodox congregation, they are amazing and disconcerting in the highest degree."[62] Kaplan was condemned by Rabbi Leo Jung, a young rabbi from Cleveland, who declared that Kaplanism, with its emphasis on nationalism, reduced the Jews to the level of "Eskimos, Poles, and Magyars."[63] Even his mother got into the act, telling him to "change—give up some of your ideas. You don't have too many followers, better try to work with Cohen again because the Center will suffer without you as well as without him. I hope my dear you will do the best as it is possible and God shall bless you that you shall live a long and happy life and then you will make happy all of us."[64]

As a consequence of one of the articles that appeared in the Jewish press, a meeting was called where Kaplan attempted to explain himself to his congregation. There was a strong show of support. Judge Rosalsky, certainly the most respected member of the board, praised Kaplan highly; and, as if to address his attackers, he said, "As much as you may strike him and the more that you stab him behind his back, the nearer will you be drawn to him." Sam Lamport, another strong supporter of Kaplan, referred to him as "one of the finest and most erudite men in the American rabbinate." However, the group wanted to hear Kaplan himself because the press was ascribing all kinds of radical ideas to him. In his remarks, Kaplan tried to be conciliatory, yet honest at the same time. "I want to make clear to you that historical traditional Judaism is what I stand for and what I work for." He said that he was using the new weapons of psychology and social science to support old verities. Then he got down to basics. Some people believed that he advocated doing away with the additional days of holidays. He explained his position, which was that the second day was not really necessary; but as long as the law (halakhah) was in effect, it must be obeyed. People had the right to express their dissatisfaction. He emphasized that his remarks were directed primarily at those who were having difficulties in their observances. To the person who observes two days and has no difficulty, he recommended no change. In essence, he said the same thing about the Sabbath. People should observe as much of the Sabbath as they can: 100 percent if possible; but, if not, then 75 percent. In other words, observe as much as you can. "If you must violate some of the Sabbath laws," he told the group, "don't feel that you have to overthrow the whole institution." He wanted to be honest about his beliefs, but at the same time to try to heal wounds he might have caused. He ended, "We all stand for a Hebrew Judaism, for a Torah Judaism, and for a Zionist Judaism. . . . We stand on tradition and history."[65]

There were many meetings during that spring of 1921, public and private. Kaplan was of two minds about the situation. On the one hand, he wanted to remain at the Center because he sincerely believed that if he left, the Center would not survive. He was willing to agree to almost any compromise no matter how unworkable it seemed. For example, at a number of meetings in May, Kaplan and the board hammered out an agreement whereby the congregation, and especially the school, would be run according to strictly Orthodox principles; but Kaplan would be free to say whatever he wanted from the pulpit. The issue of the school came up because one of the pupils in Max Kadushin's[66] class got into a discussion with Fischman, the president of the Center. She said she had been told not to reveal to her family what she had been studying in class, particularly in reference to the Bible and Mosaic authorship. Kaplan agreed that a committee would be set up to supervise the school and ensure its Orthodoxy. In a moment of profound naiveté, he wrote in his journal:

I hope that I am not compromising with myself nor with the principle of intellectual honesty by consenting to the appointment of a committee that would most likely render the instruction Orthodox. The people know my views and if they are liberal enough to tolerate me, why should I not be liberal enough to tolerate them?[67]

At times he admitted to himself that such solutions were clearly unworkable and that the only path open to him was to leave the

Center. His friends and colleagues were supportive of his leaving. Herman Rubenovitz, a Seminary graduate who had a pulpit in Boston, wrote, "The Renascence (i.e. Society for Jewish Renascence) movement demands that you free yourself from the trammels, which association with intolerant and bigoted men must of necessity impose upon you."[68] Rubenovitz suggested that he and others raise money so that a synagogue that would embody the principles Kaplan stood for could be founded. As a consequence of his feelings, in late April 1921 Kaplan asked for a year's leave of absence so he could devote himself to his writing and scholarship.[69]

Joe Cohen, the central figure on the board, wanted the Center to be Orthodox. It became increasingly clear that Kaplan was not dependable in this regard. The board members were split, with many still supporting their rabbi. On May 12 there was a meeting of the board to consider Kaplan's request for a leave. Opening the meeting, Cohen accused Kaplan in a long harangue of trying to foist a new Judaism on the Center. He referred to Kaplan's article in the *Menorah Journal* and to the Society for Jewish Renascence, both of which he said indicated that Kaplan had broken with Orthodox Judaism. Kaplan stated that he was ready to compromise. He was willing to have the Center run according to the *Shulkhan Arukh*, but he would still be free to state and to teach his views though he was not Orthodox. A committee would be appointed by the board to supervise the school. Thus, at the same time that Kaplan might preach heterodoxy from the pulpit, the children would learn Orthodoxy in the school. After about two hours, Abe Rothstein stepped in and pointed out that Kaplan had agreed to board supervision of the school. Therefore, he proposed that Kaplan be reelected rabbi. There was some wrangling about the motion, with Unterberg and Rosalsky supporting—and it carried. Kaplan's salary was to be $12,000.[70]

The issues seemed to have been settled, but they were not. In his heart of hearts Kaplan knew that the compromise was unworkable, and he continued to think about leaving the Center. The summer and the holidays came and went, and the maneuvering continued on both sides. By the end of the year, Kaplan had had his fill and had decided to resign. In his letter to Fischman, president of the board, he stated that the board knew his approach to Judaism from the start, and Cohen especially "knew me as well as I know myself." He said he did not want to take any money because "I wanted my contribution to the Center to be a whole offering to God." He found himself "hampered at every turn by the Board of Trustees" and thus felt compelled to resign.[71]

Although there were some who were happy to see Kaplan leave, his exodus, together with about half the families at the Center, put the existence of the institution in jeopardy. A few months after Kaplan left, Israel Unterberg, who had left with Kaplan, wrote to one of the board members, Ike Phillips, for a donation to a Jewish cause. Phillips, who was still obviously smarting from the split, wrote back an angry letter, giving a sense of how the "other side" felt. Phillips believed that "a number of gentlemen who are supposed to advance Judaism simply laid down on their contracts, laid down on their words, refused to pay dues, and in so many words told the handful of men who were already overburdened with responsibilities to go to hell."[72] It took many years until the Center was again on solid ground financially. In 1931 the Center incorporated itself with the new charter, stipulating that it would always be Orthodox unless 95 percent of the membership agreed that it be changed.[73]

The split at the Center had reverberations outside the synagogue itself. It certainly meant a weakening of the liberal forces within the Orthodox community. There were many traditional Jews who at this point did not perceive the Seminary as representing a new denomination. For those who had supported the Seminary and perceived themselves as Orthodox, the situation was uncomfortable. Apparently, a group of Center members, sometime after Kaplan left, came to the Seminary and asked Cyrus Adler to fire Kaplan. They threatened to withdraw their financial support if Adler did not comply with their wishes. Adler, as we know, was himself traditional, and these wealthy Jews were precisely the type he wanted to attract.[74]

Kaplan's experience at the Center is significant in understanding Kaplan the man, as well as Kaplan the ideologue of American Jewry. The experience marked a turning point in his life because he finally divorced himself from the traditional Jewish community. Perhaps he struggled so long to stay because on some level he knew that the break with the traditional sector of the Jewish community would be irreparable. With the publication of his article in the *Menorah Journal* and his dismissal of Orthodoxy as a viable alternative in America, he had, as he put it, "crossed the Rubicon" of his career. He had continuously lambasted his congregation on the economic injustices to which they were a party. When he came out flatly against Orthodoxy in his 1920 article, it was the last straw.

The fact that Kaplan lived on the level of his ideology and was rather inept politically was both his strength and his weakness. The Jewish Center began with a great vision of genuine community—a goal still to be achieved. It broke new ground in showing what a synagogue could be in America. Yet, it fell far short of what Kaplan himself could have achieved there. It became the model for a host of Jewish community centers built in the 1920s and 1930s, which only began to demonstrate Kaplan's point that people who only pray together do not really stay together on any significant level. Kaplan wanted a community, and he got a synagogue.

Notes

1. Kaplan's first major use of the term *civilization* in connection with Judaism was at the dedication of the Jewish Center on March 24, 1918. Excerpts from this speech are found in *American Jewish Chronicle* 4, no. 24 (April 1918). The article is entitled "Judaism as a Living Civilization." I shall discuss the contents of this article later. This article should not be confused with the well-known article, "The Jewish Center," *American Hebrew* 102, no. 20 (March 1918): 529.

2. Harry Glucksman, "Tendencies in the Jewish Center Movement," *National Conference of Jewish Social Service, Proceedings* (1923), 144–53. Reprinted in *Trends and Issues in Jewish Social Welfare in the United States, 1899–1958*, ed. Robert Morris and Michael Freund (Philadelphia: Jewish Publication Society, 1966), 225–30.

3. Louis Kraft, "The Jewish Center Movement," in *Mordecai M. Kaplan: An Evaluation*, ed. Ira Eisenstein and Eugene Kohn (New York: Jewish Reconstructionist Foundation, 1952), 119–35. Kraft's essay is based almost solely on Kaplan's own work, *The Future of the American Jew*, which was published in 1948.

4. *Kaplan Journal*, 3 March 1918 and 16 April 1918. The original of the Kaplan Journal is at the Jewish Theological Seminary. There is also a

typed version that covers 1913–42. The pagination in each is different. The date of any Journal entry is sufficient to locate any quotation.

5. The distinction between "eventful" and "event-making" is explained in Sidney Hook, *The Hero in History* (Boston: Beacon Press, 1950). The myth regarding Kaplan's part in creating the Central Jewish Institute (CJI) comes from a number of sources. Oscar Janowsky, in his important work *The Jewish Welfare Board Survey* (New York: Dial Press, 1948), makes it clear that he believes "that the ideological foundations of the present-day Jewish community center were laid by Mordecai Kaplan as early as 1908" (p. 244). His evidence is found in the work of Isaac Berkson, *Theories of Americanization* (New York: Columbia University, 1920), 187. For a short time, Berkson himself was director of the CJI. Berkson gives no hard evidence to back up his assertion that Kaplan conceived the idea in 1908. A careful reading of the minutes of Kehilath Jeshurun lead to the conclusion that the Talmud Torah they sought to establish was a very modest affair and was not engineered by Kaplan, who left Kehilath Jeshurun in 1908. There is no evidence that he laid out the program of the Central Jewish Institute, which is the name of the Talmud Torah after 1916.

6. For a fine study on Jews in Harlem, see Jeffrey Gurock, *When Harlem Was Jewish, 1870–1930* (New York: Columbia University Press, 1979).

7. See Kaplan's remarks on his noninvolvement with CJI in *Kaplan Journal*, 9 April 1918. For a brief summary of a speech by Kaplan in 1920 at the annual meeting of CJI, see *American Hebrew* 106, no. 14 (February 1920): 428. The title of the talk was "The Principles Underlying Community Centers."

8. On the Institutional Church, see *Encyclopedia of Religion and Ethics*, vol. 7, ed. James Hastings (New York: Charles Scribner's Sons, 1908–27), 362.

9. Goldstein resented Kaplan's heterodoxy even as a student at the Jewish Theological Seminary. It is quite ironic, therefore, that it was because of Kaplan that Goldstein entered the rabbinate. According to his biographer, Goldstein recorded in his diary that he had a "conversion experience" while listening to Kaplan preach at the funeral of Rabbi Asher, a Seminary professor who died in November of 1909. See Aaron Reichel, *The Maverick Rabbi: Rabbi Herbert Goldstein and the Institutional Synagogue* (Norfolk, Va.: Donning, 1984), 44.

10. Herbert Goldstein, "The Institutional Synagogue," *Hebrew Standard* 68, no. 8, September 15, 1916.

11. Reichel, *Maverick Rabbi*, 132.

12. A copy of the constitution of the Institutional Synagogue is found in the Yeshiva University Archives in the Institutional Synagogue Collection. I am indebted to Dr. Cohn of Yeshiva University for his gracious assistance. The other facts in this paragraph can be found in Reichel,

Maverick Rabbi, passim. The synagogue published a bulletin called *The Institutional,* which contains useful material on the 1930s. The Institutional Synagogue's building at 116th Street was later expanded to include six stories equipped with a gymnasium and a pool, as well as a large sanctuary. The building still stands on 116th Street and is now a church.

13. Kaplan himself inadvertently seems to confirm my hypothesis on the origins of the synagogue-center when he stated in his dedication address: "Let us not characterize the Jewish Center as a Club, or as a synagogue with social attractions or as a Jewish analogue of an Institutional Church" (Mordecai Kaplan, "Judaism as a Living Civilization," *American Jewish Chronicle* 4, no. 24 [April 1918]: 678).

14. Kaplan, Sermon at Dedication of the Jewish Center, 20, March 1918. Reconstructionist Rabbinical College (RRC)

15. Arthur Goren, *Dissenter in Zion—From the Writings of Judah L. Magnes* (Cambridge: Harvard University Press, 1982), 193.

16. The idea of the Jewish Center and Judaism as a civilization is articulated in Kaplan, "Judaism as a Living Civilization," 679. Some of this material also appears in Kaplan's magnum opus. See Mordecai Kaplan, *Judaism as a Civilization* (New York: Macmillan, 1934), 426.

17. *Kaplan Journal,* 10 April 1915.

18. For a discussion on Kaplan and Bible, see Mel Scult, "Mordecai Kaplan's Reinterpretation of the Torah," *Conservative Judaism* 33, no. 1 (Fall 1979): 63–67 and chapter 14 in this volume.

19. Tina Levitan, *Islands of Compassion—A History of the Jewish Hospitals of New York* (New York: Twayne Publishers, 1964), 92.

20. *Kaplan Journal,* 10 April 1915.

21. Ibid., 25 August 1917.

22. Ibid., 10 April 1915.

23. These facts on Rosalsky were taken from obituary, *New York Times,* 12 May 1936, 23; from *Who's Who in American Jewry, 1926* (New York: Jewish Biographical Bureau, 1927); and from *Kaplan Journal,* 21 April 1918. For biographical details on Schwartz, see *Who's Who, 1926.*

24. Information on Israel Unterberg was taken from obituary, *New York Times,* 2 May 1934, 21; and from *Who's Who in American Jewry, 1926.* On the Lamports, see Samuel C.'s obituary, *New York Times,* 14 September 1941; and Arthur's obituary 9 November 1940. See also Gilbert Klaperman, *The Story of Yeshiva University* (New York: Macmillan, 1969) passim. For a complete list of the board members, see *Journal of Jewish Center,* 1, no. 2 (April 1918). For remarks on the Lamports as "star workers," see Amelia Morgonroth to Mordecai Kaplan, February 1920, RRC Kaplan Archives. (Amelia Morganroth was on the Center's staff.)

25. On consulting Margolis, see *Kaplan Journal,* 2 March 1918. Also, Judith Kaplan Eisenstein, interview with author, April 1986. The issue of

mixed seating is brought up in Bernard Drachman's autobiography, in which he discusses leaving the synagogue Beth Israel-Bikur Cholim. See idem, *The Unfailing Light* (New York: Rabbincal Council of America, 1948), 197. For the matter of synagogue suffrage and equality for men and women, see *Kaplan Journal*, January 1917.

26. *Kaplan Journal*, 22 May 1917. Students of Kaplan may want to speculate whose will Kaplan is talking about here. Whether he has in mind God or the Jewish people, we see a significant sense of the transcendent.

27. Ibid., 29 August 1917.

28. For remarks on the "bourgeois type," as well as other material in this section, see *Kaplan Journal*, 9 November 1917.

29. Ibid.

30. Ibid.

31. *American Jewish Chronicle*, 8 March 1918, 491.

32. On the matter of Kaplan's salary and his dilemma, see *Kaplan Journal*, 22 July 1918. Kaplan's insistence with regard to his salary was not just a consequence of the wartime atmosphere of sacrifice in 1918. At the Society for the Advancement of Judaism he also refused a salary; there, the congregation paid only for his insurance.

33. *Journal of the Jewish Center* 1, no. 4 (April 1918).

34. The dedication is reported in *American Jewish Chronicle* 4, no. 21 (March 1918).

35. Information on the school is meager. See *Kaplan Journal*, 26 December 1918. Judith Kaplan Eisenstein provided me with these facts about the school when I interviewed her in May 1986.

36. Naomi Kaplan Wenner and Judith Kaplan Eisenstein, interview with the author, April 1975 and May 1976.

37. For observations on the Talmud class, see *Kaplan Journal*, 28 July 1919. Kaplan's Bible class is mentioned in *Journal of the Jewish Center* 2, no. 7 (October 1918).

38. See the letters from Amelia Morganroth to Mordecai Kaplan, RRC (April and May 1921).

39. For a notice of the parade, see *American Hebrew* 106, no. 26 (April 1920). Details of the music program come from Judith Kaplan Eisenstein (interview May 1986), and from *Journal of the Jewish Center* 2, no. 7 (October 1918).

40. For the sermon on preaching, see Mordecai Kaplan, "What Can Give the Jew Backbone" (Sermon delivered at the Jewish Center, 4 May 1918).

41. See, for example, *Journal of the Jewish Center* 2, no. 5 (October 1918). The probability is that the Center used a Hebrew Publishing Company edition of the Pentateuch (1913), which had a separate book that included a Hebrew-to-English text for each book of the Torah. At the back of each book, one finds the Sabbath service (probably the Adler translation) together with the Hebrew text.

42. For Wilson compared to Jacob and the angel, see Kaplan, sermon preached on 23 November 1918. For Wilson compared to Abraham, see sermon of 19 October 1918, RRC. The material from the sermons that is not in quotation marks is a summary of material in the sermons and relies heavily on Kaplan's language, although these are not direct quotations. I have followed this procedure below, staying as close as possible to Kaplan's thought when summarizing.

43. Kaplan, sermon at the Jewish Center, 30 November 1918, RRC.

44. Ibid., 29 September 1918.

45. For an enlarged definition of Zionism, see Kaplan, "What Zionism Can Give to the Jew" (sermon delivered at the Jewish Center, 24 April 1921). For a description of Zionism and not chauvinism, see Kaplan, sermon at the Jewish Center, 5 April 1919, RRC.

46. *Kaplan Journal*, 29 December 1918.

47. Kaplan, sermon at the Jewish Center, 21 April 1921, RRC.

48. Ibid., 17 May 1918.

49. Ibid., 7 December 1918; Mordecai M. Kaplan, "Judaism as a Living Civilization," *American Jewish Chronicle* 4, no. 24 (April 1918): 679.

50. Ibid.

51. "Küche, Kinder, und Kirche," *Journal of the Jewish Center* 2, no. 16 (November 1918):1; for dedication ceremonies and *Sefer Torah*, see ibid., 1, no. 6 (May 1918):1.

52. The sermon on the emancipation of women was delivered at the Jewish Center, 2 November 1918.

53. The concept of the chosenness of women is clearly in the text of the sermon, although the word *chosen* is not used there but supplied by this author. The verse is from 1 Samuel 2:16. The translations from Genesis are from Everett Fox, *In the Beginning—A New English Rendition of the Book of Genesis* (New York: Schocken, 1983). The verse in Zachariah 4:6 expresses the same thought about power and was a favorite of Kaplan's although he did not use it here: "Not by might nor by power but by My spirit, sayeth the Lord of Hosts."

54. Kaplan, "Man the Standard of All Values" (sermon delivered at the Jewish Center, 25 October 1919).

55. Kaplan, "Moral Bankruptcy of the Competitive System" (sermon delivered at the Jewish Center, 21 April 1919 [the seventh day of Passover]). The same view is expressed in 1921 in a sermon entitled, "Is Our Morale Crumbling?" Kaplan notes he is called a Bolshevik in *Kaplan Journal*, 28 July 1919. He calls Amos a "Bolshevist" in sermon at the Jewish Center, 12 April 1919, *Parshas Metzorah*. For his attack on luxury, see ibid., 14 September 1918, *Shabbes Shuvah*.

56. Kaplan, sermon at the Jewish Center, 9 November 1918. On Goldstein against radicalism, see *American Hebrew*, 106, no. 11, 30 January 1920, 317.

57. *Kaplan Journal*, 28 July 1919.

58. *Kaplan Journal*, 14 August 1918. On Louis Ginzburg's attitude, see ibid., 4 June 1941. On the quotation by G.B.S., see ibid., 7 January 1919.
59. *Kaplan Journal*, 14 August 1918.
60. Quoted in ibid., 17 May 1921.
61. Mordecai M. Kaplan, "A Program for the Reconstruction of Judaism," *Menorah Journal*, 6, no. 4 (August 1920): 182–83.
62. Bernard Drachman, Editorial, *Jewish Forum* 4, no. 1 (January 1921): 645.
63. Leo Jung, "Orthodoxy, Reform, and Kaplanism," *Jewish Forum* 4, no. 3 (April 1921): 778–83.
64. The letter from Kaplan's mother is at RRC. It is undated, but the contents make the approximate time clear.
65. The minutes of the meeting were professionally recorded. They are entitled "The Jewish Center Convention—February 9, 1921" and are found at RRC.
66. Max Kadushin went on to become a famous scholar and rabbi and was a faithful disciple of Kaplan's.
67. *Kaplan Journal*, 5 May 1921.
68. Herman H. Rubenovitz to Mordecai Kaplan, 20 January 1921, RRC.
69. Mordecai Kaplan to William Fischman, 28 April 1921, RRC.
70. *Kaplan Journal*, 12 May 1921.
71. Mordecai Kaplan to William Fischman, 16 January 1922, RRC.
72. Ike Phillips to Israel Unterberg, 5 May 1922, Unterberg file at RRC.
73. William Feinberg, interview with the author, April 1973. Feinberg was active at the Center and was one of those who stayed.
74. Rabbi Louis Finkelstein, interview with author, March 1974. Finkelstein related the incident about the delegation from the Center going to see Adler. He said that he thought Kaplan never knew of this incident. There is no way to corroborate his story.

CHAPTER 4

Kaplan and Israel Friedlaender: Expectation and Failure

Baila Round Shargel

He went through so much, he was in contact with numerous cultures and absorbed the best that was in them. Cosmopolitan in his sympathies yet intensely Jewish in his stirrings, a man of facile pen and silver tongue, a master of wit and repartee, and yet a failure.[1]

This was the recorded reaction of Mordecai M. Kaplan to the death of Israel Friedlaender while on a relief mission in the Ukraine in July 1920. It is a peculiar mixture of lavish praise for Friedlaender's personal qualities and an ultimately negative evaluation. How can we explain Kaplan's ambivalence toward his colleague?

Like most American Jews of the early twentieth century, Kaplan and Friedlaender were products of what the latter termed "a period of great physical and spiritual upheavals in the life of our people."[2] Both of them came to this country as part of the great migration that transplanted approximately one-third of eastern European Jewry in the course of a single generation. They also belonged to a small coterie of Jewish intellectuals troubled by the moral and spiritual malaise engendered by the peremptory dislocation. More specifically, they shared many academic and communal interests and traveled in the same circles.

Yet there is no evidence of personal intimacy. The voluminous archives of the Jewish Theological Seminary contain extensive correspondence between Friedlaender and his associates in New York and other cities, but none from or to Kaplan.

It is clear that, from the beginning, a certain aloofness marked their relationship. When Friedlaender joined the Seminary's faculty, Kaplan had been associated with the institution for ten years. At twenty-two he already held the rabbinical degree and a master of arts from Columbia University. These credentials, though impressive, were hardly comparable to Friedlaender's. During September 1903, the very month of his arrival in America, Friedlaender celebrated his twenty-seventh birthday. At that time he was already renowned as a Hebrew publicist, as Ahad Ha'am and Dubnow's German translator, and as a Semitics scholar awarded a doctorate by Theodor Noeldeke. Nor was the relationship initiated on an equal plane. Kaplan, a fledgling congregational rabbi, enrolled in courses at the Seminary and at Columbia. Among his instructors was Israel Friedlaender.[3] There is evidence of mutual regard. Friedlaender warmly recommended Kaplan for a Baltimore rabbinical post in 1907[4] and suggested his membership on the conference forming the new Conservative Union (United Synagogue) in 1910.[5] Kaplan, in turn, sought Friedlaender's advice on his scholarly endeavors and remained to discuss "things in general."[6]

Respect, even fondness, are then in evidence. That the relationship did not go beyond that has troubled me for many years. This essay is an attempt to set forth and analyze evidence indicating the similarities and the differences between their perspectives, in the hope of explaining Kaplan's strange verdict on Friedlaender's career.

Two caveats are in order. In pursuit of my objective, I must, first of all, limit the data to lecture notes, essays, and letters, published and unpublished, penned by Friedlaender during his years in America and Kaplan's articles and journal entries of the same period.[7] There is also the matter of sources. Neither man made life easy for his biographer. Mel Scult has noted that Kaplan intimated a debt to Dewey and Durkheim for conclusions he reached before he had even read their works.[8] I was equally frustrated by Friedlaender's reluctance to cite the sources of his social and psychological theory.[9] For these reasons, and the obvious fact that the two professors were subject to the same influences, I shall refrain from the temptation to suggest deliberate borrowings from each other, unless the subject himself seemed to suggest it.

Like others in their generation, Kaplan and Friedlaender internalized the teachings of Ahad Ha'am, especially his perception of the nature of Judaism, the current crisis in Jewish life, and the means of alleviating distress. But these two young men were especially indebted to the sage of Odessa. Kaplan always maintained that his own philosophy of Jewish life was constructed of Ahad Ha'amist building blocks. Central to his personal "Copernican Revolution" was Ahad Ha'am's insistence on the centrality of the Jewish people.[10] Friedlaender's relationship was of a more personal nature. He never met Ahad Ha'am, but the two men carried on a lengthy correspondence, first on the subject of his translation of *Al Parashat Derakhim*, later on Ahad Ha'am's planned but never executed trip to America, and intermittently on general Zionist and Jewish cultural issues.[11] Well known for his connection to the European philosopher, Friedlaender was frequently invited to lecture on this topic.

They were not, however, blind disciples of Ahad Ha'am. As religious thinkers, both men were disturbed by the absence of religion in his philosophy of Jewish life.[12]

Ahad Ha'am's special appeal can be traced to his beautiful Hebrew style and his forthright analysis of Judaism in the modern world. Especially pertinent for his American followers were his strong reservations about Jewish emancipation. Political equality and material prosperity, he argued, did not liberate the Jews of western Europe; on the contrary, their lives exhibited what he called "slavery in freedom," the surrender of their Jewish legacy for the goods of this world.

Friedlaender, also a master of the pithy phrase, raised the issue with these words: "The dawn of the Jews is the dusk of Judaism."[13] Sadly, he observed: "Judaism which stood out like a rock amidst the billow of hatred and storms of persecution is melting away like wax under the mild rays of freedom."[14]

In the opinion of all Ahad Ha'am's American followers, these rays of freedom emitted three effects that, if not confronted, would spell the end of American Judaism. The first was assimilation. In the early years of this century, the ghettos of New York and other

cities were teeming with Jewish life, yet the situation was notice-
ably fragile; the children of the immigrants were little inclined to
carry on the traditions of their fathers. Kaplan observed that the
active participants in Jewish programs were invariably foreign-born.[15]
Likewise, Friedlaender, aware of the agitation for immigration restriction, feared for the future of American Judaism after the cessa-
tion of immigration.

The expansion of American Judaism is not an organic growth from within
but a mechanic addition from without. Its gain, to use a biblical simile, is
the gain of one who puts his earnings into a bag with holes. As long as the
earnings exceed the holes, the bag seems constantly to swell. But no sooner
will the earnings have stopped than the bag will begin to shrink and will
finally collapse.[16]

Of manifest concern to both men was a second effect, which they
saw as an outgrowth of the first, the coarsening moral character of
the emerging American Jews. Kaplan's diary reveals a visceral
loathing for certain unrefined types. "These men and their wives,"
he complained, possess "but one ideal, to amass wealth."[17] Friedlaender sketched a satirical portrait of the Allrightnick: "the gau-
dily attired, slang-using, gum-chewing, movie-visiting, dollar-hunt-
ing, vulgar and uncultured, quasi-Americanized "dzentleman."[18]
    Equally distressing to the two men was a third effect, the frag-
mentation of American Jewry along generational, religious, educational, and social lines. At this period a deep chasm yawned between "uptown Jews," generally of German descent and acculturated
into American life, and "downtown Jews," the struggling immigrants of the ghetto. In a display of erudition, Friedlaender found
precedent for the attitude of the former toward the latter in Goethe's
epigram:

The German does not like the Frenchman,
But he likes to drink his wine.[19]

"The attitude of the western Jew," he observed, is the "exact reverse of it."[20] Though willing to support their eastern European
brethren in physical distress, they refuse to partake of the rich
cultural heritage cherished by the Russians.
    Similar perceptions of the problem of Judaism in America led to
advocacy of the same solutions. Primary among them was cultural

or spiritual Zionism, which, both men believed, was the ideal focal point for American Judaism.

Spiritual Zionism displayed a strongly ethical stripe, woven deeply into the fabric of each man's philosophy and pedagogy. Friedlaender's Seminary students reported that an Ahad Ha'amist interpretation of the prophets pervaded his classes in Bible.[21] His favorite biblical maxim, frequently repeated, was Zachariah 4:10: "Not by my might nor by power but by my spirit, saith the Lord of Hosts."[22]

Friedlaender was a Zionist theoretician and a Zionist leader. He attended several World Zionist congresses and served as an officer of the prewar Federation of American Zionists and the wartime Provisional Executive Council. More memorable than his organizational work were his lectures and newspaper and magazine articles on Zionist themes. The American Zionist movement disseminated several of them in pamphlet form even after it found new leaders of a more practical than "spiritual" bent.

Building upon Schecter's designation of Zionism as "the great bulwark against assimilation,"[23] Kaplan found "Zionist aspiration . . . synonymous with the revival of Judaism."[24] In his proposals for Jewish renewal, "the awakening of conscience" was as important as the awakening of Jewish consciousness.[25] Indeed, cultural Zionism always figured prominently in the philosophy and program of Reconstructionism.

Before most of their contemporaries, Kaplan and Friedlaender realized Zionism's great potential for winning otherwise indifferent young Jews for Judaism and unifying the Jewish community around a common interest. Following a visit to Yale, Kaplan noted that Zionism, alone among Jewish ideas, excited the imagination of the college students whom he addressed.[26] In his article "Jewish Nationalism, the Badge,"[27] Friedlaender proposed the novel thesis that Zionism could reconcile Orthodox and Reform Jews who differed on theological issues.

Friedlaender and Kaplan were not only cultural Zionists; they were also cultural determinists who regarded education as "social amelioration."[28] In public and private, they bemoaned the dearth of Jewish learning in America. Both of them blamed Jewish vulgarity on the poor quality of Jewish education. Friedlaender went one step further; he implied that were the situation to continue, materialism would escape all bounds and yield to criminality. It was on this basis that he argued for a Department of Semitic Studies at City College, where so many young Jews received their education. The study of Hebrew, he suggested, would prevent "the emergence of an army of Lefty Louies and Gyp the Bloods"![29]

Because of their Zionist and cultural orientation, modernist predilections, and intense desire for Jewish renewal, both men were involved in the creation of the New York Kehillah (1908–22).[30] The executives of that organization, Friedlaender among them, were eager to tackle the manifold problems of New York Jewry on a scientific basis. Therefore, they happily accepted Mordecai Kaplan's proposals for a detailed survey of Jewish education in the city. Kaplan presented the survey's findings before the Kehillah convention held in February 1910; his suggestions were incorporated into a new organ of the Kehillah, its Bureau of Education.

Friedlaender became chairman of the Kehillah's standing committee on education; Kaplan served as one of its members. This was the time when they worked most closely together. They did not always see eye to eye. For example, Friedlaender did not consider the committee qualified to disburse funds, whereas Kaplan insisted that, as an organ of a democratic body, it would bring the Bureau's plans to fruition.[31]

During the same period, Friedlaender and Kaplan also became colleagues on the Seminary faculty. When Schechter organized the institution's second branch, the Teacher's Institute, in 1909, he selected Kaplan as the principal and Friedlaender as an instructor. In 1910 Kaplan joined the rabbinical school faculty as professor of homiletics.

Their educational efforts were not confined to formal instruction. Both professors conducted classes that were not part of any curriculum. Friedlaender taught some students Arabic; with others he read the essays of Ahad Ha'am. Kaplan met with students, alumni, and people not connected with the Seminary. They discussed biblical issues and read the writings of prominent social thinkers.[32] In addition, both men were active in the Menorah Society and traveled widely to lecture on college campuses. Moreover, adult education figured prominently in their communal endeavors. Friedlaender lectured extensively before lay and rabbinical audiences; Kaplan addressed members of the YMCA and other organizations.

At every opportunity, they advanced a proposition that has retained its relevance. Disturbed at the priorities set by the communal leadership, they criticized the allocation of funds. Hospitals and synagogues were the favored beneficiaries of the magnates who controlled the purse strings. For Kaplan and Friedlaender, this was misplaced generosity. To them it was clear that education, rather than philanthropy and elaborate houses of worship, was the key to Jewish survival. Kaplan's first proposal for the reconstruction of Judaism argued boldly,

I refer to the class of Jewish philanthropists who are determined to kill Judaism with charity. They are ready to assist the Jew whenever he is in trouble, to heal him in his sickness, to send him relief if he is in want. . . . But they systematically oppose anything and everything that might strengthen Jewish consciousness or promote Jewish solidarity.[33]

This is a point that Friedlaender had been making, albeit in more measured tones, since 1905.[34]

Even when the uptown philanthropists allocated funds for Jewish schools, the two professors noted, they were careful to earmark them for other men's children. Kaplan decried the "eleemosynary character" of the Talmud Torah schools maintained by the well-to-do for children of poor immigrants[35] and also offered an invidious comparison between the National Council of Jewish Women and a mothers' meeting of the Uptown Talmud Torah. The former group cared for the education of children and poor girls in distant parts of the city, he noted, while the latter worked for the religious education of their own children.[36]

Comparable to Kaplan's democratic notions of education were Friedlaender's suggestions to the board of the Educational Alliance that the people serviced by that organization, rather than the wealthy patrons who supported it, be allowed to determine policy.[37]

To pursue a related goal of strengthening Jewish piety in the young, the two men joined forces once again. Contemporary members of Young Israel synagogues would be surprised to learn the identity of the founders of their movement. Early in this century

Israel Friedlaender and Mordecai Kaplan sent some of their students to the Lower East Side to set up religious services for young people.[38]

Despite the acknowledged similarities in the two men's interests and activities, their students were more impressed with their differences. Both professors, they agreed, were excellent pedagogues. Steeped in Jewish tradition and conversant with new trends in Jewish scholarship and contemporary social science, they also exhibited exceptional concern for individual students. Here the resemblance ended. There was a consensus that each professor expand horizons in his own peculiar fashion. Kaplan opened their minds; Friedlaender nurtured their souls.[39]

Their own words testify to the correctness of the student evaluations. Relentlessly, Kaplan pursued a goal set early in life: "arousing them (i.e. JTS students and alumni) from their apparent indifference to the fundamental questions."[40] Even before coming to America, Friedlaender set forth his objective:

My responsibility to my students is to impart to them as a basic knowledge of the Bible, knowledge which will awaken in them the *love* of Bible.[41]

The knowledge that consisted of more than book-learning, the German notion of *verstehen*, was one of Friedlaender's favorite lecture topics. This excerpt from a 1915 Menorah address found its way into print:

Jewish knowledge to me is valuable in the sense in which the word "knowledge" is employed in Hebrew. For "to know" in Hebrew (*yada*) does not merely mean to conceive intellectually, but expresses at the same time the deepest emotions of the human soul; it also means to care, to cherish, to love.[42]

Already in adolescence Kaplan and Friedlaender's contrasting temperaments were evident. Both men were born into devout families and trained from infancy in Jewish lore. At the same time they were introduced to the world of the *Haskalah*. In Praga, the Warsaw suburb where he was raised, Friedlaender learned the Bible virtually by heart and mastered the traditional commentaries. Then, in adolescence, he donned the *kapota* and made frequent visits to Hasidic *rebayyim*. Disturbed at this turn of events, his father, after a consultation with Shmarya Levin, packed the young man off to a German university.

Kaplan's father was a traditional rabbi, first in Lithuania, then in New York City. He was sufficiently enlightened to invite Arnold Ehrlich, the brilliant, radical Bible critic of uncertain Jewish credentials, to his home. Mordecai's adolescent rebellion consisted of accepting Ehrlich's position, rather than that of his father, on "the Mosaic authorship of the Torah and the historicity of the miracles."[43]

With these personality traits in mind, let us now turn to specific issues that engaged both men's attention. On two of them there was substantial agreement but discernible difference; on others, the distance between the positions was more marked. Prominent in the first category is an idea that the very names Israel Friedlaender and Mordecai M. Kaplan call to mind. That culture is the mainspring of Jewish society is the thesis of Friedlaender's most popular essay, "The Problem of Judaism in America;"[44] this notion supplied the title and substance of Kaplan's magnum opus.[45]

Over the years, Kaplan made few references to Friedlaender, yet *Judaism as a Civilization* (1934) quoted "The Problem of Judaism in America" twice, first in the preface, then in the chapter that bears the same heading as the book. The critical words were

Judaism . . . must again break the narrow frame of a creed and resume its original function as a culture, as the expression of the Jewish spirit and the whole life of the Jews.[46]

It appears that the citations were intended to give credit to Friedlaender for the book's central thesis. However, it is also possible that Kaplan treated the long-dead Friedlaender, as he did Durkheim, as an authority for a position reached independently.

The following is Friedlaender's definition of Judaism:

Judaism represents the sum total of those inner characteristics, as instincts, sentiments, convictions, and ideals, which are to a lesser or larger degree common to the individuals of the aggregate known as the Jewish people. . . . Jewry constitutes the body, Judaism the spirit or the soul of the Jewish people. . . . It finds its visible expression in a certain manner of life, such as customs, habits, and ceremonies, and in a certain spiritual productivity, such as literature, art, and the like—in short, in the two spheres, which, taken together, form what we call the culture of a nation. Judaism would thus, more exactly, represent the Jewish soul or spirit, and its outward manifestation in Jewish culture.[47]

In an address delivered at the dedication exercises of the Jewish Center in 1918, Kaplan first referred to Judaism as "not merely a religion but a civilization."[48] He invoked popular psychology to justify the new organization. Citing a current authority in the field of mental health, he noted that it was incumbent upon every civilization to provide tools for "work, play, love, and worship." He then advanced a plan for an organization capable of satisfying the occupational, recreational, aesthetic, and religious needs of the community, thereby rebuilding Jewish civilization in New York.[49]

Both statements pursued the objective of refuting Reform Judaism's credal definition of Judaism, but they did not share a common terminology. For Friedlaender, Judaism was a "culture"; for Kaplan it was a "civilization." The deviation is best explained in light of each man's background and objectives.

Anthropologists of the English-speaking world tended to use the terms interchangeably,[50] which may explain Kaplan's citation of Friedlaender's cultural definition of Judaism as if he had used the word *civilization*. As far as I can determine, he never explained why he selected that term. He did, however, register a debt to William Graham Sumner.[51] Sumner was an early twentieth-century anthropologist who developed the concept of "social heritage." Kaplan applied it to Jewish civilization, which he defined as "the sum of characteristics, usages, standards, and codes by which the Jewish people is differentiated and individualized in character from the other peoples."[52]

Unlike the British and American social thinkers at the turn of the twentieth century, their German contemporaries carefully distinguished between the two terms. According to Frederick Toennies, an important German sociologist, "culture comprises custom (*Sitte*), religion, and art; civilization comprises law and science."[53] Culture, for him, was natural and organic, the product of the folk community; it was markedly distinct from the artificial and mechanical society that constituted the civilization of the state.

Friedlaender's German education explains his preference for "culture." Moreover, both Historical Judaism, the religious philos-

ophy he embraced, and his mentor Ahad Ha'am traced the development of Judaism in organic, evolutionary terms. But Kaplan, who
drew upon the same Jewish sources, probably was not acquainted
with the distinctions of German sociology.

That Friedlaender was conversant with them was indicated in an
article published nine years after the celebrated "Problem of Judaism in America." Entitled "The Problem of Jewish Culture in America," it discussed both terms.

Culture, which is etymologically identical with *agriculture*, primarily refers to the soil and then to every other object in nature which human
endeavor has raised from its primitive natural state to a higher form of
existence. In this connotation the culture of a people largely coincides
with its *civilization*. It comprised its *manner of living*, its habits and
customs, the way it builds and furnishes its homes, takes its food, marries
its sons and daughters, buries its dead and discharges all the innumerable
functions of its external physical life. . . . In its higher application the term
culture, also in this still reflecting the Latin usage, means cultivation of
the *mind* and stands for the development of the *mental* or *spiritual* life of a
people. In this connotation culture comprises the mode of thinking (and
feeling) of a nation, its sentiments, conceptions, and ideals and the expression they find in religion, philosophy, literature, and art.[54]

There is certainly a relationship between the "spiritual productivity" of the 1907 essay and the second part of the 1915 definition.
The "customs, habits, and ceremonies" mentioned in the earlier
piece correspond to the civilizational elements designated in the
later one. In 1917 Friedlaender again distinguished between "the
rule of thinking and that of living," identifying the former with
"Torah," the latter with "material advancement."[55]

Pursuing his anti-Reform polemic, Friedlaender separated the
"cultural" from the "civilizational" elements of Judaism and argued on different premises. To vindicate the philosophy and practice of Conservative Judaism, he assumed the priority of "thinking"
over "living." A lecture series before the Eastern Council of Reform
Rabbis designated Judaism a "threefold cord. . . . Indissolubly bound
up with one another in the existence of the Jewish people are its
three 'aspects': monotheism, ceremonialism, and nationalism."[56]
Monotheism, Friedlaender suggested, was the source of Jewish
thought. It originated in the intuitive perception of the divine,
which can only be described as a "gift from heaven."[57] Monotheism

is a necessary "aspect" of Judaism, but it is never sufficient. A fragile, volatile idea, it must be "cultivated and perfected" through human institutions.[58] Through the process of cultivation and perfection were born all of the other aspects of Judaism—its ethics, its ceremonial practices, its national consciousness, and its culture. These comprise its civilization, its "manner of living." Reform Judaism, he argued, erred when it tried to sever monotheism from its support system.

This analysis proceeded from philosophical and historical arguments mustered by Jewish savants from Sa'adia Gaon to Zecharias Frankel. On another occasion, however, Friedlaender analyzed the Jewish manner of living from a different standpoint.[59] Once again the audience was largely Reform, this time the directors of the Educational Alliance. Here Friedlaender took his fellow board members to task for misunderstanding the Jews of the Lower East Side. Friedlaender did not object to classes in the practical and fine arts, the teaching of English, and lectures on current topics. But he was deeply distressed by the deliberate omission of Jewish cultural content from the programing. It was his contention that this policy actually contributed to the malaise of the immigrants. In order to prove his point, he examined the issue from a psychological and sociological standpoint.

In Friedlaender's analysis, the immigrant suffered because the values he had previously cherished, notably, "Jewish learning" and "Jewish piety," were now considered of no account. As a consequence, many of the finer Jews became "mangled human souls which are writhing in inexpressible suffering," for they had lost their "equilibrium."[60] The function of an institution established to facilitate the immigrants' transferral to America should be

the restoration of his equilibrium, in the recreation of a social environment for him which, among the puzzling conditions of the new land, would offer him that spiritual anchorage which his former environment had provided for him; in making him again the unit of a social group, the mandates of which he could obey, and in enabling him to regain the sense of security which had formerly guided him in all the functions of life.[61]

To re-create the social environment, Friedlaender proposed a series of practical steps: conducting the Sunday school and "People's Synagogue" along traditional lines, observing the Sabbath and dietary laws within the building, and creating a full cultural program of Jewish art, music, lectures, and clubs devoted to Jewish issues.[62]

Just as significant as the fact that these proposals suggested Kaplan's plans for the Jewish Center was the nature of the analysis. To examine Jewish religious institutions as instruments of social cohesion and interpersonal intercourse was to adopt the functional approach that Kaplan was working out at the same time. As I indicated previously, Friedlaender never revealed the sources of his psychological and sociological analysis, nor did he label his philosophy "pragmatic," as Kaplan was wont to do.[63] Nevertheless the memorandum to the Educational Alliance's board suggests that, even if the two men never discussed the matter, they probably read the same authors.[64]

Kaplan's position was both more consistent and more radical than Friedlaender's. The essay on the Americanization of the immigrants must have pleased him, but the exposition on monotheism must have appeared tediously old-fashioned, even infantile. In his estimation,

the youthful thinking of the race is ideological; the mature thinking is realistic. In ideological thinking, the predominant tendency is to adapt life, as far as possible, to a thought world of some kind, whether that thought world has been transmitted to us from past generations or is the result of our own mental construction. Ideas, instead of being regarded as a means to an end, become an end in themselves.[65]

In his determination to understand Judaism in a "realistic" fashion, Kaplan became Marx to Friedlaender's Hegel; he turned ideas on their heads. It was not true, he maintained, that belief in God created the Jewish civilization. The very opposite was the case. It was the "living energy" of the people, expressed in "social or ethnic experience" that gave rise to the moral values, social mores, ritual practices, and theological beliefs that constitute Jewish civilization. These, in turn, reinforced their social cohesion.

Still, he observed, times change; particularly in America, Jews face novel ideas and experiences difficult to reconcile with traditional beliefs and social mores. The young are rebellious, and the ties between generations are loosened. Jewish renewal, he was convinced, must proceed along two lines. One was the encouragement of group life through the synagogue-center. The other was the formulation of a theology that related to the life experience and intellectual outlook of an increasingly better educated Jewish population. By the end of the period under discussion, a synagogue-center was already functioning. It would take Kaplan another decade to work out his naturalistic theology.

Related to the culture/civilization issue was a second matter that reveals a small but perceptible variance in the two men's approaches. At issue was a burning question of the pre–World War I era: Are the Jews a race or a religion? Kaplan once considered it for his doctoral dissertation;[66] his first published essay (1909) dealt with the question.[67] Friedlaender's article on the subject appeared the following year.[68] Against the reformers, both writers argued that the Jews are both an ethnic and a religious community. They approached the controversial issue of racial integrity on three levels. Consulting the new science of anthropology, they reluctantly admitted that there is no such thing as a pure race. Nevertheless, Jewish history records a strong biological continuity. As Kaplan put it,

even if other races of our family stocks were grafted into the Jewish, they have all by this time been thoroughly Judaized through intermarriage with the genuine Jewish stock."[69]

Biological factors, for Friedlaender, were secondary to psychological ones:

For the purpose of our present inquiry it is enough for us to know that the Jews have always *felt* themselves as a separate race, sharply marked off from the rest of mankind. The fundamental belief which bears the entire structure of biblical and post-biblical Judaism and the expression of which fills to overflowing the Jewish liturgy and literature of all ages is the conviction that the Jews are the common descendents of Abraham.[70]

Proceeding from psychological to sociological analysis, both men maintained that what people say is less significant than what their actions indicate. According to Kaplan,

even if every Jew were to deny that the Jews form a nation, if all or the greater number of Jews were to act in a certain way towards each other which could not be explained on any other ground except nationality, which could not be explained let us say on the basis of religion pure and simple, or racial ties, they still would constitute a nation.[71]

Friedlaender agreed:

There are many Jews who deny the racial or national character of Judaism and yet betray in their actions and sentiments a deep attachment to the Jewish people as a racial community. There are others who deny the religious basis of Judaism and yet in their whole spiritual make-up bear the deep impress of the Jewish religion.[72]

To this point, the views are identical, but there followed a subtle but significant distinction. In his attempt to answer the question under discussion, Friedlaender ascribed equal valence to "race" and "religion."

In the course of 3,800 years out of the 3,900 years of the existence of our people—race and religion in Judaism were inseparable. . . . A *religious race*, i.e. a race or a nation whose distinguishing feature and whose only reason for existence is religious, is the only correct definition of the character of the Jewish community as it presents itself to us from the very beginning of its existence down to modern times.[73]

On another occasion, he expressed the idea more succinctly: "From its earliest beginnings, Judaism represented an indissoluble combination of nationalism and religion."[74]

However, when Kaplan attacked the problem on the level of the individual Jew, he arrived at a somewhat different conclusion. For him, as for Friedlaender, the most authentic Jews, the "vital" ones, defined their Judaism in both ethnic and religious terms. But he did not regard Jews who accepted only one of these definitions as equals. In his estimation, the "national" Jews existed on a higher plane than the "religious" ones. This view reflected his new sociology of Jewish life. Because of his conviction that religious expression grows out of social consciousness, he was convinced that the Jew who is attached to the Jewish people may one day develop a religious perspective. But if a person's Judaism is confined to the synagogue, then, in Kaplan's estimation, his Judaism is sterile. Kaplan compared him to a dying person with a feeble will-to-live; the national Jew, whose will-to-live is stronger, is but still alive.

More conspicuously at variance than our subjects' approach to the culture/civilization discussion and the race/religion dichotomy were certain observations on American Jewish life.

With characteristic forthrightness, Kaplan identified the nub of the problem facing the American Jewish community. It was not merely "emancipation," the code word for the exodus from the ghetto and the achievement of citizenship. It was rather the Enlightenment philosophy that made emancipation possible, abstracted and crystallized into "democracy" and "science."[75] On the first issue, Friedlaender set the agenda and Kaplan responded; on the second, the reverse was the case.

Especially during the years following his settlement in America, Friedlaender waxed optimistic about the prospects for Judaism in this democratic land, relying on precedent in the Jewish past and an idiosyncratic understanding of American politics and culture. "The Jewish-Arabic period" of the Middle Ages, he suggested, proved that a "Judaism of freedom and culture" was possible in the Diaspora.[76] Modern America, he was convinced, offered the potential for a new golden age where Jews could fully participate in society without abandoning Jewish identity and creativity. As an emigrant from Wilhelminian Germany, he was acutely aware of the difference between a government that demanded unquestioning submission and one constructed to benefit its citizens. His portrait of a state created to govern as little as possible, allowing for free expression of all its peoples, was part Dubnow, part Jefferson. Surveying the New York scene, Friedlaender concluded that American culture was still in the process of formation; hence there was no reason why Jews could not find a place.

In the great palace of American civilization we shall occupy our own corner, which we will decorate and beautify to the best of our taste and ability, and make it not only a center of attraction for the members of our family, but also an object of admiration for all the dwellers of the palace.[77]

At a meeting of the *Achavah* Club, Kaplan publicly debated Friedlaender's position on American cultural and political life;[78] two important articles continued the argument.[79] Breaking with the half century of *Wissenschaft* scholarship represented in Friedlaender's position, Kaplan questioned the value of the medieval model for "a Judaism of freedom and culture."

That Judaism flourished in Egypt during the reign of the Ptolemies, in Persia before the advent of Mohammedanism, and in Spain during the Middle Ages, is not proof that it will flourish in Western Europe and America, because the conditions are radically different.[80]

In Kaplan's estimation, Friedlaender looked down upon American culture as "crude and uncouth."[81] He doubted that young Jews shared this opinion. No matter how beautiful the "corner," it was not the place where they wished to abide. In response to Friedlaender, he insisted that "cultural Americanism is . . . exercising a much greater influence than the speaker was ready to admit."[82]

Nor did he agree with Friedlaender's analysis of the American political system. Kaplan noted that the United States government had been established to secure the rights of individuals, not groups. For this reason, he found it incompatible "with the harboring of different nationalities within a single nation."[83] Furthermore, conditions of the modern industrial era, that is, the need to curb the power of the robber barons, necessitated a strong government. Against those Jews who relied on constitutional guarantees to maintain Judaism, Kaplan argued that freedom of religion was "a mere stalking horse;"[84] other forces were at work. American democracy during the period of the "New Nationalism," he observed, was marching in the direction of increased nationalization. The social energy of a highly centralized nation would inevitably create a religion of Americanism, thereby endangering the survival of Judaism in the United States.[85]

Kaplan's insights into the nature of American democracy were original, but his judgment of Friedlaender's position was unduly severe. Despite the Dubnovian strain in his thinking, Friedlaender did not advocate the establishment of Jewish enclaves in America. I do not know how he spoke of American culture in private, but the written evidence reveals a regard for the "great ideals underlying the American commonwealth,"[86] if not the crudities of popular culture. Finally, Friedlaender did not propose a program for American Judaism but rather a vision of its potentialities.

Kaplan, blessed with over twice Friedlaender's life span, did initiate a program. Like Friedlaender and Judah Magnes,[87] he rejected Israel Zangwill's melting pot theory of acculturation and advanced the new notion of cultural pluralism associated with Horace Kallen.[88] The synagogue-center, created at the end of our period, was intended to attract all the Jews of an area and to satisfy their need for community, thirst for learning, and quest for spirituality. But he was not willing to place the Jews in a "corner," even metaphorically. His societal scheme can be compared to Mendelssohn's philosophical one, as explicated by Simon Rawidowitz.[89] The Jews would establish full-time residence in the lower story of the house where all Americans dwell; but just for them an upper floor was to be added to the building. To this they would repair in their leisure hours.

> The Jew can no longer think in terms of the Jewish civilization all the time, but he can do so at least part of the time. He should don the character of the Jewish nationality and of its civilization at least in his leisure hours and days.[90]

On the second legacy of the Enlightenment, Kaplan was equally original. "Science" denoted three issues. First was the fearless use of reason, the incisive questioning of all assumptions, even those traditionally regarded as axiomatic. Second was the application of the new social "sciences" to Jewish problems. Finally, there was the requirement to deal with "science" in its nineteenth-century meaning of *Wissenschaft des Judentums*, or the critical investigation of Jewish sources. I shall pursue these issues in reverse order.

The Jewish Theological Seminary was reorganized with a dual objective: to train rabbis and to pursue scholarship in the *Wissenschaft* tradition. Schechter lured university-educated scholars from Germany with promises of long summer vacations allowing adequate time to investigate the Geniza manuscripts, which he had brought from Cambridge, and other historical texts. Within the Seminary faculty, only Kaplan questioned the worth of the enterprise. In his opinion, the emphasis on scholarship actually interfered with what should have been the institution's primary objective, Jewish renewal in America. His journal is peppered with complaints about professors who ignored their students and misspent their energies on "stupid Geniza fragments"[91] and "dry-as-dust scholarship."[92] At one point, in frustration, he described their work as suitable only for the "crippled and maimed."[93]

In print, of course, he modified the rhetoric. But even as he protested respect for the accomplishments of the medievalists, he argued for new priorities: "Of immediate importance to Judaism is the task of reconstructing the history of our people during the first millennium of its existence."[94]

To denigrate historical study was to drive home the point that there were no useful precedents for modern Judaism. Jewish renewal, Kaplan believed, would have to proceed from other sources. To advance the study of Torah was to return to an essential of Jewish life. "The supremacy of the Torah," wrote Kaplan in 1914, "lay not in its divine authorship, rejected by the modern mind, but in the fact that Israel had always regarded it as supreme."[95] It followed that the Torah belongs at the center of any Jewish curriculum. Jewish academicians, Kaplan suggested, should investigate the ancient world rather than the Middle Ages, thereby reclaiming the Bible for Jewish scholarship. Out of a conviction that the Torah and its commentaries are the proper stuff of rabbinical training, Kaplan utilized them for his religion and homiletics courses at the Seminary.

If Kaplan ascribed little value to the "pure" science of his *Wissenschaft* predecessors and contemporaries, he readily adopted the new "applied" science of sociology. His thought, rooted in the perceptions of Ahad Ha'am and some American social thinkers, was bold and new. From it would flow the only Jewish religious philosophy constructed in America.

Kaplan's sociological approach to Judaism was suspect to the older generation of scholars,[96] but it won the respect of the next generation. It certainly was never as controversial as his grasp of the primary legacy of the Enlightenment: the demand to see all things in the light of reason and experience. Relentlessly, he pursued questions that most of his colleagues refused to touch. That the young Ginzberg accepted the documentary hypothesis on the origins of the Pentateuch[97] and that Friedlaender doubted the Mosaic authorship of the Torah can only be inferred from their writings; never did any Conservative spokesman raise these issues in public forums. Of the Seminary faculty, only Kaplan was willing to articulate a nonfundamentalist approach to Scripture and Jewish law.

Even he required coaxing. For a period of time, several of his disciples urged him to convene the Seminary community for the purpose of "agreement on general principles."[98] Finally, on June 18, 1919, he acceded to the request and, with five other men, cosigned a letter inviting alumni and students to a meeting set up "to formulate, in terms of belief and practice, the type of Judaism that we believe you profess in common with us."[99] Nothing went smoothly. Because of Ginzberg and Marx's objections, the group did not meet on Seminary premises. Kaplan presented a long paper setting forth his radical views but received little support. He later commented, "It became apparent that the time was far from ripe for any such undertaking. There were hardly any two men[100] in the room that had the same point of view."[101]

Among the dissenters was Israel Friedlaender. Before examining his position, let us briefly review his divergence from Kaplan on the role of historical research and Bible study. I have already indicated Friedlaender's unshakable conviction that Judaism could plot its course into the future only if it thoroughly understood its past. Rather than condemn research into Geniza fragments, he participated in it to the extent that his overcrowded schedule would permit. Furthermore, although he genuinely enjoyed working with young people, he displayed no preference for pedagogical training over the pursuit of learning for its own sake. This applied to all areas of Jewish scholarship, including the Bible.

On the issue of biblical scholarship, he was decidedly ambivalent. On the one hand, he introduced his students to archaeology and the Lower Criticism of the Prophets.[102] That his motives were not purely academic was indicated by the following pained outcry:

Jewish learning, distorted by bias and prejudice, has been brandished as a weapon against Judaism. We realize more clearly than ever before that we are the natural and rightful guardians of our own vineyard.[103]

On the other hand, there were areas where he feared to tread. Like Kaplan, Friedlaender admired Arnold Ehrlich's scholarship.[104] Nevertheless, he happily went along with the policy that excluded the Pentateuch from the Seminary's curriculum. Moreover, although he had studied with Wellhausen and David Hoffmann, his Jewish opponent in Berlin, he preferred not to broach the controversial issue of Higher Criticism, lest he stir up a hornet's nest.

It was not Friedlaender's fate to escape controversy in many areas. Willy-nilly, he was drawn into that important meeting of June 1919. Friedlaender was the only faculty member outside of Kaplan to sign the letter of invitation. Kaplan probably enlisted him because he had previously suggested a uniform philosophy and code of practice for United Synagogue members.[105] Neither man anticipated the furious response of Ginzberg and Marx.[106] In self-justification, Friedlaender wrote to Ginzberg, "I know and knew nothing whatever about the arrangements of the Conference, except that I was asked to sign my name to the invitation—which I gladly did."[107]

At the time of the meeting, Friedlaender responded negatively to Kaplan's proposals. The following is Rabbi Harry Cohen's résumé of his speech, recalled many years after the event:

We all waited to hear what Dr. F. would say. Dr. F. pointed that never before in our history, had any group come together to make changes in Jewish life and observance. You cannot, he said, say to the Jewish people, in the name of a small group of experts, this you should do and this you should not do, basing your decision on what you as experts believe the times demand.[108]

The meeting became a turning point in Kaplan's life. Soon after its unsatisfactory conclusion, he published his "Program for the Reconstruction of Judaism," which became the blueprint for the new Society for Jewish Renascence.

Friedlaender's rejection of Kaplan's proposals can be traced to his essentially conservative understanding of the concept of evolution. Change was inevitable, he agreed, but it must proceed slowly. "Just as historical Judaism does not believe in suddenness in the past," he had written in 1917, "so does it refuse to believe in suddenness in the future."[109] This was the essence of his response of 1919.

A willingness to await the results of "evolution" also marked his Zionist thinking. In the excitement following the Balfour Declaration, a student posed the question: Can a modern state be both "democratic" and "Jewish"? Friedlaender indicated an awareness of the problem. "The particular difficulty," he suggested, "lies in the fact that on the one hand the tradition of Judaism has constantly upheld the identity of state and religion, whereas modern thought has just as consistently opposed that identity." Nevertheless, he assured her, "I am sure that in the practical working out of our plans this difficulty will be ultimately overcome, as well as many others."[110] It is clear that Friedlaender's projections for the future, like his portrait of the past, reflected an essential romanticism.

Kaplan, by contrast, was a rationalist whose perspective rested on philosophical reasoning and sociological analysis, not romantic historiography. No inner-regulated scholar who dwelled in the world of the abstract, he rose to heights of righteous indignation at the mere mention of the miraculous and the mystical. He railed at a student who introduced kabbalistic doctrines into scriptural passages.[111] His Lithuanian horror of mysticism is revealed in a misquote from Schechter. The Seminary president once described the theology of the Historical School as "an enlightened skepticism combined with a staunch conservatism which is not even wholly devoid of a certain mystical touch."[112] When Kaplan quoted him just five years after his death, he omitted the final clause![113]

Strongly indicating his psychological distance from Friedlaender was his treatment of another problem that came to the fore after the Balfour Declaration. Like other religiously committed followers of Ahad Ha'am, Friedlaender believed that the Jewish religion, freed from non-Jewish influences, would soon become a creative force in the life of the *yishuv*. Kaplan was more realistic. Characterizing Palestine as "the religious cockpit of the world,"[114] he inquired:

Will the Jews who migrate to Palestine go there with any clear aims as to Judaism, or do we expect them to undergo a sudden metamorphosis as they are transported from their old homes? They will undoubtedly bring along with them all their intellectual shortcomings and old-world prejudices.[115]

A radical temperament and a keen perception of current problems created impatience with what he considered standpatism on the part of the Conservative leadership. Kaplan was convinced that modern conditions were so different from previous ones that the evolutionary process, touted by the Historical School, must be accelerated.

The Seminary leadership rejected out of hand his proposals to speed up the process. Most painful of all the comments must have been the biting remarks of Friedlaender, the faculty member with whom he had worked on so many projects of Jewish renewal. It is unlikely that the two men sustained a personal relationship in the tumultuous half year that lapsed between the June 1919 meeting and Friedlaender's departure for Europe.

Seven months later came the rumors, later confirmed, of Fried-laender's murder. Arriving at a crucial juncture in his own life, the news of Friedlaender's death stung Kaplan to the quick. According to his diary, the terrible event helped trigger his radical theodicy.[116] But it does not explain the harsh verdict on his colleague's life.

We cannot enter the mind of Kaplan to arrive at a definitive answer as to why he judged Friedlaender a failure. Perhaps at this time he deemed their differences in temperament and approach more significant than his essential agreement with much of Fried-laender's philosophy. Earlier journal entries had lumped Friedlaender together with Ginzberg and Marx as men who wasted their time on arcane scholarship. On other occasions, Kaplan had also indicated a lack of patience with theoreticians who glossed over obvious difficulties to project optimistic visions of the future. He certainly was cognizant of Friedlaender's personal problems, his unsuccessful efforts to balance the demands of town and gown, and the rebuffs suffered at the hands of the wartime Zionist leadership.[117]

But there is something so final and so harsh about the word *failure* that Kaplan's verdict on Friedlaender must reflect more than an acquaintance with his personal problems and discrepant views about certain theoretical concepts. We remember that Kaplan's last significant encounter with Friedlaender had been the meeting of June 1919, when Conservative leaders had rejected his proposals for a separate theology. A year later, the words of his opponents probably still rankled. For Kaplan that meeting spelled a personal failure. No man likes to think of himself in this way. We can surmise, therefore, that Kaplan projected the notion of failure onto the man whose previous statements and actions—notably the cosigning of the letter of invitation—had probably raised expectations of finding an ally on the Seminary faculty. For this reason, then, one can speculate that it was the disappointment of June 1919 rather than the catastrophe of July 1920 that triggered Kaplan's unfavorable verdict on Friedlaender's life.

Notes

1. Mordecai M. Kaplan, *Kaplan Journal*, vol. 2, 27 July 1920, 22.
2. Israel Friedlaender, *Past and Present* (New York: Burning Bush Press, 1961), 165. (Unless otherwise indicated, citations are from this, the second edition.)
3. Reported by Friedlaender in a letter to Harry Friedenwald, 19 February 1907, in the Friedenwald Papers of the Library of the Jewish Theological Seminary of America (hereafter referred to as JTSA).
4. *Ibid.*, and letter of 19 March 1907.
5. Israel Friedlaender to Herman Rubenovitz, 10 November 1910, Rubenovitz Papers of the Library of the JTSA.
6. From a conversation recorded in Kaplan's *Early Diary*, vol. 2, December 1906. I thank Mel Scult for this datum.
7. Actually to 1924, when a summary of his early thinking, *A New Approach to Jewish Life*, was published.
8. On Dewey, see "The Sociologist as Theologian: The Fundamental Assumptions of Mordecai Kaplan's Thought," *Judaism* 25, no. 3 (Summer 1976):346. The Durkheim reference is "The Origins of Kaplan's Concept of Community," an unpublished paper delivered at the Graduate Center of the City University of New York, 9 April 1986.
9. See Baila R. Shargel, *Practical Dreamer: Israel Friedlaender and the Shaping of American Judaism* (New York: Jewish Theological Seminary of America, 1985), 145–46.
10. This was the thesis of Kaplan's address to the Seminary Alumni Association in June 1909, as cited in his retrospective essay, "The Influences that Have Shaped My Life," *Reconstructionist* 8, no. 10 (June 1942): 31.
11. See *Iggerot Ahad Ha'am*. (Tel Aviv: Dvir, 1956), vols. 1, 3, 4, 5, passim.
12. Israel Friedlaender, "Zionism and the World Peace, a Rejoinder to Herbert Adams Gibbons," *Century Magazine* (April 1919): 10; and *Kaplan Journal*, vol. 1, December 1918, 94.
13. Friedlaender, *Past and Present*, 167.
14. Ibid., 166.
15. Mordecai M. Kaplan, "A Program for the Reconstruction of Judaism," *Menorah Journal* 6, no. 4 (August 1920): 182.
16. Friedlaender, *Past and Present*, 165.
17. *Kaplan Journal*, vol. 1, 25 August 1914, 73.
18. Friedlaender, *Past and Present*, 243.
19. Quoted in ibid., 275.
20. Ibid. Actually, this particular essay refers to westernized European Jews, but Friedlaender often made the same point in discussing assimilated American Jews.

21. Simon Greenberg and Max Kadushin, interviews with the author, March and November 1978.
22. See Friedlaender, "The Political Ideal of the Prophets," in *Past and Present*, 1–34.
23. *Seminary Addresses and Other Papers* (New York: Burning Bush Press, 1959), 93.
24. Kaplan, "Reconstruction of Judaism," 184.
25. Mordecai M. Kaplan, *New Approach to Jewish Life* (Bridgeport: Hartmore House, 1973), 31–34.
26. *Kaplan Journal*, vol. 1, February 1914, 49.
27. In *Jewish Daily News*, Silver Jubilee Number (1910).
28. See Arthur A. Goren, *New York Jews and the Quest for Community: The Kehillah Experiment, 1908–1922* (New York: Columbia University Press, 1970), 109.
29. Israel Friedlaender to Lee Kohns, 20 December 1912, in the Friedlaender Papers (hereafter referred to as FP) of the Library of the JTSA.
30. See Goren, *Kehillah Experiment*.
31. Ibid., 94.
32. McDougall: *Kaplan Journal*, vol. 1, January 1914, 38. Royce and James: ibid., February 1915, 136.
33. Kaplan, "Reconstruction of Judaism," 192.
34. See Israel Friedlaender, "Uptown and Downtown Zionism" (Address delivered at the "Qadimah" in the Educational Alliance, 1 March 1905), from papers in possession of Carmel Friedlaender Agranat, Jerusalem.
35. *Kaplan Journal*, vol. 1, August 1914, 95.
36. Ibid., February 1914, 53.
37. See FP, box 16.
38. Solomon Grayzel, interview with the author, March 1979.
39. See Alexander Dushkin, "Antaeus: Autobiographical Reflections," *American Jewish Archives* 21 (November 1969): 124–25; Leo Honor, "Shelosha she-hishpi'u," in *Jubilee Book of the Hebrew Teachers Union* (New York: Modern Linotype, 1944), 344–36; Morris Schussheim, "Recollections of Israel Friedlaender," *Proceedings of the Rabbinical Assembly* 9 (1945): 169.
40. *Kaplan Journal*, vol. 1, August 1914, 58.
41. Israel Friedlaender to Solomon Schechter, 7 August 1903, FP, box 8.
42. *Menorah Journal* 1 (1915): 38.
43. Mordecai M. Kaplan, "The Way I Have Come," in *Mordecai M. Kaplan: An Evaluation*, ed. Ira Eisenstein and Eugene Cohen (New York: Jewish Reconstructionist Foundation, 1952), 287.
44. Friedlaender, *Past and Present*, 159–84.
45. Mordecai M. Kaplan, *Judaism as a Civilization* (New York: Reconstructionist Press, 1934).
46. Ibid., 180, citing Friedlaender, *Past and Present*, 175.

47. Ibid., 161.
48. The speech, entitled "Judaism as a Living Civilization," was published in *The American Jewish Chronicle* 4 (April 1918). My thanks to Mel Scult for this information.
49. Ibid.
50. See A. L. Kroeber and C. Kluckhorn, *Culture: A Critical Review of Concepts and Definitions* (New York: Vintage Books, 1952), 19.
51. Kaplan, *Judaism as a Civilization*, 535.
52. Ibid., 179.
53. Quoted in Kroeber and Kluckhorn, *Culture*, 27.
54. *The Maccabean* 26 (June 1915): 120. The emphasis is Friedlaender's.
55. Israel Friedlaender, "Aspects of Historical Judaism" (a course of five lectures delivered at Temple Emanu-El, April and May 1917), FP, boxes 8 and 12, lec. 2, 6.
56. Ibid., lec. 3, 1.
57. From notes for "Aspects" lectures, FP, box 16.
58. Ibid.
59. See Israel Friedlaender, "The Americanization of the American Immigrant," in *Past and Present*, 229–45.
60. Ibid., 237.
61. Ibid., 232.
62. The proposals were never published. See FP, box 16.
63. *Kaplan Journal*, vol. 1, January 1914, 37–38.
64. Mel Scult, in "The Sociologist as Theologian," 347, mentions Charles Cooley as a social thinker read by Kaplan. Cooley's ideas seem to have influenced Friedlaender as well. See Shargel, *Practical Dreamer*, 145–46.
65. Kaplan, "Program for the Reconstruction of Judaism," 187.
66. *Kaplan Journal*, vol. 1, February 1913, 3–11.
67. Mordecai M. Kaplan, "Judaism and Nationality," *The Maccabean* 17 (August 1909): 59–64.
68. Israel Friedlaender, "Race and Religion," in *Past and Present* (1919 ed.), 431–43. This essay was not reprinted in the second edition.
69. Kaplan, "Judaism and Nationality," 60.
70. Friedlaender, *Past and Present*, 432.
71. Kaplan, "Judaism and Nationality," 59–60.
72. Friedlaender, *Past and Present*, 440.
73. Ibid., 437.
74. Friedlaender, *Past and Present* (1961 ed.), 213.
75. *Kaplan Journal*, vol. 1, March 1913, 19–23; and Mordecai M. Kaplan, "How May Judaism Be Saved?" *Menorah Journal* 2 no. 1 (Feb. 1916): 34–44.
76. Friedlaender, *Past and Present*, 170–77; 185–95.
77. Ibid., 183.
78. See Moshe Davis, "Israel Friedlaender's Minute Book of the *Achavah*

Club (1909–1912)," in *Mordecai M. Kaplan Jubilee Volume*, English sec. (New York: Jewish Theological Seminary of America, 1953), 157–213. The *Achavah* Club was a forum for Jewish intellectuals.

79. Kaplan, "How May Judaism Be Saved?" *Menorah Journal* 2, no. 1 (Feb. 1916): 34–44, and "The Future of Judaism," *Menorah Journal* 2, no. 3 (June 1916): 160–72.
80. Kaplan, "How May Judaism Be Saved?" 35.
81. *Kaplan Journal*, vol. 2, July 1920, 23.
82. Quoted in Davis, "Friedlaender's Minute Book," 205.
83. Kaplan, "How May Judaism Be Saved?" 35.
84. Kaplan, "Future of Judaism," 160.
85. Ibid., 161–63.
86. Friedlaender, *Past and Present*, 240.
87. See Goren, *New York Jews*, 47–48.
88. See Horace M. Kallen, "Democracy versus the Melting Pot: A Study of American Nationality," *The Nation* 100 (18 February 1915): 190–94; (25 February 1915): 217–20.
89. See Simon Rawidowitz, "The Philosophy of *Jerusalem*" (in Hebrew), in *Sefer Bialik*, ed. Jacob Fichmann (Tel Aviv: Hotza'at Va'ad ha-Yovel be-Hishtatfut Hotza'at 'Omanut 1934), 133.
90. Mordecai M. Kaplan, "Where Does Jewry Really Stand Today?" *Menorah Journal* 4, no. 1 (February 1918): 42.
91. *Kaplan Journal*, vol. 1, December 1918, 382.
92. Ibid., (October 1914), 91.
93. Ibid., 100.
94. Kaplan, "New Approach to Jewish Life," 48.
95. Mordecai M. Kaplan, "The Supremacy of the Torah," in *Jewish Theological Seminary Students' Annual* (New York: Jewish Theological Seminary of America, 1914), 180–92.
96. See Mel Scult, "Foundations of Jewish Education," *American Jewish Archives* (April 1986): 63.
97. Louis Ginzberg, "Law, Codification Of," *Jewish Encyclopedia*, vol. 7 (1904–1910), 635–47.
98. *Kaplan Journal*, vol. 1, December 1918, 379–81.
99. Dated June 9, 1919, Ginzberg Papers, Library of the JTSA.
100. One of the speakers was Henrietta Szold!
101. *Kaplan Journal*, vol. 1, 28 July 1919, 394.
102. Schussheim, "Recollections," 171.
103. Friedlaender, *Past and Present*, 205.
104. See his obituary, "A Great Bible Scholar, Arnold B. Ehrlich," *The Nation*, 10 January 1920, 41.
105. *Fifth Annual Report of the United Synagogue of America*, 48; and Mordecai M. Kaplan to Herman Rubenovitz, 6 November 1910, Rubenovitz papers of the Library of the JTSA.
106. Alexander Marx to Israel Friedlaender, 12 June 1919, FP; and Israel

Friedlaender to Louis Ginzberg, 13 June 1919, Ginzberg Papers of the Library of the JTSA.

107. Ibid.
108. Rabbi Harry Cohen to Morris Adler, 7 September 1955, FP, box 12.
109. Friedlaender, "Aspects of Historical Judaism," lec. 1, 4.
110. Israel Friedlaender to Margaret Elfenbein, 23 June 1918, FP.
111. Bernard Heller, "Looking Back at the Seminary," *Conservative Judaism* 23 (Spring 1969): 48–49.
112. *Studies in Judaism*, ser. 1 (Philadelphia: Jewish Publication Society, 1945), xvii.
113. Kaplan, "Program for the Reconstruction of Judaism," 183.
114. Ibid., 186.
115. Ibid.
116. *Kaplan Journal*, vol. 2, 27 July 1920, 22.
117. See Shargel, *Practical Dreamer*, chap. 2.

CHAPTER 5

Kaplan and Cyrus Adler

Richard Libowitz

Throughout their decades of service to the Jewish Theological Seminary and the Conservative movement, the relationship between Mordecai Kaplan and Cyrus Adler remained, at best, formal. While it is doubtful that either man fully appreciated the other, the frequency and volume of their well-known disagreements marked their unceasing efforts to fashion American Judaism in accordance with their respective divergent ideals.

Cyrus Adler was born in the town of Van Buren, Arkansas, in 1863. His father's illness and subsequent death caused the family to relocate in Philadelphia where Adler's maternal relatives, the Sulzbergers, were numbered among the German-Jewish elite. In an era marked by general assimilation and the growth of Reform Judaism, the young Adler was a faithful attendant of the city's oldest traditional synagogue, Mikveh Israel, where he became a disciple of that Sephardic congregation's rabbi, Sabato Morais. Adler was educated at the University of Pennsylvania and received a doctorate in Assyriology at Johns Hopkins University. He served for twenty years as assistant curator of the Smithsonian Institute, during which he began his remarkable career as leader of Jewish and general public institutions.[1]

Mordecai Kaplan was born in Swenciany, Lithuania, in 1881, the son of a talmudic scholar. The family settled in New York City in 1889. There, while attending public schools, the boy sat with tutors in preparation for rabbinical studies.[2] Kaplan entered the Jewish Theological Seminary in 1893 as the institution's first student to have received his primary education in the United States. While a seminarian, Kaplan pursued a college education, acquiring a bachelor's degree from the City College of New York and a master's degree in philosophy from Columbia University.

Kaplan's student years were completed during a period of increasing financial difficulty for the Seminary. Founded by Sabato Morais in 1886, the institution was supported by a small group of traditional and Reform Jews within the New York–Philadelphia–Baltimore corridor. These men were linked by their mutual unease over the radical direction of the Hebrew Union College and Reform Judaism. Their search for an alternate path for rabbinical education in America led them to embrace the Historical School concepts first voiced in Europe by Zecharias Frankel. The Seminary's position was never secure in its early years; by 1902 the deaths of Morais, Alexander Kohut, and other faculty members, combined with the realignment of H. Pereira Mendes and Bernard Drachman with Orthodoxy, left the school bereft of effective leadership and at the point of bankruptcy.

When it appeared that the institution would close its doors, help arrived from a most unexpected source—the largely Reform, German-Jewish, philanthropic and social leadership. Louis Marshall, Jacob Schiff, and Felix Warburg were not themselves adherents of the Seminary's theological positions, but they saw in its traditional yet Americanized alumni a means for the assimilation of the Jews streaming into the country from eastern Europe. The exotic immigrants represented both a financial burden and a social embarrassment to the uptown elite; for their part, the newcomers distrusted the *yekkes* and rejected their Reform rabbis. A cadre of Yiddish-speaking Seminary graduates could be the catalyst to bridge the gap, leading the latest arrivees to life styles more closely approaching the American norm.

Following extensive negotiations, the Schiff-Warburg group agreed to rescue the Seminary from its financial plight. Under the terms of the agreement, Solomon Schechter was summoned from England to lead the school and was given the authority to hire an entirely new faculty. Schechter would be supported by a board of trustees, half of whom would represent the financial "angels." Cyrus Adler, who was traditional in his personal practice yet thoroughly American, would serve as president of the trustees.[3]

Almost immediately, Kaplan and Adler clashed. Kaplan had expected to receive his ordination in 1902. However, the new board of trustees was anxious that his class remain in residence for an additional two years so that the reorganized institution could number sufficient students to justify the engaging of its new faculty and to graduate a class two years into Schechter's tenure. In later years, Kaplan recalled little upset among students over the additional period of study but adamant opposition to his class's placement into courses with entering students.

> I was at that time president of the student society known as the Morais-Blumenthal Society and we formulated a letter in which we asked that those of us who were about to be graduated should have our previous work taken into account and not be made to sit together with beginners. For daring to make such a request Adler came specially from Philadelphia to give us a bawling out and telling us that it was impudent on our part to send such petitions.[4]

It was an inauspicious way to begin an association.

Upon graduation, Kaplan assumed the pulpit of Kehilath Jeshurun, a prosperous Orthodox congregation on East Eighty-fifth Street. Although his professional commitments, continued studies, and expanding family life kept him busy, his rejection of Orthodox Judaism and self-dissatisfaction combined to bring him to the point of abandoning the rabbinate.

> I was so unhappy with my work that I wanted to quit. Before doing so I went to see Adler in Philadelphia. I don't remember now what made me go to him for advice. I wanted to go into selling life insurance and I probably expected him to give me the necessary recommendation. . . . When I told him what I had in mind to do he pooh-poohed the idea, and told me that when I felt depressed the best thing to do was to take a long walk and the blues would disappear. He said that that was the way he would overcome his own jimjams.[5]

In 1909, after seven years at Kehilath Jeshurun, Kaplan returned to the Jewish Theological Seminary as principal of its new Teacher's Institute; shortly thereafter, he joined the faculty of the rabbinical program as well. During his early years on the Seminary faculty,

Kaplan's scholarly endeavors followed two lines: he pursued the study of midrash, an effort in which Solomon Schechter encouraged him, and continued his investigations into the nature of Judaism, the causes of its malaise in America, and possible sources for its amelioration. In 1915 he began to publish articles in the latter area; however, these studies met with neither Schechter's approval nor Adler's.[6]

The beginning of Kaplan's career as a commentator on the Jewish situation coincided with the death of Solomon Schechter and the succession of Cyrus Adler as the Seminary's president. From the start, Adler did not appreciate Kaplan's radical views about the nature of Judaism. Looking back, Kaplan noted that "every additional article of mine that appeared in the *Menorah* helped to alienate him from me."[7]

In 1917 a group of students approached Adler about the addition of a course "on the problem of religion particularly insofar as it bears upon Judaism." Without mentioning him by name, it was clear that Mordecai Kaplan would be the instructor.

When they explained to him what kind of a new course they wanted, he put his left leg on his right leg, and sitting back, he drawled out the following: "You mean the thing they call social psychology. You know I am a rebel. I don't believe in the whole business. There is no such thing as a psychology of the Jewish people. Any one that would undertake to teach such a subject is a charlatan."[8]

The 1921 United Synagogue convention included a paper by Kaplan entitled "The Function and Organization of the Synagogue." In a critique that underscored the disparity in their viewpoints, Adler charged that Kaplan "had whittled down Judaism to what you called social inheritance, in other words, to a culture or civilization, and I find no reference to what we commonly call religion in the part of the address where one would certainly expect it." In sum, the paper was "destructive," and he warned that "I should be very sorry to think that the younger men who are entering the rabbinate come with such a point of view."[9]

Kaplan's response was mild, suggesting that "the terms we make use of have different connotations for each of us." Reacting to the charge of "whittling down" Judaism, he added, "The reason I speak of Judaism as a culture or civilization is that I want people to realize that Judaism is more inclusive than they think it is."[10]

Other disagreements followed. After one particular flare-up, Adler wrote an explanatory letter, offering insight into the several factors motivating his efforts at the Jewish Theological Seminary.

Shortly after the publication of the articles by you in the Menorah Magazine . . . we had a talk and I told you that the articles were giving me a great deal of trouble both because of interviews which people sought with me about them as well as correspondence from various parts of the country. The view that I took was that the opinions you expressed were individual, that the Seminary as a whole did not share them and was not responsible for them, but that Judaism judged men not by their opinions but by their deeds and that I had full confidence that your life was in accord with the Jewish tradition.[11]

A superficial reading of the statement might suggest Adler's summary dismissal as an orthoprax Jew essentially unconcerned with intellectual pursuits, but the letter continued with reference to another essential aspect of his administrative philosophy. "We are all modern men," he concluded: "we do not engage in inquisitions or excommunications or heresy hunting and we are brought up in the general doctrine of academic freedom."[12] This faith in academic freedom permitted—even coerced—Adler to tolerate Kaplan, personal preferences notwithstanding.

Those preferences and the distinctions between the men were highlighted during a Seminary faculty meeting in 1924. In his diary, Kaplan notes:

I had occasion to learn what, according to Adler, the Seminary stands for. . . . There are two kinds of people, he said, those who naturally accept tradition and who entertain doubts only when there is strong proof against what tradition affirms; and there are those who naturally disbelieve or doubt whatever is handed down by tradition unless they find strong proof to verify it. The policy of the Seminary requires that a man belong to the former of these types of mind. I interrupted that there was a third alternative, and that was to distinguish between such traditions as conflict with experience and those which are of the same character as the rest of human experience.[13]

As early as 1920, Stephen S. Wise had raised the possibility of Kaplan leaving the Seminary for Wise's Jewish Institute of Religion

(JIR). Uncertainty about his place within the Seminary made Kaplan a willing participant in the ongoing conversations.[14] In March 1923, Wise proposed that Kaplan offer a summer course on the psychology of religion at JIR. Adler was consulted about the invitation and spoke against it. Kaplan decided to decline the offer "on the ground that my colleagues on the faculty would consider my acceptance an act of disloyalty to the Seminary."[15] One year later, the resignation of the regular instructor prompted Wise to invite Kaplan to deliver several lectures on midrash. Kaplan accepted and, hoping that his intentions would not be misunderstood, wrote a note to Adler explaining the circumstances of the lectures.[16] From that time forward, Wise made it clear that there was a place on his faculty for Kaplan. For his part, Kaplan was the coy pursued, tentatively accepting and then declining Wise's various offers. By 1927, however, dissatisfaction with the atmosphere at the Seminary led Kaplan to accept the JIR position, and he submitted a cautiously worded letter of resignation:

Dear Dr. Adler:
Ever since I have been associated with the Jewish Theological Seminary of America as a member of the faculty, I have been pursuing various studies with the object of formulating a teachable program of Jewish life. In my opinion, neither the Orthodoxy of Samson Raphael Hirsch and Sabato Morais, nor the Reform of Abraham Geiger and Kaufman Kohler, offers a satisfactory program. But what these leaders proposed has at least the merit of being definite and consistent. It is such definiteness and consistency that I have been anxious to find in what is usually called Conservative Judaism.
    In my own humbler way, I have worked out a conception of Conservative Judaism, to the teaching of which I should now like to devote myself. That conception is based upon the principle that both the national and religious element in traditional Judaism must be conserved and developed. By omitting either of these elements, we are bound to break completely with the Judaism of the past. It is not merely in regard to the rebuilding of Palestine as a Jewish homeland that Conservative Judaism should differ from Reform, but also in regard to the retention of all that social content and cultural activity in the Diaspora, which go together with the traditional conception of Israel as a distinct people. Furthermore, Conservative Judaism should also differ radically from Orthodoxy in being prepared to reckon courageously, in all of its educational and religious activities, with the established conclusions of comparative religion and Biblical scholarship. Certainly, no study of Judaism can call itself scientific which seeks to evade those conclusions.

It was inevitable that some of the ideas which had taken root in my mind should color my teaching both at the Seminary and at the Teacher's Institute. This was known to the late Dr. Schechter, and has also been known to you and other members of the Faculty. Tho seldom was anything of a disapproving nature said to me on that subject, I could not help but sense a feeling of opposition to the spirit in which I have been teaching. A few years ago, when I published some of my views, and organized the Society for the Renascence of Judaism, that opposition bore down on me quite heavily. Since then, I have felt it my duty to avoid publishing anything that might embarrass the Seminary.

As a consequence, I have gotten into a state of mind which is by no means conducive to such creative work as I should like to do in the field of Judaism. Yet I cannot reconcile myself to a policy of drift. Being passive at the present time is not a case of letting well enough alone. In my opinion, the condition of so-called Conservative Judaism is far from being well enough. That a Conservative Jew is one who has ceased being Orthodox but has not yet become Reformed, tho said in jest, is largely true to fact. It is high time that some steps be taken to define the theoretic and practical implications of Conservative Judaism. My usefulness, however, in that capacity is bound to be curtailed unless I be free to voice my opinions concerning the spiritual needs of Jewish life, without continually having in mind that I might be jeopardizing the interests of the Seminary.

In view of all this, I deem it advisable to tender my resignation from the Seminary both as Professor of Homiletics and as Principal of the Teacher's Institute, the resignation to go into effect at the close of the academic year, or at the pleasure of the Board of Trustees.

I am deeply appreciative of all that I owe to the Seminary, and it is my heartfelt prayer that its future be glorious and blessed. I shall always be grateful to you and the other members of the faculty for the courtesies and goodwill shown me during all the years I have been at the Seminary. Tho we may differ in our views, I hope that I shall always deserve your confidence in my sincerity and devotion to the cause of Judaism.[17]

Kaplan is silent about the effect he hoped his letter of resignation would have. While he had accepted Wise's offer, there had been similar commitments on prior occasions, with Kaplan reversing himself in every instance. He had never before submitted his resignation, but a sufficiently coaxing letter from Adler could have caused another change of heart, particularly after the faculty of the Teacher's Institute requested Kaplan to reconsider.

Before posting his response, Adler consulted with Louis Marshall, his successor as president of the board of trustees. Marshall expressed some puzzlement over Kaplan's attitudes and actions and advised "delicacy in handling" the matter. He recommended the resignation be accepted but urged Adler to discuss the matter with the faculty and later present it to the board, so that any eventual action would represent "the united opinion of those who are deeply concerned in the future of the Seminary."[18]

In accordance with the advice, Adler sent Kaplan a response that its recipient deemed "suave and cold":

Dear Professor Kaplan . . .
Your letter came to me as a distinct surprise. I was not at all aware of any more difference of opinion between yourself and your colleagues during the past few years than would subsist in any College Faculty, and I think that the expression of these differences have been greatly tempered by the high regard and esteem in which you are held by your associates in the Faculty.

As I recall even in the case of the articles to which you refer, published a number of years ago, the criticism of your colleagues was directed to a considerable extent to the manner rather than to the matter, although doubtless such differences did exist in both respects. But I think you will agree that liberty of opinion does not reside in one man alone. You were criticising opinions which your colleagues held and which many other good people hold. Why be sensitive if they in turn criticized your opinions?

You say that both the national and religious element in traditional Judaism must be conserved and developed. Probably most of your colleagues agree with you on this point. It happens that I do not, ascribing maybe a different connotation to the word national than you do. But when, at any time, has your freedom in the expression of your conception of national Judaism been restrained in the slightest degree?

Of course I am the last person to dissuade you if you have a feeling of restraint in your present association and since you have not consulted with me as to the proposed step I assume it to represent a matured judgment on your part about which you did not wish to confer.

I shall therefore do as you request and present your resignation to the Board of Trustees at the earliest opportunity that I can have a meeting called. Meanwhile, I feel that I owed to you this acknowledgment and also a statement as to how your letter affected me.[19]

Adler's penultimate paragraph may have proven particularly galling; at any rate, Kaplan was sufficiently angered by the tone of the president's response to submit a further letter of clarification:

Dear Dr. Adler,
I would have preferred to have the letter in which I state the reasons for my resigning from the Seminary speak for itself, without any further comment on my part. Your reply of January 26, however, indicates that what I

said there might give the impression that I was unduly sensitive to criticism. Moreover, you seem to think that my attitude toward Jewish nationality is the main issue. I therefore find it necessary to reiterate that the question with me is not whether I could freely teach and practice the principles that differentiate Conservative Judaism from Reform. That is self-understood. The real question is whether I would be permitted to teach and practice with equal freedom those principles wherein Conservative Judaism differs from Orthodoxy. As I stated in my letter of January 19, Conservative Judaism should be "prepared to reckon courageously in all of its educational and religious activities with the established conclusions of comparative religion and Biblical scholarship. Certainly no study of Judaism can call itself scientific which seeks to evade those conclusions."

As I originally interpreted the spirit of the Seminary, it did not seem to me to be concerned either with Orthodoxy or Conservatism as such. What it stood for in my mind was a maximum of Jewishness in the mode of living, and a maximum amount of knowledge of the Jewish sources as a prerequisite to spiritual leadership. But, instead of standing for this broad principle, the Seminary has been developing a decided tendency to identify itself with Orthodoxy. The students, for example, are expected to live up to the Orthodox interpretation of the Sabbath. From what I have learned of their attitude toward this requirement, I am quite convinced that it breeds hypocrisy and cynicism among many of them. At conventions of the Rabbinic Assembly, which consists virtually of the graduates of the Seminary, our ablest graduates refrain from making any constructive suggestions that would involve a departure from Orthodoxy, lest they be considered heretics and insurgents. As a consequence, the conferences and conventions that have been held in all the years of the Assembly's existence have not resulted in a single page of printed matter dealing with the fundamental questions of Jewish life and thought. The very fact that the Seminary has been seriously considering allying itself with the Yeshivah has confirmed me in my opinion that it wants to be out and out Orthodox.

Personally, I believe this drift of the Seminary toward Orthodoxy will contribute to the further impoverishment of Jewish spiritual life in America. I am fully aware, however, that most of my associates on the Faculty do not share this view. Rather than being placed in the position of seeming to hinder what has come to be regarded as a desirable trend in the Seminary's development, I deemed it advisable to send in my resignation.[20]

This second letter would appear to have represented a final burning of the bridges, severing the last links between Mordecai Kaplan and the Jewish Theological Seminary. Yet such was not to be the case. Representatives of both the Seminary student body and the Rabbinic Assembly sought to undo that which seemed a *fait accompli*. Each group sent delegates to Kaplan's apartment, urging that he reconsider his resignation. Using the student contingent as a sounding board, Kaplan complained that "it was the general spirit of hostility which I encountered among the older alumni who were under the influence of Adler and Ginzberg rather than any specific case of interference that made my stay difficult."[21] Eventually, however, he admitted a preference to remain, "if I were assured perfect freedom to teach and publish my views, and to put into practice the implications of those views."[22] Having gained this admission, Adler was approached, petitioned, and urged to retain Kaplan in the name of academic freedom. Adler's reactions to these approaches is undocumented; however, given his fervent belief in academic freedom, it may be assumed that he was infuriated by any inference of antipathy on his part.

On February 23, 1927, Kaplan and Adler met to discuss the situation. That evening, each recorded his impressions of the session. Given the similarity of their natures, it is not surprising that each understood the other to be making concessions. Kaplan determined that Adler had shown "a decided tendency to yield," adding:

For the first time in all the years that I have known him did he display a trace of unofficial humanness in his makeup. He mentioned that for two nights his sleep was troubled on account of my resignation. He confessed to something like a note of doubt as to the wisdom of the course he had pursued during all the years he had worked for the Seminary.[23]

Adler's perception of the situation was included in a letter to his wife:

Today all or nearly all of the Professors came to see me individually and this afternoon Kaplan. I won't go into the details but for the time being the reactionists [sic] won. It seems he got the idea that I intended to dismiss him (or so he says) and hence took this step. . . . I think he was very glad to get out of an awkward situation.[24]

At any rate, the resignation was withdrawn.[25]

Although he had again elected to stay, Kaplan was aware of his tenuous status among members of the Seminary's faculty and administration. His deep involvement in the Zionist Organization of America was another nettling facet in his relationship with Adler, who has been described as one of the principal non-Zionists among

the American Jewish leadership.[26] While Kaplan, the Ahad Ha'a-
mist, believed that the hope of return to Palestine "has engendered
whatever spiritual and cultural potentialities the Jewish people still
possessed," Adler seemed "to have a phobia on the matter of Jewish
nationalism," maintaining that Zionism "has the tendency, in its
nationalistic aspect, to remove the center of gravity of Judaism from
the Torah to the land or the people."[27] While holding a "non-
Zionist" seat within the Jewish Agency for Palestine, Adler dismissed Zionism as pulling Jews away from traditional religious
practices. Kaplan claimed, "In all likelihood Zionism has had most
to do with diverting Reform from the policy of assimilation."[28]
Adler's concerns about Zionism transcended the religious, as he
explained to Felix Warburg: "In fact I stayed away from the Zionist
movement all these years for two reasons. First, because of its nonreligious character and second, because my own visits there and the
information that I had about Palestine, made me fear that the
conditions as described would be the conditions that actually would
arise."[29]

The Depression had a stringent effect upon every phase of the Seminary's operations. The bulk of correspondence between Kaplan and
Adler during the 1930s was strictly business, as the Seminary's president and the Teacher's Institute's dean struggled with lowered
budgets, salary reductions, and personnel problems. The 1930s were
also Kaplan's most fruitful literary years, marking the publication
of *Judaism as a Civilization* and *The Meaning of God in Modern
Jewish Religion*, as well as the launching of *Reconstructionist* magazine.

    At times Kaplan began to admit an appreciation for Adler. On
the latter's seventieth birthday, Kaplan confided to his diary: "In
spite of my irritation at his non-progressivism I am indebted to him
for not only tolerating me but actually smoothing my way in my
work at the Institute."[30] Six months later, however, published excerpts of an address by Kaplan attacking Jewish communal leaders
drew Adler's wrath. The key passage was the claim that

those who are in control of Jewish communal institutions, with very few
exceptions, really do not want the Jewish people to have a future. They
frankly avow the desire to see Jewish life disappear and would readily

double their contributions to Jewish philanthropies if they knew that thereby they were relieving Jews of their Judaism.[31]

Adler's scathing response reminded Kaplan that "in the various religious societies that you have endeavored to build up you have not shunned the help and cooperation of as many big businessmen as you could associate with yourself."[32] Lecturing Kaplan as he would a recalcitrant child, he added:

I do not know exactly what was in your mind, but I do feel that a man of your position who has got over the first flush of his hot-headed youth . . . has made a very serious accusation against his fellow-Jews for which you have furnished no proof.[33]

Having noted the irate protests that had reached his desk, as well as his own efforts to forestall counterattacks upon the Seminary, Adler concluded his letter with a statement of the type that usually infuriated Kaplan: "I hope that you will take this letter in the kindly sense in which it is meant."[34]

Kaplan's most significant work in the early 1930s was the completion and publication of his opus, *Judaism as a Civilization*. Adler's response to a gift copy was warm and courteous. His evaluation of its contents was as predictable as Kaplan's reaction to it.

[Adler] discharges a broadside at my book, a broadside of muddy ideas and slush phrases. We ought to cast out . . . the so-called ideologies—a word that I have come to loathe. . . . Now why should Jewish writers whine and blame the present difficulties of the Jews upon emancipation? Because this inevitably leads to the only solution, the return to Palestine. . . . But anyone must know that this cannot be the solution of the Jewish question.[35]

As the decade drew to a close, the continuing depression and worsening conditions in Europe and Mandate Palestine deepened the melancholy of the Jewish situation. Adler maintained his many offices despite advancing age and deteriorating health. Kaplan advanced his program of Jewish reconstruction but paused in his work at the Seminary to spend two years on the faculty of the Hebrew University. It was from Jerusalem that he sent congratulations upon Adler's impending seventy-fifth birthday.

I have always noted in you a sense of fairness and justice toward those who disagree with you in a certain matters, the like of which I have never encountered among people in positions of authority and leadership.[36]

Cyrus Adler died on April 7, 1940. During Adler's lifetime, Kaplan had considered him "a well-meaning martinet" whose forte was "the technicalities of academic procedure."[37] Following Adler's death, Kaplan wrote: "I cannot talk very kindly about him because he never liked me."[38] Adler's memoir, *I Have Considered the Days*, appeared posthumously.[39] Kaplan believed the book was "unhelpful" to American Jewish life and felt it should not have been published, yet he refused to include a particularly severe review of it in *Reconstructionist*. Reading that review (published elsewhere) encouraged additional reflection.

Although I owe it to Adler that I have been allowed to teach in the Seminary, he is also responsible for the ill will which most of my colleagues and members of the Seminary Board bear toward me. It is he who has gotten them to think of me as a radical and a secular nationalist. The fact is that when I credit Adler with having made it possible for me to remain at the Seminary, I am aware that it was not some profound recognition on his part of the value of what I had to give to the students that prompted him to let me alone, but rather that he was so ununderstanding and uninterested in the basic problems of Jewish life and religion that he didn't realize what I was trying to accomplish. Fundamentally what decided him to let me alone was the cliché about academic freedom which he honored too much to start proceedings against me.[40]

He also believed Adler had "banished from the Seminary the Schechterian spirit" and replaced it with the more rigid traditionalism he had learned from Sabato Morais.[41]

Kaplan's highly subjective and often contradictory descriptions of Cyrus Adler must be evaluated with an eye to the immediate situations that occasioned them. Despite his frequent proclamations of unhappiness, Kaplan remained at the Jewish Theological Seminary through and beyond the Adler years. During his quarter-century as president, Adler made numerous public defenses of his most controversial faculty member's right to speak, while separating Kaplan's positions from those of the Seminary. Clearly disagreeing with Kaplan and often angered by him, Adler never sought to remove Kaplan from his offices. Each man remained deeply committed to his own formulae for the continuation of Judaism and the betterment of the Jewish people; each was antipathetic to the other's solutions. Kaplan's contention that neither understood the other is a simplistic explanation of their differences that does little more than beg the question.

Adler understood the claims and proposals for Jewish reconstructionism to a far greater extent than Kaplan believed. What Adler lacked was not comprehension but empathy for the reforms and their rationale. He did not share Kaplan's public dismay with current conditions, his rejection of Orthodoxy, his distrust of the wealthy, nor his sense of urgency about theology. Adler had made it clear that his primary concern was praxis—an individual's thoughts were less significant than were his deeds. Kaplan demanded a set of intellectually consistent practices; he could not separate that which he knew from that which he did. His loss of faith in "Torah *mi-Sinai*" made it impossible for him to accept the continuation of many traditional beliefs and practices at the Seminary.

Kaplan extended his disquiet with Adler beyond their personal theological differences to the institutional level. Ignoring his doctorate in Assyriology and his record of scientific publication, Kaplan viewed Adler as a myopic functionary, an administrator in an office that demanded scholarly knowledge of Judaism as well as organizational skills. To Kaplan, Adler's loyalty to traditional Judaism coupled to this perceived lack of insight represented a betrayal of Solomon Schechter's vision and surrendered the Seminary to the most reactionary elements within the faculty, particularly Louis Ginzberg. These men not only opposed Kaplan's efforts but also effectively repressed independent activist thought among the Seminary's students, alumni, and faculty.

While there can be no question of the strong differences in opinion among Kaplan, Adler, and other members of the Seminary's faculty, the vehemence of Kaplan's attitudes transcend ordinary intellectual differences of opinion—even of passionately defended opinions. Kaplan did more than reject Orthodoxy, he rejected the Orthodox. Long before he had abandoned his own faithfulness to a traditional life style, he had come to regard every Orthodox rabbi with distrust. The accusation that Kaplan saw only the worst in Orthodoxy has both merit and reason. He was the son of Rabbi Israel Kaplan, a man who rejected a conspiracy to control New York City's kosher meat industry. His integrity cost Israel Kaplan his position as a *dayan* (judge) in the court of Chief Rabbi Jacob

Joseph and forced him to support his family by working as the *mashgi'ah* (supervisor) in two small poultry abattoirs. Kaplan blamed the fragility of his father's health in later years on the demands of those jobs, which required him to stand in water many hours each day. Ultimately, he blamed both his father's illness and the family's economic hardships on a hypocritical Orthodox rabbinate.

His father's sufferings were not the only cause for Kaplan's antipathy. His own appointment to the pulpit of Kehilath Jeshurun had led to protests by the Agudat HaRabbanim, which rejected the hiring of a Jewish Theological Seminary graduate by an Orthodox congregation in New York City. An eventual compromise required Kaplan to serve as "minister" of the synagogue until a recognized *rav* awarded him a *semihah* (ordination) acceptable to the protestors. Only then did he serve as rabbi. It is safe to assume that Kaplan, then in his twenties, chafed under the demeaning title.[42]

Even at the Seminary Kaplan viewed himself as the outsider; he was an ardent Zionist, a working pulpit rabbi, and a faculty member without a doctorate. Adler seemed to represent everything Kaplan was not: a man of national reputation who was comfortable in the drawing rooms of the powerful among American Jewry and was able to separate his private life from his public career. While the charge of personal jealousy should not be overstated as a factor complicating their relationship, critical remarks about a number of individuals bear tinges of envy. Kaplan felt he lacked the sort of respect accorded other faculty members, while believing his work occupied a more important place "than my colleagues or Adler would care to admit."

The Seminary is designated "Seminary." They lend it academic dignity. Finkelstein as Professor of Theology justifies its being called "Theological." Upon me falls the burden of keeping it "Jewish" so that the students might carry away from it some knowledge of how they might direct the course of Jewish life in the future.[43]

The contention that Cyrus Adler suffered Kaplan's continuing presence within the Jewish Theological Seminary either because of a reverence for academic freedom or from an insufficient understanding of the significance of Kaplan's activities is a disservice to Adler's intelligence and ignores Kaplan's own commitment to the institution. For years, Kaplan solicited contributions to the Seminary from both congregants and acquaintances and turned over many of his lecture fees to the school. In the 1930s, he resisted arguments by Ira Eisenstein, Milton Steinberg, and other young rabbis that he leave both the Seminary and Conservative Judaism proper, to establish Reconstructionism as a fourth dimension of American Judaism. Not until 1963 would he submit his retirement letter, ending the formal association that had begun seventy years earlier.

Cyrus Adler was neither an innovator nor a creative intellect; he was a brick-and-mortar individual who aided the rescue of the Seminary at the turn of the century, guided it safely through the difficult depression years, and oversaw the building of much of its present campus. His contacts ranged from academia to the highest levels of government, business, and philanthropy. His personal discipline permitted him to function simultaneously in many capacities and offices; it also enabled him to confront the various controversies that swirled around the thought and efforts of Mordecai M. Kaplan. He found a way to deflect their potential negative repercussions upon the Seminary and still maintain the formal civility that enables antagonists to serve the same institution and cause it to prosper.

Notes

1. A more complete portrait of Adler's early years is found in his memoir, *I Have Considered the Days* (Philadelphia: Jewish Publication Society, 1941).
2. For Kaplan's biographical information, see R. Libowitz, *Mordecai M. Kaplan and the Development of Reconstructionism* (Toronto: Edwin Mellen, 1983).
3. The full story of the Seminary's early history and reorganization is told by Moshe Davis, *The Emergence of Conservative Judaism* (Philadelphia: Jewish Publication Society, 1965).
4. *Kaplan Diary*, 8 April 1940, Kaplan Archives (hereafter referred to as KA), Reconstructionist Rabbinical College. Only one member of the class complied fully with the new arrangement. Kaplan attended courses during the 1902–3 academic year but, with a full-time job, was irregular in his attendance the next year and made no attempt to be "regraduated."

5. Ibid. It would seem that Adler was correct in dismissing the plaints of the young rabbi. Throughout his long life, Kaplan remained in the rabbinate and became well known for taking long walks; one wonders if Adler's prescription was their source.

6. Ibid. In 1915 Kaplan published his first article in the *Menorah Journal*. In it, he angered Schechter by disagreeing with his view about dogmas in Judaism. Kaplan later wrote, "There was a time when they thought of grooming me for the presidency [of the Seminary]," but "I made myself impossible when I began to publish my views" (ibid.).

7. Ibid.

8. *Kaplan Diary*, 19 March 1917.

9. Cyrus Adler to Mordecai Kaplan, 14 February 1921, KA.

10. Mordecai Kaplan to Cyrus Adler, 15 February 1921, KA.

11. Cyrus Adler to Mordecai Kaplan, 21 September 1923, KA; *Kaplan Diary*, 20 September 1923. See also Cyrus Adler's letter to Edwin Kaufman, 31 December 1920, Cyrus Adler Papers (hereafter referred to as CAP), Jewish Theological Seminary of America. The spark for this particular clash was the publishing of a portion of a letter written by Adler, in which he wrote, "Professor Kaplan's . . . work is to teach the art of constructing a sermon, not the knowledge of Judaism which goes into the construction of the sermon" (*Jewish Light*, September 1923).

12. Cyrus Adler to Mordecai Kaplan, 21 September 1923, KA.

13. *Kaplan Diary*, 13 February 1924.

14. In 1925 Kaplan spoke also with Julian Morgenstern about a possible move to the Hebrew Union College; they concurred that Kaplan's views were too far removed from the ethos of the Reform seminary to contemplate the transfer.

15. *Kaplan Diary*, 30 March 1923.

16. Mordecai Kaplan to Cyrus Adler, 13 October 1924, KA. See also the *Kaplan Diary*, 14 October 1924. Adler's response, dated 24 October 1924, requests that Kaplan discuss the matter with him; given the predilection of both men to preserve their papers, the lack of a written record makes it questionable whether the desired meeting occurred.

17. Mordecai Kaplan to Cyrus Adler, 19 January 1927, KA.

18. Louis Marshall to Cyrus Adler, 23 January 1927, CAP.

19. Cyrus Adler to Mordecai Kaplan, 26 January 1927, KA.

20. Mordecai Kaplan to Cyrus Adler, 31 January 1927, KA.

21. *Kaplan Diary*, 12 February 1927.

22. Ibid.

23. *Kaplan Diary*, 23 February 1927.

24. Cyrus Adler to Racie Adler, 23 February 1927, CAP. Kaplan's fear of dismissal may have been based upon the proposed merger of the Seminary and the Yeshiva, for which his continued presence on the Seminary faculty represented a major stumbling block.

25. One result of the controversy was the delay in awarding Kaplan an

honorary doctorate from the Seminary, for which he had been nominated in 1927, the twenty-fifth anniversary of his ordination.

26. See *Kaplan Diary*, 1 May 1922.
27. Mordecai M. Kaplan, *Judaism as a Civilization*, 278; *Kaplan Diary*, 9 October 1934; Cyrus Adler to Edwin Kaufman, 31 December 1920, CAP.
28. *Kaplan Diary*, 11 July 1929.
29. Cyrus Adler to Felix Warburg, 14 March 1922, CAP.
30. *Kaplan Diary*, 11 September 1933.
31. *Jewish Daily Bulletin*, 12 March 1934.
32. Cyrus Adler to Mordecai Kaplan, 16 March 1934, KA.
33. Ibid.
34. Ibid.
35. *Kaplan Diary*, 1 November 1935. Adler's review of *Judaism as a Civilization* was published in the *Jewish Day*. At the same time, in commenting on the book in a letter, Adler noted, "I believe that Judaism is a religion," but added "I have never set myself up as a censor and believe in freedom of thought and expression." (Cyrus Adler to Jacob Agus [hewitz], 20 May 1935, CAP.
36. Mordecai Kaplan to Cyrus Adler, 28 August 1938, KA.
37. *Kaplan Diary*, 18 February 1926; ibid., 10 March 1926.
38. *Kaplan Diary*, 8 April 1940.
39. Adler, *I Have Considered the Days*.
40. *Kaplan Diary*, October 1941.
41. Unmailed letter from Mordecai Kaplan to Philip Lipis, 12 September 1963, KA.
42. See Libowitz, *Mordecai M. Kaplan and the Development of Reconstruction*.
43. *Kaplan Diary*, 11 September 1933.

CHAPTER 6

Kaplan and Milton Steinberg: A Disciple's Agreements and Disagreements

Simon Noveck

In the course of his lengthy career as teacher, scholar, and religious ideologist, Mordecai Kaplan attracted a number of well-known rabbis and scholars to the Reconstructionist cause as personal disciples, members of the editorial board of the *Reconstructionist*, or as contributors to the magazine. These included such personalities as Ira Eisenstein, Eugene Kohn, Harold Weisberg, Roland Gittlesohn, Jack J. Cohen, Ludwig Nadelmann, Frank Zimmerman, and, for a time, Ben-Zion Bokser. In many instances, the influence on these men began when they were students at the Jewish Theological Seminary. Other members of the Seminary's faculty, such as Louis Ginzberg, Alexander Marx, and Israel Davidson, in spite of their many contributions to Jewish scholarship, had little to say to the students about their theological difficulties. These scholars did not usually involve themselves in the issues of the hour and shied away from religious controversies. Kaplan was the exception. He articulated doubts and raised questions long repressed in the students and helped them to formulate their own religious convictions. As a result, in the 1920s and 1930s Kaplan was immensely influential.

Numerous rabbis have testified that, if not for Kaplan, they would not have been able to remain in rabbinical school or to enter the rabbinate. In several instances, men who later served traditional congregations were excited about Kaplan's ideas and as students were supporters of Reconstructionism. Others, though not completely convinced by the Reconstructionist program, nevertheless found themselves stimulated by Kaplan's intellectual approach and by his analyses of Jewish community life and its problems. Whatever the reaction, Kaplan had a great impact on the lives and thinking of most of the students in those days.

One of the most gifted of these young men was Milton Steinberg, on whom Kaplan's influence was deep and ongoing. In 1927 in a letter on behalf of the student body to Cyrus Adler, president of the Seminary, Steinberg made it clear that "there is preeminently one man among our teachers who is responsible for what faith and courage and vision we may lay claim to. It is from him that we have acquired the hardihood to go on in a difficult and discouraging career, for it was he who has given the Judaism we are expected to teach the content and vitality we have elsewhere sought in vain."[1]

Kaplan provided Steinberg, as he did so many others in those years, with an understanding of the long-range challenges to Jewish survival and of the inadequacy of the existing religious ideologies, an interpretation of the nature of religion, and a comprehensive definition of Judaism as an evolving religious civilization, which Steinberg embraced without reservation. Kaplan also gave him a vision of an organic Jewish community much more cohesive and responsible than the existing one, an approach to Zionism and to other aspects of Jewish peoplehood, an interpretation of Jewish rituals as rites or folkways, insights into the possibilities for creative Jewish culture in the Diaspora, a rationale for public worship, a philosophy of the rabbinate, and a faith in the future of Judaism in the United States. While Steinberg was still a student, Kaplan invited him to serve as assistant rabbi at the Society for the Advancement of Judaism, but precisely because of his admiration and regard for Kaplan, Milton turned down the offer lest he become a shadow in the light of a great man. His first pulpit was in Indianapolis, where he remained for five years; when he returned to New York City, he was one of the small group that helped Kaplan launch the *Reconstructionist*. He undertook the writing of articles, editorials, and book reviews for the magazine. He also participated in the creation of new liturgical materials and often spoke on behalf of the Reconstructionist Foundation or tried to raise money for it in his congregation.

In each of his books and in many of his articles, Steinberg was outspoken in his loyalty to the Reconstructionist program. In *The Making of the Modern Jew* (1934), for example, he described the philosophy of Mordecai Kaplan as a "highly promising theory for Jewish life, . . . closely reasoned, realistic, comprehensive, and creative."[2] A number of years later the very title of his *A Partisan Guide to the Jewish Problem* (1946) indicated where he stood. "There is scarcely a nook or cranny in this book," he wrote, "in which something of Reconstructionism does not lurk." In this work Steinberg spells out his Reconstructionist convictions—the indispensability of religion in Jewish civilization, the evolving character of Judaism, the importance of ritual observance, the need for ethical teaching and reconsideration of Jewish ethical vision, and the need for creativity in Jewish culture. For him, Reconstructionism was a "tenable theory, lucid, cogent, and responsive to facts and of such a mood as to imbue Jews with a passion for Jewish living."[3]

Steinberg's ties to Kaplan were not merely intellectual; they were also emotional, involving as they did a long and close relationship based on a "continuing sense of indebtedness, affection and comradeship in ideas and purposes." Nevertheless, in spite of personal friendship and the many areas of thought for which he was indebted, there were distinctions that Steinberg reluctantly felt he had to draw between his own theological views and the religious outlook of his teacher.

One of these distinctions was the different conceptions they held about the function of religion in the modern world. Though both agreed on the indispensability of religion as the highest expression of Jewish civilization, for Kaplan religion had little to do with a fixed set of beliefs or dogmas. It was not a matter of philosophical doctrine or theological ideas to which one gave intellectual assent. Its function was rather the achieving of salvation, by which he meant finding an answer to man's needs of a social and spiritual character. This "soterical" approach, according to Kaplan, was more realistic and satisfying than one based on speculative reasoning.

Salvation or fulfillment, however, cannot be achieved in a vacuum or through experiences in the world at large but only through the more intimate experiences of one's group. For the individual Jew, the values of religion can be realized only in association with the experiences of the Jewish people and by participation in other elements of Jewish civilization—the language, literature, folkways, and arts that represent the texture of Jewish religion. Every civilization, Kaplan explained, identifies the most important elements of its life—objects, persons, places, events, days, customs—and invests them with sanctity. In the case of Judaism, these sanctified elements include the patriarchs, Moses, the prophets, the psalmists, the Torah, the Temple, the Sabbath, and the holidays. We cannot think of our religion apart from these *sancta*, anymore than we can think of the soul or personality of a human being without reference to his appearance, voice, and acts. It is through these sancta that one achieves salvation.[4]

Thus Kaplan's primary interest is in what he calls "folk religion," with its emphasis on the collective consciousness of a people rather than with the subjective feelings and experiences of individuals. Though a pragmatist who was influenced by William James, Kaplan's concern, unlike James's, is not with varieties of religious experience. Unlike Whitehead, Kaplan did not see religion as mainly a personal matter—in Whitehead's phrase, "what man does with his solitariness." Kaplan does not deny the importance of personal religion nor does he suggest that religion is lacking in personal aspects. However, for him, personal religion was, at best, supplementary, like music and the arts in a cultural education.[5] Men of genius, he admitted, are sometimes satisfied with a form of personal religion. But if religion is to provide morale and courage in meeting the problems of existence of the average individual, these must be achieved through the sancta of one's people. Kaplan is saying that religion cannot be separated from its cultural matrix; unless religion has a group to sustain it, it will not survive. Being a Jew, therefore, was associated, in his mind, with sharing the life of the Jewish people, just as being a soldier is being a member of an army.[6]

Therefore, Kaplan was not sympathetic to metaphysical speculations of any kind, at least not in the period while Steinberg was alive. Such speculations, he felt, were unnecessary except for the assumption that reality is so constituted as to guarantee men the realization of human ideals. Kaplan shared the antimetaphysical temper of twentieth-century thought, its renunciation of comprehensive aims and problems, and its avoidance of a priori speculation. Like many continental and American philosophers of religion, he subordinated abstract metaphysical problems to more practical religious considerations.

Milton Steinberg's conception of religion was based on a much more philosophical approach. To Steinberg, the essential task of religion was precisely the metaphysical goal of working out an understanding of the universe in which we live. He saw religion as consisting of four different aspects in response to four distinct human needs. The first was ritual or folkways, which to him represented a "spiritualizing device," a method of discipline, and a way of participating in a historic tradition.

The second, that of ethics, meets man's need for guidance in conduct. Steinberg believed these norms were rooted in the nature of the universe and were inescapable laws of reality. "Just as there are universal natural laws," he wrote, "there must also be laws regulating human relationships. Otherwise, there would be a gap in the unity of the universe." He did not agree with those for whom the universe was morally neutral but accepted the Jewish view that goodness is a quality objectively present in men and their conduct.

Third, religion meets the need for emotions like awe, reverence, and peace. A religion must find a place for the religious aestheticism of Santayana, for the varieties of religious experience discussed by William James, and for an inner sense of dependence and holiness. "No religion," Steinberg argued, "can be called complete that does not find room for this type of internal or subjective experience including the blinding illumination of the mystic." Religion, he declared, is "an awareness of mystery and poetry, of that which is too deep and too subtle or too vast or too grand for human comprehension." Finally, in Steinberg's view, religion should fulfill the need for a world outlook or, as he put it, a "reasoned scheme of things" to make life meaningful.[7]

Steinberg pleaded for "equilibrium and balance" in religion so that it would answer all these needs. He criticized any approach that overemphasized the emotional aspects of religion, and he protested against what he regarded as too much stress on social justice in many churches and synagogues.[8] In spite of his plea, he himself put more emphasis on *Weltanschauung* (worldview) than on other aspects. "Philosophical reflection is the beginning of piety," he said. "Religion is a matter of cosmology basically and I cannot interpret it otherwise than from that position."[9] He was convinced that the failure to achieve such a cosmology was responsible for some of the severest aberrations of his time—the upsurge of antiintellectualism; cultism and religious authoritarianism; and the latter-day worship of the state, race, or economic class, which he considered modern forms of idolatry. The fact that every great religion has produced many theologians and philosophers—Job, Philo, Augustine, Maimonides, Aquinas—indicates that an indispensable function of churches is to furnish their communicants with a philosophy of the universe. Without such a theological base a religion is "jelly."[10] For Steinberg it was regrettable that religious faith in the sense of a world outlook was being neglected by the Jewish thinkers of his time, including Kaplan. There was a great need, he insisted, for a reformulation of Jewish theology that would establish a harmony between the Jewish tradition and modern thought. In Steinberg's time (the 1930s and early 1940s), such an effort had not yet gotten under way. Jewish preaching, he suggested, tended to shy away from theology. Such questions as faith and reason, the nature of God and the ground for belief in him, and the problem of evil were not being discussed. In contemporary Jewish literature, he pointed out, very few books dealt with issues of doctrine. Indeed, rabbis and Jewish theological seminaries were resorting to books written by non-Jews for instruction in religious metaphysics and in the scientific interpretation of the Bible.[11]

Steinberg recognized that there are people who get along quite well without a philosophy of reality, to whom all abstract and nonpractical issues seem remote and artificial. But in his view, most men are concerned with such issues: "The riddle of the universe haunts them. They are anxious to find out why things are as they are, what meaning they may have, what may be the good for which mankind exists and why it is the good." Whatever our reaction to this view, he himself saw religion as *Weltanschauung*.

Thus, while in agreement on the importance of religion, Kaplan and Steinberg had different concepts of its essential goal and function. For Steinberg the belief in God and an understanding of his nature were central. For Kaplan, centrality should be accorded to the need for salvation or human fulfillment. As Steinberg himself later put it, "To me Kaplan . . . must have a different kind of mental structure than my own. He seems to be missing the main point. . . . You are dealing with two different patterns of personality."[12]

This difference in mental structure stemmed, in part, from their difference in family background and in their early intellectual training. Kaplan came from a home characterized by deep religious piety. His father, a "precocious talmudist" from a small town in the province of Vilna, arrived in the United States in 1889 and was appointed a *dayyan* in the office of the chief rabbi of New York, Jacob Joseph. It was a foregone conclusion that young Mordecai was to be a rabbi, and his early training was conducted with that aim in view. Religious observances represented for him an obligatory way of life to which he conformed as a matter of course.

Already as a young man Kaplan was disturbed by questions and doubts about Jewish tradition and went through a long period of storm and stress, which came on "with the force of a tornado."[13] Arnold Ehrlich, an original and innovative Bible scholar who was a friend of the family and often visited the Kaplan home, was partly responsible for Kaplan's inner religious conflicts. Ehrlich left many of his manuscripts with the Kaplans, which young Mordecai read with great interest. While Ehrlich's commentaries opened up to him an appreciation of the Bible as "an expression of the spiritual genius of Israel," they undermined his belief in the Mosaic authorship of the Torah and in the historicity of the miracles.[14]

Meanwhile, in 1894, a few months before his bar mitzvah, Kaplan had been admitted to the preparatory class at the Jewish Theological Seminary. As he grew older, he did not find anyone at the Seminary who could help him resolve his inner conflicts. The teachers included a number of fine scholars—Sabato Morais, Alexander Kohut, and Joseph Asher (after 1900)—but none were ready for the spiritual wrestlings of this young man. One of the courses he took was on medieval Jewish philosophy, which, in spite of its rationalist bent, did not help him to bridge the gap that divided the thought world of the Bible and Talmud from the thought world in which he lived. To Kaplan's great disappointment, these thinkers were, in his view, "devoid of any historical sense or of any conception of evolution in religion."[15] Also, his teachers seemed to ignore the questions that interested him the most: how the various biblical books came into being and the dates and historical circumstances pertaining to their writing. Thus, intellectually, Kaplan had a difficult time at the Seminary, as he was "tossed about by doubt and questioning concerning the tradition."

When, from time to time, his father studied Talmud with him Kaplan would put to him all kinds of iconoclastic questions. Though personally devout and meticulously observant, his father did nothing to make him feel that he was a sinner for refusing to accept the teachings of tradition. From early childhood the father had stressed to his young son the importance of "intellectual sincerity and moral forthrightness." Now that Mordecai was older, he would let him vent his "protests against some of the most sacred beliefs and standards" because, as he put it, he was sure his son would ultimately find his way back to Jewish loyalty. "His toleration of my outbreaks was in consonance with his emphasis on intellectual honesty."[16]

In the fall of 1900 Kaplan entered Columbia College where he studied under Nicholas Murray Butler, who two years later became president of the university. He also took courses with the famous sociologist Franklin Giddings, well known for his concept of "consciousness of kind" and later with Felix Adler for whom he wrote his master's thesis. Kaplan found many of his classes at Columbia immensely stimulating. The period of the mid-eighties and the nineties constituted something of a watershed in American history and thought. New currents of thought were flowing through the Western world and particularly in the United States. Under the impact of the Industrial Revolution, Darwin's theory of evolution and earlier discoveries in astronomy, geology, and biology, there arose the new social sciences of economics, political science, anthropology, and sociology. The period was characterized by a widespread conviction that all social phenomena could be dealt with through the same scientific methods as physics and biology.[17]

The discipline that was of particular interest to Kaplan was anthropology, not so much physical anthropology with its concern for the biological features of men, as cultural anthropology with its focus on civilization and the culture of primitive groups. *Culture* as a concept called attention to the foundation of man's behavior and thought and to problems of community, social organization, economics, and religion. In his courses at Columbia, Kaplan became acquainted with E. B. Tylor's landmark work *Primitive Culture* (1871) with its theory of animism; with the work of the American ethnologist Lewis Henry Morgan, who applied the notion of evolution to social development; and with the theories of Edward Alexander Westermarck on the nature of marriage among primitive peoples (1891) and on the history of morals. These theories seemed to Kaplan to undermine the traditional supernaturalist approach to religion, to challenge the traditional conception of God, and to raise further questions about the biblical account of revelation and the nature of creation and miracles.[18]

Kaplan was also very much influenced by his sociological studies. While scattered reflections about society and about such subjects as custom and convention, family life, and social organization went back to the Greeks, the systematic, scientific approach to social problems had its beginning in the nineteenth century with Auguste Comte and other pioneers, such as Herbert Spencer, William Graham Sumner, Lester Ward, Charles H. Cooley, and Ludwig Gumplowicz. Unlike present-day empirical sociology with its trend toward specialization and its emphasis on exactness of method, these men were all systematizers who were concerned with definitions, overall principles, and bold theories about the nature of society. Both Comte and Spencer, for example, believed that civilization as a whole was the proper subject of sociology. And all of them represented, in one way or another, the impact of evolutionary doctrine on social thinking.[19] Their emphasis on the relation of religion to group life, concepts like Gidding's notion of "consciousness of kind," Cooley's primary face-to-face groups, Sumner's stress on the importance of folkways—all made a profound impression on Kaplan. To these sociologists religion was a natural phenomenon that had nothing to do with otherworldliness or with specific beliefs in God, immortality, or reward and punishment in a hereafter. Religion was a worldly phenomenon, an aspect of social and cultural development. For the sociologists, underlying all beliefs or personal religious experiences lay the social life of the group expressed in religious observances and rites. As the needs of the community and its dominant values change, there was a corresponding shift in the beliefs and ceremonies in which these values found expression. Kaplan learned from the sociologists that the history of religion was the history of the social systems in which they were found, and that there was no one true religion or one true conception of God. As conditions changed, social interests changed and with them the religious activities that idealize these interests. All human experience must be understood in the light of its context, a conviction Kaplan later made the basis of his religious outlook.

Aside from the sociologists and the anthropologists at this time, psychologists also began to study religion in a scientific spirit. They, too, offered conceptions of the natural factors that enter into the formation of religious attitudes without appeal to a supernatural God or to revelation. The psychologists of religion confirmed for Kaplan that the individual was the product of his social environment and that the social life of the group is primary to all belief and personal religious experience. Belief in God functioned principally as a "means of fostering a sense of solidarity among members of a group."[20] For a group to have a religion in common, its members must have other interests in common.

These various naturalistic views provided Kaplan with an understanding of human nature in the individual and the group and paved the way for him to see religion as a normal and indispensable expression of that nature. But they still left him in a "turbulent state of mind," since he could not accept the traditional approach to the Bible as a divinely revealed document. What could take its place? What would he be able to preach when he had a congregation? It was with these doubts and questions that Kaplan graduated from the Seminary in 1904 and accepted an Orthodox pulpit. He was able to do so because he still adhered strictly to Jewish ritual practices. Although he found abundant teaching and preaching materials available that did not require the immediate resolution of his basic theological problems, the direction of his thinking was clearly incompatible with the Orthodox orientation expected of him.

During the next few years, three additional influences contributed to the unfolding of his thought and stimulated him to work
out a new orientation to Judaism and to the Jewish religion. The
first was the writings of the British literary critic Matthew Arnold,
who helped him to appreciate the Bible as "an expression of human
nature at its best." Kaplan began to see that no other writings could
compare with the Bible in "depth of passion for the purpose of
establishing God's kingdom or earth." Arnold's viewpoint made it
possible for him to free himself from "the need of regarding it as
supernatural and infallible." The famous critic argued that it was
not the purpose of the Bible to teach a "metaphysically correct
conception of God" but rather "to inculcate by means of popular
tales, laws, and prophetic exhortation that God is a power that
makes for righteousness—not ourselves." Arnold's alternative to
the "God of miracles" and the "God of the metaphysicians" was the
"God of experience." This alternative, which became an integral
part of Kaplan's naturalistic outlook, enabled him to remain a
rabbi.[21]

Another influence to whom Kaplan later paid tribute for producing in him "nothing less than a Copernican revolution" was Ahad
Ha'am, the father of Spiritual Zionism. In Ahad Ha'am's interpretation, the central reality in Jewish life was the people of Israel; the
meaning of God and Torah can be properly understood only in
relation to that central reality. The main concern of Judaism, therefore, was the Jewish people, its origin, its vicissitudes, and its laws.
God's metaphysical nature mattered only to a few individuals. What
God meant morally, socially, economically, and politically mattered to all of Israel's spiritual leaders, beginning with Moses.

The last major influence in Kaplan's younger years was pragmatism, the philosophical method that renders thought relevant to
man's needs. Kaplan was unable to accept William James's notion
of pluralism nor was he interested in the private religious experiences as described by James nor in his justification of supernaturalism. None of these fitted into the naturalistic approach that was
beginning to take shape in Kaplan's mind. But James's emphasis on
a practical religion without metaphysics, his concern with over-
coming evil in the world without attempting a philosophical explanation, and his emphasis on the effect that religion can have in

meeting human needs met with a positive response on Kaplan's part. Kaplan agreed with James that to have meaning an idea must be seen in the context of natural conditions and human relations.

In 1908, just at the time when Kaplan was considering the possibility of giving up the rabbinate and taking up some other profession, he received an invitation to become head of the Seminary's teacher-training program. Soon thereafter he was appointed to serve as professor of homiletics in the Seminary's rabbinical school. Confronted with the responsibility of teaching Judaism both to rabbis and to teachers, Kaplan set out to develop a new interpretation of Judaism, drawing on the various sources that had contributed to his thinking.[22]

In contrast to Kaplan's intensive early Jewish training and to his sociological and psychological interests, Milton Steinberg's upbringing was much less religious and his early intellectual studies primarily philosophical rather than sociological. Though brought up in the home of pious grandparents in Rochester, with whom his parents lived and from whom he absorbed an emotional attachment to Judaism, Steinberg received only a few years of formal Jewish education. Endowed with a logical mind and an ability to express himself well, he seemed destined to study law or to enter one of the learned professions. It never occurred to anyone in his family or to his friends that young Mikhele, as they called him, whose father was a Socialist and who took his young son to lectures at the Labor Lyceum, would become a rabbi.

As a teen-ager in New York City (to which his parents moved when he was fifteen and a half), Milton was introduced to the thought of the agnostic philosopher Herbert Spencer and to the essays of John Stuart Mill, which discussed the obstacles that the existence of evil posed to a belief in an omnipotent Providence. At the age of seventeen Steinberg, under the influence of these nonreligious thinkers, was not a synagogue goer. But prodded by his friends Myron and Ira Eisenstein, who lived on the same block in Harlem, he began to attend services at Anshe Chesed Synagogue on 114th Street and Seventh Avenue, where Jacob Kohn, a philosophically oriented rabbi, was the spiritual leader. Sensing young Steinberg's interests in philosophical matters, Kohn took him for long walks in Central Park during which he discussed with him the theistic philosophy of the Protestant thinker Borden Parker Bowne, who was waging a lifelong battle against Spencer and other materialistic philosophers. Drawing on Bowne's argument that God's existence could be proved on the basis of evidence for design in the intelligibility of the universe, Kohn tried to win young Steinberg over to religion. He also summarized for him the ideas of Josiah Royce, whose devotion to religious issues from a philosophic perspective made him a widely respected spokesman for German idealistic philosophy. Kohn tried to convince Steinberg that it was possible to believe in God even in a scientific age—that one could be rationalistic and religious at the same time. Steinberg gained from him (and from Bowne and Royce) a passion for metaphysical speculation, that is, a conviction that it is possible to interpret the nature of things in a systematic and comprehensive manner. For thinking people, Kohn pointed out, the validity of religion depended on a metaphysical system of some kind. Gradually, Steinberg's views shifted from the agnosticism of Spencer and Mill to theistic or religious metaphysics; and from the social philosophy of Eugene Debs, Morris Hilquist, and the Socialists, about whom he had learned from his father, to the problems of the Jewish community.[23]

In the classes of Morris Raphael Cohen at City College, Steinberg had a chance to defend his newly acquired religious convictions. Like Mill and Spencer before him, Cohen lacked feeling or respect for organized religion and went out of his way to shock the students with his antireligious views. For Cohen, there was no logical force in the theistic argument that the universe "must have a person as its cause, designer, or director." In his view, all forms of theism were anthropomorphic, and it was "blind arrogance," he said, "to put one's confidence in such a personalistic explanation."[24] While many of the students violently disagreed, Milton alone had the courage to do so publicly. Drawing on the knowledge he had acquired of Royce and Bowne and from his discussions with Jacob Kohn, as well as his command of the Bible and Graetz's history (having read all of the volumes), Steinberg undertook to debate with the professor. In these early philosophical debates, Steinberg strengthened his religious convictions and, as a result, made the decision to enter the Jewish Theological Seminary and study for the rabbinate.[25]

While at the Seminary, like Kaplan, he too was disappointed that his studies did not help him find answers to his unresolved theological doubts. During his first year, he was "filled with ups and downs" and was "alternately elated and depressed." On a half-dozen occasions he was on the point of withdrawing. Years later, in a letter to a young rabbinical student, Steinberg suggested that such doubts were nothing to be ashamed of. "Quite the contrary," he affirmed, "every man of soul in the seminary must traverse this particular bit of wilderness. The only men I knew who didn't have this experience were rabbinical oxen. While mental disturbances are no guarantee of effectiveness in the rabbinate, I certainly think that the absence of them is a serious reflection in any student."[26]

During those years, Steinberg also took courses in the philosophy department of the Columbia Graduate School. These included Frederick Woodbridge's famous course on Greek philosophy, a survey of the leading ideas of speculative thought from the Greeks to Henri Bergson, a course on recent philosophical thought in the United States, and one on religious philosophy with Herbert Schneider. From these classes Steinberg acquired a good working knowledge of the history of Western philosophy and of Hellenistic religious thought. Judging by the books in his library, passages underlined, and summaries at the back of each volume, he had a special interest in the philosophers of the American Golden Age: Peirce, James, Royce, Santayana, Dewey, and Whitehead. Though critical of established religions, these men, except for Dewey, were all interested in the problem of faith and in reconciling scientific and technological advances with religious insight. Aside from the Golden Age philosophers, Steinberg was most interested in such speculative and metaphysical thinkers as Bergson and Schopenhauer, on whom he wrote his master's thesis.[27] If throughout his life Steinberg tried to teach Judaism from a philosophical perspective and if his interest was always in the metaphysical aspect when the trend in twentieth-century philosophy was in other directions, the reason goes back to these early studies. Kaplan, though not unacquainted with philosophical literature, was influenced more by his early anthropological and sociological studies. Steinberg, with all his devotion to organizations and causes working for Jewish survival, saw religion primarily as a need of the individual in quest of truth and rightness rather than as a reflection of the sancta of the group.

Given their different backgrounds, the approaches to the problem of God of Kaplan and Steinberg inevitably were quite different. Kaplan's concept, which is revolutionary in the history of Jewish thought, envisions God in nonpersonal terms. God is not an entity, not a personal being who reveals himself in a supernatural way, but is a divine quality of the universe. Kaplan identifies as God all the relationships and tendencies in the universe that make human life worthwhile, the "sum of the animating, organizing forces and relationships which are forever making a cosmos out of a chaos."[28] God is just as real, Kaplan insists, if we think of him as a quality or as an organizing force as our conceiving of him as an entity or being.[29] The latter notion, in Kaplan's view, is no longer compatible with the scientific stage of civilization in which we find ourselves. According to Kaplan, when we say we believe in God we mean that nature is so constituted as to enable man to achieve salvation. The cosmos is not blind, indifferent, and meaningless but contains forces and tendencies that make for man's fulfillment. Just as there are conditions in the cosmos propitious to physical life, so too there are conditions propitious to life abundant or salvation. As an organic totality integrated by cosmic laws, the cosmos is a source of value. To view the universe in this way is, for Kaplan, to believe in God.

The human being, too, is so constituted as to make for the realization of ideals. God manifests himself in a person's sense of responsibility; in his striving to transform conditions under which he lives; in his spirit of cooperation; in his sense of unity, creativity, and worth. The word God, then, is symbolically expressive of the highest ideals for which men strive. Godhood for Kaplan can have no meaning apart from these human ideals of truth, goodness, and beauty interwoven in a pattern of holiness. Kaplan also suggested that we substitute for the notion of a permanent being the concept of process. God is the process that makes for life abundant or salvation. Kaplan envisaged this process as more than physical, or psychological, or social. It is "superfactual, superexperiential, and transnatural."[30] God is not apart from the world but rather the power in the world that makes for human salvation. Kaplan was convinced that a belief in God conceived in this way could function in our day exactly as in the past—as an affirmation that life has value. It implies, as the God-idea always has, that reality is so constituted as to endorse and guarantee the realization of our ideals.[31]

Beginning in the early 1940s, Steinberg was openly critical of the Kaplanian approach. In an essay in the *Reconstructionist* in March 1941, he replied to an article in an earlier issue in which Eugene Kohn had presented the Kaplanian view of God. A concept of God, Kohn had written, was important not for what it says about the metaphysical nature of the deity but for how it functions in the life of the Jewish people.

Steinberg respected the motives behind this conviction of the futility of metaphysical speculation. But for him, the riddle of the universe was not so readily dismissed. Faith was not only a psychological and ethical venture but also an affirmation concerning the ultimate nature of things. By this "open disagreement" Steinberg wanted to assert that the Kaplan-Kohn envisagement of God was not essential to a Reconstructionist affirmation. In his opinion, the Kaplan-Kohn view represented "an inadequate theism." For a God who is merely an aspect of reality, the sum total of life-enhancing forces, is not enough of a God. Not only traditional religionists, Steinberg noted, but sophisticated philosophers like Royce and Bergson looked upon God, among other things, as a "principle of explanation through which an obscure universe takes on lucidity." Moreover, the God of Jewish history is the creator not of one aspect of reality but of the whole of it. To Steinberg, therefore, the theology of a God who is a "process at work in the universe" might well lead to the bizarre necessity of positioning a second Godhead. The Kaplan-Kohn concept seemed to Steinberg to be merely a name without any objective reality to correspond to it.[32] As he confided to Rabbi Jacob Kohn, he did not derive his theology from Kaplan:

It is one of Kaplan's limitations that he has almost no metaphysical interest, perhaps no metaphysical sensitivity. To him God is a concept, at least so he always speaks of God, rather than an existential reality, the reality of all realities, the *vrai vérité*. Or to put it otherwise, to Kaplan God represents the psychological and sociological consequences of the God idea rather than the cosmic *Ding-an-sich*. It is for its sociology of Jewish life that I am a Reconstructionist, not for the clarity or the utility of Kaplan's theology. I have often challenged Kaplan on that point. His response is that metaphysics is "personal" religion as opposed to the tradition-sanctioned group expression. I have never been able to see the value or the validity of the distinction he makes.[33]

Steinberg was convinced that it is possible for modern man to have a God who is more than an idea but is the reality of all realities—the source, sanction, and guarantee of man's moral aspiration. Such a God, he insisted, is inescapable both on intellectual and moral grounds. This public assertion of theological difference with his teacher by no means indicated any alienation from the Reconstructionist cause or any diminution of his personal affection for Dr. Kaplan:

With all my reservations as to Kaplan's theology, with all my awareness of emotional bias in him, I am at home only in the Reconstructionist group. Conservative Judaism is, for want of a philosophy, jellyfish in character. Reconstructionism for all its inadequacies is to me an adequate sociology, the only one in contemporary Jewish life which takes cognizance of all aspects of Jewish tradition.[34]

In *Basic Judaism* and in his theological essays, Steinberg set forth his theistic views in philosophical terms. Judaism is undogmatic, he wrote, allowing for various conceptions of God, as transcendent or immanent, as an abstract principle of being as with Maimonides and the kabbalistic mystics, or as supremely personal. We cannot know God completely. Concerning the essence of God—what he is in himself—we can only guess. Moses, the psalmists, Ibn Gabirol, Maimonides, the Kabbalists, he pointed out, have all affirmed in their own way that our ignorance of God is greater than our knowledge. Yet though our ignorance is "stupendous and irremediable," it should not be exaggerated.[35] "It is not total. We know enough to have some insight into the scheme of things and a considerable idea of how we ought to comport ourselves. God is one and not many, as among the pagans; one and not two, as among the Zoroastrians; and one and not none as the atheists declare." Judaism, says Steinberg, "protests against the proposition that God is only a human conception or a useful fiction or that his name may properly be assigned to the highest value a man cherishes. Judaism affirms that

God's existence is independent of man and that he is actual and real, the creator, lawgiver, guide of history, keeper, liberator, and savior." In Steinberg's envisionment, God is an entity or being, not the sum of those forces that make for the enhancement of life, as Kaplan taught. God is spirit, reason, and moral will—the essence and ground of all things. He is the mind of the universe, contemplating and ordering all things. He possesses infinite consciousness before which all things are forever present.[36]

Steinberg did not pretend that there was anything radically novel in his viewpoint. The student of philosophy, he said, would find its antecedents in both Jewish and philosophical thought, in rabbinic works, and in the works of the Stoics, the Neoplatonists, Hegel, and Bergson.[37] In essence, Steinberg's was the conventional theistic outlook—that is, that the ultimate ground of things is a supreme reality, which is the source of everything other than itself and which has the character of a perfect being. In several respects, however, his concept deviated from that of traditional Judaism. He believed, for example, that God manifests himself in natural law and its regularity rather than in miracles, which for him were part of the "folklore" of a time "when people did not have the same awareness of causal relations as we do." "My position," he wrote in reply to an inquiry from one of his younger congregants, "is very close to that of Spinoza. To me God is revealed in the regularity of nature, a regularity which does not allow for the suspension of nature."[38] Nor did Steinberg believe in providence in the traditional or Maimonidean sense. For him, the Bergsonian analogue of a "hand pushing through the sand," which denies absolute equity in the fate of every individual, seemed "thoroughly adequate." He accepted the view that "there is a direction behind the whole but no necessary meaning to the accidents which befall the individual component." It was enough for Steinberg to know that "there is a power which makes for freedom, sentience, creativity, and righteousness even though in the case of individuals the grains may fall helter-skelter.[39]

Each person envisages God according to his ability and his outlook—the simple, the sophisticated, the rationalist, the mystic, the traditionalist, the moralist, each in his own way. Some emphasize God's apartness from the world, his otherness; others his nearness and in-ness. In Steinberg's view, only one envisagement comes close to catching the simultaneous immanence and transcendence of God. That is the figure of God as father. Steinberg admits that this metaphor, while better than others, suffers from being heavily anthropomorphic. "There is then no adequate description of God. None of our allegories can be the full truth or anymore than a 'dark and garbled hint.' "[40] Nevertheless,

> only the postulate of God explains the world with any measure of adequacy; only it makes its salient characteristics intelligible; only it renders comprehensible the soul of man invested with sanity, moral yearning, and sensitivity—a phenomenon which otherwise must remain an anomaly. Only it offers an accounting for the law-abiding quality of the cosmos, for the fact that it is cosmos and not chaos.[41]

Another theological issue that Steinberg approached in a different way from his teacher was that of the problem of evil. For Kaplan, attempts by traditional theologians to justify suffering and evil in the world represented a futile enterprise, since no intellectually satisfying explanation is possible. Kaplan describes those who crave an answer to this problem as "metaphysicians with a boundless intellectual appetite," afflicted with a "false hunger."[42] Such a goal can only drag religion down, when its purpose should be an affirmation of life's worthwhileness. While evil is real, we should not portray it as the essential nature of reality. The direction of our life's current should be toward the good; evil is an obstruction that resists the current but cannot stop it. We must, therefore, shift from the field of thought to the field of action and ask not how life can be considered good when there is so much evil in the world, but What must I do to make the world better? This possibility of transcending evil by focusing on the good and by transferring the problem from the realm of speculative thought to that of purposive action applies not only to ills external to ourselves but also to our own personal shortcomings. Human suffering is due either to man's failure, willful or unconscious, to reckon with the physical or biological ills of nature or with those moral laws of responsibility that are an extension of the cosmic process and that are divine insofar as they make for man's creative survival.

Kaplan, then, did not confront the problem of evil in a theological sense. Monumental evil was something to be overcome, not explained. For him it was not intrinsic but accidental. Kaplan really has no theological explanation for evil, though he sometimes talked about it in metaphysical terms. He does not really make an effort intellectually to confront the evil in the world. Essentially, Kaplan's approach is that of Pragmatists like William James, for whom the problem is also a practical, not a speculative one. For James, too, the question to be considered is not why evil exists but what we can do to lessen the amount of it in the world.

Steinberg took just the opposite approach. He recognized that Kaplan and the Pragmatists may be correct in their belief that no completely satisfactory answer to this problem will be forthcoming. But to try was surely as human as to strive for the elimination of evil. We cannot avoid asking a metaphysical "why" when faced by radical evil and tragedy. To comprehend our options, some attempt to understand evil metaphysically is needed, in addition to our efforts to overcome it practically. From early youth until his last days, Steinberg was constantly trying to understand this problem philosophically. One of his earliest memories as a nine-year-old boy was a lecture his father took him to by Professor Walter Rauschenbush of the Rochester Theological Seminary. Rauschenbush raised the question of why God permitted the occurrence of poverty, exploitation, and wars. "And if war does break out," Rauschenbush asked, "why does God not stop it?"[43] The problem fascinated Steinberg; and while he recognized, as he grew older, that one cannot entirely account for evil, particularly for natural disasters like floods and earthquakes, he was convinced the effort must be made. His first published article was on the Ezra Apocalypse, which dealt with God's relationship to the undefined power of evil. In *As a Driven Leaf* (1939), the climactic event that severed the last cord binding Elisha to his people dealt with the same problem.[44] Among Steinberg's early theological writings, one of his most interesting essays was entitled "God and the World's Evil." Written in a vivid and colorful style, the article reflected his optimistic outlook on man.

In his effort to justify God's ways, Steinberg considered the various theories that had appeared in Jewish and philosophical tradition and found most of them unacceptable. The interpretation most attractive to him was one based on the theory of emergent evolution, suggested by the English zoologist and philosopher C. L. Morgan and developed by Samuel Alexander. These philosophers pointed to distinct levels in nature reaching up from the mineral, to the animal, to the level of spirit. An "emergent," according to Morgan, introduces a novelty that cannot be predicted from the factors already at work in a process. At critical stages, new modes of relationship come into being that cannot be interpreted in terms of the factors operating on a lower level. Steinberg, too, saw life as a kind of "evolutionary ladder." Men are "kin to the mineral, prisoners of time and space, near relatives to the plant, exposed to attack and hunger" and like animals engaged in a competitive struggle. In light of this, evil is the "persistence of the circumstances of lower strata in higher." The whole evolutionary record is the "tale of the hang-over of restraints" and the "saga of life's continuous victory over them." The heritage of the beast is still powerful in man. He can be irrational, cruel, and destructive. But he has the intellect and skills to emancipate himself and the moral insights to overcome his destructive tendencies.[45]

Steinberg did not assert that this was the only possible interpretation of evil. Nor did he assume that the solution he put forth would be to anyone's complete satisfaction. But even if only partially satisfactory, the God-factor was still indicated, for it left less unexplained than was true of atheism.

Can one pray to Steinberg's God? "Not," he said, "if prayer is to obtain from God what one cannot get oneself." But prayer has other purposes—to express adoration and reverence for the power and wisdom behind the world, to express thanksgiving for what life and the universe have brought us, to affirm individual and communal ideals and, in time of grief, a sense of peace and resignation. In other words, to Steinberg prayer does not have the purpose of affecting the outside world, but rather is a means of expressing or influencing one's thoughts and ideas. When one prays, he is taken out of himself for a moment, grows less selfish, and "views himself against the background of the infinite universe. Such an experience is a divine one and through it man becomes almost a God."[46]

Kaplan, too, suggests that by becoming aware of the power transcending ourselves that makes for salvation and of our relationships to one another we induce them to function most efficiently. The purpose of worship and prayer is to produce such awareness. He quotes William James, who describes prayer as "the vital act by which the entire mind seeks to save itself by clinging to the principle from which it draws its life." For Kaplan, since God is immanent in man, there must be something in the individual human being that is part of God. When a man prays, "that part of him which is the actualized element in him addresses itself to that part which is potential." Prayer, says Kaplan quoting Franz Rosenzweig, is its own fulfillment: "the soul prays for the power to pray."[47]

While there was little difference between master and disciple on the nature of prayer, the two did not completely see eye to eye on some of the proposed revisions of the traditional book. These differences emerged in 1943 when they began working together on the Reconstructionist Sabbath prayer book. Steinberg was more liberal than many of his colleagues in the Rabbinical Assembly on this subject but more of a traditionalist than were his fellow editors, Kaplan, Ira Eisenstein, and Eugene Kohn. In Steinberg's view, departures from traditional norms were justified only "when clearly and demonstrably indicated by intellectual or ethical necessity." For him, every deviation had to be justified on the ground that there was no intellectually or morally honest alternative. His coeditors, it seemed to him, were prepared to make innovations not only on the basis of integrity but also on that of aesthetic preference. While theoretically they agreed that "the presumption is always in favor of the tradition," it now became apparent to him that he and they understood the phrase differently. Thus they were ready, on literary taste alone, to eliminate certain passages in the Sabbath morning service. For ideological reasons, all references to the election of Israel were removed. Steinberg was unwilling to accept references to Israel's superiority over other peoples, but he saw no difficulty with the idea that the Jewish people had a religious mission. He had misgivings about the traditional expression "Thou hast chosen us from among the nations" because it claimed "an exclusive mission, drawing invidious contrasts between it and other people who were also called to God's service." But he felt that while the verb *bahar* (he chose) should be retained, phrases such as *mi-kol ha-*

amim (from among other peoples) should be deleted. In addition, Steinberg would have preferred to keep the Amidah in the Musaf.[48] His point of view on these matters was not accepted.

When advance proofs of the main part of the new prayer book reached Steinberg, he wrote Kaplan to congratulate him on a "mighty achievement." Steinberg described himself as "deeply moved, delighted, and exhilarated" by the new book, but he made clear in a postscript that he had his dissents, "sometimes significant ones, from some of the things in the text." They were, however, "overshadowed by my approval."[49] Steinberg continued to collaborate on the final stages of the publication, making several contributions to the supplementary prayers.

Nevertheless, when Kaplan decided the following year to issue a new High Holiday prayer book, Steinberg decided not to participate, describing himself as "still scarred" by his experience with the Sabbath prayer book.[50] Kaplan was somewhat taken aback by this statement; but "since a matter of conscience was involved," he suggested that Steinberg "must be guided by his own ideas and emotions." Six months later, however, in April 1948, to Steinberg's surprise Kaplan paid him a personal visit and asked him to reconsider his decision. After "careful, deliberate thought," Steinberg decided against this. Their differences were still unresolved, he explained. But he did release a statement of commendation of the new High Holiday prayer book to which he was sympathetic, even though he could not underwrite it in detail.[51]

The religious ideas of Milton Steinberg summarized thus far, including his critique of Kaplan, were all formulated during the 1930s and early 1940s and represent Steinberg's theological thinking up to the fall of 1947. They were based on sporadic readings between other projects and, as he himself recognized, needed maturing through more reading and reflection. However, at the end of 1947, Steinberg, for the first time, cleared the way for an intensive program of readings in religious philosophy. He sensed, more strongly than was true of Kaplan, that the new philosophical trends that had developed since the war constituted a challenge to a "rationalist-pragmatist metaphysics." Until then Steinberg had looked upon himself as a "modernist" with a faith in intellect, a confidence in the essential goodness of man and the remediability of evil, and with a strong sense of the reality of progress as part of the scheme of things. But now he recognized that at least among intellectuals a new climate was developing: a disenchantment with liberal culture and a reevaluation of such established beliefs as rationalism, humanism, faith in progress, science, the use of intelligence in human affairs, and the perfectibility of human nature.[52] The works of Kierkegaard, Barth, and Brunner were being widely read, as were those of existentialist writers, such as Buber and Berdyaev. While these men exerted only limited influence in academic philosophical circles in the United States, they were having a decided impact on Protestant theology. Steinberg sensed that they might also have implications for Judaism. He was not sure whether religious existentialism and Barthianism were merely fads that would disappear in a few years; or whether, as it turned out, they represented a basic change in the intellectual climate. Either way, he thought, he ought to bring himself up to date.

Contemporary religious philosophy consisted of a sprawling variety of methods and concepts, and he resolved to work through the thicket of conflicting positions. Aside from reading the existentialists and the neo-Orthodox, he wanted to familiarize himself with the diverse schools—realist metaphysics, neo-Thomism, post–liberal theology—and to deepen his knowledge of the Pragmatists. But most important for Steinberg were the metaphysical philosophers and theologians. Steinberg had several reasons for this interest. First, he hoped to write a long-deferred book on the theoretical beliefs of Judaism. Theism as a philosophic doctrine had been losing ground since the middle of the seventeenth century and for many philosophers had become an unacceptable view. He planned to call the book *An Anatomy of Faith* and hoped it would provide the same analysis for religious faith that *The Making of the Modern Jew* had provided for Jewish survival. Second, Steinberg hoped for an appointment to teach theology at the Seminary. He was convinced that the Seminary had withheld recognizing him as a potential member of its staff because he had not published enough in the field. Finally, there was the need to clarify, in his own mind, his theological differences with Kaplan. Kaplan was aware of Steinberg's metaphysical approach; but in *The Future of the American*

Jew, which appeared in 1948, his teacher reiterated his conviction that metaphysics was unnecessary. Steinberg needed to keep abreast of the field so he could defend his own point of view.

Did Steinberg revise his theological orientation as a result of these readings? There are critics who maintain that a change in the pattern of his convictions was under way, that is, a rethinking of his position and a shift of orientation. These critics insist that Steinberg had reached a turning point in his intellectual life, in which "he came to share with the Bible, Pascal, Kierkegaard, Buber, and Franz Rosenzweig the conviction that the religious life begins not with a judgment of rational assent but with an unconditional act of faith."[53] Will Herberg, with whom Steinberg read philosophical texts in his last years, went so far as to say that "the entire cast of his thought was transformed in this period. The kind of cosmic optimism he had accepted earlier now became an abomination to him."[54] This meant, according to some of these critics, Steinberg's gradual alienation from the Reconstructionist movement and the beginning of a parting of the ways.

In fact, as a result of the war and its horrors and the new psychiatry with its emphasis on the blind, irrational drives in man, Steinberg did modify his view of human nature, but not as radically as some would contend. Though completely aware that reason was being rejected by many postwar thinkers as an instrument for attaining truth, Steinberg held on to his rationalistic approach to the end. He recognized that some of the basic assumptions of liberalism —faith in education and critical intelligence, as taught by Dewey, and the optimism of the Social Gospel movement, as expounded by Rauschenbusch—may have to be revised. He rejected the nineteenth-century notion of the inevitability of progress in favor of a more tempered appraisal of the human being, one more in consonance with the realism of the Bible. But he did not in any way lose his interest in metaphysics nor change his views about Kaplan's theology. During these last years, Steinberg studied Peirce's evolutionary metaphysics with its emphasis on the role of chance as a factor in the universe and read *Process and Reality* by Whitehead, whose notion of a finite, growing God intrigued him. He was also influenced by the work of Charles Hartshorne, whose purpose was to demonstrate the possibility of a neo-classical concept of God that avoided contradictions, was philosophically tenable, and yet retained its religious value. Steinberg credited Hartshorne's social conception of theism for emancipating him "from servitude to the classical metaphysicians and their God who in his rigid eternal sameness is not God at all, certainly not the God of whom Scripture maketh proclamation nor whom the human heart requires."[55] Steinberg's convictions about religious metaphysics and his new enthusiasm for the notion of a nonabsolute God are evident in the paper he prepared for the Rabbinical Assembly convention in June 1949, entitled "Theological Issues of the Hour." After surveying the decline of reason in modern thought, the anti-intellectualism, the new emphasis on revelation, and the return of transcendentalism, Steinberg again warns, as he had many times before, against the "evasion of metaphysics." On this score, he felt, the effort of William James must be judged a failure: "Refusing on pragmatist principles to venture any definition of the relation among the plural elements in his pluralist universe, he leaves that universe not only unexplained but even unthinkable."[56]

Steinberg was also critical of John Dewey, who refused as a matter of principle to answer the most common questions asked of the philosopher: What is the scheme of things? "If there is one thing which is quite clear," Steinberg reiterated, "it is that human beings are insatiably curious about metaphysics. You can't stop them from speculating on it." To insist that this was an illegitimate demand was a contradiction in terms. In Steinberg's opinion, Dewey failed to recognize the relationship between human morality and convictions as to the ultimates in life. "Dewey wanted the benefits of religion without the risk and the gamble."[57]

This lack of interest in ultimates was, in Steinberg's judgment, "the most serious deficiency in Kaplanian theology." To Steinberg, Kaplan's approach was a "theology without a metaphysics"; it was, therefore, "not a theology at all but an account of the psychological and ethical consequences of affirming one." Philosophical speculation concerning God and his existence and nature, according to Kaplan, was "personal" rather than "folk religion," irrelevant to any serious human interest, a "flight of the imagination but without real significance."[58]

In reply, Steinberg posed several questions: "Why," he asks, "is an interest as widespread and persistent as the metaphysical dismissed as merely personal religion of a less worthy sort than folk? Again, is it true that faith is willed but not reasoned? Is it not the case that it is most generally something of both? Still again, is it merely theological reflection which is circular and indecisive? Is it not so with all thought about anything at all?" What proposition in any universe of discourse can be demonstrated completely? Why should theology be derogated while other disciplines liable to similar deficiencies are spared?[59] Because Kaplan had refused any description of his God as what God is, not in his implications but in himself; because he spoke so generally to the God-idea rather than of God; because "he shrinks God to the sum of those aspects which enhance man's life, these being all of God which he regards as mattering to man"—because of all this, according to Steinberg,

the actuality of God is brought under question. It is asked: does God really exist or is He only man's notion? Is there anything objective which corresponds to the subjective conception? And who adds up "the sum" in "the sum total of forces that make for salvation"? Is the sum added up "out there" or in the human imagination? The universe is left unexplained. To say of God that He is a power within the scheme of things leaves the scheme altogether unaccounted for. . . . A need arises for another God beyond and in addition to Dr. Kaplan's who shall account for the world in which they find themselves, concerning which they are insatiably curious. Something alarmingly close to tribalism in religion is revived. A God possessed of metaphysical standing, a Being who is also a principle of explanation for reality, must be beyond the parochialism of time and space, of nation and creed. He has to be distorted before He can be exploited for particularist purposes. But a God who is all relativist, especially such a God as Kaplan's who tends to be a function of social life, "an aspect of a particular civilization," is in imminent peril of breaking down into a plurality of deities, each civilization possessing and being informed by its own.[60]

The case for religion without metaphysics, Steinberg assured his colleagues, could not conceivably be presented with greater piety, skill, and integrity than by Kaplan. But he does not go far enough, said Steinberg: "God-in-Himself is needed, too, as a principle of explanation and because otherwise the God idea itself is emptied of content and potency." Steinberg did not mean that all religious people must be metaphysicians, but he was convinced that at the core of every person's belief there ought to be "something ontological, some affirmation whether naive or sophisticated . . . concerning the ultimate nature of things."[61] Whether these criticisms should be described as "in limited areas of theology," in the words of Ira Eisenstein; as a "molehill of difference," according to Kaplan; or as "a crucial difference of great significance," as defined by Arthur Cohen, depends on the importance one attaches to metaphysics and Jewish theology.[62] Steinberg himself referred to his criticisms of Kaplanian theology as the "gravest reservation from the prevailing position."[63]

If Steinberg had lived and continued his readings in process philosophy, as is likely; if he had continued to explore the concept of a finite God; and, at the same time, if Kaplan or one of his other disciples had developed a metaphysical basis for Kaplan's theories along the lines of process philosophy, it is quite possible that theologically the two would have come much closer together. Most of the process philosophers, such as Hartshorne, Whitehead, and even Peirce, were not supernaturalists; and their concept of a limited God, limited in his power, as Steinberg thought, would probably not have been far removed from Kaplan's God, who also is only an aspect of the universe—that aspect which makes for man's salvation. However, whatever the differences in their visions, there is no evidence that Steinberg was becoming alienated from the movement and would have broken out of the Reconstructionist confines. As Ira Eisenstein has pointed out, the areas of agreement between Steinberg and Kaplan were far greater than the areas of disagreement.

To celebrate the fifteenth anniversary of the *Reconstructionist*, Steinberg wrote an article entitled "The Test of Time." It would appear in March 1950, just ten days before his death. While candid about the "defects" and "weaknesses" of the movement, Steinberg reiterated in the article his loyalty to the Reconstructionist cause:

The bulk of Reconstructionism, theory, program, implementation seems to me to stand up under the test of the years and indeed to have been validated by it. Before us, then, is an instance, not too frequent in human affairs, of a latter time which not only need not be shamed by the former but which has reason, modest and restrained, but reason nonetheless, to take pride in it and, taking pride, to reaffirm commitments and objectivity.

One of Steinberg's most important contributions to theological thinking lies in his criticisms of Kaplanian theology. The ongoing debate between the two men on the need for metaphysics, the nature of religion, the meaning of God, the problem of evil, and on revisions of the prayer book has surely enriched Reconstructionist thought and the religious life of American Jews. In due time, it may lead to the development of a metaphysical foundation for Kaplan's seminal and influential reinterpretation of Judaism.

Notes

1. Milton Steinberg to Cyrus Adler, 2 November 1927.
2. Milton Steinberg, *The Making of the Modern Jew* (New York: Behrman House, 1952), 306.
3. Milton Steinberg, *A Partisan Guide to the Jewish Problem* (Indianapolis: Bobbs Merrill, 1945), chaps 11 and 12. See especially pp. 174, 182, 187, 188–90, 191, 195.
4. Mordecai M. Kaplan, *The Meaning of God in Modern Jewish Religion* (New York: Behrman's Jewish Book House, 1937), 333; idem, *The Greater Judaism in the Making: A Study of the Evolution of Judaism* (New York: The Reconstructionist Press, 1960), 459–60.
5. Mordecai M. Kaplan, *Judaism as a Civilization* (New York: Macmillan, 1934), 343.
6. Ibid., 342–43.
7. Milton Steinberg, *A Believing Jew* (New York: Harcourt, Brace, 1951), 65–70.
8. Ibid., 64–65.
9. Milton Steinberg to Eugene Kohn, 15 August 1946.
10. "The Uses of Faith," unpublished article prepared for the *Nation*, May 1948.
11. Steinberg, *A Partisan Guide*, 184.
12. Milton Steinberg: "New Currents in Religious Thought," lecture 2, p. 30 (unpublished transcript). This passage is deleted in Arthur Cohen's paraphrased version of these lectures in *An Anatomy of Faith* (New York: Harcourt, Brace, 1960).
13. "The Way I Have Come," in *Mordecai M. Kaplan: An Evaluation*, ed. Ira Eisenstein and Eugene Kohn (New York: Jewish Reconstructionist Foundation, 1952), 285, 286, 289, 290. See also Mordecai M. Kaplan, "The Influences That Have Shaped My Life," *Reconstructionist* 8, no. 10 (June 26, 1942); 28-20; idem, "A Heart of Wisdom," *Reconstructionist* 17 no. 16 (May 1951).

14. Kaplan, "Way I Have Come," 289.
15. Ibid.
16. Kaplan, "Influences," 30.
17. For an analysis of "The Delineation of Supernaturalism," see Merle Curti, *The Growth of American Thought* (New York: Harper and Brothers, 1943), chap. 21. On the new science of anthropology, see *Encyclopedia Britannica, Macropedia*, vol. 27, s.v. "social sciences," 365–84.
18. For the implications of anthropology for the study of religion, see John Macquarrie, *Twentieth-Century Religious Thought: Frontiers of Philosophy and Theology* (New York: Scribner, 1981), 95–115; Harold Weisberg in *Mordecai M. Kaplan: An Evaluation*, ed. Ira Eisenstein and Eugene Kohn (New York: Jewish Reconstructionist Foundation, 1952), 158–59 and Kaplan, *Judaism as a Civilization*, 39.
19. *Contemporary Social Theory*, ed. Harry Elmer Barnes, Howard Becker, and Frances Bennett Becker, (New York: Appleton-Century, 1940), chap 1; and *An Introduction to the History of Sociology*, ed. Harry Elmer Barnes (New York: Appleton-Century, 1940), part 2.
20. Edward S. Ames, *The Psychology of Religious Experience* (Boston and New York: Houghton-Mifflin, 1910). For a list of books on the psychology of religion, many of which Kaplan undoubtedly read, see Horace L. Friess and Herbert Schneider, *Religion in Various Cultures* (New York: Henry Holt, 1932), 499.
21. Kaplan, "Way I Have Come," 296–97.
22. Ibid., 299.
23. Simon Noveck, *Milton Steinberg: Portrait of a Rabbi* (New York: Ktav, 1978), 1–17.
24. *The Campus* (City College of New York newspaper), 26 April 1921.
25. Noveck, *Milton Steinberg*, 18–21.
26. Milton Steinberg to Mordecai Brill, 21 December 1932.
27. Noveck, *Milton Steinberg*, 33–35.
28. Kaplan, *Meaning of God*, 76.
29. Ibid., 25.
30. Mordecai M. Kaplan, *The Future of the American Jew*, (New York: Macmillan, 1948), 183.
31. Kaplan, *Meaning of God*, 26.
32. *Reconstructionist* (March 1941).
33. Milton Steinberg to Jacob Kohn, n.d.
34. Ibid.
35. Milton Steinberg, *Basic Judaism* (New York: Harcourt Brace, 1947), 39–41.
36. Ibid., 42–49.
37. Steinberg, *A Believing Jew*, 18-20.
38. Milton Steinberg to Lloyd Schapes, 2 March 1942.
39. Milton Steinberg to L. Richard Cipes, 16 January 1939.

40. Steinberg, *Basic Judaism*, 49–53.
41. Milton Steinberg, *Anatomy of Faith*, ed. with intro. by Arthur A. Cohen. (New York: Harcourt, Brace, 1960), p. 115.
42. Kaplan, *Future of the American Jew* 243; idem, *Judaism as a Civilization* 329–30.
43. Milton Steinberg, *Only Human—The Eternal Alibi*, ed. Bernard Mandelbaum (New York: Bloch, 1963), 22.
44. Milton Steinberg, *As a Driven Leaf* (Indianapolis: Bobbs Merrill, 1939), 248–50.
45. Steinberg, *A Believing Jew*, 25–29.
46. Steinberg, *Only Human*, 103–5.
47. Kaplan, *Future of the American Jew*, 183–85.
48. Noveck, *Milton Steinberg*, 180–81.
49. Ibid., 181.
50. Milton Steinberg to Mordecai Kaplan, November 1947. Steinberg later explained that when he described himself as "still scarred" by his experience with the Sabbath prayer book, he did not refer to the prayer book as a whole, about which "I have always been and am still ardent," See Noveck, *Milton Steinberg*, 315.
51. Noveck, *Milton Steinberg*, 188.
52. Harold Weisberg, "Ideologies of American Jews" in *The American Jew: A Reappraisal*, ed. Oscar I. Janowsky (Philadelphia: Jewish Publication Society, 1964), 340–41.
53. Arthur A. Cohen, *Conservative Judaism* (Summer 1960): 16; David Silverman, unpublished lecture at Emanuel Synagogue in Hartford, Conn., 1963.
54. Review of *A Believing Jew*, in *Commentary*, May 1951.
55. Milton Steinberg, "Theological Problems of the Hour," *Rabbinical Assembly of America: Proceedings*, 1949, 376–77.
56. Ibid., 378.
57. For Steinberg's view of John Dewey, see "New Currents in Religious Thought," 18–27, especially 24 and 27.
58. Steinberg, "Theological Problems," 378–79.
59. Ibid.
60. Ibid., 380.
61. Ibid., 381.
62. Ira Eisenstein and Arthur A. Cohen, *Conservative Judaism* (Summer 1960). Mordecai M. Kaplan, *Reconstructionist* (19 May 1950).
63. Milton Steinberg, "The Test of Time," *Reconstructionist* (March 1950).

PART THREE

Intellectual Contemporaries

CHAPTER 7

Kaplan and John Dewey

Allan Lazaroff

Mordecai Kaplan has long been linked in the popular Jewish mind with the great American philosopher John Dewey.[1] In spite of this common association, there has been no scholarly research on the similarities between them nor an analysis of the influence of Dewey on his younger contemporary. If similarities and influences were found, it would constitute a significant religious application of Dewey's generally secularist philosophy. Dewey's direct influence on Kaplan is difficult to trace, however, because most early twentieth-century American reformers were Deweyites before they ever read Dewey.[2] This essay will concentrate on the similarities and differences between Dewey and Kaplan that emerge from their many published writings and will only briefly consider the question of direct influence.

One similarity between Dewey and Kaplan was their pragmatism and concern with action as well as theory. Dewey argued that the customary separation of ends from means had turned experimental hypotheses into absolute ideals. He criticized the abstractness of classical philosophy and the otherworldliness of the historic religions because both had led to passivity and inaction in this-worldly matters.[3] He emphasized active involvement and practical subjects,

This paper is part of a project supported by a Senior Research Fellowship from the John Dewey Foundation and the Center for Dewey Studies at Southern Illinois University. The author is most grateful for this support.

such as education, not only in his writings but also in his own life. He supervised a laboratory school in Chicago, for example, and he continued to lead and to participate vigorously in many organizations and social causes throughout his long life.

Kaplan was also concerned with activity and pragmatic consequences, not just theory. His functional rationalism claimed that Judaism needed working hypotheses, not immutable creeds; thus, he shared Dewey's opposition to abstract philosophy and religious otherworldliness. Kaplan maintained that Judaism from the Pharisaic period onward had become otherworldly and therefore was in need of reconstruction in modern times.[4] As for those who contended that traditional Judaism was already this-worldly, Kaplan dismissed them as apologists, much as Dewey dismissed those religious modernists who sought to play down the otherworldliness of Christianity.[5] Like Dewey, Kaplan did not just write about the importance of practical affairs. He was an activist who founded his own synagogue, for example, and led many community efforts and professional organizations. For him as for Dewey, the practical pursuit of education was a central and lifelong endeavor. The title and contents of Kaplan's last book, *If Not Now, When?* (1973), indicate his continuing impatience, even in his nineties, to implement his projected reconstruction of the Jewish people. For both Dewey and Kaplan, the problem with supernaturalism was not so much its theoretical irrationality as its negative practical and social effects.[6]

Hence, the thought of Dewey and Kaplan, in contrast to that of William James, is essentially social, reflecting the influence of the social sciences, such as sociology, social psychology, and anthropology, on early twentieth-century intellectuals.[7] According to Dewey, the very process of inquiry is cooperative as well as experimental. Further, his moral philosophy of shared experience both begins and ends in society. Culture, thought, and science are conditioned by social and other surroundings, and in turn a goal of science is to influence and direct social life. Dewey's fondest dream was the application of scientific method to social problems.[8] Similarly, for Kaplan religion and Judaism are social both in origin and effect. Religion and Judaism arise as the collective self-consciousness of the group, and their goal is to criticize, formulate, and direct group life for the greater self-realization of their members.[9] Kaplan was a Jewish social engineer who sought to reorganize Jewish life in all its aspects following modern scientific and pragmatic procedures. His first book, *Judaism as a Civilization* (1934), emerged from courses he was teaching Jewish social workers.

Dewey and Kaplan's pervasive social concern reflects their basic humanism and anthropocentrism.[10] In opposition to a traditional overbearing theocentrism, on the one hand, and to an impersonal natural necessity, on the other,[11] they both spoke of the importance of the human personality; of the centrality of human freedom, effort, and responsibility; and of the nobility and significance of human purposes and ideal ends. They are consequently melioristic about the potential for human betterment and have been criticized for slighting the evil and tragedy in the world. Such a criticism, however, is not justified. Both recognized tragedy and suffering, but they typically sought a moderate reaction to it that would avoid either a stultifying pessimism about irredeemable evil or a romantic optimism about inevitable progress. These extremes, they felt, could paralyze human effort: utopian optimism by leading to complacency or disillusionment, and radical pessimism by arousing feelings of futility and despair that extinguish hope. Criticism of Kaplan and Dewey on this issue has tended to push them unfairly into the optimists' camp; in fact, however, they both carefully characterized their moderate positions as "meliorism."[12] Kaplan, perhaps because of his slight inclination toward metaphysics, edged closer to optimism than Dewey. Yet both insisted that existence is a mixture of evil and good and that the important issue is not an illusory metaphysical or theological problem but rather the practical problem of courageously using human inquiry and intelligence to reduce the evil. Hence, their litmus test for any theory of evil is their usual pragmatic one, namely, its effect on human action. For both of them, gratuitous evil and suffering is a problem that, because of its seriousness, requires all the more the application of scientific method for its redress.[13] If it seems that this meliorism is not a very satisfying response to the enormity of gratuitous suffering, especially in a post-Holocaust age, the recent popularity of the basically Reconstructionist book by Howard Kushner, *When Bad Things Happen to Good People* (1981), suggests that this courageous attitude to suffering does indeed strike a responsive chord.

Dewey's humanism and meliorism, which could be called a social faith in human intelligence, also expressed itself in his religion of democracy. Democracy had become the logical extension of his earlier Christianity. If Christianity were the search for truth, Dewey argued, then Christianity was really democracy, since, as we saw, the scientific search for truth is social and democratic.[14] Democracy and science also go hand in hand because of the correspondence between the thought of a culture and the structure of its society. In the Middle Ages, feudal society was hierarchically structured and so medieval theology and philosophy were hierarchically structured as well. Similarly, in modern times the open inquiry and cooperative experimentation of science require an open, cooperative, and democratic society. The democracy that Dewey intended was not a technical political system but an almost metaphysical social ideal, perhaps best realized in something like the small communities of Dewey's childhood New England.[15] This commitment to democracy, as well as his pragmatism, contributed to the distinctively American character of Dewey's philosophy. This characteristic is exemplified in his adulation of American heroes such as Thomas Jefferson and Ralph Waldo Emerson. Dewey also admired the way the United States separated, not just the state and church, but also political citizenship and economic participation from cultural traditions and nationality, and he considered this separation an important American contribution to government and democracy.[16]

Kaplan agreed with Dewey that a culture reflects its surrounding society. Judaism in the Middle Ages was supernatural, Kaplan said, because medieval culture in general was supernatural. Similarly, Judaism in modern America must reflect the democracy of modern America. This democratic brand of Judaism meant that Kaplan was for the common Jew as Dewey was for the common man. It also meant that Kaplan was as characteristically American in his outlook as Dewey was. He wanted to create a distinctively American Judaism that even gave priority to Americanism over Judaism. Probably having in mind the American separation that Dewey had noted between political citizenship and cultural nationality, Kaplan contended that it was especially a democratic society such as the United States that could allow Jewish diaspora life as a subcommunity, in this case as a hyphenated Jewish-Americanism.[17]

So deep was Kaplan's commitment to American democracy that he called it a religion, as Dewey had, and he even composed a worship service for it. This commitment to democracy lay behind Kaplan's rejection of the "chosen people" concept, for peoples, like individuals, are equal. Kaplan called democracy a religion worthy of such commitment because it helps individuals and peoples achieve self-realization, which he designates salvation. Individual self-fulfillment for both Dewey and Kaplan can take place only in society. They denounced the dualism that made the self and society seem opposed to each other, and they criticized both individualism and Marxism.[18]

Dewey and Kaplan saw a continuum not only between the individual and society but between the local and larger community and between the nation and the international community. In this continuum of human associations beyond the individual, they agree, the various social forms and structures are judged by their functionality relative to changing circumstances. The local community should be the basic form of association. The modern nation-state may at times be significant, but both deny it any absolute importance. Militant territorial nationalism had indeed proven belligerent, malignant, and dangerous.[19] In its place they both favored "cultural nationality," to use Dewey's term, or, in Kaplan's words, "cultural nationhood" or "transnationalism." This allowed ethnic groups to exist as minorities in other states because, as Dewey says, not all nationalities can economically acquire territory or, as Kaplan explains it, because even the people of territorial states extend beyond their borders. Cultural nationality or nationhood thus furthers democracy and international peace.[20]

Hence, for both Dewey and Kaplan, Zionism is essentially cultural, not political, and they saw this cultural nationalism as an important contribution of Judaism to the world. Kaplan argued that the Jewish tradition of ethical nationhood allowed Judaism to moderate and adjust to modern nationalism better than other religions could. Before the establishment of the State of Israel, Kaplan even advocated only cultural and religious autonomy for Jews in Palestine, not national political sovereignty. The cultural character of Kaplan's nationalism is also underlined in his frequent admonition that Jews must save Judaism before it can save them, an indication of his debt to the cultural Zionism of Ahad Ha'am.[21]

The continuum between the individual and society that diminishes the significance of the political nation is typical of the unity that Dewey sees in all of experience. There is no special scientific, aesthetic, or religious experience or realm; there is simply experience, which may have different qualities. There is as well no separation between education and the school, on the one hand, and everyday experience and society, on the other.[22] Following a similar Hegelian opposition to dualisms, Dewey frequently takes a third position between two extremes in many of the arguments in his books and articles. He even defines intelligence as mediation between the old and the new. Negatively, he censures institutional religions because of both the metaphysical dualism inherent in their supernaturalism and the social dualism inherent in their sectarianism and priesthood. Traditional religions were thus not only unscientific but also divisive and undemocratic.[23]

This theme of the continuum and unity in life appears in Kaplan's thought as well. He noted his inability from the beginning to divide reality into absolute contrasts. A sin, for example, is at the same time against God, against oneself, and against others. Hence, Kaplan often took a third or mean position between the extremes of a dualism. His major work, *Judaism as a Civilization*, contends that his religious culturalism solves the problems of neo-Orthodoxy on the one hand and Reformism on the other. He proposed the position of transnaturalism between supernaturalism and naturalism, and he situated Reconstructionism in America between the extremes of Zionism and integrationism.[24] As with Dewey, so with Kaplan the third alternative he so frequently advocates is no simple, moderate combination but is rather more like a transcending synthesis. Hence, he had argued early in his career for a Jewish center to replace the contemporary synagogue that set religion apart and perpetuated a dualism of sacred and profane. In his later thought, polarity is an important aspect of the universe that the self-conscious individual overcomes in moral responsibility. Kaplan similarly resisted for decades making Reconstructionism just another Jewish religious denomination. He saw it primarily as a unifying umbrella over the existing divisions in American Jewish life.[25]

The similarities between Kaplan and Dewey seem to indicate that Kaplan was part of the early twentieth-century revolt against formalism in America of which Dewey was the philosophical spokesman.[26] There is, however, a certain formalism and even a residue of traditional absolutism in Kaplan's writings that distinguish him from Dewey. This distinction is evident in some of the same areas in which the two of them seem to be so similar.

The first area of similarity between them was their pragmatism and emphasis on action. For Dewey, this involved a thorough relativism and an opposition to the quest for certainty that rules out any absolutism whatsoever. According to Dewey, for example, there is no basic, innate human nature. Acquired human habits and institutions are more fixed than any inborn human nature and instincts.[27]

For all of Kaplan's pragmatism and functionalism, relativism was for him only the closest approach to absolute truth, and religions were still particular embodiments of universal truths. Kaplan was what Dewey called an "approximationist," one who affirms that there are absolute truths to which we are getting closer. Kaplan felt, for example, that there is an essential human nature with certain needs and wants, although he later emphasized its infinite potentialities.[28] Furthermore, while Kaplan admired "realist" philosophers, such as Aristotle, as opposed to ideologues or "ideationists," like Plato, he appreciated the need of the Jewish community for an ideology and rationale; and he himself sought to formulate a complete and integrated system of thought.[29] He also turned for such an ideology to the work of the liberal German-Jewish philosopher Hermann Cohen, in spite of the latter's proclivity toward "ideationism." One of Kaplan's last books was thus an English epitome of Cohen's philosophy of Judaism and commentary on it.[30]

Another similarity already noted between Dewey and Kaplan was that both supported cultural nationalism, but they arrived at this position from different starting points. Dewey came from the broader perspective of always enlarging experience for everyone, and he had no particular attachment to any specific group or culture. He was concerned with the whole community and advocated the interracial ideal of each culture contributing and enriching the whole through its own individual traditions. This did not mean that everyone would eventually become alike, for he opposed the anonymous homogeneity and distasteful uniformity of the melting-pot metaphor. He was, however, also against released time from public schools because it was limiting and factious instead of broadening. The rituals and institutions of religious groups may have been significant in the past, Dewey felt, but in modern times they were only divisive and rigid preservers of outworn ideologies. Culturalism could further become not only divisive but dangerous when, united with political nationalism, it involves patriotism and the honor we associate with the individual person.[31]

Kaplan, on the other hand, began with the centrality of Jewish peoplehood, and he called the awareness of this centrality a "Copernican revolution," a term Dewey also used. For Kaplan and the Reconstructionists, the analogy between a people and an individual person was positive, not negative. Peoples, like individuals, have a right to exist and their soul is their religion. From sociology Kaplan learned that peoples preserve their identity through their *sancta*, that is, through their sacred objects, literature, events, and persons. Thus, these sancta are also positive for Kaplan and are as important today as they were in the past. Yet, like Dewey and most Jewish groups at the time, the Reconstructionists did not support the proposal for released time from New York City public schools, and Kaplan did not favor Jewish day schools in place of public schools.[32]

A third similarity between Dewey and Kaplan was their humanism and anthropocentricism. Dewey, however, eventually rejected the label of humanistic because, as elaborated by F. C. S. Schiller, it carried a connotation of isolating humanity from the rest of nature. Dewey instead affirmed the continuity of the human and the natural and opposed the dualism of spirit and matter, of soul and body, as he opposed all dualisms. He allowed the use of the word *soul*, for example, to indicate the qualities and properties of psychophysical activities organized as a unity, not to indicate any traditional mythic animism.[33]

In contrast to Dewey, Kaplan admired Schiller's humanism. Kaplan did say that humanism was not enough, but he was criticizing humanism then from the theological perspective. From the opposite anthropocentric perspective, he clearly distinguished the human from the natural and the spiritual from the physical. He dwells at length, for example, on the superiority of spiritual over natural selection, and he speaks of the soul as the infinitely creative plus in human beings beyond nature.[34]

At the same time, Kaplan insists that the spiritual and rational is neither supernatural nor transcendent because this would have negative implications regarding nature. He maintains that his functional rationalism deprecates all ontological dualisms. Kaplan's transnaturalism is thus more appropriately not a dualism but rather a distinction between a higher and lower form of being. Even if it were a dualism, however, dualisms and rival ontologies, such as idealism and materialism, are compatible with naturalism as a method. Since Kaplan says that both realms, the spiritual and the physical, are known in human experience, both are naturalistic in a broad epistemological sense of naturalism. It might thus have sufficed for Kaplan to have retained the term *naturalism* for all his philosophy. He often calls his theory of religion "transnaturalism," however, as though to emphasize that the spiritual and rational are beyond nature while yet reckoning with it.[35]

It is because of Kaplan's preference for the term *transnatural* over *natural* as a designation for the realm of greatest concern to him that naturalism has not been specified here as an area of agreement between Dewey and Kaplan. Both Dewey and Kaplan were interested primarily in the human and the social, but since Kaplan called the human and the social transnaturalistic and a higher realm and Dewey considered it naturalistic, the issue of naturalism seems more of a difference between them rather than a similarity. The naturalism that both of them shared was more a negative opposition to both traditional religious supernaturalism and traditional philosophical transcendence. It is true that Kaplan considered naturalism, along with nationalism, as one of the two greatest challenges of the modern world, but as he responded to the challenge of nationalism with his cultural transnationalism, so he responded to the challenge of naturalism with transnaturalism. Whereas, however, Kaplan's cultural transnationalism is similar to Dewey's views on nationality, as noted previously, Kaplan's transnaturalism is quite distinct from Dewey's naturalism. If there were a compelling need to pin a label on Kaplan, religious humanism would fit more than religious naturalism, especially in contrasting him to Dewey.[36] Beyond this contrast, however, Kaplan could still be considered, as he usually is, a religious naturalist—but only in the broadest sense of naturalism. On the other hand, an additional characteristic that both Kaplan and Dewey do share is their intellectual independence and the ensuing difficulty in pinning any of our traditional philosophical labels on either of them.

This transnaturalistic distinction that Kaplan maintains between the spiritual and the natural characterizes not only his description of humanity but also his account of the concepts of God and values, and on these topics he differs even more from Dewey. On the topic of God, Kaplan denies "even an incidental resemblance" between the sense in which he uses the term *God* and the sense in which Dewey used it.[37] For Kaplan, God is the correlative of human beings, with society as an intermediary between them. Human self-transcendence indicates a power or process that is in the world and yet transcends it, making for human transcendence and salvation. This power is God.[38] Dewey also felt that the universe is friendly to human beings and that a proper sense of humility leads individuals to realize their dependence on forces beyond their control. He opposed atheism as well as supernaturalism, and he used the term *God* to refer to the unification of ideal possibilities with the actual, that is, to the functional effect of furthering good in human life.[39]

It is nevertheless evident that Kaplan's concept of God differs from Dewey's in several ways. It differs first because of this transnaturalism, in which, according to Kaplan, both God and humanity are part of a spiritual creative plus beyond nature—God is a cosmic plus; the soul a human plus, whereas Dewey, of course, opposed the division between mind and matter and between consciousness and physical nature, as he opposed all dualisms whatsoever.[40] Second, Kaplan's concept of God differs from Dewey's in that Kaplan followed Matthew Arnold's definition of God as an enduring power, not ourselves, making for righteousness. God for Kaplan is a power —or process or function or field of operation—correlative with humanity but beyond it. God is the guarantee for the realization of ethical ideals in this world and so encourages people to strive for this realization. Dewey, on the other hand, insists that there is no antecedent ideal or guarantee of the ideal in reality, even though the universe is cooperative. God is identical with the human actualization of the ideal. He is not a correlative of it, nor is he any sort of power not ourselves. Dewey's use of the term *God*, over the protests of colleagues, was part of his attempt to harness religious motivation for the intelligent formulation and actualization of ideals, but he emphasized that this did not require any antecedent being.[41]

Third, Kaplan calls God the organicity of the world. Organicity, the mutual influence and interaction between a totality and its parts, was transferred by Kaplan from biological organisms to social units, such as communities, and eventually to the cosmos. This organicity—a fourth dimension besides beauty, truth, and goodness —characterizes the holy, the transnatural, and hence God and indicates Kaplan's pervasive teleological vitalism.[42] In contrast, Dewey denied that organicity and correlativity were either social or cosmic principles.[43] Finally, Kaplan acknowledged legitimate mysticism as the awareness of the mystery of life that spells God, that is behind phenomena, and that helps humanity transcend itself. For Dewey, mystical experience was a normal occurrence that did not in itself convey special knowledge about existence or being.[44]

Transnaturalism also sharply distinguishes Kaplan's views on ethics from those of Dewey. Unlike Dewey and many naturalists, Kaplan consistently denied that the *ought* can be derived from what is. Values for Kaplan are in a special category, in the spiritual realm, and they are experienced through wisdom, not reason or Deweyan intelligence. In addition to sciences such as sociology and psychology that describe facts, Kaplan advocated a prescriptive science of values, to be called *soterics*, that would help humanity transcend and master itself and so achieve salvation. This association with salvation indicates how the realm of values is rooted in religion. Values for Dewey, on the other hand, are not different from other ends. They are naturalistic hypotheses that are not dualistically marked off into a special realm.[45]

The differences between Kaplan and Dewey on the topics of God and values suggest a major difference between them concerning religion. Kaplan after all is basically a religious thinker and an expositor of Judaism, whereas Dewey is a philosopher for whom religion is at best peripheral. Both rebelled as young men against the traditional religion of their homes, but they chose different paths after this rebellion. Dewey forsook organized religion altogether and turned to reconstructing philosophy. Religion, he said, was not a philosophical problem for him, so he seemed to neglect it.[46] Kaplan also considered leaving religion as a young man, in his case because of his rabbinic problems with his congregation.[47] Instead, remaining on the faculty of the Jewish Theological Seminary, he turned to reconstructing Judaism and the Jewish people, much as Dewey wrote of reconstructing philosophy.

There are thus some rough parallels between the role of philosophy for Dewey and the role of religion for Kaplan. Dewey said that philosophy formulates a coming to self-consciousness of our civilization, and Kaplan called the role of religion practically the same as that of self-consciousness.[48] According to Dewey, philosophy is occupied with criticizing and clarifying the values of its society, and it must now perform this function deliberately and openly.[49] Kaplan almost identifies religion with ethics and values,[50] and he also argues that the change and adaptation of Judaism to modern society must be deliberate.[51] Dewey referred to philosophy as a method, and Kaplan called his Reconstructionism a method as well.[52]

What Kaplan says about religion thus bears a rough similarity to what Dewey says about philosophy, but it has much less similarity to what Dewey says about religion. Both Dewey and Kaplan do address their liberal philosophy of religion not to believers but to humanists, secularists, and naturalists who would not otherwise be religious. Further, they both claim that there is no such thing as substantive religion in general and that religion instead is qualitative. For Kaplan, however, the particular religions are qualities of different cultures. It is through the religious quality of its culture that a community and people and its individual members can achieve self-realization and hence salvation, for a religion is like the soul or ego of a people. The particular historic religions are consequently as important today as they were in the past and need only be restructured democratically to answer contemporary needs. This is why Kaplan urged Jews to reconstruct Jewish society so that Judaism can aid them in their own self-realization.[53]

For Dewey, on the other hand, the religious is a quality of individual experience, although the most important effect of its emotional impact is the support of social progress. This quality of experience, the adjectively religious, is the unification of the self toward inclusive ideal ends presented by the imagination as worthy of choice. Dewey hoped that this unification would result in religious fervor being channeled from outmoded rites and dogmas to scientific social practices.[54]

Thus, religion was more social and traditional for Kaplan, while more individualistic for Dewey.[55] Since Dewey and Kaplan shared a profound social concern, this individualistic character of religion for Dewey reinforces the view that religion was not a major factor in Dewey's thought.[56] The difference between Dewey and Kaplan regarding religion is also reflected in their attitudes toward Catholicism and Protestantism. Kaplan admired Catholicism as the original self-consciousness of collective Christendom, and he even held it up as a model for Judaism—not, of course, for its authoritarianism or supernaturalism but for its tangibility, visibility, and communal organization. More specifically, the unassimilable Catholic community in America provided a model of cultural hyphenism for the American Jewish community. In contrast, Kaplan thought Protestant individualism to be more socially negative and destructive.[57] Dewey remained adamantly opposed to all the historic religions because of their dualisms and their rigid dogmas and rites, although he acknowledged that they had helped form communities in the past. Nevertheless, he considered Protestant individualism a distinct improvement over Catholic institutionalism, and his reduction of the religious to a "natural piety" and an inner attitude of unification is Protestant in character.[58]

Finally, as Dewey had a very traditional view of the historic religions, Kaplan had a rather traditional view of philosophy—this situation being the obverse of religion serving the same function for Kaplan that philosophy did for Dewey. That is, both Dewey and Kaplan pragmatically opposed both traditional religion and philosophy, but as Dewey pragmatically reconstructed philosophy, Kaplan pragmatically reconstructed the Jewish religion. As this left Dewey with his traditional view of the historic religions, which he opposed, it also left Kaplan with his traditional view of philosophy, to which he also felt some antipathy. Kaplan had indeed originally spoken admiringly of realist philosophers such as Aristotle and Bergson, but he came to refer to his own realism as functional rationalism, not philosophy. He thought of philosophy as more abstract and defined it as "the immaculate conception of thought not sired by experience," reserving it generally, although not rigorously, for an "ideationism" and rational idealism such as that of Plato and Hegel.[59] He distinguished, for example, the philosophical religious personality interested in mathematical and physical truth from the prophet who is concerned with the improvement and salvation of human beings through social justice and peace.[60]

I have shown, therefore, that Dewey's philosophy and Kaplan's thought share several broad areas of similarity, but that they also differ significantly in some of those areas and that they differ quite essentially in their views on ethics, God, and religion. Following this systematic comparison, I turn briefly now to the other factor involved in the common association of Dewey and Kaplan, which I noted at the beginning—namely, the issue of Dewey's direct influence on Kaplan, who was the younger of the two by some twenty-one years.[61] The question is difficult; the evidence is sometimes conflicting; and it is not certain that a study of Kaplan's extensive diaries, journals, and correspondence, which is beyond the scope of this essay, will clarify the matter.

On the positive side, it would seem likely that Dewey influenced Kaplan considerably because, as Whitehead wrote at the end of the 1930s, it was a "period subject to Dewey's influence."[62] Kaplan credited Dewey with teaching him to think pragmatically and functionally about life in general and about education in particular, and he used Dewey's *Democracy and Education* (1916) as the basic text in the education course he taught at the Hebrew University in Jerusalem.[63] He even took the name for his movement, Reconstructionism, from Dewey's book *Reconstruction in Philosophy* (1920).[64] Altogether, Kaplan's library contains fifteen books by Dewey, comprising most of Dewey's major works, as well as another six books either about Dewey or containing an important article by him,[65] indicating that Dewey's influence on Kaplan was more direct than indirect. Kaplan also uses phrases common in Dewey's writings and mentions historical figures, such as Bacon and Emerson, that Dewey had dwelt on.

On the other hand, the essential differences between them on the religious topics so important to Kaplan probably explain why Kaplan complained that Dewey's writings, unlike most books and articles, did not give him any ideas he could use. Reading Dewey, Kaplan grumbled, gave him heartache instead and made him painfully aware of the irrelevance of most of his problems.[66] Protests such as this incline one toward Mel Scult's suggestion that the chief pragmatic influence on Kaplan in his early years was William James.[67] Indeed, combined with the sociological tendencies Kaplan absorbed, this Jamesian pragmatism might have resulted in Kaplan's adopting a position similar to that of Dewey, without necessarily reflecting much of Dewey's direct influence.

Nevertheless, even if James was more of a formative source for Kaplan's pragmatism in the early years, the general similarities between Dewey and Kaplan I have described and the other information discussed earlier indicate that Dewey's influence on Kaplan was significant at a later stage in areas other than religion and ethics. Even in religion, Kaplan may have applied to his own theory some of what Dewey said not about religion but about philosophy. Hence, if Kaplan's thought seems a significant religious application of Dewey's generally secular philosophy, as we mentioned at the beginning of this essay, it is indeed those aspects of Dewey's philosophy that deal with topics other than religion and ethics that Kaplan utilizes in dealing with religion.

All this would help account for the popular tendency to associate Kaplan with Dewey. At the same time, it would have been natural for this popular association between Dewey and Kaplan to be greater than what would be justified either by the similarities between them or by Dewey's influence on Kaplan. Since Dewey was the authoritative New York intellectual of that time and symbolized the reform spirit of the age, a New York intellectual and reformer like Kaplan would be more closely linked to Dewey than the actual similarities and influence might warrant.

In conclusion, then, Kaplan and Dewey are similar in their pragmatism and activism, their social and scientific concern, their humanism and meliorism, their cultural nationalism, their Americanism and devotion to democracy, and their moderate synthesizing of dualisms into new, unified, middle ways. Kaplan differs from Dewey in his slight residual absolutism, his emphasis on peoplehood, his vitalistic transnaturalism that characterizes people, God, and values as a higher level of being, and his concern with the reconstruction of Jewish religion instead of philosophy as the basic means for individual and community self-realization. While the similarities and a few other details suggest that Dewey significantly influenced Kaplan within the limits of their specified differences, this historical question of influence deserves further and more biographical study.

One final note. One of the differences between Kaplan and Dewey is the residual absolutism and formalism in Kaplan's thought, but this difference means that Kaplan corrected a problem for which Dewey was criticized. Dewey's fear of fixed ends and rigid dogmas, it was maintained, inhibited him from even modest theorizing about specific social programs.[68] Kaplan, on the other hand, had many formal and specific proposals for the organization of the Jewish community. Yet, in spite of this advantageous difference from Dewey, Kaplan's Reconstructionism still did not flourish in the postwar period when Dewey's influence sharply declined. By then the age of humanistic science and social engineering evidently had already given way to a new era. Today, however, there is a resurgence of interest in Dewey, and one wonders whether the similarities between Kaplan and Dewey will lead to a renewed interest in Kaplan's Reconstructionism as well.

Notes

1. For examples, see Arthur Hertzberg's introduction to the reprint of Kaplan's *Judaism as a Civilization* (New York: Jewish Publication Society and Reconstructionist Press, 1981), xx, xxxii; Charles S. Liebman, "Reconstructionism in American Jewish Life," *American Jewish Year Book, 1970,* vol. 71, 6, 51; Richard L. Rubenstein, "Reconstructionism and the Problem of Evil," in his *After Auschwitz* (Indianapolis: Bobbs-Merrill, 1966), 85, 89, 90; Joseph L. Blau, *Modern Varieties of Judaism* (New York: Columbia University Press, 1964), 169. At the Jewish Theological Seminary, where Kaplan taught, criticism of Dewey was understood by the students to be really directed at Kaplan.

2. Eric F. Goldman, *Rendezvous with Destiny: A History of Modern American Reform* (New York: Random House, Vintage Books, 1977), 123.

3. *The Early Works of John Dewey*, vol. 4, *1893–1894*, ed. Jo Ann Boydston (Carbondale: Southern Illinois University Press, 1971), 211; introduction to Corliss Lamont, *The Illusion of Immortality*, 3d ed. (New York: Philosophical Library, 1959), xi.
4. Mordecai M. Kaplan, "Toward a Reconstruction of Judaism," *Menorah Journal* 13, no. 2 (April 1927): 123; idem, *The Greater Judaism in the Making: A Study of the Modern Evolution of Judaism* (New York: Reconstructionist Press, 1960), 73–75.
5. John Dewey, "One Current Religious Problem," *Journal of Philosophy* 33, no. 12 (June 1936): 325; Mordecai M. Kaplan, *Judaism in Transition* (New York: Covici-Friede, 1936), 18–20. Later, in *The Religion of Ethical Nationhood* (New York: Macmillan, 1970), 189, Kaplan says that the rabbis, in *Avot* 1:17, anticipated Dewey's emphasis on the pragmatic aspect of study.
6. John Dewey, *A Common Faith* (New Haven: Yale University Press, 1934), 80; Mordecai M. Kaplan, *The Meaning of God in Modern Jewish Religion* (New York: Behrman's Jewish Book House, 1937), 119–20, 280.
7. In Dewey, this may have been the influence of George Herbert Mead. See Israel Scheffler, *Four Pragmatists: A Critical Introduction to Peirce, James, Mead, and Dewey* (New York: Humanities Press, 1974), 149–50, 187. In Kaplan, it was the influence of sociologists such as Durkheim. See Mordecai M. Kaplan, "Reply," *Reconstructionist* 36, no. 12 (December 1970): 13.
8. John Dewey, *Liberalism and Social Action* (1935; reprint, New York: G. P. Putnam's Sons, Perigee Books, 1980), 67, 71, 83; idem, *Reconstruction in Philosophy*, enl. ed. (Boston: Beacon Press, 1948), v, xxvii; idem, *Human Nature and Conduct: An Introduction to Social Psychology* (New York: Random House, Modern Library, 1930), 287.
9. Mordecai M. Kaplan, *Judaism as a Civilization: Toward a Reconstruction of American-Jewish Life* (1934; reprint, New York: Schocken, 1967), 320, 327–28, 345.
10. John Dewey, *The Public and Its Problems* (1927; reprint, Denver: Alan Swallow, n.d.), 168, 176; Kaplan, "Reconstruction of Judaism," 123; Mordecai M. Kaplan, *Judaism without Supernaturalism* (New York: Reconstructionist Press, 1958), 26, 188; idem, *Religion of Ethical Nationhood*, 8–10.
11. See Morris R. Cohen, "Some Difficulties in John Dewey's Anthropocentric Naturalism," in his *Studies in Philosophy and Science* (New York: Henry Holt, 1949), 140–42; Kaplan, *Judaism in Transition*, ix–x, 256–57; idem, "Judaism and Intercultural Contacts," in *Modern Trends in World Religions*, ed. A. Eustace Hayden (Chicago: University of Chicago Press, 1934), 179–80.
12. Dewey, *Human Nature and Conduct*, 259–66; idem, *Reconstruction in Philosophy*, 177–79; Mordecai M. Kaplan, *The Future of the American Jew* (1948; reprint, New York: Reconstructionist Press, 1967), 296–301;

idem, *Questions Jews Ask: Reconstructionist Answers*, rev. ed. (New York: Reconstructionist Press, 1966), 115–26.

13. Dewey, *Common Faith*, 45–47; Kaplan, *Meaning of God*, 63–76, 84, 134, 144–45; idem, *Future of the American Jew*, 234–39. Perhaps the best-known critic of Dewey in this regard is Reinhold Niebuhr, *The Nature and Destiny of Man*, 2 vols. (New York: Charles Scribner's Sons, 1941, 1943), 1:110–14, 2:237 (a remarkable misunderstanding of Dewey, by the way). Standard critics of Kaplan on this issue are Richard L. Rubenstein, "Reconstructionism and the Problem of Evil," in his *After Auschwitz*, 89–90; and Arthur A. Cohen, *The Natural and Supernatural Jew: An Historical and Theological Introduction* (New York: Random House, Pantheon Books, 1962), 213–14, n. 13. An Orthodox criticism is mounted by Eliezer Berkovits, *Major Themes in Modern Philosophies of Judaism* (New York: Ktav, 1974), 159.

    Kaplan, it should be noted, joins Orthodox Jews in denying that the Holocaust, while unprecedented, is unique and qualitatively different from earlier Jewish massacres and suffering. This indicates that the really moderate position of Kaplan and Dewey on evil has certain similarities to a traditional Jewish view. See, for example, Michael Wyschogrod, *Body of Faith: Judaism as Corporeal Election* (Minneapolis: Seabury Press, 1983), 14–15.

14. John Dewey, "Christianity and Democracy," in *The Early Works: 1893–1894*, vol. 4, 4–9.

15. Dewey, *Reconstruction in Philosophy*, 53–66; idem, *Public and Its Problems*, 111, 143, 148–49, 211–15; Joseph Ratner, ed., *Characters and Events: Popular Essays in Social and Political Philosophy*, 2 vols. (New York: Henry Holt, 1929), 2:849.

16. *Characters and Events*, 2:643.

17. Kaplan, *Judaism as a Civilization*, 216; idem, *Future of the American Jew*, 435–36, 520–22, 537; idem, "Toward a Reconstruction of Judaism," 130. See also the last section of Liebman, "Reconstructionism" on Reconstructionism as folk religion.

18. Kaplan, *Meaning of God*, 112–13, 284; idem, *Judaism as a Civilization*, 283, 474–76; idem, *Questions Jews Ask*, 433; John Dewey, *Democracy and Education: An Introduction to the Philosophy of Education* (New York: Macmillan, 1916), 122–23; idem, *Liberalism and Social Action*, 5, 77–78, 81, 84–85.

19. Dewey, *Public and Its Problems*, 8, 43, 71; Kaplan, *Future of the American Jew*, 18–20.

20. Kaplan, *Judaism without Supernaturalism*, 221–23; idem, *Greater Judaism*, 454–55; idem, *Questions Jews Ask*, 406, 488; John Dewey, "The Principle of Nationality," in *The Middle Works: 1899–1924*, vol. 10, 1916–1917, ed. Jo Ann Boydston (Carbondale: Southern Illinois University Press, 1980), 291 (orig. in *Menorah Journal* 3); Samuel B. Finkel,

"American Jews and the Hebrew University," *American Jewish Yearbook*, vol. 39 (1937–38), 198–99.

21. Kaplan, "Reconstruction of Judaism," 130; idem, *Future of the American Jew*, 125; Ira Eisenstein, "Mordecai M. Kaplan and His Teachers," in *Mordecai M. Kaplan: An Evaluation*, ed. Ira Eisenstein and Eugene Kohn (New York: Jewish Reconstructionist Foundation, 1952), 23–24.

22. Dewey, *Common Faith*, 10; idem, *Democracy and Education*, 358; idem, *Experience and Nature*, 2d ed. (La Salle, Ill.: Open Court, 1929), 329.

23. Dewey, *Human Nature and Conduct*, 301; idem, *Liberalism and Social Action*, 48–50; idem, "Religion and Our Schools," in *Characters and Events*, 2:508–9, 514.

24. Kaplan, *Meaning of God*, 172; idem, *Questions Jews Ask*, 38; idem, "A Heart of Wisdom," *Reconstructionist* 17, no. 6 (May 1951): 13.

25. Kaplan, *Judaism as a Civilization*, pp. 291–92, 425–28; idem, *Future of the American Jew*, xviii, 111; idem, *Greater Judaism*, 499; idem, "A Program for the Reconstruction of Judaism," *Menorah Journal* 6, no. 4 (August 1920): 190, 196.

26. See Morton White, *Social Thought in America: The Revolt Against Formalism* (Boston: Beacon Press, 1957).

27. Dewey, *Human Nature and Conduct*, 85–89, 101–3.

28. Kaplan, *Questions Jews Ask*, 91–92, 148–50; idem, *Judaism without Supernaturalism*, 118; idem, "How to Live Creatively as a Jew," in *Moments of Personal Discovery*, ed. R. M. MacIver (1952; reprint, New York: Kennikat Press, 1969), 99. On the consistency of relative scientific confirmation with absolute ideal truth, as in Peirce, see Scheffler, *Four Pragmatists*, 112, 116.

In *Judaism as a Civilization*, 307, Kaplan seems to deny that there are absolute truths, but he evidently means there that the knowledge or truths *our minds gain* are not absolute, not that there are no absolute truths at all.

29. Kaplan, "Program for Reconstruction of Judaism," 188; idem, *Judaism without Supernaturalism*, 118; idem, "Reply," 13–14. See also Sidney Morgenbesser and David Sidorsky, "Reconstructionism and the Naturalistic Tradition in America," *Reconstructionist* 21, no. 1 (February 1955): 39–41. Kaplan was evidently prodded into more speculation on theological topics by complaints about the lack of such in his writings. See, for example, Milton Steinberg, *Anatomy of Faith*, ed. Arthur A. Cohen (New York: Harcourt Brace, 1960), 181–82, 248–49.

30. Mordecai M. Kaplan, *The Purpose and Meaning of Jewish Existence* (Philadelphia: Jewish Publication Society of America, 1964). Kaplan called Cohen and Ahad Ha'am the two most outstanding recent Jewish thinkers. When he boasted later in the same volume that the most influential philosopher of his day was Jewish, he was probably referring

to Bergson. See A. Eustace Haydon, ed., *Modern Trends in World Religions*, 16–18, 180.

31. John Dewey, *Characters and Events*, 2:466–67, 801–3; idem, "Principle of Nationality," 288–89; George Dykhuizen, *The Life and Mind of John Dewey*, ed. Jo Ann Boydston (Carbondale: Southern Illinois University Press, 1973), 143–44, 275–77, 295.

32. Kaplan, "Reconstruction of Judaism," 130; idem, *Judaism as a Civilization*, 323–25, 489; idem, *Questions Jews Ask*, chap. 1 and 174–75; idem, *Judaism without Supernaturalism*, 68; idem, "How to Live Creatively as a Jew," 95–98; *Reconstructionist* 6, no. 1 (February 1940): 4–6.

33. Corliss Lamont, "New Light on Dewey's *Common Faith*," *Journal of Philosophy* 58 (1961): 26; Dewey, *Experience and Nature*, 249–50.

34. Mordecai M. Kaplan, "Jewish Religion as Wisdom," *Reconstructionist* 33, no. 18 (January 1968): 9, or idem, *Religion of Ethical Nationhood*, 22–23; idem, *Meaning of God*, 320–29; idem, *Judaism without Supernaturalism*, 119–20; idem, *Future of the American Jew*, 247–55; idem, *Judaism as a Civilization*, 315; idem, "The Human Person," *Reconstructionist* 32, no. 13 (November 11, 1966): 9.

35. Kaplan, *Questions Jews Ask*, 95; idem, *Future of the American Jew*, 183; idem, *Judaism without Supernaturalism*, 10; idem, *Judaism as a Civilization*, 317; idem, *Religion of Ethical Nationhood*, 4; idem, *If Not Now, When? Toward a Reconstitution of the Jewish People: Conversations between Mordecai M. Kaplan and Arthur A. Cohen* (New York: Schocken, 1973), 93. On the broad sense of naturalism as a method compatible with different ontologies, see Arthur Danto's article "Naturalism," in *The Encyclopedia of Philosophy* (1967) 5:448–50.

36. Eliezer Berkovits suggests the terms "pananthropomorphism" or "pananthropoism" for Kaplan's transnaturalism. See his *Major Themes*, 182–85.

37. Mordecai M. Kaplan, "When Is a Religion Authentic?" *Reconstructionist* 30, no. 11 (October 1964): 16–17.

38. Kaplan, *Questions Jews Ask*, 95–96, 103, 128; idem, "Human Person," 9, 12.

39. Dewey, *Human Nature and Conduct*, 266–67; idem, *Common Faith*, 24–25, 42, 50–52, 55; idem, "A God or the God?" *Christian Century* 50, no. 6 (February 1933): 196.

40. Kaplan, "Human Person," 9; Dewey, *Experience and Nature*, 95, 318.

41. Kaplan, *Purpose and Meaning of Jewish Existence*, vi, 324; idem, *Meaning of God*, 29, 323–24; John Dewey, Edwin E. Aubrey, and Henry N. Wieman, "Is John Dewey a Theist?" *Christian Century* 51 (1934): 1550–51; Sidney Hook, "Some Memories of John Dewey," *Contemporary* 14, no. 3 (September 1952): 253. For Arnold's definition of God, see, for example, Matthew Arnold, *Literature and Dogma* (New York: n.p., 1883), 52, 348.

Kaplan evidently got the notion of correlative terms, such as "teacher-pupil," from Hermann Cohen, for he considered it Cohen's most original contribution to religion. Kaplan, *Purpose and Meaning of Jewish Existence*, 107.

42. Kaplan, *Greater Judaism*, 498–99; idem, *Religion of Ethical Nationhood*, 79; idem, *If Not Now, When?* 89; idem, *Purpose and Meaning of Jewish Existence*, 230–31; idem, "The Unsolved Problem of Evil," *Reconstructionist* 29, no. 8 (May 1963): 14; Harold C. Weisberg, "Mordecai M. Kaplan's Theory of Religion," in *Mordecai M. Kaplan*, 172.

43. Dewey, *Reconstruction in Philosophy*, 187–92; idem, "The Subject Matter of Metaphysical Inquiry," in *On Experience, Nature, and Freedom: Representative Selections*, ed. Richard J. Bernstein (Indianapolis: Liberal Arts Press, 1960), 212–13, 222.

44. Kaplan, *Questions Jews Ask*, 179, 466–67; Mel Scult, "The Sociologist as Theologian: The Fundamental Assumptions of Mordecai Kaplan's Thought," *Judaism* 25, no. 3 (1976): 347; Dewey, *Common Faith*, 35–38.

45. Kaplan, "Reply," 14; idem, "Jewish Religion as Wisdom," 8–12; idem, "Our Religious Vocation," *Reconstructionist* 27, no. 20 (February 1962): 10; John Dewey, *The Quest for Certainty: A Study of the Relation between Knowledge and Action* (New York: G. P. Putnam's Sons, 1929; Capricorn Books, 1960), chap. 10, 269–71. See also Morgenbesser and Sidorsky, "Reconstructionism and the Naturalistic Tradition," p. 40.

46. Max Eastman, *Great Companions* (New York: Farrar, Straus, and Cudahy, 1959), 257, 261; Robert B. Williams, ed., *John Dewey: Recollections* (Washington, D.C.: University Press of America, 1982), 76. On Dewey's early religious development, see Dykhuizen, *Life and Mind of John Dewey*, 6, 8, 22, 33, 47, 50, 65, 73–74, 100.

47. Mordecai M. Kaplan, "The Influences that Have Shaped My Life," *Reconstructionist* 8, no. 10 (June 1942): 30–31.

48. John Dewey, "Philosophy and Civilization," in *John Dewey: The Essential Writings*, ed. David Sidorsky (New York: Harper & Row, Harper Torchbooks, 1977), 11 (originally in Dewey, *Philosophy and Civilization*, 1931); Kaplan, *Judaism as a Civilization*, 345; idem, *Judaism without Supernaturalism*, 16.

49. Dewey, *Reconstruction in Philosophy*, 26; idem, *Experience and Nature*, 322.

50. Kaplan, *Questions Jews Ask*, 134–40; idem, *If Not Now, When?* 85; Liebman, "Reconstructionism," 231. Kaplan's purpose in identifying religion and ethics was not to reduce religion to philosophical ethics but rather to bring ethics over from philosophy to religion.

51. Kaplan, *Judaism as a Civilization*, 514; idem, "The Meaning of Reconstructionism," *Reconstructionist* 6, no. 1 (February 1940): 18; Ira Eisenstein, "Mordecai M. Kaplan," in *Great Jewish Thinkers of the Twentieth Century*, ed. Simon Noveck (B'nai-B'rith Department of Adult

Jewish Education, 1963), 263–64. Blau calls this the basic principle of Reconstructionism in his *Modern Varieties of Judaism*, 184–85.

52. John Dewey, "The Relation of Philosophy to Theology," in *The Early Works, 1893–1894*, vol. 4, 365; Kaplan, *Judaism without Supernaturalism*, 209.

53. Kaplan, "Reconstruction of Judaism," 129–30; idem, "Judaism and Intercultural Contacts," 183; idem, *Judaism as a Civilization;* 201–02; idem, *Questions Jews Ask*, 497; idem, *Purpose and Meaning of Jewish Existence*, 54; idem, "What Is Judaism?" *Menorah Journal* 1, no. 5 (December 1915): 313–14.

54. Dewey, *Common Faith*, 26–27, 33, 50, 71, 79.

55. On the surprisingly individualistic character of the "religious" that Dewey discusses in *A Common Faith* (1934), his major and latest statement on religion, see John Herman Randall, Jr., "The Religion of Shared Experience," in *The Philosopher of the Common Man: Essays in Honor of John Dewey to Celebrate his Eightieth Birthday* (New York: G. P. Putnam's Sons, 1940), 139. In Dewey's *Human Nature and Conduct* (1922), on the other hand, this individualistic religious attitude also involves a sense of community and the whole (see 301–2).

56. It has been argued that, like art, religion became more important for Dewey as he came to appreciate more the role of consummation in experience. Interestingly, what there is that is positive about religion in Dewey's books other than *A Common Faith* is consummatory not only in being unifying and integrative but also in occurring as an inspirational flourish at or near the end of the works. See, for example, the concluding paragraphs of *Reconstruction in Philosophy* and *Human Nature and Conduct* and the next-to-last section of *The Quest for Certainty*. Still, art is central for Dewey because, in addition to being consummatory, it also serves an important social role as a basic means of communication. The same cannot be said of religion. Hence, Dewey had to be almost forced to compose his brief book on religion, a statement that cannot be made about his major work on art published the same year.

57. Mordecai M. Kaplan, "How May Judaism Be Saved," *Menorah Journal* 2, no. 1 (February 1916): 42; idem, "Judaism and Christianity," *Menorah Journal* 2, no. 2 (April 1916): 114; idem, *Judaism as a Civilization*, 217–18; idem, *Future of the American Jew*, 99, 101, 121; idem, *Questions Jews Ask*, 201, 281–82.

In the Protestant Ecumenical movement Kaplan saw an effort to achieve a communal unity that transcended creedal differences. (See idem, *Questions Jews Ask*, 30–31). Since such a church would not be authoritarian, as Roman Catholicism is, Kaplan suggested it as a model for a future world Jewish community and made some other positive statements about Protestantism as well. (See idem, *Judaism without Supernaturalism*, 61, 65, 205.) Yet, while his opinion of Protestantism improved, he retained his admiration for Catholic social organization. In a letter to Raphael Jospe dated 19 February 1967, Kaplan still urges that Jews be organized locally into communities like the parishes and dioceses of the Catholics and, he now adds, some of the Protestant denominations. The author wishes to thank Dr. Jospe for providing him with a copy of this letter.

58. Dewey, *Common Faith*, 30, 67–68; *Characters and Events*, 2:516, 832. The distinction between Catholicism and Protestantism as being respectively more social or more individualistic is used here because it is suggested by both Kaplan and Dewey, but the author does not want to be understood as necessarily agreeing with the distinction. Randall (see note 55) mentions one Protestant aspect of Dewey's religious thought that applies to Kaplan as well, namely, its lay protest against the professional priesthood. Kaplan wanted to be called leader, not rabbi, when he began the Society for the Advancement of Judaism.

59. Kaplan, "A Program for the Reconstruction of Judaism," 188; idem, *Purpose and Meaning of Jewish Existence*, vii, 62; Charles E. Vernoff, "Supernatural and Transnatural—An Encounter of Religious Perspectives: The Theological Problematic in the Modern Judaic Worldview of Mordecai M. Kaplan," (Ph.D. diss., University of California, Santa Barbara, 1979), 438, n. 1.

Religious philosophy that is based on experience, however, even if it has a significant element of "ideationism," is essential as an ideology and rationale providing Jews and Judaism with a sense of purpose and meaning. (See Kaplan, *Future of the American Jew*, 167–68.) Hence, Kaplan turned to the religious philosophy of Hermann Cohen for such a Jewish ideology.

60. Kaplan, *Questions Jews Ask*, 228–29; idem, "How Man Comes to Know God," *Proceedings of the Rabbinical Assembly of America, 1941–1944*, 8:265–66.

61. Kaplan and Dewey share some strikingly similar biographical details. Both lived long, active, and productive lives, Kaplan to age 102, Dewey to age 92. Both were exceedingly prolific authors and continued writing and publishing into their last years—Kaplan into his nineties and Dewey into his eighties.

As for their personal lives, Kaplan had four daughters and Dewey had three daughters and a surviving son (two other sons died as children). Each remarried in his old age after the death of his first wife.

Most significantly, they both taught education and philosophy for a couple of decades within two or three blocks of each other in Morningside Heights in Manhattan, Kaplan as dean of the Teacher's Institute at the Jewish Theological Seminary and Dewey at Teacher's College and in the philosophy department at Columbia University. For a few years (1939–45), they even lived across the street from each other at Central Park West and Eighty-ninth Street. Yet Ira Eisenstein, Kaplan's son-in-law, has written to the author that he knows of no personal contact between Kaplan and Dewey. Both were personally shy.

62. Quoted in Paul Arthur Schilpp, ed., *The Philosophy of John Dewey* (New York: Tudor Publishing, Library of Living Philosophers, 1939), 477–78.

63. Richard Libowitz, *Mordecai M. Kaplan and the Development of Reconstructionism* (New York: Edwin Mellen Press, 1983), 38.

64. Mordecai M. Kaplan to Raphael Jospe, 19 February 1967.

65. Kaplan's personal library is now housed at the Reconstructionist Rabbinical College in Wyncote, Pennsylvania, outside Philadelphia. The college's librarian, Sue Frank, provided a list of the books in Kaplan's library by or about Dewey.

66. Libowitz, *Mordecai M. Kaplan*, 204, from an entry in Kaplan's main diary, dated 9 June 1931.

67. Scult, "Sociologist as Theologian," 346.

68. Morton White, *Social Thought in America* (Boston: Beacon Press, 1968), 244–45.

CHAPTER 8

Kaplan and
Henry Nelson Wieman

Emanuel S. Goldsmith

Mordecai M. Kaplan (1881–1983) and Henry Nelson Wieman (1884–1975) were two of the outstanding religious thinkers of the twentieth century. One a Jew and the other a Protestant, they were representatives of their respective traditions as well as pioneers on the frontier of the continuing human quest for the divine. Kaplan and Wieman were radical modernists who wholeheartedly embraced religious liberalism, naturalism, empiricism, and process thought and gave expression to the American spirit in theology and the philosophy of religion. Defending their faiths from atheism and humanism, on the one hand, and from fundamentalism and literalism, on the other, their approaches were both reconstructive and innovative. They bequeathed to future generations rich legacies of understanding and insight that will continue to grow in significance as people search for new religious truths, as well as for the relevance of their inherited traditions.

The childhood years of Kaplan in New York City and of Wieman in Missouri were similar in that while they grew up in intensely religious homes, the religiosity of their parents was probing, intel-

This paper was originally presented at the conference on Influences in the Reconfiguration of Modern Judaism sponsored by the Council for the World's Religions in Stansstad, Switzerland, 1–5 September 1988.

lectual, and nondogmatic. They were thus able in later years to distinguish what they considered to be the deep and abiding concerns of religious conviction and devotion from religious formalism and institutionalism. Even as a child Kaplan realized that although Jewish religious observance was believed to have been dictated by God, its real significance was not intrinsic but lay in its ability to relate the Jew to the Jewish people. "Whether I was reciting the brief thanksgiving prayer on opening the eyes, or the prayers on going to bed, or various prayers and benedictions during the day, they all had one meaning for me—that of being a Jew."[1]

The major influence in Kaplan's life was his father. Rabbi Israel Kaplan was an adherent of the Lithuanian Musar movement, founded by Rabbi Israel Salanter, which emphasized the ethical element in religion as of greater significance than piety or scholarship. While strictly observant, Kaplan's father was committed to intellectual honesty and tolerated his son's deviations from traditional standards and beliefs. When they studied Talmud together and Mordecai took exception to statements in the text or the commentaries, his father would pinch his son's cheek and say, "You don't let yourself be fooled, my son."[2]

The primary religious influence on Wieman was his mother, who shaped his religious development by the strength of her faith.[3] Although his father was a Presbyterian minister, his parents did not indoctrinate their son in their religion, and whatever he received from them seemed to be caught by contagion rather than taught. He did not, for example, automatically identify religion with the church. "The business of keeping the church going is the most religious religion there is. But it was never the religion of my mother or father, although he was a clergyman."[4]

Both Wieman and Kaplan recalled experiences in their formative years that were crucial for their religious development. While conducting a religious service together with fellow students when he was sixteen, Kaplan experienced a religious illumination. "The Psalms, which I had up to that time been in the habit of reciting mechanically as part of the daily prayers, suddenly became for me alight with meaning, and, for the first time, I experienced the reality of God."[5] On an April evening during his senior year in college, Wieman sat alone in his room and looked out over the

Missouri River. Suddenly it came over him that he wanted to devote his life not to journalism, as he had been planning, but to the philosophy of religion. "The new purpose took hold of me with overwhelming force and satisfaction. . . . this new idea seemed to release an urge that had been blocked and I was joyously exuberant over this new plan."[6]

Not having been taught to identify religion with particular beliefs or institutions, Wieman felt no distress when challenged to alter his beliefs by new ideas, such as Darwin's theory of evolution.[7] Kaplan, on the other hand, was troubled by the problems that modern thought posed to traditional religion and specifically to the writings of the medieval Jewish theologians in which he sought answers to his perplexities. He became aware that the medieval theologians lacked a historical sense and an awareness of evolution in religion. His faith in the Mosaic authorship of the Torah and in the historicity of the biblical miracles was eventually undermined and replaced with an evolutionary and historical approach.[8]

Kaplan and Wieman began their work during the heyday of American religious liberalism, which lasted from the turn of the century until the beginning of the Second World War. In addition to the growth of modern science, a major factor in the rise of liberalism was the development of modern historical and literary research on religion and the Bible. Although exposed to modern religious scholarship, neither Kaplan nor Wieman was particularly attracted to textual or historical study. During a year of study in Germany, Wieman heard the great historians Wilhelm Windelband and Ernest Troeltsch. He felt that Windelband's philosophical systematizing and classifying was done at the expense of depth and constructiveness. His reaction to Troeltsch was that, despite the great importance of his historical study of religion, it could not provide any direction for living.[9] Kaplan's attitude to modern Jewish scholarship was similar, and his scholarly recension of an ethical treatise by Moshe Hayyim Luzzatto appears to have been his sole foray into the world of textual scholarship. He was generally distrustful of those scholars who live so thoroughly in the past that it serves for them as an authority that blinds them to the needs of the present and with which they attack changes dictated by practical or rational considerations.[10]

The religious liberals of the early twentieth century continued the work of the Enlightenment and adjusted religion to modern science, philosophy, and history. They domesticated religious ideas and carried forward the "confrontation between traditional orthodoxies and the new grounds for religious skepticism exposed during the nineteenth century."[11] American religious liberalism, in particular, was characterized by ethical passion and a preoccupation with religious experience. Its underlying motifs were continuity (emphasis on the immanence rather than the transcendence of God), autonomy (the centrality of personal religious experience rather than the appeal to external authority), and dynamism (the stress on evolution in nature and history rather than the traditional appeal to static categories).[12]

While clearly within the broad stream of American religious liberalism, Wieman and Kaplan were critical of certain liberal presuppositions. As modernistic liberals or radical modernizers, they took scientific method, scholarly discipline, empirical fact, and prevailing forms of philosophy as their points of departure.[13] Although aware of much in Judaism and Christianity that should be retained in modern times, they felt that their traditions had to be evaluated in the light of modern science, philosophy, psychology, and sociology. Nothing was to be adhered to unless its relevance could be made apparent.[14] As modernists they advocated "the conscious, intended adaptation of religious ideas to modern culture."[15] For them, God was immanent in cultural evolution, and society was progressively moving toward realization of the kingdom of God, even if such a goal might never actually be attained.[16]

In the period under discussion, liberalism was represented in the Jewish community chiefly by the Reform movement. Reformers taught that Judaism had attained the highest development of the God-idea and was, therefore, superior to all other religions. Kaplan felt that such a claim could not be substantiated by historical fact. The Reform movement also stressed ethical commitment to the detriment of ritual practice. Kaplan chided it for having thus reduced Judaism to a philosophy of religion. In addition, the Reform movement renounced Jewish nationalism and insisted that the Jews were merely a religious community. Kaplan accused it of thereby severing Judaism from the texture of Jewish experience and of a failure to understand the full implications of religion and community. A community, according to Kaplan, was not merely a society. A community implied living in common as well as believing in common. The Reform movement, he contended, had failed to assimilate recent studies of the nature and history of religion, and its theology and sociology were hopelessly anachronistic. It had given free scope to intellectual inquiry without taking advantage of that freedom to understand the nature and purpose of religion and peoplehood.[17] The main function of religion, as Kaplan saw it, was to enable a group to adjust to its environment and make the most of its life. "The scientific spirit has invaded the entire domain of human thinking. Even theology is giving way to the science of religion to which it bears the same relation as alchemy to chemistry."[18]

Wieman's major quarrel with Protestant religious liberalism, like Kaplan's with Reform Judaism, was based on what he perceived to be its misunderstanding of the true nature of religion. He attacked what he saw as its subjectivism and sentimentalism. These, he felt, were the results of an inadequate understanding of the nature of religious experience and a failure to treat such experience scientifically.[19] To him, religious experience "when not controlled and directed by devotion to something well-defined and distinguished and assuredly known to be the present source of human good" was "futile sentimentalism" and "promiscuity in religious living."[20] Belief in what seemed helpful without other evidence was to him a religion of wishful fancy. He sought objective evidence of God in nature and human life.[21] He advocated a theocentric faith in which the actuality of God rather than human ideas about God would be the object of salvation.

Despite their reservations about religious liberalism, Kaplan and Wieman were, broadly speaking, members of the religious liberal camp. Kaplan, for example, while concerned with the preservation of those elements of the Jewish past that had contemporary significance and with the integrity and continuity of Jewish civilization, also insisted on "the responsibility of the living generation to evaluate tradition and to reject what is not relevant to contemporary needs, or in accord with the best in modern thought."[22] Advocates of liberal religion, said Wieman, had to oppose a faith that assumes that the problems of human life have been solved by the religious personalities and traditions of the past. Liberal religion had to be based on questions rather than answers, and any answers it provided had to be seen as tentative. It had to be committed "not to a belief but to the actuality which a belief seeks to apprehend; not to a problem solved but to a problem in process of being solved; not to an answer given but to a question being asked and an answer found more or less adequate to the question."[23] He believed that liberal religion was based on faith that demanded tests of reason for its affirmations. "As in science, every discovery only opens the way for further inquiry."[24]

Generally speaking, religious liberalism emphasized subjective belief and appealed to religious experience for evidence of God. This emphasis, however, frequently led to the denial of the objective reality of God. Along with their opposition to idealism's tendency to objectify subjective human ideals, Wieman and Kaplan were also opposed to the extreme forms of humanism that deny all objective reality to the divine aspects of experience. "Does the idealism of humanism give us the deepest and most characteristic quality of religion which enables it to pour into human life something of great value which cannot be got in morality or art or politics or industry or home life or anywhere else?" asked Wieman.[25] "Human effort can be efficacious in bringing a desired possibility to pass only when there is some order in which and with which men can work to that end. . . . God is that order of existence and possibility which includes the possibility of greatest value to be attained, which makes it a possibility and in adjustment to which human effort is efficacious in achieving it, but without which human effort would be entirely futile and foolish."[26]

Kaplan deemed the humanistic interpretation of life inadequate because of its failure to express or foster the feeling that man's ethical aspirations are part of a cosmic urge. "Without the conviction that the world contains all that is necessary for human salvation, the assumptions necessary for ethical living remain cold hypotheses lacking all dynamic power."[27] Spiritual religion differs from humanism in its assumption that the cosmos is in rapport with the human quest for fulfillment. It stresses that "the universe is not only interrelated but divine, in that it is so constituted to help man in his striving after salvation."[28] Despite these misgivings, however, Kaplan and Wieman are properly designated religious humanists, since both accorded centrality in religion to the human need for salvation or transformation and both rejected supernaturalism.

Kaplan and Wieman belonged to that sector of American religious liberalism that embraced theistic or religious naturalism. They conceded that naturalism had formerly been incompatible with religion because it reduced all life and thought to operations of matter and physicochemical causes, and left no room for belief in the reality of God and spiritual values.[29] In countering the belief in a supernatural power that exists in a realm beyond space and time, the older naturalism had failed to point to the creative, transforming, or spiritual element in the midst of actual events and inherent in the temporal world. The type of naturalism espoused by Wieman and Kaplan recognized qualitative distinctions between lower and higher orders of being. It allowed for creative or emergent evolution and for the autonomous functioning of mind and spirit. It conceived of truth, justice, and love as operating in their own right and helping to bring order out of chaos.[30] People could thus have a faith and devotion to "a power, resident in events, that transforms the world in ways better than the human mind can imagine. . . . This power demands of man not only the faith of self-giving, but also obedience to the moral law and the practical setting up of all conditions within his ability that facilitate the transformation of creativity."[31]

Wieman and Kaplan were also empirical theologians who sought an anchor for religious faith independent of revelation and tradition and found it in the scientific methods of reason, observation, and experimentation. The empirical method in theology bases all claims to, and interpretations of, knowledge on personal experience. Such experience may, however, embrace all that has been "enjoyed and suffered." Empirical theology also insists on a method of religious inquiry that is accessible to all. "Recent empiricism," as James A. Martin, Jr., points out, "while retaining the notion that scientific knowledge must begin and end with public experience, has not conceived of such experience narrowly in terms of mere sensation and association. Affective, volitional, and valuational elements are seen to be parts of the whole. And the significance of experimenta-

tion, or experimentalism, as the most fruitful method for the explo-
ration and organization of experience has been emphasized."[32]
Wieman insisted, therefore, that God must be found in human life
and that reason must serve as a guide to the classification and
testing of religious concepts. To Wieman, "the canons of rational
consistency are important," writes Daniel D. Williams, "not because all experience can be presented in a rational scheme, but as
man's protection against illusion, nonsense, and the imposition of
untestable doctrines upon his religious search for truth."[33]

For Kaplan, the effect of trying to preserve Jewish religion in its
traditional form, without adequately reckoning with modern experience, was to make Jewish religion an anachronism in the modern
world. Jewish religion had to be based "not on what our ancestors
have told of their experience with God, but on our own experience
with God."[34] His study of the evolution of Jewish religion led him
to realize that "although medieval Jewish theology believed it was
merely reaffirming the Jew's allegiance to traditional beliefs, it
indirectly paid sufficient homage to reason to prepare the way for a
type of religion in which reason—in a sense sufficiently large to
include our deeper insights and intuitions—is the only guide and
authority."[35] To Kaplan, any conception of God based on delusion
partook of idolatry. Anti-intellectualism and irrationalism in the
form of romanticism and mysticism were to him distortions of truth
and the sense of reality.[36]

Kaplan and Wieman were process theologians influenced by the
thought of such philosophers as Henri Bergson, Samuel Alexander,
C. Lloyd Morgan, John E. Boodin, George Herbert Mead, and Alfred
North Whitehead. Process philosophy emphasizes both process, or
becoming, and relations, or relativity. It contends that the entire
universe is in a state of change or process and stresses the theme of
relationship.[37] *Time, change, becoming, growth, organicity,* and
creativity are frequently used terms. Wieman has been called "the
theologian par excellence of man's experiential encounter with the
concrete actuality of God's being as this issues in creative, transfor-
mative, and redemptive processes."[38] According to Wieman, it is
only God *in* human life, rather than at the beginning, bottom, top,
or end of it, who can be a matter of religious concern. It is also only
"when God is sought and found in the midst of the concrete situa-

tion where we are that he can be known through action." Action, Wieman emphasizes, "is the only way in which we come to know anything in truth, but especially any reality in its character of commanding our supreme devotion and absolute self-commitment."[39] Kaplan emphasized that modern scientific and philosophic thought views all of reality as dynamic and as energy in action. To speak of God as process is "to select, out of the infinite processes in the universe, that complex of forces and relationships which makes for the highest fulfillment of man as a human being and identify it by the term 'God.' "[40]

Wieman and Kaplan also shared a deep concern with the concept of value. Religion is actually concerned with value in two senses. It involves the choice, appreciation, and adoration of value or the source of value, and it posits a faith in the universe as hospitable to value.[41] Kaplan placed the term *God* in the category of value, which is related to wisdom, rather than in the category of fact, which is related to reason and intelligence. Values, he insisted, are actually as real as visible and tangible facts.[42] "As psychic and social facts or realities, values are far more potent as fact makers or factors, in the sense of producing results. The God concept, properly understood as a factor in ordering the life of men and nations, is the most potent and creative factor in human existence."[43]

Wieman contended that, as a supreme value, God is a perceptible natural process.[44] The term *God* is a name for the growth of meaning and value in the world, and values are the data by which God is sought and found. Although God is always greater than "the specific objects of human desire and aversion," God and the highest human values are identical.[45] He warned that "the creative source of value must come first in man's devotion, while the specific values apprehended through the narrow slit of human awareness must come second, if we are to find the way of our deliverance and the way of human fulfillment."[46] John E. Smith observes that Wieman's position rests on two central theses: "His claim that God is truly present in perceived experience is intended to avoid reducing God to a mere concept or ideal. His interpretation of God as the source of human good or value, on the other hand, seeks to avoid confusing God with the whole of reality."[47]

The approaches of Wieman and Kaplan were not only axiological, or concerned with values, but also soteriological, or concerned with salvation. As theologians they introduced such concepts as salvation, redemption, deliverance, transformation, and metamorphosis into empirical and process thought. To both of them, salvation is a this-worldly social as well as individual reality that must be understood in terms of human needs. For Wieman, salvation is the life of aspiration in which the deepest need of human nature finds fulfillment. This need is "the need of bringing to fulfillment that multiplication of responses which arise in a man over and above his established habits. . . . It is to interact with ever more of the world round about him."[48] Modern persons can, therefore, find their salvation only through the social world in which they participate, and social reconstruction is the modern road to salvation.[49] Psychologically, salvation is emergence "from inner conflict or stagnation to progressive integration of personality; from personal powers confined to personal powers released; from a disjunct personality to a conjunct one; from a sense of insecurity to a profound and indestructible peace; from specific objectives that imprison and perish, to a total objective that is eternal; from bondage to an established social pattern of life, to a pattern that opens out into an illimitable realm of possible value and meaning."[50] The salvation of society involves rearranging institutions, ideals, and customs in order to "restore mutual support and release growth of meaning."[51] The salvation of the individual and the salvation of society are interrelated. "The salvation sought is the salvation of man, psychologically, socially, historically. It is the salvation of human life in its total movement of history, society, and individual existence."[52]

Religion's major responsibility, according to Wieman, is to point to the way of salvation.[53] And the salvation that affords deepest satisfaction and maximum realization of human potentialities is found in a creativity that reconstructs personality, society, and history by generating insights and expanding horizons. It operates through creative intercommunication among individuals, peoples, and cultures. This creativity expands the range of what an individual can know, control, appreciate as good, and distinguish as evil, and the depth and scope of what he can appreciate and understand about himself and about the unique individuality of other persons and peoples.[54]

Religion, according to Kaplan, is man's conscious quest for salvation or the achievement of his human destiny.[55] The proper task of religion is not to prove the existence of God but to assist people in their quest for self-fulfillment or salvation.[56] Salvation is "the achievement of such personality in the individual and of such society in the collective, as to augment the measure of integrity, responsibility, and creativity in the world."[57] It is the maximum fulfillment of those capacities that entitle people to be described as created in the divine image.[58] It is the effort to improve oneself and one's environment and as such is prophetic of human destiny and a manifestation of the divine in human life.[59] It is the capacity to play a conscious role in the evolution of self as well as the urge to transformation and metamorphosis.[60]

The concept of salvation, according to Kaplan, is rooted in the objective psychological need to be needed, which is experienced as the need to be accepted and loved. To be needed a person must be honest, creative, just, and ready to serve. Every person may be creative because insofar as he produces more than he consumes he contributes to making life worthwhile for all.[61] The need to be needed applies to nations as well as to individuals. To achieve salvation, human beings must strive for world peace, ethical nationhood, and individual happiness.[62] For the individual, salvation also consists of the satisfaction of the three primary needs: health, love, and creativity. For society, furthering salvation involves seeing to it that every person has the economic and cultural opportunities necessary for maximum self-fulfillment.[63]

The word *God* may become a device with which to conceal from oneself and from others the true character of one's faith.[64] Wieman and Kaplan sought to specify the distinguishing characteristics of God. For Wieman, the word *God* refers to a kind of communication —"the kind which creates appreciative understanding of the individuality of persons and peoples when they allow it to operate in their lives, creating society, sustaining all these in their being and increasing the values in them, when required conditions are present. This operative presence creates in each individual his capacity to love and appreciate and understand the individuality of others."[65] Such communication occurs between persons all the time to some degree. But to be radically transforming, it must rise to a high level and overcome the counterprocesses that ordinarily obstruct and suppress it. When such communication rises to a level of power and dominance, it endows life with all of its great values.[66]

God is the process of creative good or creativity which, in the form of creative interchange and internal integration, operates to transform human life in a way that it could not do by itself. It delivers human life from evil and conveys it to the greatest good human life can ever attain.[67] Wieman insisted that God can never be a person or a personality. "It is a logical fallacy to call God a person if any of his essential powers are different in kind from those essential to, and definitive of, the human being. This is so because the established meaning of the word 'personality' is to designate the characteristics which are distinctive and essential to the human being."[68] There is a creativity that personality may undergo but not perform. It is this creativity that progressively creates personality through community. "Either God exercises the power of creativity progressively creating personality, in which case he cannot be a personality because he is then exercising the creativity no person can exercise but can only undergo; or else, if he is a personality he is himself a creature of this creativity. A God who is a creature of an ontologically prior creativity is properly called an idol."[69]

Creative interchange can be readily observed in the growth of young children, where it creates mind, personality, and, through "symbolized meanings," a community with others.[70] It is in the form of symbolized meanings conveyed by language that values reach the human mind. Language may be distinguished from the signs to which lower animals respond by its ability to carry symbolized meanings that can expand indefinitely in terms of values, knowledge, skills, and power.[71] Creative interchange may be said to create the universe, since it makes possible whatever experience of the universe people can have. "It creates the human mind and in that way creates the world relative to the human mind."[72] Because it creates us and sustains us at the human level and gives us all the values human beings can have, creative interchange is the one basic and most precious good all human beings share.[73]

To Kaplan, nature's God, or Godhood, is identical with the totality of creative processes in man and nature that make for self-transcendence and self-perfection.[74] "Divinity is that aspect of the whole of nature, both in the universe and in man, which impels mankind to create a better and happier world and every individual to make the most of his own life."[75] God is "the functioning in nature of the eternally creative process, which, by bringing order out of chaos and good out of evil, actuates man to self-fulfillment."[76]

Kaplan sought to divorce the God-idea from mythology, anthropomorphism, and supernaturalism and to identify it with "all human conduct that strives for the creative survival of the human species in a warless world."[77] Since we can now understand the moral aspect of social existence that impels us to fulfill ourselves as human beings, we can freely reject the supernatural elements of traditional religion.[78] We can find God in the urge to truth, honesty, empathy, loyalty, justice, freedom, and good will.[79] Religion must be purged of (1) "an attitude of credulity which renders the mind susceptible to irrational and superstitious beliefs in luck, fate or sinister consequences"; (2) "the belief that salvation is the exclusive prerogative of one's own religion"; (3) "intellectual fixation on some past stage in the history of one's religion as one of divine revelation, and the nostalgic hope for a return to that period"; (4) "inability to think of God in any but anthropomorphic or authropopathic terms"; (5) "inability to identify divinity with the natural processes of body or mind"; (6) "belief in divine reward and punishment not only for social sins but also for ritual transgressions and unbelief"; (7) "otherworldliness, or the assumption that man cannot possibly achieve his destiny in the world"; (8) "the dichotomy of body and soul as a rationale for asceticism which is pleasing to God"; (9) "abnormal mysticism which is a perversion of normal mysticism."[80]

Although Kaplan emphasized moral responsibility and conscience as the principal manifestations of Godhood in human life, he sought to prove that ethical traits are the subjective expressions of objective processes in nature. "The theory of reciprocal responsibility is the conscious human manifestation of the principle whereby everything in nature is both cause and effect of everything else. It corresponds with the universal law of polarity whereby everything in the universe, from the minutest electron to the vastest star, is both self-active and interactive, independent and interdependent."[81] "The cosmic process of universal reciprocity outside the human mind comes to be God only when it is experienced as cosmic interdependence, and, in the world, as moral responsibility."[82] Human nature is an extension of cosmic processes while conscience, which dictates to man what he should do and induces remorse for failure, is actually the "semi-conscious intellectual effort to experience Divinity without recourse to anthropomorphic terms, rational propositions or mystic ecstasy."[83]

Kaplan stressed the significance of group, or public, religion as essentially an expression of response to human needs. Group religion is an aspect of wisdom or the concern with value and as such responds to the need to be needed. The need to be needed is identical with the need to transcend oneself, or to experience the holiness of life. Transcendence, or holiness, is actually the human equivalent of what in nature is known as organicity, or the process by which anything is more than the sum of its parts. God is the incremental plus of organic human society. "The process of organicity, functioning *self-consciously* in organic human societies, is God as the power that makes for salvation."[84] The God of Israel "represents the power of salvation which the collective self-consciousness generates by means of its organic function, and which is inherently akin to that which makes the cosmos or nature as a whole, possible."[85]

To Kaplan, the idea of God is a correlate of the idea of salvation or self-fulfillment. It reflects awareness of the organicity of the universe and assumes that there is enough in the world to meet men's needs but not enough to satiate their lusts and greeds.[86] Historically, the term *god* denoted any value or good that answered a need. "The unique God denotes the fulfillment of all human needs."[87] Such fulfillment depends on the functioning of conscience and moral responsibility. Religion is not a response to an intellectual need but to the human need to be needed. "It is not a matter of reflection but a matter of responsibility."[88] The term *God* is not a substantive but a functional noun denoting something exceptional and therefore transcendental or transnatural. It denotes the experience of holiness, which is related to the functioning of conscience.[89]

Both Wieman and Kaplan grappled significantly with the problem of evil. By denying the traditional conception of divine omnipotence, they were able to rescue divine beneficence without resorting to, and glorifying in, paradox. Wieman stated unequivocally that although creativity creates mind, culture, and history, it does not create the monstrous evils in the world. Evil results from counterprocesses and obstructions to creativity.[90] Creative interchange creates all the positive values of human existence, but the self-destructive processes result from what obstructs creativity and operates in opposition to it.[91] Most importantly, whatever evil exists, people can always choose between better or worse. The responsibility to know what is better and to commit oneself to it devolves upon all of us. "Whether the good is mighty or weak over against the evil, it is the best there is and blessedness is found in living for it even in error and defeat."[92]

For Kaplan, evil was religion's worst quandary and the source of its crisis in the modern world. Theology's attempt to understand evil intellectually and to resign people to it actually contributes to the worsening of the human situation. Religion is too preoccupied with justifying "God's ways" and with preaching resignation, instead of actively seeking an end to exploitation and war. The various attempts to account for evil are erroneous because they derive from the incorrect notion that God is a being like man. For Kaplan, insofar as Godhood is the correlate of humanity's efforts to improve human life, God is a process. The creativity manifest in human responsibility, integrity, and loyalty or love constitutes the Godhood or divinity of the cosmos. This perspective shifts attention from metaphysical speculation to man's inhumanity to man.[93] "If God, conceived as function, denotes whatever is of ultimate value to mankind, he cannot be represented as a personal Being infinite in power and goodness, which is a contradiction in terms."[94] Theodicies that attempt to justify God's ways are meaningless and replete with inconsistencies. "Nature is infinite chaos, with all its evils forever being vanquished by creativity, which is God as infinite goodness. . . . The power of God is inexhaustible but not infinite."[95] Kaplan's position was based on his analysis of the empirically verifiable functioning of conscience. The function of conscience, the "pain of the human spirit," is not to promote speculation about

God or reconcile humanity to man-made evil but to eliminate the causes of such evil and help bring about God's kingdom on earth. Conscience is thus also the revelation of God in the human spirit.[96]

Kaplan and Wieman gave a great deal of thought to the practical aspects of religion and especially to religious education and worship. Kaplan spoke of the creative expansion of Torah based on a conception of this-worldly salvation. It would have to deal, from the standpoint of ethics and religion, "with all those higher needs of the human spirit which have come to be better understood by reason of the general advances in the knowledge of human nature."[97] The primary purpose of education should be to get people to want only what they absolutely need physically, socially, and spiritually. As a lifelong process, Jewish education should deal with the subject of ecology and include topics such as the elimination of war, ethical nationhood, and individual freedom.[98] Kaplan was disturbed by the fact that present-day organized Jewish life gives little encouragement to the consideration of religion from an intellectual point of view. It is, therefore, necessary to stimulate interest in such problems as are dealt with in theology and philosophy of religion and to cultivate religion as an integral element in human culture.[99]

In order for Jewish education to be a source of self-fulfillment, it has to deal with the fact that the human mind evolves, as people's needs multiply and means are found to satisfy those needs. Religious traditions must, therefore, be transmitted not in their own terms but in terms that make them contemporaneous and subject to the process of conscious, ongoing interpretation.[100] Moreover, "the Jew as an individual must reckon with his individuality, with a sense of freedom which he must not renounce nor even play down. He must insist upon his right to do his own thinking and to refuse to be brainwashed." Jewish education should emphasize wisdom rather than faith, since "the very nature of religion and God can be demonstrated as having greater validity in terms of human experience, instead of in terms of faith, which is experience by proxy."[101]

Wieman stressed the need to understand religion not only as a set of answers but also as a question or problem that is part of the totality of human life and that we may not escape even if we reject all answers thus far given. Religion must, therefore, be taught in the same way that every other subject is taught.[102] The Bible, for example, must be approached neither as a book of answers to religious questions nor as literature but as a book of inquiry containing the history of a religiously gifted people. Answers found in the Bible should be treated as incomplete and subject to correction.[103] The problem of religion should be viewed both in its social context and as internal to individual personality.[104]

Wieman wrote that "empirical theology opens the way for hope, because it can show that if creativity and its demands are studied and searched, and if its demands are accepted, it can and will transform human life toward the greater and deeper satisfactions of life and save man from self-destruction and from the mechanization of life which occurs when action is not inspired and guided by appreciation of individuality. . . . Creativity at the human level operates as people learn from one another and then are transformed by the unconscious integration in each individual of what he gets from others."[105] Mutual learning takes place on the superficial level of knowledge, skills, and techniques, as well as on the deeper level of creative interchange. Such mutual learning in depth, "creative interchange which creates appreciative understanding at the deeper levels, must itself become our ruling loyalty and dominant motivation."[106]

Kaplan believed that worship fulfills essential needs of human nature by affirming the meaning of life and the primacy of moral and spiritual values and by giving reality, purpose, and self-consciousness to the collective spirit of a people. It provides a glimpse into the unity, creativity, and worthwhileness of life.[107] According to him, "prayer aims at deriving from the Process that constitutes God, the power that would strengthen the forces and relationships by which we fulfill ourselves as persons."[108] Nevertheless, Kaplan advocated emphasizing the study rather than the prayer element in worship. Worship, he felt, should be used to study God's laws in nature and in human life.[109]

The deep personal needs of the religious man, according to Wieman, are for "salvation and transformation, for deep communion and appreciative understanding, for answered prayer and the kingdom of love. . . . It can be demonstrated how creativity meets these needs; it cannot be demonstrated how a supernatural person and

almighty power does so."[110] The purpose of worship is to keep the
religious problem in the forefront of human life.[111] In prayer we
attempt to renew and deepen our commitment and to submit ourselves more completely to the direction and control of what can
creatively transform us.[112] When one worships profoundly and sincerely, with his or her personality organized around a prayer, the
prayer becomes an ingredient in the experience of creative interchange and transformation. "The outcome of this creative transformation will have a character it would not have if this petition had
not been an ingredient in the total process of creativity. In this way
prayer can be truly effective in producing consequences."[113] Thus,
prayer may be defined as "that voluntarily established attitude of
the personality which enables connections of value to grow far
beyond the scope of ordinary instrumentalities of consciousness"
and "enables the work of God to go on more abundantly and
blessedly."[114]

Wieman and Kaplan did not fail to apply their approaches to the
attitudes of their respective religions to other faiths. "The value of
the Christian message," said Wieman, "lies in what it can contribute to promoting creative interchange between parent and child,
husband and wife, human associations of all kinds, cultures and
peoples. When not applied to human living in this way, the Christian message becomes a tyranny of dogma, a barrier to creative
interchange, and source of great evil, as history demonstrates."[115]
Diverse temperaments, traditions, and regional interests require different forms of religion. The different forms of religion need not be
reduced to one form only. But if conflicting interests are to be
brought into greater interdependence, the various forms of religion
must have a ruling commitment to a creative interchange that can
bring conflicts under control.[116]

Kaplan wrote of the sancta of a people or church as the persons,
events, texts, places, and so on, through which it helps those who
belong to it achieve salvation. The sancta of each people or church
naturally mean more to its members than those of any other group.
Whether the sancta of one group are more ethical or spiritual than
the sancta of another is beside the point. "The fact is that such
comparison is not only odious but unwarranted, because the sancta
of no religion or civilization are so fixed or static as to be incapable

of development and revaluation."[117] Since every religion aspires to be a means of salvation to its own people or church, the assumption that one's own religion is the only religion is obsolete. No religion can be absolutely more or less true than another. "Though, at some particular time or place, one religion may be more helpful to its own adherents than another religion is to the adherents of that religion, that condition may be reversed before long."[118] Each religion exists in its own right and has no need to justify itself by asserting its superiority over other religions. "If a devout Christian tells me that he finds in the adoration of the personality of Jesus all the inspiration that he requires for living a life that satisfies his spiritual needs, I cannot as a Jew say this attitude is not true, although I am so conditioned that I could not possibly find it true in my own experience. On the other hand, If I say to him that I can find in the Torah literature of the Jew the reflection of an attitude toward life more satisfying than any I could find in the New Testament or elsewhere, I, too, am speaking the truth, and my religion is as true as his."[119] Each religion exists in its own right and should not have to justify its existence by any assertion of superiority.

Thus, for both Kaplan and Wieman the future of interfaith goodwill depends on something other than tolerance between groups. The way to deal with diversity is for each faith to heed the voice of conscience and the dictates of moral responsibility, and to relate to other faiths in the spirit of creative intercommunication and mutual learning in depth. It is a tribute to the diversity and openness of American society that these two religious thinkers of diverse traditions could not only come to know and appreciate each other's work but to publicly acknowledge their mutual admiration and respect. Kaplan was a diligent student of Wieman's writings and recommended them to his students. In the classes in philosophy of religion that he taught at the Jewish Theological Seminary, he sometimes utilized Wieman's books as texts. Wieman, for his part, said that he was certain that Kaplan's thought was on the right track and that, sooner or later, the dominant form of religion by which people find salvation would be developed along the lines indicated by Kaplan.[120]

The ideological convergence of the Judaism of Mordecai M. Kaplan and the Christianity of Henry Nelson Wieman constitutes a significant development in American religious thought. The two thinkers remained remarkably loyal to the presuppositions of modernist liberalism during careers that extended beyond the emergence of crisis theology, neo-Orthodoxy, existentialism, and the death-of-God theology. While their thoughts continued to evolve and to absorb insights from new developments in philosophy and the social sciences, the two thinkers remained firmly rooted in the basic outlooks they developed quite early in their careers. Refusing to succumb to despair about human nature and the possibility of progress, they continued to affirm the interdependence of religion and culture and to require of their respective faiths both intellectual honesty and moral action consonant with belief.[121] In the tradition of a significant sector of American religious thinking, they were "free theologians" seeking both self-understanding and insight into the issues of their day through creative thinking about God.[122] They grappled critically and imaginatively with human experience so that it might provide new religious vision and hope. Such reflection has often played a unifying and constructive role in the history of religion. The ideologies of Kaplan and Wieman may indeed play such a role in the future.

Notes

1. Mordecai M. Kaplan, "The Way I Have Come," in *Mordecai M. Kaplan: An Evaluation*, ed. I. Eisenstein and E. Kohn (New York: Jewish Reconstructionist Foundation, 1952), 287.
2. Mordecai M. Kaplan, "The Influences that Have Shaped My Life," *Reconstructionist* 8, no. 10 (June 1942): 30.
3. Henry Nelson Wieman, "Intellectual Autobiography," in *The Empirical Theology of Henry Nelson Wieman*, ed. R. W. Bretall (New York: MacMillan, 1963), 6.
4. Henry Nelson Wieman, "Theocentric Religion," in *Contemporary American Theology*, vol. 1, ed. V. Ferm (New York: Round Table Press, 1932), 340.
5. Kaplan, "Influences," 29.
6. Wieman, "Theocentric Religion," 342.
7. Ibid., 341.
8. Kaplan, "The Way I Have Come," 287.
9. Wieman, "Theocentric Religion," 343f; cf. James C. Livingston, *Mod-*

ern Christian Thought From the Enlightenment to Vatican II (New York: Macmillan, 1971), 429.

10. Mordecai M. Kaplan, *The Greater Judaism in the Making* (New York: Reconstructionist Press, 1960), 353.

11. Sidney E. Ahlstrom, *A Religious History of the American People* (New Haven: Yale University Press, 1983), 783.

12. Kenneth Cauthen, *The Impact of American Religious Liberalism* (New York: Harper & Row, 1962), 25.

13. Ahlstrom, *Religious History*, 782f.

14. Cauthen, *American Religious Liberalism*, 29.

15. William R. Hutchison, *The Modernist Impulse in American Prostestantism* (Cambridge: Harvard University Press, 1976) 2.

16. Ibid.

17. Mordecai M. Kaplan, *Judaism as a Civilization* (New York: Macmillan, 1934), 115.

18. Mordecai M. Kaplan, "The Future of Judaism," *Menorah Journal* 2, no. 3 (June 1916): 169.

19. Henry Nelson Wieman [with Walter M. Horton], *The Growth of Religion* (Chicago: Willet, Clark, 1938), 248.

20. Henry Nelson Wieman, "Neo-Orthodoxy and Contemporary Religious Reaction," in *Religious Liberals Reply*, ed. H. N. Wieman et al. (Boston: Beacon Press, 1947), 6f.

21. Henry Nelson Wieman, *The Issues of Life* (New York: Abingdon Press, 1930), 168f; cf. idem, "Theocentric Religion," 346.

22. Mordecai M. Kaplan, *Questions Jews Ask: Reconstructionist Answers* (New York: Reconstructionist Press, 1956), 443.

23. Henry Nelson Wieman, *Intellectual Foundation of Faith* (New York: Philosophical Library, 1961), 2.

24. Ibid., 2, 201.

25. Wieman, *Growth of Religion*, 251.

26. Wieman, *Issues of Life*, 163.

27. Mordecai M. Kaplan, *The Meaning of God in Modern Jewish Religion* (New York: Behrman's Jewish Book House, 1937), 245.

28. Mordecai M. Kaplan, *The Future of the American Jew* (New York: Macmillan, 1948), 193.

29. Kaplan, *Questions Jews Ask*, 95.

30. Ibid.

31. Henry Nelson Wieman, *The Directive in History* (Boston: Beacon Press, 1949), 59.

32. James A. Martin, Jr., *Empirical Philosophies of Religion* (New York: King's Crown Press, 1945), 2.

33. Daniel D. Williams, "Wieman as a Christian Theologian," in *Empirical Theology of Henry Nelson Wieman*, ed. R. W. Bretall (see n. 3), 79.

34. Kaplan, *Future of the American Jew*, 210.

35. Kaplan, *Judaism as a Civilization*, 382.

36. Mordecai M. Kaplan, *The Religion of Ethical Nationhood* (New York: Macmillan, 1970), 66.

37. Charles Hartshorne, "Introduction," in *Philosophers of Process*, ed. D. Browning (New York: Random House, 1965), v; cf. James R. Gray, *Modern Process Thought* (Washington, D.C.: University Press of America, 1982), xi.

38. Bernard E. Loomer, "Wieman's Stature as a Contemporary Theologian," in *Empirical Theology of Henry Nelson Wieman*, ed. R. W. Bretall (see n. 3), 395.

39. Wieman, *Growth of Religion*, 347.

40. Kaplan, *Questions Jews Ask*, 103.

41. Edgar S. Brightman, *A Philosophy of Religion* (Englewood Cliffs, N.J.: Prentice-Hall, 1940), 86.

42. Kaplan, *Religion of Ethical Nationhood*, 48.

43. Ibid., 23.

44. Martin, *Empirical Philosophies*, 6.

45. Wieman, *Growth of Religion*, 267.

46. Henry Nelson Wieman, *The Source of Human Good* (Chicago: Chicago University Press, 1946), 39.

47. John E. Smith, "Philosophy of Religion," in *Religion*, ed. P. Ramsey (Englewood Cliffs, N.J.: Prentice-Hall, 1965), 380.

48. Henry Nelson Wieman, *The Wrestle of Religion with Truth* (New York: Macmillan, 1927), 123f.

49. Henry Nelson Wieman [with R. W. Wieman], *Normative Psychology of Religion* (New York: Crowell, 1935), 99f.

50. Ibid., 171.

51. Ibid., 172.

52. Wieman, *Intellectual Foundation of Faith*, 169.

53. Ibid., 80.

54. Ibid., 7f.

55. Kaplan, *Future of the American Jew*, 172.

56. Kaplan, *Religion of Ethical Nationhood*, 21.

57. Mordecai M. Kaplan, "Religion in a New Key," *Reconstructionist* 26, no. 1 (February 1960): 17.

58. Kaplan, *Questions Jews Ask*, 126.

59. Ibid., 480.

60. Kaplan, "Religion in a New Key," 18.

61. Kaplan, *Religion of Ethical Nationhood*, 49.

62. Mordecai M. Kaplan, *If Not Now, When? Toward a Reconstruction of the Jewish People: Conversations between Mordecai M. Kaplan and Arthur A. Cohen* (New York: Schocken, 1973), 80.

63. Kaplan, *Future of the American Jew*, 206.

64. Wieman, *Intellectual Foundation of Faith*, 47.

65. Ibid., 52.

66. Ibid., 55.

67. Ibid., 53.
68. Ibid., 58.
69. Ibid., 66.
70. Henry Nelson Wieman, "Appendix," in *Creative Interchange*, ed. J. A. Broyer and W. S. Minor (Carbondale: Southern Illinois University Press, 1982), 447.
71. Ibid., 447.
72. Henry Nelson Wieman, *Man's Ultimate Commitment* (Carbondale: Southern Illinois University Press, 1958), 31.
73. Wieman, "Appendix," 447.
74. Kaplan, *Religion of Ethical Nationhood*, 109.
75. Ibid., 75.
76. Ibid., 10.
77. Ibid., 82.
78. Ibid., 70.
79. Mordecai M. Kaplan, "Between Two Worlds," in *Varieties of Jewish Belief*, ed. I. Eisenstein (New York: Reconstructionist Press, 1966), 141.
80. Kaplan, *Religion of Ethical Nationhood*, 86f.
81. Ibid., 34f.
82. Ibid., 48.
83. Ibid., 71.
84. Kaplan, *If Not Now, When?* 38.
85. Mordecai M. Kaplan, "Our God as Our Collective Conscience," *Reconstructionist* 41, no. 1 (February 1975): 14.
86. Kaplan, *If Not Now, When?* 14.
87. Ibid., 79.
88. Ibid., 119.
89. Ibid., 89.
90. Wieman, "Appendix," 446.
91. Ibid., 446.
92. Wieman, *Intellectual Foundation of Faith*, 120f; cf. David Wesley Soper, *Men Who Shape Belief* (Philadelphia: The Westminster Press, 1955) 190.
93. Mordecai M. Kaplan, "The Unresolved Problem of Evil," *Reconstructionist* 29, no. 7 (May 1963): 6–11; ibid., 29, no. 8 (May 1963): 11–16.
94. Kaplan, *Religion of Ethical Nationhood*, 51.
95. Ibid.
96. Kaplan, "Unresolved Problem of Evil," 15.
97. Kaplan, *Questions Jews Ask*, 389.
98. Mordecai M. Kaplan, "What is Jewish Consciousness?" *Reconstructionist* 38, no. 6 (September 1972): 11.
99. Kaplan, *Future of the American Jew*, 166f.
100. Kaplan, *If Not Now, When?* 98.
101. Ibid., 55, 96.

102. Wieman, *Man's Ultimate Commitment*, 196.

103. Ibid., 200.

104. Wieman, *Intellectual Foundation of Faith*, 181.

105. Henry Nelson Wieman, "Reply to Williams," in *The Emperical Theology of Henry Nelson Wieman*, ed. R. W. Bretall, (see n. 3) 102.

106. Ibid., 104.

107. Kaplan, *Judaism as a Civilization*, 347.

108. Kaplan, *Questions Jews Ask*, 104.

109. Mordecai M. Kaplan, *Not So Random Thoughts* (New York: Reconstructionist Press, 1966), 210.

110. Wieman, *Man's Ultimate Commitment*, 178.

111. Wieman, *Intellectual Foundation of Faith*, 21.

112. Ibid., 71.

113. Ibid., 77f.

114. Wieman, *Growth of Religion*, 380.

115. Henry Nelson Wieman, *Religious Inquiry* (Boston: Beacon Press, 1968), 21.

116. Ibid., 33f.

117. Mordecai M. Kaplan, *Judaism without Supernaturalism* (New York: Reconstructionist Press, 1958), 74.

118. Ibid., 75.

119. Mordecai M. Kaplan, *Judaism in Transition* (New York: Covici-Friede, 1936), 282.

120. Henry Nelson Wieman, "Mordecai M. Kaplan's Idea of God," in *Mordecai M. Kaplan: An Evaluation*, ed. I. Eisenstein and E. Kohn (see n. 1), 210.

121. Cf. Hutchison, *Modernist Impulse*, 310.

122. Cf. Frederick Sontag and John K. Roth, *The American Religious Experience* (New York: Harper & Row, 1972), 340.

Ahad Ha-Am in Kaplan: Roads Crossing and Parting

Meir Ben-Horin

It is widely accepted that Kaplan was an Ahad Ha-Amian. Rabbi Samuel M. Blumenfield, who from 1954 to 1968 served as director of the Department of Education and Culture of the World Zionist Organization—American Section, coined the phrase the "Ahad Ha-Am of American Jewry."[1] In his tribute to Kaplan, Gerson D. Cohen, chancellor of the Jewish Theological Seminary of America, saw him, in part, as attempting "to articulate a new Zionism to America, a vision of Ahad Ha-Amism brought to these shores that spoke of aliyah as well as the continued creativity of the Diaspora."[2] Professor Arnold J. Band of UCLA linked Kaplan and Ahad Ha-Am, without a hint at qualification. In his contribution to a recent volume of essays on Ahad Ha-Am, he asserts that "Chaim Weizmann, David Ben-Gurion, Berl Katznelson, and Mordecai Kaplan turned to Ahad Ha-Am's writings for ideological support."[3] But another contributor to the same volume, Evyatar Friesel, who based his interpretation on an entry of 4 October 1914 in Kaplan's journal, leaves no doubt about the need to revise the blanket judgment. "Mordecai Kaplan," he comments, "clear-minded and skeptical, wrote in his diary in 1914 that the purest expression of Ahad Ha-Amism in America was the Bureau of Education of the Kehillah in New York. Led by Samson Benderly, the Bureau aimed to impart a national Jewish education, whose secularism Kaplan considered both wrong and futureless. Mordecai Kaplan kept those doubts about Ahad Ha-Amism to himself."[4] Broader in scope is Gideon Shimoni's recognition that while Kaplan's notion of the centrality of Zion in *Judaism as a Civilization* "brought him very close to Ahad Ha-Am's cultural Zionism," the difference between his view and Ahad Ha-Am's is "substantial." Kaplan's affirmation of the Diaspora went far beyond that of Ahad Ha-Am, "both in the religious orientation of his 'Reconstructionist' Judaism and in his insistence on the parallel value of a Diaspora Jewish life 'in two civilizations.' "[5]

Students of Kaplan's writings will not find it difficult to document his acknowledgment of Ahad Ha-Am's influence on his thinking. At the age of almost ninety, Kaplan in 1970 still held himself indebted to Ahad Ha-Am and, therefore, dedicated *The Religion of Ethical Nationhood*, published that year, not only to Schechter and Brandeis but, first of all, "to the memory of Ahad Ha-Am (Asher Ginzberg) who revealed to me the spiritual reality of the Jewish people." Some thirty years earlier, those who came to pay tribute to Kaplan on the occasion of his sixtieth birthday heard him reflect on his development as a loyal Jew: "As for myself, the Zionist movement and particularly the Ahad Ha-Amist conception of the Jewish people as a living organism, animated by an irresistible will to live, enabled me to find spiritual anchorage."[6] Some twenty-five years later, in an interview aired over CBS and published as "Reconstructionism in Brief," Kaplan spoke of the influences that determined his new conception of Judaism: "One was that of Ahad Ha-Am and the other was that of John Dewey. Ahad Ha-Am enabled me to shift the center of gravity in Judaism from theology to peoplehood. John Dewey taught me how to think straight on any subject."[7] Perhaps Kaplan's first reference to Ahad Ha-Am may be found under the date of 19 August 1905. That day Kaplan, age twenty-four, recorded in unpublished reflections entitled "Communings with the Spirit" his conviction that "Achad Ha-Am's [sic] conception of nationality plus [Matthew] Arnold's interpretation of Israel's (ancient) genius for righteousness contain that which could form a positive expression of the Jewish spirit. All it wants, is definiteness and detail."[8]

However, even these few passages make it clear, explicitly or implicitly, that as far as Kaplan was concerned, Ahad Ha-Am needed to be supplemented. In some respects, Schechter, Brandeis, and Dewey, along with Henry Sidgwick[9] and Emile Durkheim,[10] led Kaplan along the path of his life. However, Arnold loomed larger than all the others combined, except the Jewish classics from the Bible to the present. Kaplan's declarations of indebtedness to Ahad Ha-Am were always, it seems, dogged by additions, reservations, criticisms, and outright rejection.

A text taken from Kaplan's journal documents this point effectively. In the summer of 1955, Kaplan reread Ahad Ha-Am for the purpose of defending him against a powerfully telling critique by Baruch Kurzweil.[11] In August 1955, Kaplan observed in a journal entry that the more he reread, the more he realized the extent of his indebtedness to Ahad Ha-Am:

Although I arrived at the idea of unity in diversity . . . on the basis of premises derived from my studies of the nature of religion, he deserves the credit for having started me thinking along lines that inevitably led to that conclusion. To my great surprise I came across in Vol. I of his essays the very same recognition of the principle of religious pluralism in Judaism. I am quite sure that when I first read those essays over forty years ago, that principle made little, if any, impression on me.[12]

But in the wake of this expression of dependence follows unequivocal criticism: "On further reflection I find myself not so sure that Ahad Ha-Am was altogether clear in his own mind as to what he meant by the will to live of the Jewish people." In his initial essay, Ahad Ha-Am says that, with the assumption of individual reward and punishment and belief in the world to come, "the Jews lost the collective will to live. How does that jibe with his thesis that Jewish survival was made possible by the extraordinary will to live of the Jews as a people?" To be consistent, he should have "treated the idea of God as that onto which the Jews projected their collective will to live."[13] This collective quality of the Jewish will to live was never lost in the concepts of *Kiddush ha-Shem* and *Hillul ha-Shem* (sanctification and desecration of the holy name).

The following day Kaplan was still preoccupied with Ahad Ha-Am. Although disappointed by another find, Kaplan's language now is not only vigorous but virtually gleeful, like that of anyone making a pleasurable discovery:

I am quite disillusioned to find that Ahad Ha-Am, too, has his Achilles heel. I have found it in his essay "Divre Shalom [words of peace]" where, at one time, to use a pugilistic analogy, he slugs away wildly, and, at another time, pulls his punches. An example of the first tactic is his statement that "religion is genuinely such only when its adherents believe in its divine origin." An example of the second tactic is his saying that to speak of reforming a religion is to utter a paradox like speaking of freezing fire.[14]

With regard to the first assumption, Kaplan credits Ahad Ha-Am with sincerity,

but I question his sincerity with regard to the assumption that religion admits only of unconscious change. His reasoning on that point in that essay is nothing less than sophistry. . . . What he recommends coincides with the paradoxical position of the majority opinion in the Conservative movement, namely, a conscious effort to act unconsciously in the matter of Jewish law.[15]

This criticism notwithstanding, Kaplan published his apologia of Ahad Ha-Am which, incidentally, required three or four drafts.

There can be no question, then, about Kaplan's preoccupation with Ahad Ha-Am and, indeed, about his discipleship. Nor can it be denied that criticism, disavowal, and outright disapproval pervade Kaplan's passages that deal with Ahad Ha-Am. Convergences commingle with sharp dissent. The overall impression is one of ambivalence or, positively, of dependence against the background of intellectual independence. Characteristic of Kaplan's discipleship is his supervening self-emancipation from all his masters, including tradition itself, along with an ongoing attachment to them in bonds of gratitude and affection. This is true of his relationship with Conservative Judaism and the Seminary; it is true also of his relationship with Martin Buber.[16]

By way of further documentation, this paper will show Kaplan's independence and distance from Ahad Ha-Am by comparing what the two thinkers have to say about a third—Moses Mendelssohn.

The locus classicus in Ahad Ha-Am's writings appears in the short essay "Dor Tahpukhot" (Age of transformation), the title of a monograph by Simon Bernfeld (1897).[17] Minor reservations notwithstanding, Ahad Ha-Am was pleased with his friend's work on Mendelssohn's times because it offers an objective view of the controversial German-Jewish sage. Enough time, Ahad Ha-Am noted, had elapsed so that an unbiased judgment on Mendelssohn's place in history was possible. Mendelssohn need not be seen as a hero in Thomas Carlyle's sense, as a maker of history, a "great man," or a kind of "divinity" that creates his epoch in his image. Nor does he have to be seen as a sort of demon who came to destroy the world and was the source of all evil. Along with other "heroes" who were neither world builders nor world destroyers but rather ordinary folk, "with traits good and bad and with limited power," Mendelssohn could be recognized for what he really was: neither a Moses nor a messiah nor a traitor but a common man. Ahad Ha-Am offered this assessment:

One of these imaginary heroes . . . was Rabbi Moses Mendelssohn—that dear and honest man who never sought to achieve greatness and who was not capable of greatness. Had he lived some generations earlier, in Italy or in Holland, his name would now be known and honored as one of the Jewish sages who wrote scholarly books, such as YaShaR of Candia [Joseph Solomon Delmedigo, 1591–1655] or Rabbi Manasseh ben-Israel [1604–1657], and not more. But his time and place brought it about, without any intention or effort on his part, that he should become a tall figure surrounded by men of action of his times. Thus the entire revolution which commenced in his lifetime and continued long after his death was named after him, despite the fact that actually his role in it was at most "like a chip of the beam." And so the RaMBeMaN [Rabbi Mosheh Ben Menahem—Mendelssohn's acronym] first became a savior angel, a second (or third) Moses. . . . Then, with the rise of the reaction against those generations, he became the demon of demons, a betrayer of his people and a "troubler of Israel." This despite the fact that he was neither one nor the other but rather a gentle and sensitive soul, replete with knowledge and good taste but also weak, devoid of any ambition and capacity for great deeds, for reforming the world, for destroying or building up.[18]

In his letter of 4 May 1897 to Bernfeld, Ahad Ha-Am thanked the author for "Dor Tahpukhot" and observed that "you are the first in our literature to return to Mendelssohn his true character: not one of the divinities nor the demon of demons . . . but a simple, thoughtful, and talented human being."[19]

Kaplan took Mendelssohn more seriously. To be sure, he did not accept his Orthodoxy. Nor did he think that Mendelssohn had found the solution to the conflict between faith and reason: "Though uncommonly gifted as a thinker and writer, [Mendelssohn] was unable to achieve a satisfactory ideological adjustment between traditional Judaism and the European secular culture of which he was a leading spokesman." Mendelssohn was, in fact, less successful in reconciling his Judaism with his own rationalistic world outlook "than the medieval Jewish theologians had been in their attempt to resolve the conflict between Jewish tradition and Greek philosophy."[20] Mendelssohn's idea that Judaism knows no dogmas is entirely inconsistent with his avowal of faith in the Torah's supernatural origin. Hence, he cannot be regarded as the father of modern Reform Judaism.[21] Yet, we have in him "the first representative Jew" of the Enlightenment, which "constituted a more adventurous reliance upon reason and experience and a more daring revolt against political and religious authoritarianism than mankind had ever known. The revolt against the political regime prepared the way for modern nationalism and, incidentally, for the Jewish emancipation."[22] But whether consistent or not with Mendelssohn's idea that Judaism had no dogmas, "Jewish religion unquestionably turned a new corner." By thus identifying loyalty to Judaism with action rather than with thought, Mendelssohn "provided those Jews for whom the traditional creed [of Maimonides] had become irksome the release they were seeking."[23]

Kaplan believed that Mendelssohn was impelled by "a deeply felt, though unformulated, urge to reconstruct Judaism, to readjust it to the needs of a newer day, which he was the first in Jewry to experience."[24] Mendelssohn legitimized the dictates of reason, but he failed to show how these could be synthesized with the laws of the Torah. He recognized the Torah as legislation revealed for the Jewish people at Sinai, but he regarded the universal religion of reason and righteousness as not revealed. To say that Judaism has no dogmas, therefore, amounted to saying that "henceforth Judaism should not be expected to function as a means to other-worldly salvation. It should function as the Jews' way of life in this world."

In the words of Eva Jospe,

Despite these reflections [on salvation in the beyond], Mendelssohn was less interested in purely theoretical speculation, with its esoteric abstractions, than in a practical philosophy with its potential for guiding men toward a purposefully lived, hence "happy" life. And this, in turn, motivated him "to search for truth, to love beauty, to desire the good, to do the best." Subsequently, he looked among the existing philosophical systems for the one whose *Weltweisheit* could be turned into *Lebensweisheit*, a set of values by which to live and to become what men were meant to be: enlightenedly humane, hence genuinely human.[25]

Ahad Ha-Am dismissed Mendelssohn as just another distinguished scholar or sage, distinguished but not particularly unusual or rare. His language in the cited passage borders on the sarcastic and certainly deposes Mendelssohn from any pedestal on which he might have been placed. To Ahad Ha-Am, Mendelssohn was not a minor prophet of Ahad Ha-Amian culturalist secularism, ethical nationalism, and "spiritual center" Zionism. Perhaps it is not unreasonable to surmise that Mendelssohn's Orthodoxy made him in Ahad Ha-Am's eyes merge with earlier Orthodox rabbis, so as to become almost indistinguishable from their multitude. By contrast, the very same Orthodoxy in practice did not prevent Kaplan from acknowledging Mendelssohn's contribution to Jewish intellectual emancipation. It did not keep him from embracing Mendelssohn as a forerunner of his own efforts at reconstructing Judaism. Ahad Ha-Am made no contribution to Jewish religious renascence. Dogmatic secularist that he was, he could not see that others wrestling with this issue might achieve at least a small measure of success. For Kaplan, on the other hand, struggling with the meaning of God constituted the supreme task and the supreme opportunity of life, particularly of Jewish life. A majority of his journal entries may be compared to a painter's, sculptor's, or composer's preliminary sketches— the artist's tentative trials and errors, his toyings, as it were, with images and ideas that gained possession of his mind. Hence, Kaplan was able to accept Mendelssohn as a a teacher and a fellow wrestler with the idea of God, and he could do so with a sense of gratitude and in full independence. In Ahad Ha-Am as well, he could see a teacher and a fellow wrestler with the meaning of Judaism in the modern world, and he did so with a sense of reverence and in full independence.

Some elements of Ahad Ha-Amist thinking were readily absorbed into the complex of Kaplan's religious philosophy. Among these must be counted the centrality in Judaism of Jewish peoplehood; the notion of the Jewish people as the creator of Jewish culture and especially of Hebrew literature; the emphasis on the renewal of the Jewish people's creativity in all spheres of modern culture; the revival of Hebrew as the Jewish national, historic language; and the reeducation of the Jewish people for survival in the modern world. Above all, and not always sufficiently noted, is the adoption by Kaplan of Ahad Ha-Am's "method."

The greatest compliment Kaplan paid Ahad Ha-Am came, I believe, not in the dedication of *The Religion of Ethical Nationhood* nor in the various expressions of general indebtedness but in his paper entitled "The God Idea in Judaism," which goes back to the mid-thirties.[26] In this essay, Kaplan formulated "the process of interpretation whereby the God idea of Jewish tradition might be transformed into a vital element in a modern Jewish ideology." The method wherewith to do this will be found "by analyzing the method whereby Ahad Ha-Am succeeds in proving that the Moses tradition can continue to function as a vital element in the modern Jewish consciousness."[27] "Much in our religious tradition" might be rendered "dynamic" by applying to it Ahad Ha-Am's procedure, in which four steps or "propositions" may be distinguished.

First, Moses is treated like Goethe's Werther. "The idea of Moses was much more of an efficient cause in Jewish life than if there had been an actual man by the name of Moses." (Kaplan does not here expressly deny the historicity of Moses.) Second, the Moses idea and its influence "implies that it answered to some deep urge in the nature of the Jewish people." This idea is "an uncompromising passion for righteousness." The proper inference to be drawn from this historic fact is "that in the inner life of the Jewish people at its best there asserted itself a love of justice and righteousness that was the first of its kind in human annals." Third, "this urge to righteousness is an extremely desirable tendency" and should be fostered in our time. Fourth, "it is advisable to have the idea Moses [sic] continue to figure in the Jewish consciousness as a means of lending moral momentum and sanction to the urge to righteousness."[28]

To Kaplan, the consequences for the traditional conception of God are clear. "If Moses is writ large over every page of the Pentateuch, . . . God is writ large over every page of our national literature." If one's purpose is to cultivate a Jewish consciousness, he cannot be ignored, "for God is one assumed reality which has occupied the focus of its attention ever since it has been in existence." But today many Jews opt for omitting him from consideration rather

than believing in the God of "the Jewish consciousness in its formative stage." Such omission is "unfortunate and hurtful to the future
of Judaism." It follows that to move toward a solution of this "inner
problem of Jewish life," the God idea must be treated "in the same
way as Ahad Ha-Am treats the idea of Moses." Kaplan, therefore,
proceeds to formulate four propositions that parallel Ahad Ha-Am's
four steps.

First, "even if in actual fact there did not exist such a being as
the God spoken of in the Jewish writings, there is no gainsaying the
fact that the conception of God has . . . been more active as an
efficient cause in the life of the Jewish people than any other single
idea or even group of ideas." Second, the God idea answered to some
"powerful urge in the soul of the Jewish people," namely, the universal urge "to salvation, or self-fulfillment, or living oneself out to
the full." The uniquely Jewish aspect of this urge to salvation is its
articulation "through the unshakable faith that the whole of existence is so conditioned as to make salvation attainable." This faith
is expressed in the "belief that God is one, the creator of the universe, and the lawgiver of mankind." Third, this faith is so important that it should be fostered "at all costs." Fourth, the God idea
will gradually come to refer not to "an entity identifiable by the
senses or the imagination, but [to] a conception which helps the
mind to hold together in organized fashion a nexus of truths about
the nature of reality, truths that give meaning and purpose to
human life."[29] God, ultimately, is "that Power in the world which
impels [human beings] to make it what it should be."[30]

In the mid-fifties, Kaplan had occasion to elaborate his idea that
Reconstructionism "is a *method*, rather than a series of affirmations
or conclusions concerning Jewish life or thought." It is "a method
of dealing with Judaism . . . as the sum of all those manifestations
of the Jewish people which are the result of its will to live and to
make the most of life."[31] The adoption of Ahad Ha-Am's method,
therefore, shows how important Ahad Ha-Am really was to Kaplan,
irrespective of particular agreements or disagreements or approval
or rejection. It is the centrality of method that remains the primary
ingredient in the crossing and the parting of the roads that bound
Kaplan to Ahad Ha-Am and that separated the two.

The final paragraph on Ahad Ha-Am in Kaplan's *The Greater*

Judaism in the Making speaks of this separation. Here, Kaplan regrets, rather sadly, that Ahad Ha-Am failed to appreciate Jewish religion as a strongly felt force and that he failed to search for "a deeper understanding of the belief in God." Because of this failure, Kaplan is convinced, Ahad Ha-Am fell short of attaining the status of a modern Maimonides, "guiding us out of our most troublesome perplexities."[32] Unwilling to leave the task unattended, Kaplan felt compelled to undertake it himself. In doing so he had to follow the method wherever it led him. The daring to do so and to persist in the effort despite great odds is also part of Ahad Ha-Am's legacy.

It is, perhaps, permissible to indulge in some speculation on the direction in which Ahad Ha-Am's thinking might have moved, beyond secularism, had he accepted Cyrus Adler's invitation to deliver at the Dropsie College for Hebrew and Cognate Learning in Philadelphia ten lectures on the history of Jewish ethics, or a subject related to it, during the academic term 1911–12 or in March or April 1912.[33] He might have met Kaplan and might have taken note of the younger man's evolving thought. Perhaps the possibility of understanding God in nonsupernaturalist terms might have evoked in him a favorable response. It is not beyond reason to speculate that he might have accepted the ideas that led to the creation by Kaplan of the Society for Jewish Renascence in 1920 and of the Society for the Advancement of Judaism in 1922. However, Ahad Ha-Am never came to Dropsie College and to the United States, and an exchange of indebtednesses never occurred; thus, all such posthistoric speculation is futile. It is safe to say that Kaplan, contrary to the opinions of some, was not an American Ahad Ha-Am.[34]

In conclusion, the reevaluation of Kaplan as a Jewish theologian must begin with the revision of an unqualified linkage with Ahad Ha-Am, who stands for Jewish nationalist secularism, along with a revised judgment of Kaplan's alleged naturalism, sociologism, pragmatism, and humanism. Elements of these entered into the much larger whole that is Kaplanism or transnaturalism. They are not, severally or collectively, coextensive with it. Moreover, a full appreciation of Kaplan's work must begin with a detailed study of his use of biblical, talmudic, and post-talmudic texts and what he made of all the Jewish sources he cited in his published works and his journal. These are the first and most important influences on the mind of this thinker who, above all, was and wanted to be known as a rabbi.

Notes

1. Samuel M. Blumenfield, "Mordecai M. Kaplan—Ahad Ha-Am of American Jewry," in *"Thou Shalt Teach": Selected Essays of Samuel M. Blumenfield*, ed. Judah Pilch (New York: Department of Education and Culture, World Zionist Organization—American Section, 1973), 174–82; see also idem, *Hevrah ve-Hinnukh be-Yahadut America* (Society and Education in American Jewry) (Jerusalem: M. Newman, 1965), 232–39.
2. Gershon D. Cohen, quoted in Reconstructionist 49, no. 9 (June 1984): 21.
3. Arnold J. Band, "The Ahad Ha-Am and Berdyczewski Polarity," in *At the Crossroads: Essays on Ahad Ha-Am*, ed. Jacques Kornberg (Albany: State University of New York Press, 1983), 58.
4. Evyatar Friesel, "Ahad Ha-Amism in American Zionist Thought," in *Essays on Ahad Ha-Am*, ed. Jacques Kornberg, (see n. 3) 138. Later, Kaplan certainly made no secret of his deviation from Ahad Ha-Am. For example, in *The Future of the American Jew* (New York: Macmillan, 1948), Kaplan distances himself from central ingredients of Ahad Ha-Am's cultural Zionism. Kaplan's language is blunt:

> Ahad Ha-Am's program for Eretz Yisrael, lacking the essential elements of large-scale immigration and international recognition, could not have developed Eretz Yisrael into a history-making center of Jewish life. Ahad Ha-Am has the correct intuition, when he envisaged Eretz Yisrael as a focal and integrating center of Jewish revival throughout the world, but he erred in his conception of the way that goal was to be attained. He put his faith in a hand-picked selection of highly qualified persons who . . . would choose to migrate to Eretz Yisrael in order to re-create there the Jewish civilization. However, history is not made in this way (132).

But already in *Judaism as a Civilization* (1934; reprint, New York: Thomas Yoseloff, 1957), he minced no words in rejecting a position Ahad Ha-Am had taken:

> With all due deference to Ahad Ha-Am, one cannot but regard as chimerical and unpsychologic his effort to bring about a renascence of the Jewish people by urging the substitution of loyalty and devotion to the Jewish national being in place of the individualistic yearning for personal salvation. . . . Once men have learned to reckon with the individual as an end rather than as a means in appraising the value of any social ideal or program, it is reactionary to ask the individual to sink back into his former subservience (282).

5. Gideon Shimoni, "Ideological Perspectives," in *Zionism in Transition*, ed. Moshe Davis (New York: Arno Press, 1980), 34. Alfred Gottschalk, in *"Ahad Ha-Am, the Bible, and the Bible Tradition"* (Ph.D. diss., University of Southern California, 1965 [photo-offset]), flatly states that "the Reconstructionist position in Jewish religious thought, barring its Americanism, is Ahad Ha-Amism." But he adds that Kaplan "goes beyond Ahad Ha-Am . . . in consciously urging a religious orientation to life, affirming the holiness of life and its supreme worth" (3ff.).
6. Kaplan, "The Influences that Have Shaped My Life," *Reconstructionist* 8, no. 10 (June 1942): 31.
7. Mordecai M. Kaplan, "Reconstructionism in Brief," *Jewish Spectator* 31, no. 7 (September 1966): 10. Curiously enough, he omitted Matthew Arnold (see n. 8).
8. See Meir Ben-Horin, "Defining God: Arnoldian Elements in Kaplan's Theology," *Jewish Social Studies* 43, nos. 3–4 (Summer-Fall 1981): 191.
9. See Kaplan's master's thesis, entitled "Ethical System of Henry Sidgwick," available in the Rare Books and Manuscript Library of Columbia University's Butler Library. The thesis, in longhand, was signed by Kaplan on 28 February 1902.
10. See Kaplan, *Judaism as a Civilization*, 307, 333f, where passages from Durkheim's *The Elementary Forms of the Religious Life* (1912) are cited. In 1971, in his first lecture at the Reconstructionist Rabbinical College in Philadelphia, Kaplan made this book required reading for his students.
11. Mordecai M. Kaplan, "Anti-Maimunism in Modern Dress—A Reply to Baruch Kurzweil's Attack on Ahad Ha-Am," *Judaism*, 4, no. 4 (Fall 1955): 303–12.
12. *Kaplan Journal*, 25 July 1955.
13. Ibid., 26 July 1955.
14. Ibid.
15. *Kaplan Journal*, 5 September 1955.
16. See Meir Ben-Horin, *Transnature's God: Studies in the Theology of Mordecai M. Kaplan*, (forthcoming), chap. 3, "Kaplan and Buber—Tensions and Harmonies."
17. Reprinted in *Kol Kitvey Ahad Ha-Am* (Ahad Ha-Am's collected writings) (Jerusalem: Hotsa'ah Ivrit, 1949), 268f.
18. Ibid., 269.
19. *Iggerot Ahad Ha-Am* (Ahad Ha-Am's letters), vol. 1 (1896–98) (Jerusalem-Berlin: Yavneh-Moriah, 1923), 87.
20. Mordecai M. Kaplan, *The Greater Judaism in the Making: A Study of the Modern Evolution of Judaism* (New York: Reconstructionist Press, 1960), 182.
21. Ibid., 190.
22. Ibid., 183.

23. Kaplan, *Future of the American Jew*, 245.
24. Mordecai M. Kaplan, *Judaism in Transition* (New York: Covici-Friede, 1936), 207.
25. Quoted in ibid., 231; see also Mordecai M. Kaplan, "The Place of Dogma in Judaism," in *Proceedings of the Rabbinical Assembly* vol. 4 (1933), 280–300.
26. Mordecai M. Kaplan, "The God Idea in Judaism," in *The Jewish Reconstructionist Papers*, ed. Mordecai M. Kaplan (New York: Behrman's Jewish Book House, 1936), 88–100.
27. Ibid., 88.
28. Ibid., 89f.
29. Ibid., 90–92.
30. Ibid., 99.
31. Mordecai M. Kaplan, *Questions Jews Ask: Reconstructionist Answers* (New York: Reconstructionist Press, 1956), 80f.
32. Kaplan, *Greater Judaism in the Making*, 431.
33. Meir Ben-Horin, "Cyrus Adler and Ahad Ha-Am Correspondence (1910–1913)," *The Seventy-fifth Anniversary Volume of the Jewish Quarterly Review* (Philadelphia: Jewish Quarterly Review, 1967), 47–59.
34. See Friesel, "Ahad Ha-Amism," 134. Friesel writes that the most important interpreter of Ahad Ha-Am among American Zionists was Israel Friedlaender.

CHAPTER 10

Kaplan, Abraham Joshua Heschel, and Martin Buber: Three Approaches to Jewish Revival

S. Daniel Breslauer

Modernity has forced a new agenda upon Jewish thinkers. While medieval Jewish philosophy sought to demonstrate the existence of God and the primacy of the Sinaitic revelation, modern Jews have investigated the meaning of religion for the human believer and the responsiveness of revelation to the needs of each Jew.[1] Reform Judaism, Jewish Orthodoxy, Zionism, and the Conservative movement in Judaism represent alternative modern responses to this challenge. Mordecai M. Kaplan's relationship to his contemporary theologians derives from his views of these options. In an optimistic statement, he affirms a "greater Judaism in the making" that will emerge "out of the welter of the four mutually conflicting versions of Judaism."[2] Kaplan's various writings, in diverse ways and with complex arguments, sketch out a programmatic agenda for that greater Judaism. The four alternative, "mutually conflicting" visions of Judaism must be taken seriously as points of departure for a new Jewish thinking. For Kaplan, Reform Judaism pointed to the need for an ideology that will express the "collective consciousness" of the Jewish people.[3] Orthodoxy, even in its "atomized conception of Jewish collective life," revealed the urgency for "a creative unity, whether it be political, cultural, or religious," binding world Jewry into one community.[4] Zionism, while lacking "vitality and viability" because of its distance from Jewish religious tradition, nevertheless provided a model of practical and relevant Jewish action in the modern world.[5] This agenda—the creation of a revitalized Jewish ideology, a creative Jewish community, and relevant Jewish practice—linked Kaplan to other contemporary Jewish theologians. The present study will examine how this agenda evolved with respect to Kaplan, Martin Buber, and Abraham Joshua Heschel.

In addition, Kaplan shared a common orientation with Conservative Judaism—the movement with which he has been most closely associated—whose humanistic goal was the survival and enhancement of the Jewish people.[6] A humanistic approach to Jewish religion, however, was not restricted either to Kaplan or to Conservatism. Indeed, it is the mark of any modern theological approach to Judaism. Traditional and nontraditional Jewish thinkers alike have confronted the human problems facing modern Jews in affirming their heritage. Whereas biblical and medieval Jewish thinkers were primarily concerned with belief in God and developed complex proofs for metaphysical affirmation of God's existence, modern Jewish thinkers have placed humanity at the center of their ruminations. The Jewish people and the Jewish person, as well as the dynamics of being human rather than the dynamics of the divine, provide the themes of Judaic theology in the contemporary world. Kaplan comes into contact with other contemporary Jewish theologians through his focus on the needs of humanity combined with a reevaluation of Jewish ideology, Jewish community, and Jewish religious practice.

Kaplan's point of departure was the reverse of traditional Judaism's emphasis on God's need for humanity. He insisted, instead, that a modern Jew "must experience God's relevance to man."[7] From this perspective, the human need outweighs the divine. Kaplan's program for reviving Jewish theological ideology, Jewish community, and Jewish practice took this shift in emphasis seriously. Experience must teach the meaning of God as a reality for each Jew; experience must provide the ties of unity among Jews; experience must be the criterion on which each Jew builds a pattern of religious practice. Many theologians who oppose Kaplan's pragmatism agree with him in focusing on the centrality of Jewish experience when renewing modern Jewish religious life.

Thus Martin Buber, into whose views Kaplan demonstrated keener insight than Buber himself appreciated, also focused on the human side of the divine-human equation. Fearing that his dialogical emphasis would be misunderstood, Buber insisted that God needs humanity only insofar as humanity requires the divine need. Relationship, for Buber, demands mutuality. If human beings are to engage in relationship, then God must allow them mutuality. The divine must be self-limiting; God provides a need for each person that "constitutes the mystery of man's creation."[8] While Buber focuses on the human side, he emphasizes the divine need for humanity as the way in which God provides meaning to each person. Such an emphasis corresponds to the outlook of Conservative Judaism as Kaplan understood it. Buber also analyzed Jewish community, Zionism, and even Jewish religious practice in ways that Kaplan could understand and translate into his own theological language.[9] Buber's apparent difference from Kaplan arises from the practical program each creates rather than from a difference concerning Jewish renewal.

The same might also be said of Abraham Joshua Heschel, who seemed to delight in polemic and exaggerated his differences from other thinkers, especially from Kaplan. Nevertheless, his approach to theology emphasized the divine need for humanity, a religious basis for community and Zionism, and a creative revival of Jewish practice. His vision of modern Judaism, when stripped of its rhetoric, shows a striking resemblance to the concerns Kaplan articulates.

Heschel, in contrast to both Buber and Kaplan, concentrates on "God in search of man."[10] In an explicit rejection of a humanistic focus, he declares that "it is a sure way of missing Him when they think that God is an answer to a human need."[11] Heschel lovingly details God's involvement in human history, God's suffering together with humanity. At the same time, Heschel does not deny mutuality. He recognizes that God's need for humanity answers a deep human need as well. No less than Buber and Kaplan, Heschel acknowledges that human beings need to be needed and that God's search for humanity enables each person to become a more realized self.[12] Despite this balanced understanding, Heschel often polemicizes against views what seem to be one-sided caricatures of Buber or Kaplan. A more reasoned study of Kaplan will reveal the weaknesses in Heschel's self-separation from other thinkers.

Therefore, Buber, Heschel, and Kaplan share a common perspective. Nevertheless, while all approached the question of Jewish revival fully aware of the divine need for humanity, they emphasized a different ingredient that was needed for that revival. Kaplan offered a programmatic agenda for renewing Jewish life; Buber constructed a paradigm of mutuality by which to judge attempts at establishing a renewal of Judaism; Heschel's theological perspective created an atmosphere of devotion necessary for modern religious consciousness. By comparing their views, it may be possible to synthesize a new set of guidelines for constructing a modern Jewish theology.

Mordecai Kaplan approached theology as a practical rather than a theoretical problem in the creation of a vital modern Judaism. The transition from traditional Judaism to contemporary Jewish thinking must, he suggested, take account of the historical changes in Jewish belief. He noted that biblical Judaism emphasized human creativity and mutuality between God and the Jewish people.[13] However, that principle of mutuality became obscured, as social, political, and economic necessities shaped Judaism into an increasingly authoritarian mold in the course of history. In the Middle Ages, human initiative took the form of rabbinic decrees, or *takkanot*. The threat of modernity inhibited even that expression of independence, and the Jew became more and more of a passive servant to the divine. Modern Jews rejected this model and questioned traditional faith not because they disbelieved in God, but because Judaism ignores God's relevance for individuals seeking self-fulfillment. Modern Jews do not need to recapture a "lost faith in God" but rather to discover divine relevance to their quest for independence.[14]

The practical problem has become that of formulating new ways of conceiving God. Kaplan offered the following theological innovation: God is relevant as the source of human values and as the means by which Jews realize the necessity for honesty, responsibility, and loyalty. In this conception, Kaplan suggested, Jews can discover the importance of the God-idea for their personal development. Human beings need such a view of God as the basis for ethical and moral maturation.[15]

God must be defined in terms of the human experience of self-transcendence. Kaplan defined the idea of God he believed was most relevant for modern Jews by studying how people grew toward their fullest potential, the fulfillment of which he designates as "salvation." God, for Kaplan, as for traditional Judaism, denoted that compelling force in the universe enabling salvation. Because salvation, however, refers to a this-worldly personal self-actualization, a theology must be built on an analysis of moments of self-expression. In such moments, human beings recognize that they are aided by a more than human set of forces. Nature and circumstances combine to enable self-realization. By calling this "transnatural" combination of forces that makes possible human actualization *God*, Kaplan claims to have identified a deity confirmed by human experience, whose reality will "influence the conduct of people" because it verifies human ideals.[16] In this view, the practical meaning of God depends upon human intellectual effort in constructing a viable God-idea.

Kaplan's practicality finds expression in his approach to Jewish community no less than in his theology. Jews have become disillusioned not only with the Jewish religion but with the Jewish community as well. Democracy has taught them to be suspicious of leaders who demand uncritical obedience to external authority. Every effort to establish an autocratic, uniform standard of Jewish life leads to sectarian division. Orthodoxy splinters Jewish life when it overlooks the voluntaristic nature of contemporary religious affiliation. No call for the revival of Jewish community can succeed unless it appeals for voluntary, not dogmatic, acceptance by each individual Jew.

In connection with this practical approach to Jewish social organization, Kaplan offers an extended explanation of the biblical view of covenant. He interprets the notion as one based on an affirmation of human initiative. When a community asserts that its identity derives from a covenant agreement, it claims that communal unity springs not from accidental traits (such as birth or geography) but from a self-conscious decision. Jewish communal identity, insofar as it remains true to the symbolic meaning of covenant, affirms the freedom of individual Jews because loyalty to this community reflects personal, voluntary association with a group, rather than blind "ancestor worship" or nationalism. Jewish peoplehood, understood in this way, is a unique type of social organization, indelibly democratic. In contrast to more authoritarian forms of social unity, its very nature depends upon choice and intellectual assent.[17]

Kaplan applies this biblical model to modern Jewish life in his "covenant proposal" for the future structure of Judaism.[18] Jews, as individuals and as a people, must enter into a new communal agreement. The various Jewish agencies—whether Zionist or religious—should form a democratic, communal body to formulate and cause to be ratified a new constitution for the Jewish people that would transcend loyalty to any particular political state, but which would organize local, national, and international Jewry into a coherent unity.

Kaplan considers this new communal body a moral advance within human social organization to be derived from the Jewish notion of *halakhah*, as law designed for living. In his view of the *halakhic* process, every Jew contributes to the growth of Jewish law because the true legislating authority in Judaism, from his standpoint, is the Jewish people as a whole. A restructured Jewish community with the power to enact meaningful, modern legislation would demonstrate the creative possibility of a tradition renewing itself from within. Participation in Jewish lawmaking would teach the individual Jew the importance of personal decision-making, thus offering each Jew an opportunity to grow in democratic responsibility.[19]

Kaplan's call for a democratic forum of Jewish legislation points to his recognition of the importance of the primacy of practice. A new approach to Jewish religious law must evolve new guidelines for Jewish behavior. Kaplan demanded that Jewish practice be revised through a voluntary, democratic process. The formation of a new

covenantal constitution will solve the problem by including Jews
who rejected an imposed tradition by providing a democratic source
of those laws that govern Jewish living.

When outlining the elements required by his proposed covenantal constitution, Kaplan insisted that there must be "unity without
cultic uniformity."[20] This insistence reflects a reality of modern
Jewish life. Kaplan's insight that religion must be pragmatically
justified finds support in contemporary Jewish behavior. Jews follow
only those religious practices that have personal significance to
them.[21] Jews become uncomfortable with those practices that seem
to thwart or reverse modern efforts at self-development. The transformation of Jewish practice for the sake of pragmatic ends—whether
done consciously or unconsciously—presents a problem for both
traditionalists and nontraditionalists. Traditionalists, despite their
commitment to continuity with the past, must cope with the necessity for change. Nontraditionalists, despite their acceptance of major changes in religious practice, must discover a means of ensuring
their continued links with a historical identity.

Kaplan's view of Jewish practice generally emphasizes the double
contribution that religion makes to individual development and
that the individual makes to humanity. On the one hand, religious
practice and symbolism binds an individual to a particular social
group. An individual learns to share with others and to place the
group at the center of personal concern. The individual learns that
self-actualization is impossible unless done within the larger unit
for the sake of a cause larger than the self. Religion teaches that life
is worthwhile not only by stressing the importance of the individual
but by showing how the individual is important for the group.[22]
This altruism expresses itself most clearly when individuals act not
merely for the good of the parochial group but for all humanity.
The two motivations are not mutually exclusive; acting for the
sake of one's community not only increases the possibility of self-
actualization but also advances the good of every human community.

Kaplan notes the interaction of benefits. An individual's altruism
influences the local community and humanity at large. At the same
time, the group serves the individual. Not only does religion identify the individual with the community but expects the community

to serve the individual. Communal worship, for example, has two purposes—that of selecting and symbolizing those elements of reality that help one attain certain ideals and that of identifying oneself with a community that holds those ideals. Such self-identification includes a recognition of the obligations an individual owes to society. These obligations become compelling, however, only if the society facilitates individual growth. Such a symbiosis indicates that the society itself is to be judged by virtue of the ideals it holds and the way in which it serves individuals who seek to realize those ideals. A religion must provide its members with symbols and rituals that satisfy their spiritual needs.[23]

As in the case of community and theology, Kaplan's approach to the problem of religious practice tended to be concrete and practical. Individuals should accept those rituals and symbols having personal meaning, reserving the right to reject meaningless ones. This approach creates a "voluntaristic Jewish religion" that is "diverse in belief and practice." Kaplan realized that this call, if heeded, would result in ritual diversity and undermine a uniform code of Jewish behavior. That consequence seems a price worth paying, since not only did he find the idea of a uniform code of Jewish practice unrealistic but differences "in personal taste, aptitudes and interests renders it undesirable." Jewish communal life would become less able to respond to individual needs were it to impose a single standard of religious practice.[24]

Kaplan's three-fold practical agenda—creating a viable theology, communal identity, and revitalizing Jewish practice—links him with other modern Jewish thinkers. Martin Buber and Abraham Joshua Heschel, in particular, shared this set of objectives, although they pursued them in radically different ways. Kaplan's relationship to them may be clarified by noting how the common agenda was transformed by the distinctive approaches taken by each thinker.

When Mordecai Kaplan sought to analyze Martin Buber as a philosopher, he translated Buber's theological paradigm into a practical program appropriate for Buber's peculiar intellectual and historical context.[25] Kaplan recognized the practical implications of Buber's position that the philosopher of dialogue himself overlooked, but he misunderstood Buber's intention. While Buber did seek the inner transformation of Jews, he did not—as he himself vigorously contended to Kaplan—set out to do this through a transformation of traditional Judaism. Whereas Kaplan offered a program for Jewish reconstruction, Buber pointed to the I-Thou encounter as the touchstone for authentic Jewish life in the future. Buber's concern was less that of reviving Jewish tradition as the basis for individual self-fulfillment than creating a setting within which true meeting could take place. Kaplan's self-conscious and consistent involvement with Jewish tradition caused him to misinterpret Buber's more tangential association with Judaism.

For Kaplan, the agenda itself and the means of carrying it out sprang from a love of the Jewish tradition; his struggle to revive that tradition led him to formulate his philosophy of religion. In reverse manner, Buber's concern for genuine encounter, lyrically expressed in *I and Thou*, led him to investigate those basic Jewish issues central to Kaplan. While Kaplan's vision of a renewed Judaism precedes his analysis of the human situation that calls it forth, Buber's Judaism flows from his ideal of a renewed humanity.

That ideal, developed in detail in Buber's *I and Thou*, and expounded throughout Buber's later corpus, emphasizes the everyday possibilities for genuine meeting. When interhuman encounter takes place and human beings interact with one another or with other manifestations of creation, whether animate or inanimate, they step into a fuller sphere of being. Moments of such encounter include a meeting not only with creatures but also with the creator, not only with this specific other whom I face at this moment but with the eternal Thou, from whose face I cannot turn. While Kaplan used a humanistic standard of salvation—self-realization— through a list of specific human values, Buber's goal of genuine I-Thou dialogue precluded concrete definition. Encounter is an opportunity, rather than any set of specific goals of self-actualization. God's relevance comes from his eternal presence that makes I-Thou meeting possible, not from a definable role in "salvation" as Kaplan understood it.

This difference shapes the way Buber's understanding of God, community, and Jewish perspective differed from that of Kaplan. Although both thinkers moved beyond God's need for humanity to humanity's need of the deity, Kaplan contended that pragmatic necessity dictates such a move. Buber's uneasiness with the claim that God needs humanity, however, stemmed from his reluctance to define God's limitations. He refused, therefore, to create a functional definition of deity. Because God entails more than human experience can understand, Buber criticized those who "confine God to a producing function." Admitting the importance of declaring that God needs humanity and that humanity needs God, Buber contends, nevertheless, that the only valid rationale for speaking of the importance of human action in the "divine becoming," or of God as process in living relationship with humanity, lies in an insistence on the relevance of the human deed to God. The mutuality of the divine and the human becomes for him a metaphor symbolizing the infinite significance of human actions.[26] Despite his philosophy's similarity to Kaplan's humanism, Buber established a paradigm of authentic being rather than a program by which to construct a viable concept of God.

This difference in theology led, necessarily, to a different understanding of Jewish community. Buber and Kaplan seem to agree on the indispensability of community for personal development. Buber, however, saw community less as an instrument for personal growth than as an opportunity for genuine encounter, claiming that a modern "theophany" can take place solely within the context of community even though only the individual and not the collectivity can "enter . . . into the dialogue of the ages."[27] All community —including Jewish community—justifies itself insofar as it grows out of and stimulates true encounter.

For Buber, the revival of Jewish community depended upon Jewish dedication to the common goal of interhuman encounter, as exemplified by the biblical concept of covenant. Buber considered covenant, as presented in the Hebrew Bible, as the basis of true community. Israel became a true community by becoming "partners in the covenant." Through the covenant every aspect of human life was oriented toward a truly human interaction. Because of covenant, Buber claimed, Jews realized that the purpose of communal life was to realize justice through a concrete human civilization. Jewish distinctiveness—whether illustrated by a contrast between Abraham and Noah or by rituals such as that of the first fruits—lay in pointing the way toward a life of encounter not only for individuals but for collectivities.[28] Public ritual no less than private openness contributes to the possibility for interhuman meeting.

Jews can revive such public occasions for interhuman meeting, not merely by reviewing their religious past but also by strengthening their social life in the present. Zionism, Buber claimed, may be a creative agent in that effort. Like Kaplan, Buber looked beyond political Zionism toward a revival of the Jewish people. His ideal, however, emphasized dialogical encounter, rather than the democratic process Kaplan portrays. Buber did not ignore the danger of parochialism nor the lack of democratic openness in Zionism as a historical movement. While Kaplan offered a political program for the construction of a democratic community, Buber proposed a humanistic criterion for community. Applying his paradigm to Zionism, he found the movement wanting because it has shown "too little feeling for the world and world history" and has instead embarked on a narrow nationalism that in fact "leads to de-judaization under a Jewish banner."[29] Buber opposed this narrowness, not as Kaplan might because it betrayed the democratic impulse but because it obstructed genuine meeting.

While Kaplan conceived of modern Jewish community in terms of a new political mechanism, Buber saw the problem in terms of reevaluating the meaning of community. The solution to Kaplan was to be found in restructuring social institutions. Buber, however, denies institutions such power. "Community," he averred, "is where community happens." The Jewish task was not to create more institutions but to work—to allow community to occur.[30] The equivalent of Kaplan's agenda for a "New Zionism" or a "religion of ethical nationhood" was for Buber the task of becoming open to dialogue and the birth of community.

Buber's emphasis on allowing encounter to occur naturally rather than to promote its revival artificially also held for his approach to Jewish ritual. At first glance, Buber seemed to reject the validity of all religious rituals; indeed, Buber's response to Kaplan's summary of his thoughts apparently confirms this view. Buber's repudiation of any desire to rebuild a modern Judaism suggested that he had lost hope in the viability of traditional Jewish practice. On closer inspection, however, his understanding of Jewish religious practice is less negative.[31] Buber's insistence that religious practice lead to moments of genuine meeting prevented him from offering a specific set of new ritual guidelines such as those Kaplan suggests. Instead, he examines the meaning of rites and religious practices, in general, and those of the Jews, in particular, to find the basis for their continuing significance. All religious practice holds the potential for initiating an I-Thou encounter. Attention to the realm of the spirit opens doors to genuine meeting. Prayer, rituals, and commandments have no intrinsic value but do offer new opportunities for engagement with divine reality. Such actions do not constitute the "truth" of religion but do point to the essential act: "standing and withstanding in the abyss of the real reciprocal relation with the mystery of God."[32]

Buber interpreted the laws given at Sinai, for example, as "pointing beyond themselves into the sphere of the 'holy.'" As tools leading to encounter, Jewish laws served a valuable purpose. In this view, the crisis of Jewish law lay not in its becoming irrelevant or misunderstood by new generations, but in detaching the "holy" from the life experience of those who follow the law. Of course, laws help form and shape community. To Buber, their primary justification, however, came from their ability to revive true communal life, to reawaken genuine encounter.[33] On the basis of this understanding of how Jewish religious practice functioned in the past, Buber suggests the meaning of ritual and religious life in religion today.

While Kaplan provided a practical program for Jewish religious practice, Buber's paradigmatic criteria suggests a purely spiritual yardstick of religious vitality. The practical implications of Buber's religious paradigm does conform to Kaplan's program. Ritual has significance through its inner meaning, not as rote obedience. Jewish practice flows from personal living and, therefore, cannot be imposed as an absolute, uniform, and inflexible requirement. Understood in this way, religious practices need not be uniform. Since Buber holds that the rituals of "an ancient treasure" may once again become living vessels of religious life, Buber could surely approve of Kaplan's reconstruction of Jewish religious practice.

Not only Jewish practice but every aspect of Buber's paradigm of dialogue may be applied to Kaplan's program of Jewish renewal. The dialogic paradigm complements that program with a broader aim and a more general goal—the renewal of the living vitality of Jewish religion. Buber's approach appeals to those who reject Kaplan's specific suggestions but accept his insight that modernity demands a dramatic Jewish renewal. While Buber's theories may offer a less comprehensive plan of Jewish action, his views of God, Jewish community, and the relevance of Jewish practice offer greater scope for different personal responses than does Kaplan's programmatic agenda.

One might think that Abraham Heschel, like Martin Buber, differed from Kaplan by offering a paradigm of Jewish life rather than a program for Jewish renewal. Certainly, Heschel's response to specific programs, such as liturgical change, would support such a view. Heschel insisted that while Jewish liturgy has always been flexible and that while expectations of maximal Jewish practice are unrealistic, revitalization depended on changing attitudes, not on changing the substance of Jewish religious behavior. This approach might seem to advocate the need for a new paradigm of Jewish living, one drawn, perhaps, from eastern European Hasidism, a movement that Heschel once referred to as a "Jewish golden age." Yet Heschel differed from both Buber and Kaplan in evoking an attitude rather than a paradigm, seeking response rather than emulation, and inviting wonder and awe rather than a changed worldview or a transformed system of Judaism.

Like Buber and Kaplan, Heschel recognized the humanistic shift in modern religious consciousness. Unlike them, he condemned this shift as a move toward selfishness. He rejected the self-centeredness of contemporary thinking, even while giving a central place to the discussion of "needs." Unlike Kaplan, Heschel did not offer ways in which Judaism can satisfy human needs but concentrated solely on "the need to be needed," in light of which human beings find self-realization by living beyond themselves. An idea of God must begin by demanding transcendence of self before it can achieve actualization of the self.[34] Heschel sought to awaken "a surprise in the soul" so that Jews could intuit the experience of covenant, the meaning of which he interpreted as "God is in need of man." His major purpose was to remind readers that the human being has significance only because of the lasting divine need for human existence.[35]

Kaplan and Heschel have more in common theologically than Heschel could admit. They concur on the problems raised by the modern condition, on the mutuality of needs linking the divine and the human, and on the necessity for a revival of spiritual sensitivity. Heschel's dissent from Kaplan lay more in style than in content. Kaplan appealed to human reason and translated Jewish concepts into rational categories. Heschel considered the only effective program for reviving Judaism to be stimulating a transcendence of reason—an intimation of the human condition that comes from introspection, not scientific analysis. Heschel feared the deification of reason; Kaplan feared the obfuscation of emotionalism. Heschel decorated his rational arguments with poetic ornamentation; Kaplan's admission of the importance of spirituality was couched in rationalistic form.

Heschel's understanding of Jewish communal identity reveals a similar relationship to Kaplan's approach. Like Buber and Kaplan, Heschel acknowledged that covenant implies community. The Bible defies understanding if Israel's national consciousness is ignored: "It is not as individuals but as the people Israel that we can find an approach to the prophets. The Bible lives within those who live within the covenant."[36] His concern, however, was that nationalistic slogans could replace a genuine commitment to the people of Israel as the servants of God, so he sought to awaken a sense of Israel's purpose and destiny rather than to reorganize Jewish communal structure. The June 1967 war and the reaction of non-Jews who ignored Israel's danger but condemned its success stimulated him to a lyrical celebration of Jewish peoplehood, but even then Heschel warned that "we must beware lest the place of David becomes a commonplace."[37] Heschel contended that the most practical path toward Jewish community consists of reshaping Jewish self-understanding. Rather than create a paradigm of community, "community means community of concern"; rather than devise a program for communal life, Heschel insisted that both paradigm and program will flow from a transformed perspective on Jewish religion.[38]

Heschel's moral activism seems to contradict this attitudinal bias. Heschel took a stand on many questions of practical concern. He actively supported fair housing, the rights of the aged and the oppressed, an end to the Vietnam War, and the cause of Soviet Jews. However, this political creativity concerned issues of conscience, that is, problems dependent for their solution on changing attitudes. Thus, Heschel's social activism grew out of a theological commitment. He devoted his efforts to evoking symbols and theology rather than stimulating the building of institutions.

In contrast to Buber and Kaplan, Heschel's agenda grew out of a trust that religion at its deepest level could reform human consciousness. Heschel's dedicated call to renew the force and appeal of Jewish religious practice reveals the central thrust of his theological program: to transform Jewish perspective. Contending that a revival of Judaism depends on creating a devotional attitude, he advocated that Jewish symbolism and religious practice be seen as ways to include this attitude, and he utilized his own command of language to that end.[39] Heschel believed that only renewed Jewish piety could overcome the threat of modernity.

That devotional orientation points to the major distinction between Heschel and Kaplan and explains Heschel's objections to many of Kaplan's liturgical innovations. Heschel's veiled polemic against Kaplan was directed against his pragmatic changes, which were considered a misguided attempt to revive Jewish religion. Heschel declared—in words echoing a conversation with Kaplan—that "a revision of the prayer book will not solve the crisis of prayer. What we need is a revision of the soul, a new heart rather than a new text."[40] He insisted on turning to the "God of Abraham, Isaac, and Jacob" rather than the "God of John Dewey." He warned against regarding Jewish religious practice as "folkways" because folkways are "relevant to man," while commandments, *mitzvot*, are relevant to God.

More is at stake here than Heschel's devotional attitude. Heschel contended that deliberate changes in the direction of making religion more relevant to man reflect a compromise with decadent civilization—the corrupt and self-serving society in which we live. These criticisms flow from his contention that a program to revive Jewish life cannot regard Judaism as a civilization, since "Judaism is the art of surpassing civilization."[41] Jews must change their perspective on Western culture if they wish to contribute to its growth. Kaplan begins by accepting Western values and seeks to find how Judaism advances them. Heschel sees Judaism as an alternative to Western culture and insists a critical attitude toward that culture is the point of departure for any Jewish response to modernity.

Heschel's approach is oriented toward attitude rather than program, to perspective rather than paradigm. Thus, Heschel rejects the need for a new prayer book while insisting on liturgical revival. Not a fundamentalist, Heschel realizes the limits of maximalism: "the power to observe depends on the situation."[42] The solution to a decline in observance, however, does not consist in making more changes. Renewal cannot come from tinkering with specific practices but from a total reformulation of one's worldview.

A modern view of contemporary Jewish religion must take Kaplan's program of renewal seriously, since it not only encapsulates the major trends of modern Jewish thought but offers a practical response to them. Kaplan recognizes that modern Jews approach their relationship to Judaism and God differently than did Jews in earlier times. Jewish renewal presupposes God's relevance to humanity, the importance of covenant as cementing ties in Jewish community, and Jewish religious practice as expressive both of individual diversity and a will toward unity. Kaplan's insight that these presuppositions should not merely be taken as theoretical constructs but must be translated into concrete programs is the point of departure for any successful attempt to reawaken Jewish life.

Kaplan's solutions, however, often apply to a limited circle of Jews. For those who consider rationalism definitive, Kaplan's definition of God may be appealing. Others, like Heschel, who seek an alternative perspective to that of scientific knowledge, will not find Kaplan's God-idea a helpful restatement of their struggle for salvation. Those who, with Buber, view political life with skepticism will distrust Kaplan's political optimism. A new view of Jewish covenant must combine Kaplan's programmatic realism with the broader concerns for a paradigm of community and the religious perspective of Buber and Heschel.

Kaplan's understanding of Jewish life encompassed the need for a practical program for Jewish renewal. His actual program differed significantly from the programs that could arise from Buber's view of communal mutuality or Heschel's pietistic perspective. A reconstruction of contemporary Judaism that learns from Heschel and Buber, no less than from Kaplan, would base its theology on the broad sensitivity that Heschel evokes and its communal identity on the wide mutuality of Buber's ideal. Combined with these values, Kaplan's pragmatic understanding of Jewish practice and a renewed way of living as a Jew would be deepened in theory and become a realistic option for contemporary Jews.

Notes

1. See the various discussions by Zeev Levi in his *On the Relationship between Jewish and General Philosophy* (in Hebrew) (Tel Aviv: Hakibbutz Hamme'uḥad, 1982), esp. 231–40. He also notes the humanism in thinkers such as Kaplan, Heschel, and Buber in his "The Status of Man: Rosenzweig and Buber," *Daat* 12 (1984): 82. See also the entire discussion in Eliezer Schweid, "The Reconstruction of Jewish Religion out of Secular Culture," in this book, as well as his *Judaism and Secular Culture* (in Hebrew) (Tel Aviv: Hakibbutz Hamme'uḥad, 1981).
2. Mordecai M. Kaplan, *The Greater Judaism in the Making: A Study of the Modern Evolution of Judaism* (New York: Reconstructionist Press, 1960), 450.
3. Ibid., 289.
4. Ibid., 335–36, 348.
5. Ibid., 449.
6. Ibid., 366–67.
7. Mordecai M. Kaplan, *The Religion of Ethical Nationhood: Judaism's Contribution to World Peace* (New York: Macmillan, 1970), 17, 47–49, 103.
8. Martin Buber, *Eclipse of God* (New York: Harper & Row, 1952), 138. Cf. idem, *I and Thou*, trans. Walter Kaufmann (New York: Charles Scribner's Sons, 1970), 130; and the introductory passages in idem, *On Judaism*, ed. Nahum N. Glatzer (New York: Schocken, 1967), 6–9. See also S. Daniel Breslauer, *The Chrysalis of Religion: A Guide to the Jewishness of Buber's "I and Thou"* (Nashville: Abingdon, 1980).
9. Mordecai M. Kaplan, "Buber's Evaluation of Philosophic Thought and Religious Tradition," in *The Philosophy of Martin Buber*, ed. Paul Arthur Schilpp and Maurice Friedman, *The Library of Living Philosophers*, vol. 12 (La Salle, Ill.: Open Court Press, 1967), 248–72; cf. Buber's response on ibid., 744.

10. See Abraham Joshua Heschel, *Man Is Not Alone: A Philosophy of Religion* (New York: Farrar, Straus & Giroux, 1951), 233–34, 241, 248, 257, 269; and idem, *God in Search of Man: A Philosophy of Judaism* (New York: Harper & Row, 1966), 161–69, 286–91; and throughout idem, *Who Is Man?* (Stanford, Calif.: Stanford University Press, 1965). Cf. S. Daniel Breslauer, *The Ecumenical Perspective and the Modernization of Jewish Religion* (Missoula, Mont.: Scholars Press, 1978).
11. Heschel, *Man Is Not Alone*, 233–34.
12. See ibid., 241, 248, 257, 269; and Heschel, *God in Search of Man*, 161–69, 286–91; and idem, *Who Is Man?*, passim.
13. Kaplan, *Greater Judaism*, 509.
14. Mordecai Kaplan, *If Not Now, When? Toward A Reconstruction of the Jewish People: Conversations between Mordecai M. Kaplan and Arthur A. Cohen* (New York: Schocken, 1973), 67. Note as well the explicit contention that belief in God does not come through reasoning but "by experiencing God's power in making life worth living" (idem, *The Future of the American Jew* [1948; reprint, New York: Reconstructionist Press, 1967], 259).
15. See Kaplan, *If Not Now, When?* 67, 68, 86, 120; idem, *Judaism without Supernaturalism* (New York: Reconstructionist Press, 1958), 110; idem, *Questions Jews Ask: Reconstructionist Answers* (New York: Reconstructionist Press, 1956), 84, 87, 94, 103; and idem, *The Meaning of God in Modern Jewish Religion* (New York: Reconstructionist Press, 1962), 26–30, 82–83.
16. Kaplan, *Greater Judaism*, 457–59, 473, 490–91.
17. See idem, *Judaism as a Civilization: Toward a Reconstruction of American Jewish Life* (1934; reprint, New York: Schocken, 1967), 258–59; idem, *Judaism without Supernaturalism*, 155, 230–36; and idem, *Questions Jews Ask*, 50.
18. See Kaplan, *Judaism without Supernaturalism*, 192–205, for the explication of the "covenant proposal"; other treatments of the same idea can be found in idem, *A New Zionism*, 2d enl. ed. (New York: Reconstructionist Press, 1959); idem, *If Not Now, When?* 23; idem, *Future of the American Jew*, 54, 114, 392; and idem, *Questions Jews Ask*, 48–50, 402.
19. See Kaplan, *Future of the American Jew*, 429–535. On Kaplan's approach to *halakhah*, see the following essays in Ronald A. Brauner, ed., *Jewish Civilization: Essays and Studies*, vol. 2 (Philadelphia: Reconstructionist Rabbinical College, 1981): Mel Scult, "Halakhah and Authority in the Early Kaplan," 101–10; Meir Ben-Horin, "Perspectives on Halakhah," 113–26; Jack J. Cohen, "Toward an Ideology for Post-Halakhic Jews," 127–44; Ira Eisenstein, "Mordecai M. Kaplan and Halakhah," 145–54; Richard Hirsh, "Mordecai Kaplan's Approach to Jewish Law," 155–69; Sidney H. Schwarz, "Catholic Israel and Halakhic

Change," 171–81; and Charles Vernoff, "Toward a Transnatural Judaic Theology of Halakhah," 195–205.

20. Kaplan, *Religion of Ethical Nationhood*, 11.

21. See Breslauer, *Ecumenical Perspective*.

22. See Kaplan, *New Zionism*, 98, 112, 115; idem, *Greater Judaism*, 453, 468.

23. Kaplan, *Judaism as a Civilization*, 347; idem, *If Not Now, When?* 38–39; and idem, *Future of the American Jew*, 418.

24. Kaplan, *Judaism without Supernaturalism*, 116; idem, *New Zionism*, 92; and idem, *Future of the American Jew*, 420–21 (see the entire discussion on ritualism on 413–28).

25. See note 9, as well as the discussion of this exchange and a study of the intellectual ties and personal mismeeting between the two thinkers in Meir Ben-Horin, "Kaplan and Buber—Tensions and Harmonies," in *Jewish Civilization: Essays and Studies*, vol. 1, ed. Ronald A. Brauner (Philadelphia: Reconstruction Rabbinical College, 1979), 227–84.

26. See Buber, *Eclipse of God*, 21; and idem, *On Judaism*, 86.

27. Martin Buber, *Between Man and Man* [afterword by the author and introduction by Maurice Friedman], trans. Ronald Gregor Smith and Maurice Friedman (New York: Macmillan, 1965), 7, 80.

28. See Buber, *On Judaism*, 77, 174, 193; and idem, *Kingship of God*, 3d enl. ed., trans. Richard Scheimann (New York: Harper & Row, 1967); idem, *Moses: The Revelation and the Covenant* (New York: Harper & Row, 1958), esp. 112; and idem, *On the Bible*, ed. Nahum N. Glatzer (New York: Schocken, 1968), 22–43, 80–91, 122–30.

29. Martin Buber, *On Zion: The History of an Idea*, trans. Stanley Grafman (London: Horowitz, 1973), 123. Idem, *Israel and the World: Essays in a Time of Crisis*, 2d. ed. (New York: Schocken, 1963), 157.

30. Buber, *Between Man and Man*, 31. Cf. idem, *Pointing the Way: Collected Essays*, ed. and trans. Maurice Friedman (New York: Harper & Row, 1957).

31. See Breslauer, *Chrysalis of Religion*, 68–97.

32. Buber, *Pointing the Way*, 113.

33. See Buber, *Eclipse of God*, 104; idem, *On Judaism*, 80, 91–93; and idem, *The Origin and Meaning of Hasidism*, ed. and trans. Maurice Friedman (New York: Horizon Press, 1960), 94.

34. See the discussion in Heschel, *Man Is Not Alone*, 217–27, 257–60, 269–70; and idem, *God in Search of Man*, 349–51, 396–400.

35. On these themes, see Abraham Joshua Heschel, *The Earth Is the Lord's* (New York: Harper & Row, 1966), 92; idem, *A Passion for Truth* (New York: Farrar, Straus & Giroux, 1973), passim; idem, *God in Search of Man*, 213; idem, *Man Is Not Alone*, 214–15, 241, 248; and idem, *Who Is Man?*, 61, 75.

36. Heschel, *God in Search of Man*, 255.

37. Abraham Joshua Heschel, *Israel: An Echo of Eternity* (New York: Farrar, Straus & Giroux, 1967), 34.

38. Ibid., 211.

39. See Edward K. Kaplan, "Form and Content in Abraham J. Heschel's Poetic Style," *Central Conference of American Rabbis Journal* 18, no. 2 (1971): 28–39; idem, "Language and Reality in Abraham J. Heschel's Philosophy of Religion," *Journal of the American Academy of Religion* 41, no. 1 (1973): 94–113; and idem, "Heschel's Poetics of Religious Thinking," in *Abraham Joshua Heschel: Exploring His Life and Thought,* ed. John C. Merkle (New York: Macmillan, 1985), 103–19.

40. Abraham Joshua Heschel, *Man's Quest for God: Studies in Prayer and Symbolism* (New York: Charles Scribner's Sons, 1954), 83.

41. Ibid., 88, 114; and idem., *The Insecurity of Freedom: Essays on Human Existence* (New York: Farrar, Straus & Giroux, 1967), 225–26, 233.

42. Heschel, *God in Search of Man,* 102–5, 301. Cf. his remarks in idem, *The Sabbath: Its Meaning for Modern Man,* expanded ed. (New York: Harper & Row, 1966), 17; and in idem, *Insecurity of Freedom,* 206–7.

PART FOUR

Reinterpreting Judaism

CHAPTER II

A Critical Assessment of Kaplan's Ideas of Salvation

Harold M. Schulweis

The critics of Mordecai Kaplan's philosophic efforts were persistent in their accusations of his purported neglect of metaphysics. Of what value is "an account of the psychological and ethical consequences" of affirming a theology without the metaphysical substructure that deals with "things as a whole" and without the belief that there is "something ontological, some affirmation . . . concerning the ultimate nature of things"?[1] A theology that does not offer God as "the only tenable explanation of the universe"[2] and that does not deal with the problems of theodicy, sin, resurrection, and proofs for the existence and attributes of the deity is no theology at all.

The task of this article is to analyze Kaplan's *soterics* as a metaphysical theology. Not that his metaphysical analysis concerns itself with being qua being; nor with speculation over ultimate or first principles; nor with the traditional schoolman's preoccupation with the transcendental nature of God, freedom, and immortality. But in his theory of salvation, we confront an empirical metaphysics, a philosophic anthropology that searches for the pervasive traits of the natural world and of human nature. Upon these concepts of maximum generality, Kaplan constructed an ethics and theology. The root metaphors of Kaplan's metaphysics are biological and

257

organic, not mechanistic or discrete; its method, scientific; its conclusions, probabilistic, heuristic, and in principle verifiable. His
metaphysics stresses growth, creativity, and process. His theology is
naturalistically and humanistically oriented.

Before analyzing Kaplan's soterical approach, it must be set in
historical perspective. It arose as a response to the insolubility of
the traditional problem inherent in positing the existence and character of a supernatural God. The problem may be stated thus: if
there exists an antecedent Being, wholly independent of human
beings, of whom no spatiotemporal attributes may be legitimately
predicated and whose nature lies outside the realm of human experience, in what sense can such a reality be said to be known by
human persons or be meaningful to them? The very incomprehensi-
bleness, in human terms, of such a supernatural God denies the
conditions for its confirmation or rejection. The supernaturalist's
claim turns impregnable not by virtue of its irresistible logic but
because of its "logically meaningless" formulation.

The religious naturalist enters the scene unable to accept a supernatural God on faith. Like Kaplan, he may hold at least one unverifiable presupposition. But while his assumptions are heuristic principles or hypotheses, subject at all times to questions and rejection
should they prove unworkable or fruitless, the claims of orthodox
theologians have actual ontological references, in which the Being
referred to is given absolute existential status not subject to doubt.
The religious naturalist is convinced that the source of the meaningful attributes of God is discovered through experiences between
human beings and between the rest of the natural world, experiences that are often the same but can vary from group to group and
from place to place. In the very search of mankind for God, the
religious naturalist seeks his clues as to the nature of the divine
itself. He may come to know that when men claim to have experienced a revelation of a supernatural Being, they often confuse the
reality of the experience with the experience of reality. He may
come to know that "the Ethiopians make their gods black and snub-
nosed, while the Thracians give theirs red hair and blue eyes"
(Xenophanes); but he dismisses none of these. For the religious
naturalist also knows that the process of reifying man's characteris-

tics, values, and ideals reveals its sancta, aspiration levels, success criteria, and ethical rationale.

Kaplan's theological approach was based on the conviction that "by shifting the orientation from the God-concept, a point intended to be outside human experience, to the idea of man, we are likely to make more headway with the problem of salvation."[3] To cite Feuerbach: "If we are to understand religion, we must take as subject what has been taken for predicate and vice-versa."[4] The human being as an *animal symbolicum* pictures God and therein enters the world of possibility, oughts, and should-be. In worship, he extols those elements that better his life and seeks strength to eliminate the evils that plague it. In his struggle to find himself through this symbolic dimension, he can become more truly human and, thereby, appreciate the divinity in and between him and the world.

The truly revolutionary character of Kaplan's soterical approach, however, is not in this general application of his naturalism but in his humanistic interpretation of personal salvation. The quest for divinity in the world at large entails the discovery within oneself of that which will better one's personal life. "From out of my depths, I call unto Divinity." Only to the extent to which one consciously realizes every humanizing potentiality in oneself and others will one attain a measure of personal salvation and an experience and understanding of Godliness. Kaplan's soterics is the study of the nature and method of achieving this end.

It is Kaplan's belief that soterics can be a framework for salvation for all people, regardless of varying personal viewpoints, because it is based on two elemental and compulsory factors in human nature itself: *the will to live* and its corollary, *the will to maximum life*. In the latter, the principle of self-realization is centered in the development of the productive personality of the self on every level:

1. On the level of vitalities, the self is an organism of biogenic needs (such as hunger and sex) and sociogenic needs (the socially acquired needs, such as belonging to a group or having status). The ascetic, otherworldly philosophies that deny these

primary and secondary needs are, from the point of view of soterics, inimical to healthful growth and salvation.

2. On the level of reason and intelligence, the self functions as a mediator of conflicting interests in order to harmonize and channel the variety of experiences impinging on it. Like the Aristotelian "mean" and the Platonic "sense of justice," the rational exercise allows each impulse a measure of gratification consistent with the total welfare. It is the crucial instrument recognizing the innate potentialities of the self and its enlargement.

3. On the level of morale, the self is said to "harbor the values of the spirit of holiness," "the kingdom of ends."[5] On this level, courage supplies the emotive charge that transforms man's ethical and intellectual commitments into action. The dramatization of the search for self-actualization is celebrated through ritual and prayer; and the realm of purposes is recognized, articulated, and made conscious.

Soterics is a this-worldly "normative science of human life in all its aspects, from the standpoint of verifiable experience."[6] It is a form of art in which the diverse levels of human living, as described above, are integrated and each dimension given its weight according to the desired goal of the total health, happiness, and creativity of the individual. The religious personality is conceived as an artist molding his self into the highest form, impelled by the soteric imperative, as described by Plotinus:

Withdraw into your self and look. And if you do not find yourself beautiful yet, act as does the creator of a statue that is to be made beautiful; he cuts away here, he smooths there, he makes this line lighter, this other purer, until a lovely face has grown upon his work. So do you also: cut away all that is excessive, straighten all that is crooked, bring light to all that is overcast, labor to make all one glow of beauty, and never cease carving your statue until there shall shine out on you from it the godlike splendor of virtue, until you shall see the perfect goodness established in the stainless shrine.[7]

In his conception of salvation as the attainment of the maximum good through the development of the inherent possibilities or potentialities of the organism, Kaplan has been more influenced by the contributions of recent psychiatry than by the romantic, idealistic metaphysics of self-realization. An increasing number of philosophically oriented psychologists, such as Fromm, Horney, Sullivan, and Goldstein, have leaned heavily on the urge in man to self-realization in order to justify the goal and direction of their therapy. They appear to be as concerned with the reeducation of the individual personality toward this end as with treatment aimed at simple adjustment to existing conditions.

Kurt Goldstein, a psychiatric pathologist, refers to the observation that "an organism is governed by the tendency to actualize as much as possible the individual capacities" and argues that this tendency is "the only drive by which the life of the organism is determined."[8] Karen Horney concurs: "Man, by his very nature and of his own accord, strives toward self-realization, . . . and his set of values evolves from such striving."[9] Erich Fromm articulates the same concept when he states the aim of psychiatric therapy to be "the optimal development of a person's potentialities and the realization of his individuality,"[10] his justification being the belief that "all organisms have an inherent tendency to actualize their specific potentialities."[11]

The relationship between health and salvation (that is, self-realization) is not entirely new in religious philosophy. It is no mere etymological accident that the term *salvation* in so many languages is integrally related to the idea of healing.[12] The central idea of salvation is "making whole," a "re-establishment of a whole thing that was broken, disrupted, disintegrated."[13] This has been given a naturalistic cast in Kaplan's soterics. The integrated development of the self-productive personality is understood in religious terms as the quintessential ingredient in spiritual growth and the realization of the divine principle in man.

At this point, certain questions may be raised: First, if the realization of "maximum life" is inherent in the nature of man, why the need for Kaplan's "soterical imperative" to bring it about? Why recommend any action in accordance with human nature, since it is apparently that which no one can avoid doing? The answer may lie in understanding that the drive for maximum life or self-realization is a generalized one inherent in human nature, but it comprises many specific levels of activity on the part of the self, which requires mediation. Self-consciousness and the use of reason are necessary for at least two reasons: to learn the best and surest way to satisfy specific impulses and to learn how to integrate the demands of any one impulse to the total welfare of the organism at any given time. Thus, for Kaplan, the degree to which the individual can succeed in attaining his salvation depends upon the extent to which he has both sensitivity and self-awareness. The need to possess these traits is what persuades Kaplan to call for the "artistic dimension" in man to achieve his measure of the divine.

Second, is the concept of self-realization too ambiguous to be of value as a basis for soterics? Whether one acts one way or the other, some natural capacity will be realized. For the goal of actualizing all the latent capacities of man, no methodological directive is offered so as to judge conflicting directions of fulfillment. As Henry Sidgwick, commenting on the self-realization theories of Green and Spencer, put it, "the sinner realizes capabilities, in this broad sense (of self-realization), as much as the saint."[14]

In answer, it should be said that the concept of maximum life of self-realization is not the sole characteristic of man, but rather represents that which is essentially human in man's nature. Salvation does not depend on the fulfillment of any and every impulse indiscriminately but the fulfillment of the potential of an organism in such a healthful fashion as will aid the individual in achieving the maximum good. How this maximum good is defined will depend on the individual's culture and the culture's institutions at any given stage. In a complex society such as ours, where differing criteria of self-realization coexist, the problem of choosing from particular modes of behavior is aggravated. Horney and Fromm, for example, invoke "creativity," "spontaneity," or "productivity" as standards to distinguish behavior leading to healthy development from behavior leading to stagnant or self-destructive conditions. Unfortunately, these concepts (creativity, and so on) are in turn defined as that which is self-fulfilling or that which leads to further growth and development. Clearly the argument is circular, and the need for clearly defined criteria is not obviated.

The proponents of the self-realization theory seem to have a pragmatic solution to this problem, implying experimentation and trial and error. While the positive characterization and criteria of self-realization remain ambiguous, the negative aspects (such as ill-health and anxiety phenomena) are more precise. Where self-realization is not in the direction of general health and well-being, the organism will manifest symptoms of disorder. Be it a subjective report of unhappiness, or a specialist's diagnosis of neurotic traits, or the appearance of psychosomatic ills, something will raise a red flag. Whether growth is healthful or inimical, therefore, is not a matter of caprice but is rooted in the constitutive demands of the organism.

Further, there are curative powers in the organism, such that, when the proper corrective directives are applied by oneself or a specialist, the organism will respond with well-being. Karen Horney points to "curative forces inherent in the mind as well as the body, and that in cases of disorder of body or mind, the physician merely gives a helping hand to remove the harmful and to support the healing forces."[15] In the language of Kaplan, the "psychoanalyst and the artist have in common the giving of new form to what is, by identifying what is and eliciting from it that which can and ought to be."[16]

Yet even if we establish a degree of internal consistency in the theory of self-realization, the existence of an urge to self-realization is far from being accepted as a verified datum by the entire scientific world. The consequences of this doubtful status for soterics will be discussed further in the context of the more fundamental principle —the will to live.

If the self-realization principle of soterics is characteristic of the distinctively human species, it may be said that the will to live is common to all living forms. The nature of this Spinozistic "endeavor to preserve one's own being," however, is not clear. Examples of its manifestations offered by Kaplan lead one to assume that it is intended by him as an empirical datum. "The healing of a wound, whether in a tree or in a living being, is a manifestation of an organic urge."[17] Since it is innate and, in its original form, "not meant to be conceived of as a conscious purpose of living beings,"[18] this will would appear in human beings as a generalized instinct— a complex, purposeful, motivating force, "a faculty of acting in such a way as to produce certain ends without previous education in their performance."[19]

Kaplan would ground both the will to live and the will to examine life (self-realization) in human nature, in the organism itself. These data are intended to serve as a reliable, generic base for a normative universe of discourse among all mankind, regardless of the differing forms of specific societies. Thus, while given societies would supply varying norms in the achievement of salvation, the entire world would still be in a position to judge their efficacy.

As for the self-realization principle, agreement about the existence of a general self-preservative urge in organisms is far from settled in psychological literature. Erich Fromm may state that "the desire to live is inherent in every organism and man cannot help wanting to live regardless of what he would like to think about";[20] but another eminent psychologist, Karl Menninger, argues that "the best theory to account for all the presently known facts is Freud's hypothesis of a death instinct."[21] And Muzafer Sherif writes what might apply to both the preceding: "Such dramatic-sounding instincts as the instincts of death and destruction cannot be subjected to the check of controlled investigation."[22] Therefore, from an empirical point of view, considerable doubt is cast upon the urge to self-preservation as the grounds for normative unity. The difficulty with this self-preservation urge lies in making it a generalized designation of reactions to specifically bodily demands or deficits, which, in fact, may only coincidentally have self-preservative value. To reify as motive that which may well be a contingent by-product is as unwarranted as the claim of a purposeful perpetuation of the species on the basis of a mating or sex instinct.

Further, the unqualified will to live may easily be perverted into a pathological drive, an unfettered egoism destructive of the nobler social values. It is in this respect that Kurt Goldstein views the self-preservative drive as "essentially characteristic of a sick people," as symptomatic of "anomalous life, of the decay of life." While it may be that "sometimes the normal organism also tends primarily to avoid catastrophe, . . . this takes place under inadequate conditions and is not at all usual behavior."[23] Anticipating such difficulties, Kaplan has sought to argue that the self that is being preserved includes the higher "ideal self" of social values, as well as the self of the vitalities. "The truth is," he writes, "that the will to live is bi-polar. It is as given to self-spending as to self-preservation."[24] By thus subsuming the socially imposed nature of the self under the single category of the preservation of self, Kaplan intends to avoid the embarrassment that confronted those Idealistic philosophers who formulated reasonably similar self-realization theories (Bosanquet, Green, Bradley, and Royce). But some strength is sapped from the effort to make self-preservation stem from the original nature of the organism itself. There is a measure of truth in Mill's statement that "every respectable attribute of humanity is the result not of instinct but of the victory over instinct."[25]

Even were there no question concerning the empirical status of these life urges, a major gap in the position would exist all the same. The empirically verified character of human nature in no way entails or guarantees agreement that human nature ought to be fulfilled. In any normative system, there is a logical priority of value to fact. Were it established that a death instinct does, in fact, operate, it is doubtful that Kaplan would legitimate it as a normative base. Kaplan assigns a telic significance to the will to live and the will to self-realization, namely, that their purpose lies not simply in their fulfillment. That argument does not make the leap from the descriptive to the normative any the less unwarranted.

It would be regrettable were our difficulties with both the will to live and the will to maximum life to cause us to overlook the genuine contributions soterics may make as a "common hypothetical method of achieving salvation," as Kaplan puts it. Recognizing the problems, it appears reasonable to suggest the abandonment of these "wills" treated as verified data and their adoption as hypothetical outgrowths of a metaphysical substructure, the basic presuppositions of Kaplan's ethics and theology. This metaphysical substructure would contain at least three major presuppositions:

1. There exist certain universal biological, psychological, and social needs and interests in man.
2. The integrated gratification of these needs and interests is a value.
3. The world is so salvation-conditioned as to enable their gratification.

Such metaphysical presuppositions are, of course, not subjects for verification in the scientific sense because the nature of these presuppositions has nothing to do with truth or falsity but rather with pragmatic efficacy. Unlike the unverifiable propositions of super-naturalism, they make no claim to ontological status. Their use is regulative and heuristic, not substantive and constitutive. They are subject to rejection should they not prove fruitful.

Soterical presuppositions may be vindicated on the same grounds as are the principles of induction or of the uniformity of nature made by science itself. It has more than once been pointed out that "all knowledge which on a basis of experience tells us something about what is not experienced is based upon a belief (an inductive principle) which experience cannot confirm or confute, yet which . . . appears to be as firmly rooted in us as many facts of experience."[26]

To understand Kaplan's claims as regulative invites several observations. First, requisite for the construction of a universal ethics, "a kind of valuational Esperanto," is the recognition of certain universal needs (innate) and interests (acquired). This might well direct the attention of soterics to such well-accepted but simpler biological drives as hunger, sex, and thirst and to such social-psychological interests as status and role-taking. The generalized formulations of the will to live and the will to maximum life would be considered hypotheses subject to further study. Investigation in this direction may also lead to a clearer understanding of the nature of the self, a basic category in the soterics of Kaplan, for the essence of value appears to be judged in terms of the activities and behavior contributory to the actualization of the self's natural tendencies. It is the self that experiences desires and impulses and seeks their satisfaction. It is the self that, in a manner of speaking, is also experienced, becoming an object unto itself, in that it evaluates the consequences of its behavior and organizes its value system. The self might be said, then, to contain the material, formal, final, and efficient causes of its being. This is the distinctively humanistic element in soterics, portraying as it does the self as an active agent, an artist creating its salvation, in proper contrast with the passive role of the self that awaits otherworldly salvation.

Further study into this vital category is made necessary by soterics, since the self is so complex and multifunctional in nature.

What is the proper balance in the assignment of value to the varying aspects of the self as both an egoistic and altruistic being?

Second, therefore, in stating that the source of value lies in the integrated satisfaction of the needs and interests of the organism, Kaplan proposes an indissoluble relationship between salvation and health. Physical and mental hygiene and the religious ethics of soterics are not related by analogy alone. What is healthful and what is moral are integrally related. With the successful advent of psychiatric therapy, that relationship between mental and moral hygiene has been reinforced. Many an unethical act is understood as a manifestation of illness, for example, compulsive gambling, sadistic behavior, alcoholism, psychopathic murder, and kleptomania. These vices are now increasingly examined as illnesses. Murder and theft are evil, but they are additionally understood in terms of their consequences for the total functioning organism. The penetration of psychiatry and its methods and therapy into the fields previously monopolized by abstract analyses or dogmatic theology is in keeping with the soterical emphasis on total (mental, physical, and moral) health as a central concern for personal salvation.

Third, the soterical presupposition of a salvation-conditioned universe so patterned as to contain the means of satisfying man's craving for self-realization elicits a natural piety toward those powers within the universe. Appreciation of the distinguishable powers for human salvation does not eliminate the reality of evil. It affirms not that reality is good but that goodness is real.[27] The "givenness" of societal and nonhuman environments that man takes as contributory to value denies the theological claim that the universe is essentially hostile to human ends. In the same spirit as Kaplan, Van der Leeuw extols the universe as good by pointing to "water and trees, the fruit of the fields and beasts in the forest [as] bringers of salvation; the force issuing from their power transforms the gloom of life into joy and happiness. . . . Culture too is 'salvation,' that is, a deed which is willed or volitional."[28]

Kaplan refers to this presupposition as a soterical "inference," an acknowledged "willed faith" that is pragmatically understood. Much as adequacy, intersubjectivity, and consistency serve to vindicate

268   HAROLD M. SCHULWEIS

the inductive principle, so the purposes of salvation justify the sentiment that "man's cosmos is en rapport with the human will to salvation."[29] The moral optimism of such a salvation principle is, like the principle of induction, motivational and directive. It offers a structure of expectancies creating belief in the possibilities of human experience that serve to inspire people to achieve that end. This morale is intended to keep persons strong. Kaplan asserts that "insofar as the belief in God makes a difference in a person's life or in the life of a group, it must have consequences in the domain of effectiveness."[30] How can a working principle that sustains human endeavor, whether in science or religion, not incline us to interpret reality as somehow amenable to the aspirations of men?

John Stuart Mill stated unequivocally the problematic in the naturalist's reconstruction of traditional supernaturalism:

It needs to be considered whether in order to obtain the effective morale resulting from supernaturalist faith, it is necessary to travel beyond the boundaries of the world which we inhabit; or whether the idealization of our earthly life, the cultivation of a high conception of what it may be made, is not capable of supplying a poetry, and in the best sense of the word a religion, equally fitted to exalt the feeling and, with the same aid from education, still better calculated to ennoble the conduct, than any belief respecting unseen powers."[31]

Once a man is informed that faith in a salvational cosmos is an instrument that gains for us moral optimism and strengthens our hearts, does his awareness reduce the efficacy of prayer? Will anyone recite *geshem* (the prayer for rain) knowing full well that no palpable favors will ensue, that it may only serve to direct those feelings of gratitude to an indispensable natural force?

The religious naturalist must recognize the problem. It is too late for him to turn back and pretend that neither philosophy nor science has made its inroads. Those religious personalities committed to a naturalist position cannot afford the luxury of bemoaning the loss of a certain type of morale attendant on the supernaturalist's faith, the more so since many other consequences of such belief are entirely dysfunctional.

The reconstructing naturalist needs instead to invade new areas of morale and to plan new interpretations of symbols and rites so as to compensate for the loss of comfort and ease afforded by facile conformity to convention. The observation of sociologist Robert Merton is of interest in this respect:

Those functionalists who . . . attend only to the effects of such symbolic practices (rituals) upon the individual state of mind . . . neglect the fact that these very practices may on occasion take the place of more effective alternatives. And those theorists who refer to the indispensability of standardized practices or prevailing institutions because of their observed function in reinforcing common sentiments must look first to functional substitutes before arriving at a conclusion, more often premature than confirmed.[32]

It is this fruitful direction that soterics impells us to explore.

In the midst of public religious apathy and in the sight of piece-meal emendations, false sentiments, and half-truths, the religious naturalist needs to base his morale on the wisdom of the past and the vision of a future. In the words of Emerson, "The sun shines today also. There is more food and flax in the fields. There are new lands, new men, new thoughts; let us demand our own works and laws and worship."[33]

Notes

1. Milton Steinberg, "Theological Problems of the Hour," in *Rabbinical Assembly Proceedings* (New York: Rabbinical Assembly of America, 1949), 378.
2. Milton Steinberg, *The Common Sense of Religious Faith* (New York: Jewish Reconstructionist Foundation, 1947), 12.
3. From an unpublished manuscript by Mordecai M. Kaplan, entitled "The Art of Being Human." Kaplan Archives, Reconstructionist Rabbinical College.
4. L. Feuerbach, quoted in H. Hoffding, *History of Modern Philosophy*, vol. 2 (London: Macmillan, 1915), 277.
5. Kaplan, "Art of Being Human," 60a.
6. Ibid., 33.
7. Plotinus, quoted in *The Essence of Plotinus*, trans. Stephen Mackenna (New York: Oxford University Press, 1934), 49.
8. Kurt Goldstein, *The Organism* (New York: American Book, 1939), 196.
9. Karen Horney, *Neurosis and Human Growth* (New York: W. W. Norton, 1950), 15.
10. Erich Fromm, *Psycholanalysis and Religion* (New Haven: Yale University Press, 1950), 74.

11. Ibid., 20.
12. *Saos* in Greek; *salvus* in Latin; *Heil* in German. Interestingly, too, *soteriology*, in the study of hygiene, refers to laws of health.
13. Paul Tillich, "The Relation of Religion to Health" (Paper presented at University Seminar on Religion, Columbia University, 1945–46), 349.
14. Henry Sidgwick, *Lectures on the Ethics of T. H. Green, H. Spencer, and J. Martineau* (London: Macmillan, 1902), 64.
15. Horney, *Neurosis and Human Growth*, 348.
16. Kaplan, "Art of Being Human," 112.
17. Mordecai M. Kaplan, "Towards a Philosophy of Cultural Integration," in *Approaches to Group Understanding*, ed. Bryson et al. (New York: Harper & Brothers, 1947), 603.
18. Mordecai M. Kaplan, "The Need for Normative Unity in Higher Education," in *Goals for American Education*, ed. Lyman Bryson, Louis Finkelstein, and R. M. MacIver (New York: Harper & Brothers, 1950), 308.
19. William James, *Principles of Psychology*, vol. 2 (New York: Henry Holt, 1931), 383.
20. Erich Fromm, *Man for Himself* (New York: Harcourt Brace, 1938), 13.
21. Karl Menninger, *Man against Himself* (New York: Harcourt Brace, 1938), 13.
22. Muzafer Sherif, *An Outline of Social Psychology* (New York: Harper & Brothers, 1948), 20.
23. Goldstein, *Organism*, 197.
24. Kaplan, "Need for Normative Unity," 312.
25. John Stuart Mill, "Essay on Nature," in *Three Essays on Religion* (New York: Henry Holt, 1874), 46.
26. Bertrand Russell, *Problems of Philosophy* (New York: Oxford University Press, 1948), 69.
27. All the more puzzling is Henry Wieman's claim that Dr. Kaplan identifies the universe with God or goodness and is thus "forced to defend his belief in the goodness of the universe against the facts of evil" (*Review of Religion* 14, no. 1 [November 1949]: 51).
28. G. Van der Leeuw, *Religion in Essence and in Manifestation* (London: Allen and Unwin, 1938), 101, 104.
29. Mordecai M. Kaplan, *The Future of the American Jew* (New York: Macmillan, 1948), 193.
30. Kaplan, "Art of Being Human," 75.
31. Mill, "The Utility of Religion," in *Three Essays*, (see n. 25), 105.
32. Robert Merton, *Social Theory and Social Structure* (Glencoe, Ill.: Free Press, 1949), 37.
33. Ralph Waldo Emerson, quoted in Morris R. Cohen, *A Dreamer's Journey* (Boston: Beacon Press, 1949), 180.

CHAPTER 12

Kaplan's Approach to Metaphysics

William E. Kaufman

Writing about Kaplan's theology in his book *Anatomy of Faith*, Milton Steinberg contended that "it is precisely in Kaplan's dispatch of the metaphysical problem that I have always had my most grievous difficulties with his thought. It makes a great deal of difference to me whether God is an entity, a being in himself, an aspect of reality, or a useful fiction."[1] In contrast, Harold Schulweis interprets Kaplan's thought as an "empirical metaphysics, which employs concepts of maximum generality in searching for the pervasive traits of the natural world and of human nature."[2] Clearly, Steinberg and Schulweis are operating with different conceptions of metaphysics. The first step in evaluating Kaplan's approach to metaphysics, therefore, is to reflect on the nature and diversity of the metaphysical enterprise itself.

The term *metaphysics* may be defined as "philosophical inquiry into being or reality".[3] Since Kaplan's method was pragmatic, his primary concern was not an analysis of being qua being. Nor was he interested in speculative philosophy as Whitehead defined it, namely, "the endeavor to frame a coherent, logical, necessary system of general ideas in terms of which every element in our experience can be interpreted."[4] Metaphysics is not the name of a simple single activity; diverse metaphysicians have had diverse intellectual ambitions.[5] There are many modes of inquiry into the nature of reality. Bearing in mind the diversity of metaphysical styles, my aim in this essay is to determine the type of metaphysical inquiry Kaplan engages in, the role it plays in his thought, and his unique approach to it.

The basic metaphysical decision of a philosopher is his choice of categories, the way he carves up reality and the basic presuppositions with which he operates. As philosophers survey the various entities about which discourse is possible, they usually conclude that entities of a certain sort are more important than entities of other sorts.

Even a cursory reading of Kaplan's works yields the realization that he prefers terms such as *power, force,* or *process* to anthropomorphic ways of speaking about God or ultimate reality. Consider, for example, these passages:

It is sufficient that God should mean to us the sum of the animating, organizing forces and relationships which are forever making a cosmos out of chaos.[6]

Thinking of God as a process rather than an entity in no way tends to make Him less real.[7]

In the foregoing passages, Kaplan has not dispatched the metaphysical issue, as Steinberg had claimed. Rather, what Kaplan was groping for was a new and distinctively "modern" metaphysics, utilizing categories such as "force" and "process" rather than notions of personal agency. The problems involved in Kaplan's choice of categories I shall consider below. The point I wish to establish now is that Kaplan did make metaphysical decisions in the choice of the categories he employed to interpret reality.

In his *attitude* toward metaphysics, however, Kaplan was ambivalent. Consider, for example, this statement:

That we cannot know what Divinity is apart from our idea of it should not be surprising. There is nothing we can possibly know apart from our idea of it. We are told, for instance, that matter is frozen energy. Yet how helpful is this definition to us? What do we really know about energy except the way it functions?[8]

Kaplan here is advocating a pragmatic or functional approach to the idea of God that seems antithetical to metaphysics.

Now let us reflect on another passage in Kaplan's writings:

Nature is infinite chaos, with all its evils forever being vanquished by creativity, which is God as infinite goodness. That is the conclusion arrived at through wisdom that is mature. The power of God is inexhaustible but not infinite.[9]

In the foregoing passage, Kaplan is clearly making metaphysical claims. In fact, it is only as a metaphysical statement that this passage makes sense. If it is intended as a scientific cosmological statement, it is manifestly untrue. On a purely immanent level, it is simply false that creativity shall forever conquer chaos in the universe. According to the concept of entropy and the second law of thermodynamics, the universe will ultimately run down. Bertrand Russell graphically depicts his view that the scientifically disclosed universe is ultimately destined for extinction:

That man is the product of causes which had no prevision of the end they were achieving; that his origin, his growth, his hopes and fears, his loves and his beliefs, are but the outcome of accidental collocations of atoms; that no fire, no heroism, no intensity of thought and feeling can preserve an individual beyond the grave; that all the labors of the ages, all the devotion, all the inspiration, all the noonday brightness of human genius, are destined to extinction in the vast death of the solar system, and that the whole temple of man's achievement must eventually be buried beneath the debris of a universe in ruins—all these things, if not quite beyond dispute, are yet so nearly certain that no philosophy which rejects them can hope to stand.[10]

In our present cosmic epoch, it is most probably untrue, on an immanent level, that creativity will forever conquer chaos. Kaplan's assertion that creativity will conquer chaos can, therefore, only be justified on a metaphysical level. Some concepts of Whiteheadian process philosophy suggest ways of dealing metaphysically with this problematic aspect of Kaplan's thought.

The concept of "process," according to Whitehead, signifies that the fundamental characteristic of nature is "passage" or "creative advance." Creative advance, or creativity, for Whitehead is one of the formative elements in the world. In *Religion in the Making*, Whitehead identifies the formative elements in the world as follows:

1. The creativity whereby the actual world has the character of temporal passage to novelty.

2. The realm of ideal entities or forms, not actual but exemplified in everything actual.

3. The actual but non-temporal entity whereby the indeterminacy of mere creativity is transmuted into a determinate freedom. This non-temporal entity is what men call God—the supreme God of rational religion.[11]

Why does Whitehead find it necessary to introduce God as a factor in the world? Whitehead sees the world as a vast network of momentary events coming into being and lapsing into the past. Each new event must take account of other events that make up its world and must do so in a definite way, for without definiteness there can be no actuality. Now, if the form of definiteness derived only from the past, each event would exhibit no freedom or spontaneity. Thus, the form of definiteness must be derived from the realm of possibility. But the realm of possibility is purely abstract; it lacks agency. Whitehead maintains that there must be an agency that mediates between these abstract forms, or pure possibilities, and the actual world. This agency, for Whitehead, is God, who envisages the abstract forms of definiteness in such a way as to establish their relevance to each new situation in the world. God thus establishes what-is-not as relevant to what is and thereby lures the world toward new forms of realization. God, for Whitehead, represents the call to possibility, the lure of novelty toward unrealized ideals beyond what the past compels us to become. This description of the not-yet impinging on the now, the lure of novelty, the freedom of self-transcendence, the attainment of value—these are the elements in immediate experience that Whitehead sees as manifestations of God.

Whitehead also maintains that God has an ultimate harmonizing function. For Whitehead, only if God is an everlasting actual entity who transcends the rest of actuality is it possible to maintain that creativity will forever conquer chaos. This is so by virtue of creative events achieving "objective immortality" after they perish, by being preserved and transmuted in the harmony of God's experience.

Although Kaplan's theology requires something like a Whiteheadian framework for its metaphysical completion, this does not mean that Kaplan would have accepted all the details of such a conceptual system. The principal difference between Whitehead and Kaplan on metaphysics is as follows: Whitehead, like Kaplan, frequently uses locutions such as "aspect of the universe" or "factor in the universe" to refer to God. The obvious question, then, is whether Whitehead's thought is an example of "naturalistic" theism. Victor Lowe, a leading authority on Whitehead, writes, "The summary reply to this question is to point out that Whitehead always conceives of God as being an actual entity; we may not say 'aspect' and stop. He transcends the world as much as he is immanent in the world."[12] This does not mean that Whitehead was a supernaturalist. But he did maintain that God was an actual entity transcending the rest of actuality. Kaplan, in contrast, *was* content with locutions referring to God, such as "aspect of the universe." Furthermore, Kaplan did not wish to identify God as an entity of any kind, as he stated explicitly in the statement quoted previously: "Thinking of God as a process rather than as an entity in no way tends to make Him less real."[13]

God for Kaplan is more akin to Whitehead's notion of creativity than to Whitehead's idea of God, for Whitehead's "creativity" is analogous to Kaplan's concept of God as "the inexhaustible fund of creative potentiality in nature."[14] Kaplan's claim that the creative potentiality is *inexhaustible* can only be justified metaphysically; as we have seen, scientifically this potentiality may not be unlimited. The comparison and contrast with process theology shows that Kaplan's effort to stay clear of conceiving God as an entity raises questions of the status of God in his thought.

Can Kaplan's God, which by his own definition is not an identifiable entity but rather creativity as potential and in process, be rendered intelligible? Kaplan alternates between two nouns in speaking of God: "power" (potential creativity) and "process." Belief in God, Kaplan writes, is faith "in the existence of a power in the world that furthers man's salvation. This is the faith that reality, the cosmos, or whatever constitutes for us the universe in which we move and have our being, is so constituted that it both urges us on and helps us to achieve our salvation, provided, of course, we learn to know and understand enough about that reality to be able to conform to its demands."[15]

The foregoing is so obviously a metaphysical statement that one wonders how anyone could deny that Kaplan has a metaphysics.

He speaks about "reality" or the "cosmos" and predicates of it an urge that impels man to fulfillment or salvation. The uniqueness of Kaplan's scheme is that it is a *participatory metaphysics;* that is, man must participate in the reality to know it (he must learn to "know and understand" enough about it to conform to its demands).

For Kaplan, then, God functions as the power or process that impels us to make the best use of our lives. It can be known only by participation, by allowing it to function in our lives. The key question is, What is the metaphysical status of this God-idea for Kaplan? If humankind were to perish in a nuclear war, does God die? In other words, is God merely a function of the human quest for salvation; or, to put it in Kaplan's terminology, is God *only* a correlative term—that is, correlative to man?

In an article entitled "When Is a Religion Authentic?" Kaplan distinguishes his notion of God from that of John Dewey. Whereas for John Dewey the term *God* is merely "an emotional symbol for the object of human idealism,"[16] Kaplan asserts that his use of the term *God* has "both a correlative meaning and a substantive meaning. The correlative meaning is the one it has from the standpoint of what it affirms concerning salvation. The substantive meaning is the one it has from the standpoint of what it affirms concerning the cosmos independently of its relation to man."[17]

Kaplan maintains that the distinction he draws between the "correlative" and the "substantive" uses of the term *God* parallels Maimonides's distinction between the divine attributes and essence. It is well known that Maimonides felt that only two types of predicates can be used concerning God: negative attributes and attributes of action. The essence of God remains *unknowable.* Kaplan reinterprets Maimonides's attributes of action to reflect the discernment of the existence of God "in the functioning of moral responsibility and in His attribute as the Power that makes for man's salvation."[18]

This is Kaplan's interpretation of the "correlative" meaning of the term *God.* The "substantive" meaning of God is the cosmic process of ontological polarity, which undergirds the human sense of responsibility that Kaplan came to regard as the path to human salvation. Kaplan explains:

Salvation is the maximum harmonious functioning of a person's physical, mental, social, moral, and spiritual powers. Such harmonious functioning consists in man's conscious fulfillment of nature's most inclusive cosmic process of ontological polarity. This is the process which underlies all other cosmic polarities, present in nature and identified in physics, chemistry, biology, psychology, and sociology. That is the process whereby everything in the universe possesses an individuality of its own and at the same time interacts with whatever is in its field. When this cosmic synthesis of individuation and interaction functions in the individual, or in society, as independence and interdependence, it is experienced as a sense of responsibility, or as conscience.[19]

Accordingly, for Kaplan, God as ontological polarity is to moral responsibility as light is to color, or as the law of gravity is to the falling of the apple. Where, then, one might ask, is the sense of mystery with which Maimonides approached the unfathomable essence of God? How does Kaplan pursue the parallel he wants to establish between his metaphysics and "the doctrine concerning God's essence and attributes dealt with by Maimonides"?[20] It is interesting to note precisely where Kaplan locates the mystery. Kaplan writes that "the ultimate connection between ontological polarity and man's salvation must forever remain a mystery."[21] It is precisely in the connection between the substantive and the correlative aspects of God that Kaplan locates the ontological mystery rather than, as Maimonides does, in the essence of God itself.

Kaplan's effort to ground the correlative or functional aspect of God in the substantive nature of the deity surely confirms that metaphysics played a considerable role in his theology. If Kaplan were only interested in the pragmatic aspects of human salvation, he would not have attempted to ground his soteriology in a metaphysical understanding of God as ontological polarity. The status of *God* for Kaplan is not merely a function of human soteriology but also a cosmic reality independent of man. Like Maimonides, Kaplan realized that the metaphysical quest ultimately issues in a mystery, which Kaplan locates in the ultimate connection between ontological polarity and man's salvation.

The fact that Kaplan locates the mystery where he does indicates that he was unclear about the precise connection between God as the creative cosmic process and God as the power that makes for human salvation. Although in terms of metaphysical status, God as substantive is independent of man, God is not independent of nature. God is either a law of nature, such as ontological polarity, or the creative potential within nature, or the creative process of nature—the term *God* takes on each of these meanings in Kaplan's theology. There is thus a lack of integration among the various terms Kaplan uses for God and between God's substantive and correlative aspects.

The status of God in Kaplan's theology is thus highly ambiguous. Clearly, Kaplan wanted to assert that God is more than simply a function of nature, as manifested in his use of the term *transnaturalism* to characterize his theology. Yet, he would not go as far as Whitehead and envisage God as an actual entity transcending the rest of actuality. Kaplan would have considered the notion of God as an actual entity to be a reification of a process. The problem is that Kaplan needed a notion of God as a "super-process" transcending nature in order to be clear of the scientific concepts of entropy and the second law of thermodynamics. He comes closest to such a notion when he refers to the "inexhaustible" power of God; but for the most part, God for Kaplan is an aspect or process within nature. As such, the metaphysical status of God in Kaplan's thought remains problematic.

In his book *The Return to Cosmology: Postmodern Science and the Theology of Nature*,[22] Stephen Toulmin maintains that mythology is not merely a thing of the past, exemplified by the personification or anthropomorphic thinking that created Atlas, Ceres, Wotan, and Poseidon. In contrast to the ancient anthropomorphic myths, the myths of the twentieth century, Toulmin holds, are not so much anthropomorphic as mechanomorphic.[23] When we think of the universe as a machine or when we remove words like *force* or *energy* from their clearly defined scientific contexts and apply them to the universe as a whole, we are not thinking scientifically but mythically. The question thus arises as to whether Kaplan has merely replaced anthropomorphic mythology with what Toulmin calls "scientific mythology."

On the face of it, Kaplan surely uses scientific terms such as *process*, *force*, and *energy* and employs constructs such as ontological polarity to characterize the universe as a whole. Has Kaplan then merely replaced an anthropomorphic myth with a mechano-morphic myth?

Kaplan ultimately falls back on organic rather than mechanical analogies in his metaphysical claims. Clearly, he rejects anthropo-morphic mythological thinking when he writes, "We cannot con-ceive of God any more as a sort of invisible superman, displaying the same psychological traits as a man, but on a larger scale. We cannot think of him as loving, pitying, rewarding, punishing, etc."[24] But Kaplan does not wish to go to the other extreme and to think about God and the universe in purely mechanical terms. He contin-ues: "Many have therefore abandoned altogether the conception of a personal God, and prefer to think of ultimate reality in terms of force, energy, and similar concepts. Such an attitude is, however, erroneous. It violates completely our sense of the sacredness of life. It is irrelevant to human ideals and the quest for salvation."[25]

Thus, Kaplan does not think of God as process, force, or ontolog-ical polarity *simpliciter*. He uses an organic metaphor to steer a middle course between anthropomorphism and mechanomorphism when he maintains that "there is something divine in human per-sonality, in that it is the instrument through which the creative life of the world effects the evolution of the human race."[26]

Here Kaplan approximates the organic view of process philoso-phy. In the above passage he is closer to Bergson's process metaphys-ics than to Whitehead's, the "creative life of the world" being analogous to Bergson's *élan vital*, or "vital force." Use of organic metaphors, such as "life of the universe" or "vital force" are, of course, also forms of scientific mythology, since virtually all scien-tists today reject vitalism as a scientific hypothesis. Therefore, it can be evaluated only as a metaphysical, and not as a scientific, claim.

W. H. Walsh provides a useful analysis of the criteria to be used in evaluating metaphysical claims. The task of the metaphysician, he asserts, is to give "a connected account of the world as a whole."[27] No scientific theory can claim to cover all the facts because there is no agreement about what all the facts are. Metaphysical statements are, therefore, neither true nor false in any simple noncontroversial sense. Rather, what we look for in a metaphysical theory is illumi-nation and new insight into the way we see the world, in much the same way as we regard a literary theory as illuminating or not. At the heart of a metaphysical theory is a choice or commitment as to what sorts of things are basic and fundamental rather than derivative and secondary.

Kaplan's metaphysical choice is a decision to accept the organic metaphor of God as "the creative life of the universe" as the most illuminating metaphor because it does the most justice to that factor in the nature of life, "which expresses itself in human personality, which evokes ideals, which sends men on the quest of personal and social salvation."[28] This, too, is the significance of Kaplan's transnaturalism; it represents the fact that Kaplan sees nature as transcending the mechanical. As Kaplan explains, "The soul is the creative plus in human nature, as God is the creative plus of nature as a whole. God represents the inexhaustible fund of creative potentiality in nature by virtue of which it transcends the mechanical."[29]

Kaplan's approach to metaphysics is soteriological. He chooses those metaphysical or universal factors in the world that he believed would be most generative of human ideals and most evocative for the human quest for salvation. In some passages, he sees the pervasive characteristics of the universe as "the sum of the animating, organizing forces and relationships which are forever making a cosmos out of chaos." In other passages, he sees the pervasive universal trend as the creative process of nature or as "ontological polarity." Ultimately, he sees the metaphysical essence as "the creative life of the world" that evokes the human striving for salvation. But there can be no doubt that his claims that there exist such pervasive characteristics as ontological polarity and organicity in the universe are clearly and indubitably metaphysical statements.

To summarize, Kaplan cannot be accused of dispatching the metaphysical issue. Rather, he was constantly striving to formulate in various ways a metaphysical view of the universe that would furnish a foundation for his fundamental claim that the universe is so constituted as to enable man to achieve salvation—a claim that is itself a metaphysical assertion. Kaplan thus shares with the process theologians the quest for those ultimate factors in the cosmic process that generate and support humankind in its search for the values and the ideals that render life worth living.

Notes

1. Milton Steinberg, *Anatomy of Faith*, ed. Arthur A. Cohen (New York: Harcourt Brace, 1960), 248.
2. Harold Schulweis, "Kaplan's Theory of Soterics," in *Mordecai M. Kaplan: An Evaluation* (New York: Reconstructionist Foundation, 1952), 263.
3. Robert N. Beck, *Perspectives in Philosophy* (New York: Holt, Rinehart & Winston, 1975), 564.
4. Alfred North Whitehead, *Process and Reality* (New York: Harper & Brothers, 1929), 4.
5. See W. H. Walsh, *Metaphysics* (New York: Harcourt Brace and World, 1962), 17ff.
6. Mordecai M. Kaplan, *The Meaning of God in Modern Jewish Religion* (New York: Reconstructionist Press, 1962), 76.
7. Mordecai M. Kaplan, *The Future of the American Jew* (1948; reprint, New York: Reconstructionist Press, 1967), 183.
8. Mordecai M. Kaplan, "The Meaning of God for the Contemporary Jew," in *Tradition and Contemporary Experience*, ed. Alfred Jospe (New York: Schocken, 1970), 70–71.
9. Mordecai M. Kaplan, *The Religion of Ethical Nationhood* (New York: Macmillan, 1970), 51.
10. Bertrand Russell, "A Free Man's Worship," in *Why I Am Not a Christian* (New York: Simon & Schuster, 1957), 107.
11. Alfred North Whitehead, *Religion in the Making* (New York: Meridian, 1960), 88.
12. Victor Lowe, *Understanding Whitehead* (Baltimore: Johns Hopkins University Press, 1956), 105.
13. Kaplan, *Future of the American Jew*, 183.
14. Kaplan, *Religion of Ethical Nationhood*, 91.
15. Kaplan, *Future of the American Jew*, 182.
16. Mordecai M. Kaplan, "When Is a Religion Authentic?" *Reconstructionist* 30, no. 11 October 2, 1964): 16–17.
17. Ibid., 17.
18. Ibid., 16.
19. Ibid., 15.
20. Ibid., 16.
21. Ibid.
22. Stephen Toulmin, *The Return to Cosmology: Postmodern Science and the Theology of Nature* (Berkley: University of California Press, 1982).
23. Ibid., 24.
24. Kaplan, *Meaning of God*, 88.

25. Ibid.
26. Ibid., 89.
27. Walsh, *Metaphysics*, 77.
28. Kaplan, *Meaning of God*, 89.
29. Kaplan, *Religion of Ethical Nationhood*, 91.

CHAPTER 13

Kaplan and Process Theology

Jacob J. Staub

No aspect of the teachings of Mordecai M. Kaplan has provoked more powerful reactions than his theology, and no aspect of his writings is in greater need of amplification and clarification. His discussions of God have attracted a faithful and passionate group of followers. For them, the naturalistic idiom of Reconstructionist theology has led to a commitment to a life of Jewish practice and belief long after faith in traditional teachings has been lost. On the other hand, Kaplan's critics have accused him of everything from fuzzy thinking to atheism and have resorted to the dubious assertion that his forays into theology have removed him from the realm of authentically Jewish discourse.

The question of the Jewish authenticity of Kaplan's theology will not be the primary subject of this paper. Those who understand and accept Kaplan's vision of the evolving nature of Jewish civilization *and* those who have troubled to study the history of Jewish thought know full well that any attempt to extract a single, consistent, "authentic" essence from all of the various theological formulations by Jewish teachers through the ages is a perilous task indeed.

Jewish history presents us with such unwieldy paradoxes as the dominance of the uncompromising naturalism of Maimonides's negative theology on one side of the Pyrenees precisely when, just several hundred miles away, the Hasidei Ashkenaz were reacting to the First Crusade with a theology that denied the existence of natural law and portrayed God as involved in the most particular of occurrences. At the time, neither side would have admitted the legitimacy of the other's most beloved beliefs; and yet, subsequently, Jews incorporated aspects of each side into their theologies. No flourish of rhetoric nor any homily on the unchanging nature of Jewish monotheism can convince the serious student of Jewish intellectual history that Moses' conception of God was identical to that of Rabbi Akiva, or that the theological speculations of the *yordei merkavah* were more or less faithful to the biblical and rabbinic ideas of God than were the logical arguments of Sa'adia Gaon or the midnight auditions of Joseph Karo.

The fact is that Jews' descriptions of God have varied widely based on variations in their personal temperaments, their individual and collective experiences, and the cultural influences to which they have been subject. In light of this, the most appropriate and useful evaluation of the theology of any Jewish thinker, Kaplan included, will deal with its self-consistency and its ability to provide a convincing framework within which Jews can pursue Jewish lives. It is the experiences of Jewish people in history—and not a rigidly defined conceptual standard—that render the final verdict about whether a given theological approach provides a meaningful system for Jewish living.

Applying these criteria to Kaplan's writings, even the sympathetic reader is struck by the unsystematic nature of Kaplan's theological reflections. Kaplan, of course, would have been the first to admit that he was not primarily engaged in metaphysical speculation. He believed that the proponents of what he saw as the outmoded system of traditional, eastern European beliefs were doomed to fail in their attempts to convince modern, Western Jews of the ongoing relevance of those beliefs. In seeking to adapt the Jewish heritage to the radically unprecedented situation of the twentieth century, he enthusiastically adopted the then-current philosophy of pragmatism as the vehicle for that adaptation.

Thus, wedded as he was to a pragmatic search for the means to human salvation that admitted that we can know only what we experience, Kaplan focused on our intuition of transcendence, on our experience of a process that impels us to strive for life-abundant, and on our sense that the cosmos is in rapport with the human quest. We know the presence of God, he affirmed repeatedly, when it is manifest in our lives and behavior—and not via abstract metaphysical speculation nor through faith in the witness and teachings of preceding generations.

Given this pragmatic approach, it should not surprise the student of Kaplan that he never embarked upon the construction of a systematic portrait of the nature of the universe and God's relation to it. He attempted to chart questions of transcendence by mapping the interiorities of concrete human experience—the only source, according to the pragmatic approach, of valid knowledge. Those who mistake this approach for Kaplan's denial or avoidance of the "objective" reality of God fail to understand Kaplan's approach to objectivity itself. For him, abstract theories about God's nature were epistemologically suspect; in relating God's reality to the concrete realities of the human quest for salvation, he sought not to undercut but rather to bolster his readers' belief in God.

In the process of articulating his prescription for how we can make God manifest, however, Kaplan was led—against his will, it sometimes seems—to make affirmations that exceed the limits of the certainties of human experience. That God is the creative life of the universe, the sum of forces making cosmos out of chaos; that God is immanent insofar as all parts of the universe act upon each other and is transcendent insofar as the whole acts upon each part; that reality is so constituted as to enable people to achieve salvation; that God strives to redeem us and impels us to pursue self-transcendence; that God is a cosmic process that includes and exceeds all other physical, biological, chemical, physiological, and social processes—these are metaphysical assertions that beg for clarification and systematization. As statements of faith, they require no demonstration. But if they are to be persuasive and compelling—the stuff by which purposive lives can be lived—they ought to be shown to be self-consistent and reasonably related to the reality that people encounter in their lives.

In fact, however, such Kaplanian images of God are far from being self-evidently consistent, nor do they obviously accord with the experience of reality many people have. As poetic metaphors, they masterfully evoke images of a greater divine force coursing through the natural world. They do not cause a contemporary Jew to stumble over assertions of supernatural divine intervention or of a royal, personal figure sitting above, controlling events according to a divine plan. Thus, they are effective in opening up glimpses of transcendence to contemporary Jews whose secularized upbringing has left no room for a supernaturalistic belief in God. Unless these metaphors, however, can be interwoven into a more consistent system that sustains the individual through the vicissitudes of his or her life, the moving poetry of communal prayer will end up being discarded in the intensive-care units of hospitals and the conference rooms in which ethical decisions are made. Some of the questions raised when one assembles Kaplan's assorted statements about God are as follows.

1. What does it mean to say that the divine creative life of the universe includes all other processes and that it organizes cosmos out of chaos? How does God relate to the world? Is God manifest everywhere—in nature's malevolent aspects as well as in its benevolent aspects? In human failures as well as in human successes? Sometimes Kaplan speaks about God as the sum; at other times, he contrasts the divine forces that make for cosmos with the chaos that has yet to manifest divinity.

Thus, the reader of Kaplan is left to wonder whether the God process is an all-inclusive unity, or if it is one complex of processes among others. Such an ambiguity has obvious consequences for the Kaplanian worldview. One might choose to assume that he sought to portray in a contemporary idiom the paradox that much of preceding Jewish thought has rested on—namely, that God is both within the world and beyond it. Even within that paradox, however, we still want to know whether the divine embraces the bad with the good, or if the divine is an ally in our quest that struggles as we do with that which is not yet divine.

2. On what ground does Kaplan stand when he affirms that the basic human hungers are essentially or primarily noble? While it is pragmatically and homiletically effective to stress our quest for freedom and justice, for example, in order to cultivate those qualities, such a strategy ought to be based on a consistent truth-claim. On what credible basis, however, can Kaplan regard evils, as he does, as no more than obstacles that cannot resist the divine cur-

rent, that are only real in the sense that darkness is the absence of light?

The work of psychologists in this century—not to mention the clear emergence of radical evil on the world political scene—would lead us to the contrary conclusion: that people's ignoble impulses are every bit as real as their striving for nobility. Thus, the God that we may come to know through our experiences of transcendence may be pragmatically assumed to be real, but consistency would require the admission by similar means of the existence of evil forces—either on which God has no effect or which in some sense should *also* be regarded as divine.

3. On what basis can we be confident that the so-called divine processes are more than human projections upon a universe that is value-neutral? When the reality of God is experienced in luminous moments, we can affirm the reality of that experience. Unless one can account, however, for occasional or intermittent flashes of divine illumination in terms of a symbolic picture of the universe that accords with that experience, luminous moments do not in themselves render God persuasively present as a real force in the world and in our lives.

To a great extent, the predicate theology that has been developed by Harold Schulweis clarifies Kaplan's thought by identifying divinity with the divine predicates and by denying the reality of a divine subject. For Schulweis, God is manifest when divine things happen, and there is no divine subject to whom we may attribute the existence of evil. If he is read as constructing a midrash on Kaplan, Schulweis can be seen to have eliminated all of those problematic passages in which Kaplan implies the existence of a subject-process that must be correlated with all of reality. Since, as Schulweis argues, God-language is necessarily and admittedly a metaphorical description of a transcendent reality beyond accurate description, it is best to focus on those occasions and actions that make the divine manifest. In doing so, one avoids becoming mired in metaphysical excuses for the apparently imperfect universe in which we find ourselves.

Schulweis (and Kaplan) stand on firm and traditional Jewish theological ground in asserting God's ultimately ineffable nature and in concentrating rather on those moments in which the influences of a God who is beyond definition can, nevertheless, be located. That was the position of Maimonides, who ruled out all positive attributions to God except attributes of divine action, and who defined attributes of action as qualities that we attribute to God because the effects of God's causation are such that, if they were caused by a human being, that person would be said to possess those qualities. Both the Maimonidean and the Kaplanian positions maintain a startling level of agnosticism about God's essential nature, while firmly insisting on attributing qualities to God that are derived from human experience.

Thus, predicate theology is no more vulnerable to the charge of avoiding a direct discussion of God's nature than is Maimonides's negative theology. The comparison with the Maimonidean approach, however, is instructive in illumining other problems in Kaplan's and Schulweis's approaches. Whereas the Rambam developed a coherent portrait of the universe through which each attribute of action could be viewed as a partial and ultimately inaccurate reflection of God's unity, Kaplan did not. In clarifying Kaplan, Schulweis also highlights the weakness of Kaplan's theological approach. In what sense, we ask, can we affirm the unity of the divine predicates, and from where does that unity derive? Without an affirmation and description of the reality out of which the predicates emerge, without a God that is at least a functional noun, we are left at most with a power or a set of powers not ourselves that can be of assistance to us in our quests. However, that falls considerably short of providing us with the confidence that our efforts will succeed in the face of an apparently indifferent universe.

The difficulties inherent in providing a coherent portrait of the cosmos in which the divine predicates are supposed to function can be seen, however, to follow directly from the incongruity of overlaying a twentieth-century conception of God upon a traditional, premodern metaphysics. In reducing God's direct role in the governance of the world and in questioning the literal truth of biblical and midrashic images of God, medieval Jewish philosophers, such as Maimonides, exaggerated the chasm between the divine and human realms. God, for them, was not only beyond human knowledge; God was also utterly and absolutely other. For Maimonides, any literal attribution of a human quality to God was idolatrous. Attributes of action derived from human experience could be applied to God and thus serve as a model for human imitation, but they were not to be believed literally. Instead, knowledge of and communion with God was to be acquired through the cumulative negation of every nondivine association with God.

Such a radical distinction between the divine and the human is not Kaplan's or Schulweis's objective. The God they seek to describe is one who reflects twentieth-century images of power and sanctity. Such a God does not rule majestically from on high as an absolute, mysterious monarch but rather reflects more modern notions of empathy and alliance with humanity. The premodern otherness of God was located in images that reflected the social and political values of their time—values that are no longer current. God as stern but merciful father; God as potter molding creatures without restriction; God as the source of the otherness that humans experience in a world impermeable to human understanding; God as the perfect, self-contained One unconcerned with and unaffected by anything else—these are not the images the theologians of our day seek to recover. Thus, when we seek the source of Kaplan's powers or Schulweis's predicates, we should take care that we are not assuming the necessity of positing such a source to be radically other. Rather, the coherent portrait of the cosmos required to ground their theologies is to be found in the work of process theologians of this century.

Beginning with an affirmation of the *ultimate* value of this world and using human experience as the basis for the construction of metaphysics and theology, process theologians, such as A. N. Whitehead and Charles Hartshorne, have provided a radical alternative to the classical ways of speaking about God. Whereas classical "monopolar" theology (in Hartshorne's term) exalts an utterly transcendent and ultimately impassive God while denigrating this world, Hartshorne's "dipolar" God is very much the paradigmatic supercase of what this-worldly Jews would affirm as perfections. God is portrayed as absolute in existence but relative in actuality, as abstractly independent but actually radically dependent on creatures.

In process theology, the reality of experience-events is primarily social and sympathetic. Becoming includes and generates being. This is a perspective that reflects a modern, posttraditional understanding of reality. It systematically explains how everything is contained within God without being controlled by God (since perfect power is not coercive) and how God can be said to be cognizant of, and in sympathy with, all existent things. It does much of Schulweis's work for him by locating actuality in concrete events and by defining abstract experience and personhood—human and divine—as no more than the constant threads that successive events share in common. It provides a way to speak of God as a process on which we depend and to which we can relate, without abstracting God from the experienced universe.

By affirming that reality is progressive and that God—as the perfect process—is ever changing and growing, ever surpassing past perfections in the innovations of the universe's component parts, and ever providing us with new possibilities for enjoyment, process theology provides the appropriate metaphysical correlate to the affirmation of the *evolutionary* nature of Jewish civilization. Even the perfect divine predicates need not be hypostatized as unchanging and everlasting. The reality of God and its manifestations are themselves subject to an ongoing, continuous process of becoming. There is thus divine warrant for opposing the status quo, for continually striving to surpass the accomplishments of the past and present.

Whitehead's vision of the function of culture is also a promising way to develop Kaplan's understanding of the necessity for Jewish civilization. Not all possibilities are available at each moment of creative synthesis. One's civilizational heritage opens up certain possibilities for enjoyment that would not otherwise be available. Experiencing the concrete reality of Jewish sancta allows for a creative synthesis that builds upon the enjoyment and insights of others.

Such a theological framework represents a radical departure from both classical Jewish theology and from the popular beliefs on which most Jews have been raised. It requires a wrenching reorientation to begin to think of God as in perpetual process, involved in and substantially affected by the undetermined unfolding of concrete events—and not only as a removed "governor" decreeing from above.

Yet the framework of process theology reflects much of what many contemporary Jews actually believe about the empathic and progressive nature of reality and makes coherent much of what Kaplan chose to say more casually about the nature and reality of God.

Nevertheless, however useful process theology may be in elaborating Kaplan's theology and in resolving, through dipolarity, many of his apparent contradictions, it must be noted that the works of Whitehead, Hartshorne, and Schubert Ogden are not entirely harmonious with the thrust of Kaplan's vision. Kaplan's God-process is one that is only described as making for the good, for life-abundant, for cosmos over chaos, for the strength that we need to overcome adversity and create community. He refers to God as the sum of all processes in the abstract; but when he cites instances of divine manifestations, he is selective. For this reason, Schulweis's predicate theology can be said to explicate him fairly.

This is not identical to Hartshorne's God, who is said to provide present experience-events with possibilities, acting to persuade or lure entities to make the most beneficial choices but acting primarily through a radical sympathy for all things, no matter how they choose to self-create. In constructing an all-inclusive metaphysics, process theologians seem bound to include everything within the God-process—evil as well as good—so that God's all-embracing love, as the sum of all concretions, extends to all humans, for example, equally. The all-empathic God is not only nonjudgmental; God also makes no guarantees that any goal will ever be reached. To the contrary, God is radically dependent on us to create the future over which God has no control and which will actually constitute God.

Thus, Schulweis is not entirely wrong when he claims that Hartshorne's "neoclassical subject theology" offers us an amoral God. The morality of the God of process theology is that of love, knowledge, memory, and empathy. The God who is the source of *all* possibilities is no more the cause of good than evil, no matter where the divine sympathies lie. Perfect power, according to this way of thinking, allows sympathetically for freedom and innovation—as the highest form of morality. This is primarily a God of love rather than of justice, a responsive and dependent God whose present and future reality is conditioned by and includes the memory of all of our deeds. It is not the God of Isaianic or Kaplanian righteousness. It is a God who is present not only when we actualize Schulweis's predicates but when we fail to do so as well.

Thus, the use of process theology to explicate and systematize Kaplan's thinking must necessarily be selective. A faithful explication will not allow for an empathic, nonjudgmental God who cares about us but who does not, in some sense, represent the imperative to seek righteousness. In firm Jewish tradition, the Kaplanian perspective chooses to identify the divine with a prophetic and rabbinic ethics rather than with an all-inclusive embrace of the totality of all things—even at the expense of an account of the world that makes complete sense.

It remains an open question, then, whether such a perspective can be made to harmonize with the move from the classical monopolar God to one of dipolarity. That is, it remains to be explored whether a process theology can be developed that both locates the divine at both poles of the continuum and yet preserves the God of righteousness. Those who seek to reduce the classical chasm between God and creation, who understand ultimate reality as process rather than stasis, may have to choose between an absolutely empathic and an absolutely righteous God. Kaplan, when he is interpreted through the lens of process theology, can be seen never to have made that choice, leading to many of the contradictions mentioned in this essay.

That choice, however, should not be assumed to be inevitable. Our rabbinic and medieval predecessors notwithstanding, the identification of divine perfection with immutability is anything but obvious. Indeed, one suspects that many have held on to that equation for God after abandoning it with reference to nondivine reality because of the fear that the floodgates of chaos will be opened by an admission that ultimate things change, too. In fact, a continual process of teshuvah, of turning and returning on a lifelong journey toward God, may prove to be more firmly grounded in the imitation of a God who is in a continual process of divine unfolding—a God of becoming and being, a God of absolute responsiveness and dependence—than in the imitation of a God so perfect as to be beyond our ability to know. Cosmologically and spiritually, our ancestors' world revolved around a fixed center. It is our challenge to adapt their wisdom to the very different images of the external and internal world current in our day.

If there is a compelling reason to follow Kaplan in seeking alternatives to traditional, supernaturalistic theology, it is not, as Kaplan claimed, that people find it unconvincing. It is clear that many do find it convincing. It is rather that our affirmation of secularity, of this-worldliness, of the ultimate value of lives lived in this universe requires a theology that locates God in and of this world—as the source of our efforts at self-integration and social liberation. A transnaturalistic process theology is no more demonstrable than a supernaturalistic one; it does promise, however, an articulation that correlates with the confidence that we profess in the purposes of our lives.

Select Bibliography

Caraway, James E. *God as Dynamic Actuality: A Preliminary Study of the Process Theologies of John B. Cobb, Jr. and Schubert M. Ogden.* Washington, D.C.: University Press of America, 1978.

Cargas, Harry J., and Bernard Lee. *Religious Experience and Process Theology.* New York: Paulist Press, 1976.

Cobb, John B., Jr. *A Christian Natural Theology Based on the Thought of Alfred North Whitehead.* Philadelphia: Westminster Press, 1965.

Cobb, John B., Jr., and David Ray Griffin. *Process Theology: An Introductory Exposition.* Philadelphia: Westminster Press, 1976.

Cousins, Ewert H., ed. *Process Theology.* New York: Newman Press, 1973.

Ford, Lewis S., ed. *Two Process Philosophers: Hartshorne's Encounter with Whitehead* (AAR Studies in Religion, no. 5). Tallahassee, Fla.: American Academy of Religion, 1973.

Hartshorne, Charles. *The Logic of Perfection.* Lasalle, Ill.: Open Court Publishing, 1962.

———. *Beyond Humanism: Essays in the Philosophy of Nature.* Gloucester, Mass.: Peter Smith, 1975.

Ogden, Schubert M. *The Reality of God and Other Essays.* New York: Harper & Row, 1966.

———. *On Theology.* New York: Harper & Row, 1986.

Schulweis, Harold M. *Evil and the Morality of God.* Cincinnati: Hebrew Union College Press, 1984.

Whitehead, Alfred North. *Process and Reality.* Edited by David Ray Griffin and Donald W. Sherburne. New York: Free Press, 1978.

CHAPTER 14

Kaplan's Reinterpretation
of the Bible

Mel Scult

We associate Mordecai Kaplan with the concept of Jewish peoplehood, with Judaism as a civilization, and with his lifelong search
for the meaning of God in human experience, but rarely is Kaplan
perceived as an interpreter of the Bible. To be sure, he frequently
bases his arguments on Torah texts, and we do find explications of
his concept of Torah.[1] However, nowhere in print do we find a
systematic discussion of his biblical theology, of the more well-
known biblical narratives, and of the major critical problems that
confront the student of the Bible.

The many rabbis who have studied with Kaplan are, however,
well aware of his views on every aspect of Bible study, for it was in
his classes at the Jewish Theological Seminary, particularly in his
courses on homiletics, that Kaplan examined the Torah with his
students.[2] He insisted that before his students could preach they had
to have something to say; this meant studying the Bible and philosophy of religion. In addition to teaching at the Seminary, Kaplan
sometimes gave courses at other institutions. In the years 1915–16,
he taught a course entitled "Interpretation of the Bible" at Teacher's College of Columbia University. The course was repeated again
with a slightly different emphasis in 1918.[3] Year after year Kaplan

preached weekly, first at the Jewish Center and later at the Society for the Advancement of Judaism.

The only effort to set forth Kaplan's method of biblical interpretation was made by Eugene Kohn, a student at the Jewish Theological Seminary when Kaplan began teaching homiletics.[4] In his essay "Mordecai Kaplan as Exegete," Kohn rightly ties Kaplan's understanding of the Bible to the problems of the preacher. More than anything else Kaplan wanted to make the text relevant. The need for a further elaboration of Kaplan's method is recognized by Kohn when, at the end of his essay, he wrote, "We have not yet, for example, produced a single Bible commentary that is based on the reinterpretive approach (i.e. Kaplan's method)."[5] The commentary that Kohn wanted was indeed begun by Kaplan himself, unbeknownst apparently even to those closest to him. Thus, we will be able to see the specifics of Kaplan's method, not as one can imagine he *might* have done it but as he did it.

Kaplan dissented from traditional modes of thought while still an adolescent. His first doubts centered on his understanding of the Bible, particularly the matter of biblical miracles.[6] Arnold B. Ehrlich, the Bible scholar who frequented the Kaplan household at the time, was a primary force in molding Kaplan's attitudes. Many years later Kaplan wrote, "He [Ehrlich] taught me to penetrate through the vast layers of traditional commentaries to the rock-bottom original intent of the biblical authors. In doing so, he undermined my belief in the Mosaic authorship of the Torah and in the historicity of miracles."[7]

Ehrlich, who was working on a Bible commentary, came to consult Kaplan's father about the way in which certain biblical terms were used in the Talmud. He shared his insights and discoveries with the Kaplans. The young Kaplan would take these ideas and argue with his classmates at the Seminary over the points Ehrlich had made.

Ehrlich was a rather eccentric man whose work, although not generally well known, is still valued by Bible scholars.[8] He came to the United States in 1875 but was never able to secure a teaching position with a Jewish institution because, while in Germany, he had worked with Franz Delitzsch on a Hebrew translation of the New Testament that was to be used for missionary purposes. Harry Orlinsky, a noted Bible scholar in his own right, describes Ehrlich as an "utterly egocentric personality . . . never in doubt that he was absolutely right in his understanding of the preserved Hebrew text . . . [and] if he could not solve a difficulty, it was because the difficulty was insolvable."[9] The point is perhaps also illustrated by an epigram that Ehrlich quoted from a medieval Muslim writer on the title page of his commentary *Mikra Kiphshuto—The Bible According to Its Literal Meaning*. The epigram reads "He who has the truth is the majority, even if he is alone." The title page also contains a dating of the volume not in the Jewish or Christian mode but counting from the Declaration of Independence. It may be that Ehrlich, in his stubborn independence of mind and in his love for America, served as a role model for the young Kaplan.

Ehrlich wrote his commentary in Hebrew because he was intent on bringing to Jews the significant results of modern biblical criticism. He believed that he had a unique service to perform for both Jews and Christians. The Jews, Ehrlich explained in his introduction, hesitated to amend the text because they considered each letter sacred. Thus, the results of modern scientific research were not used by Jews in their attempts to understand the Scriptures. Ehrlich alludes to S. D. Luzzatto, the Italian-Jewish exegete of the early nineteenth century, as the only traditional Jew who was willing to amend the text when necessary. The Christians, on the other hand, who are so ready to explore the text scientifically, only consider it holy in relationship to their own Scriptures, according to Ehrlich, and do not know the postbiblical Jewish sources that might help them in understanding the text. Thus Ehrlich, through his extensive knowledge of Hebrew and of biblical criticism, believed he could bring to both sets of readers a more valid understanding of the literal meaning of the biblical text.[10]

Regarding Ehrlich's strengths and weaknesses, Orlinsky has the following to say: He was a "master of the Hebrew language . . . [and] his emendations were consistently of superior quality to those proposed by the vast majority of his contemporaries but they were too frequently quite unnecessary, and purely conjectural, rarely based on a sound understanding of the versions."[11] It seemed to some scholars that Ehrlich sometimes changed the text almost as if he were correcting a student's composition, as, for example, his changing of the word *baṛah* (created) in Genesis 1:3 to *baḍah* (imagined or contemplated).[12] Ehrlich seemed to spend his time elucidating what to other scholars might seem obvious. In Genesis 1:2, the most difficult word is *meraḥefet* (hovered) or perhaps *tohu va-vohu* (unformed and void). Ehrlich, however, wrote more than half a page on the word *hay'etah* (was) in the phrase "the earth *was* unformed and void." He attempted to show that the word *hay'etah* indicated an equivalence between the earth and the void, rather than an object that had a certain quality.[13] Thus, the verse is intended to say (as the new Jewish Publication Society translation indicates), "the earth *being* unformed and void with darkness over the surface of the deep." To explain the deeper meaning of what seems obvious—was Ehrlich's way and his strength.

In his introduction, Ehrlich explained that he was a man "of little faith," so that when the evidence was clear he could face the fact that parts of the Pentateuch come from different periods— sometimes hundreds of years apart.[14] Although relatively unconcerned with tracing the different documents through the Pentateuch, he does note their existence.[15] He maintained that although the patriarchs believed in one God who was all-powerful, they did not deny the existence of other gods.[16] He also assumed that because the story of the golden calf was not mentioned by the prophets that it was postexilic.[17] He believed that both the priestly code and the Book of Deuteronomy were "very late."[18] Though he tends to be a secularist, Ehrlich gave clear evidence of his great love for the Jewish people and of his feeling that they have a unique mission to perform in bringing the message of the Torah to the world.[19]

Kaplan easily accepted the multiple authorship of the Bible and the results of biblical criticism. For Kaplan, the main theme of the Bible is the groping of the Jews as a collectivity for meaning and values. In all these ways, Ehrlich was a major formative influence in Kaplan's life. Before we can fully understand Kaplan's contribution to the study of the Bible and the conflicts he encountered, we must note the state of biblical scholarship in the early years of the twentieth century and the atmosphere in which Kaplan worked.

At the beginning of our century, Jewish scholars found it difficult
to avoid the challenges offered by Christian biblical critics. Julius
Wellhausen, the most prominent Protestant Bible scholar, postulated a slow evolutionary development of Israelite religion from a
primitive animism in the patriarchal period to the ethical monotheism of the literary prophets. The document known as the Pentateuch
is thus the product of many hands and was given its final shape in
the time of Ezra (fifth century B.C.E.). Jews reacted in a number of
different ways. Traditional Jews totally ignored the German-Protes-
tant critics and never took the whole enterprise of biblical criticism
seriously. On the other end of the spectrum, secular Jewish nation-
alists believed that the Bible was the record of Israel's spiritual
groping and revealed the soul of Israel rather than the word of God
in any direct sense. Ahad Ha-Am thus did not hesitate to call for a
more scientific investigation and reinterpretation of the Scriptures.
Some leaders of Reform Judaism followed in Abraham Geiger's steps
and accepted the critical view. Kaufman Kohler, in his *Jewish
Theology*, accepted the composite nature of the Pentateuch but
launched a vigorous attack on Christian scholars who denigrated
the nature of Mosaic religion.[20] Isaac M. Wise (1819–1900), the first
president of the Hebrew Union College, on the other hand, had
attacked the critics and maintained that the Pentateuch was thoroughly Mosaic even though some portions were set down immediately after the death of Moses.[21]

The founders of the Jewish Theological Seminary were generally
agreed that the scientific method could be applied to the textual
study of the Prophets and the Wisdom literature but not to the
Pentateuch. Alexander Kohut (1842–94) spoke for the Seminary
when he wrote, "to us the Pentateuch is a *noli me tangere!* Hands
off! We disclaim all honor of handling the sharp knife which cuts
the Bible into a thousand pieces."[22] Sabato Morais (1823–97), the
first president of the Seminary, stated, "I read my Bible without the
spectacles of Wellhausen."[23] Indeed, the very founding of the Seminary is tied to a reassertion of the traditional view of the Torah and
its origin. Cyrus Adler quoted approvingly the following statement
made by Morais:

At the basis of our Seminary lies the belief that Moses was in all truth
inspired by the living God to promulgate the laws for the government of a

people sanctified to an imperishable mission; that the same laws, embodied in the Pentateuch, have unavoidably a local and a general application. . . . The traditions of the fathers are therefore coeval with the written statutes of the five Holy Books.[24]

With the reorganization of the Seminary in 1902 and the arrival on the scene of Solomon Schechter many things changed, but the attitudes and policies respecting the Pentateuch did not. Schechter's well-known statement that higher criticism was higher anti-Semitism was part of a speech he gave at a dinner honoring Kaufman Kohler, who had just become president of the Hebrew Union College. In his speech, Schechter did not spell out the details of his position. At one point he seemed to be saying that in some way the critics were taking the Bible away from the Jews and minimizing the Jewish contribution to mankind. "The Bible is our sole raison d'être," wrote Schechter, "and it is just this which the higher anti-Semitism is seeking to destroy, denying all our claims for the past, and leaving us without hope for the future."[25] He may be referring here to the contention made by some that Israelite monotheism was derivative and constituted an extension of other Near Eastern cultures, rather than a radically new phenomenon. In another speech, Schechter attacked Wellhausen head-on, not because of his theories of composite authorship, but rather for his explicit anti-Semitism. In his well-known statement endorsing Zionism delivered in 1906, Schechter quotes the following from Wellhausen:

The persistency of the [Jewish] race may, of course, prove a harder thing to overcome than Spinoza has supposed; but nevertheless, he will be found to have spoken truly in declaring that the so-called emancipation of the Jews must inevitably lead to the extinction of Judaism wherever the process is extended beyond the political to the social sphere.[26]

Before Schechter came to the Seminary he lived and taught in England. In January 1899, he delivered a lecture entitled "The Study of the Bible," the occasion being his appointment as professor of Hebrew in the University College of London. In this essay, Schechter is much more moderate regarding biblical criticism than in his later statements. Respecting his attitudes toward the critics, he says, "Nor, I trust, have I ever given way to anybody in my respect for most of the leaders of the various schools of Bible criticism, lower as well as higher." He believed that the scientific analysis of the

Bible was "one of the finest intellectual feats of this century."[27] What he wanted, however, was a more critical attitude toward the critics but by no means a complete dismissal. "That tradition cannot be maintained in all its statements need not be denied," he said, "The question at present, however, is not as it was with the older schools, whether tradition was possibly mistaken in this or that respect, but whether it contains elements of truth at all. . . . As somebody has remarked, if tradition is not infallible, neither are any of its critics."[28]

Thus, we see that, for whatever reasons, Schechter's statements on biblical criticism after he became head of the Seminary were much more conservative than before his arrival in America. Even in his more extreme condemnations, he seems to be more concerned with the denigration of Mosaic religion than with source theory per se. Nonetheless, when he was about to hire Israel Friedlaender for the Seminary faculty, he made it clear to Friedlaender that although he accepted the critical view of the Pentateuch, he was not to teach it.[29] Schechter set the curricular policy for the rabbinical school, continued by Adler and Finkelstein, which excluded the systematic scientific study of the Pentateuch.

The other members of the faculty, though they readily applied the tools of historical scholarship to post-biblical tradition, were hesitant to apply this method to the Bible. On the origin of Pentateuchal Judaism, the position of Louis Ginzberg, the leading member of the faculty, was ambiguous. In his article on law codes in the *Jewish Encyclopedia*, Ginzberg states that "the laws [in Ex. 21–23:19] originated a long time prior to the date at which the code was committed to writing."[30] He goes on to say that "the Deuteronomic Code, notwithstanding its many peculiarities, cannot properly be designated as a new code; it represents rather a revised and improved edition of the Book of the Covenant, made in conformity with the new ideas of the time." Louis Finkelstein as well as Ginzberg's own son, Eli Ginzberg, both report that the great talmudist regretted having written the *Jewish Encyclopedia* article. The truth of the matter is probably that Ginzberg was of two minds. His critical faculties told him that elements in the Pentateuchal codes were obviously not all Mosaic; yet, his deep commitment to traditional Judaism and to the Jewish community led him to take strong public stands against biblical criticism.

Before Ginzberg came to the Seminary, he was considered for a position by Isaac M. Wise at the Hebrew Union College. Wise never made it completely clear why he selected Henry Malter over Ginzberg. One graduate of the class of 1896 at Hebrew Union College heard from a friend who was on the board of governors at the time that Wise had been excited about Ginzberg, but decided not to recommend his appointment after he heard that Ginzberg inclined favorably to the Wellhausen interpretation of the Pentateuch.[31]

Nevertheless, in a number of public statements Ginzberg clearly and unambiguously condemned biblical criticism. In an article published in 1922, entitled "Bible Interpretation: The Jewish Attitude," Ginzberg is quoted as saying, "The philosophic premises [of biblical criticism] exclude a divine ordering of the universe and deny the possibility of God appearing to man. Consequently the theory of creation must be regarded as a myth; theophanies in any form are impossible and revelation is assumed not to be an historical fact. With all these assumptions Judaism is in entire disagreement."[32]

Kaplan, on the other hand, made it quite clear in both his public and private statements that he accepted composite authorship; that some parts of the Pentateuch were postexilic in origin; and that these "facts" did not in any way impair Jewish life or undermine the centrality and importance of the Torah. In 1914 Kaplan wrote an article entitled "The Supremacy of the Torah," in which he maintained that biblical criticism did not in any way weaken the authority of the Scriptures.[33] Rather than answering the critics, Kaplan simply set them aside. For him the status of the Torah was not a matter of its origin but of its place in the history of the Jewish people. Whether or not it was to remain supreme in the future was a consequence of the compelling force of the ideas in the Torah. If the Torah's authority could be maintained in this functional way, then no statement about its origin would be threatening. Function was compelling; origin was not.

At this early point of his life, Kaplan was still rather traditional in many of his views. The following quotation illustrates this point as well as Kaplan's functional interpretation of the Torah's authority:

Traditional belief as to the origin of the Torah is not the sole support of its supremacy. If this is found to give way, the one derived from its having rendered Israel the instrument of divine revelation is no less effective in maintaining its pre-eminence.[34]

Kaplan was vigorously attacked in the Jewish press because of his acceptance of biblical criticism, despite his repeated statements that he upheld the Torah's supremacy. He was called a heretic,[35] and one editorial demanded that he resign from the Seminary because he could no longer teach traditional Judaism.[36] As one paper put it, "Professor Kaplan by denying that God has given the Torah to Israel and also that the belief in the Messiah is fallacious [sic] has destroyed the most solid foundations of the traditional faith."[37] The organized Orthodox rabbinate called a special meeting at one point in order to condemn Kaplan and his followers, whom they called "the half-Orthodox."[38] From time to time Kaplan did receive letters of support for his position,[39] but from his colleagues at the Seminary and from the leaders of the Conservative movement he encountered either cold acceptance or open hostility.[40]

To accept the composite authorship of the Pentateuch, Kaplan had to face the problem of revelation. Here, as with other issues, Kaplan's explanation is functional in nature. If the Torah is a composite document, then obviously it was not totally revealed to Moses. The Torah, however, remains divine in "a derivative way," to use Kaplan's phrase. It comes from God in the sense that "it represents the embodiment in Jewish life of ultimate moral and spiritual forces, the divine character of which reason is ready to affirm, [and] in no way conflicts with the results of modern biblical studies, and on the contrary is rather confirmed by them."[41] The Torah is to be considered eternal in Kaplan's view, even though it is not directly revealed by God. For the Torah to be eternal means that it "must never cease functioning as a standard in Jewish life."[42] The continued application takes place through reinterpretation (derash), which reveals the secondary meaning of the holy text.[43] This secondary meaning changes from age to age as people relate the text to their own particular experiences.

Kaplan, always concerned with continuity in Judaism, wanted to be sure that his theory of interpretation did not legitimate any and all changes in the meaning of basic concepts. Central notions, such as revelation, must not be changed beyond recognition. There must be a basic continuity of identity that links our present interpretations with those of the past. This identity did not mean the "sameness of doctrine" but "constancy of ratio between experience on the one hand and Judaism's reaction toward experience on the other."[44] If we can find beliefs that engender in us the same reactions that traditional beliefs engendered in our forefathers, then we obviously have the continuity of identity we are seeking. Thus, Kaplan dismissed the allegorical method of interpretation wherein the simple or primary meaning is completely erased. In the allegorical method, usually identified with Philo, "the facts disappear entirely, the unities of character and incident [are] entirely ignored, and the entire content turned upside down."[45]

It should be clear by this time that Kaplan did not treat tradition lightly, nor was he attempting simply to change ancient notions into modern ones. His method, a type of demythologizing, was thus a translation or rendering of a thought from one system into another. If the belief embodied in a mythic system has been adequately translated, we should upon adopting the translation hold attitudes analogous to the ancients and see implications for our thought and behavior analogous to theirs without the necessity of adopting identical notions. Calling such an interpretation *functional* means that the implications and the behavior that flow from the concept should in every case be similar, even though the content of the reinterpretation might look very different.

The concept of translation as a description of Kaplan's method allows us to retain a pluralistic image of biblical interpretation. Just as a statement may be translated into many languages other than the original, so with the archaic beliefs we are discussing. The translation of biblical thought into Maimonides's Aristotelian system is thus no less valid intrinsically than Kaplan's translation into modern terms. At the same time, we can still measure the adequacy of these different translations to ascertain the degree to which they give a faithful rendering of the original. We would look at Maimonides's translation to see whether key notions function the same way in his system as they do in the original. One of the advantages of this notion of interpretation is that it is not necessary to choose between a traditional translation and a contemporary one, because both may function equally well under different circumstances. After all, rabbinic interpretation (midrash) is as much a translation as is our own rendering.

Kaplan's functional interpretation is not a facile criticism of traditional thought by modern values but rather an attempt to bring the traditional back into our lives in a way that is genuinely operative. Kaplan's critics are wrong, therefore, when they accuse him of a slavish acceptance of contemporary values. One critic, reacting against what he considers to be Kaplan's one-sidedness, states that Judaism should not "capitulate to a scientific naturalistic imperialism but [there should be] a mutually active critique of Judaism by these values and conversely of these values by Judaism."[46] It will become clear that this "mutually active critique" is precisely what Kaplan was striving for in his work on the Bible.

Before exploring some examples of Kaplan's interpretations of the Bible, a word is in order about my sources. Kaplan used the Bible as a point of departure in everything he wrote. I mentioned above that he used his homiletics courses at the Seminary as an opportunity to explore the Pentateuch from a philosophical point of view. It is consequently surprising that nowhere in the great corpus of Kaplan's published works do we find a systematic exposition of the Pentateuch, either in its narrative or legal portions. The two manuscripts on the Bible mentioned previously are quite different in character.[47] The older one contains a verse commentary covering the first fifteen chapters of the Book of Genesis. In addition to this verse commentary, there is an exposition of the themes in each weekly portion; the more recent work drops the verse commentary and contains comments on the whole Pentateuch according to the weekly *sidra*. I shall also use material from an unpublished work, entitled "The Meaning of Religion,"[48] and material from Kaplan's journal.

Kaplan never presented himself as a Bible scholar. His knowledge of ancient Near Eastern non-Jewish languages and literatures was limited and derived mostly from secondary sources. He was acquainted with the discoveries of archaeologists but, again, he had no deep interest or expertise in this area. Indeed, it may be that his insecurity in the area of Bible studies explains why he never dealt with this area systematically in his published works. Kaplan's value as a biblical interpreter flows from intuitions and keen insights, as well as from his talent as a preacher. Making the text relevant was his ultimate, but not his sole, purpose.

First, let us explore Kaplan's perceptions about the ways in which the biblical mind functions. He tells us that the ancients frequently were not able to deal with their own subjective states but constantly felt impelled to objectify and reify their feelings. In Kaplan's words,

The ancients, with their limited self knowledge, could not regard their inner drives as subjective experience. Whatever inner force was beyond their control was to them as much of an objective and external fact as the things they saw around them. Like the external world the irresistible inner promptings of the heart or the will could not, they thought, but come from some deity.[49]

Seeing biblical statements as projections is not unique to Kaplan. Among Jewish thinkers, however, he is rare in holding this view and is imaginative in furnishing instances that might be seen as projections. Commenting on the Garden of Eden story, Kaplan notes that "God's keen disappointment in creation is, in fact, Israel's resentment at the way in which the human being often spoils God's beautiful world."[50] In commenting on the story of Jacob's encounter with the angel, Kaplan points out that an encounter with demons was well within the limits of propriety to ancient Israelites. He gives a modern interpretation rather than dismissing this as a piece of superstition, interpreting the ancient belief in demons as a crude way of accounting for the unconscious and the uncontrollable forces in human nature. He then adds the following: "The latest outbreak of the demonic forces in the world that left Israel limping is very much in need of being countered by the faith that Israel will not only survive but come away from the tragic experience with renewed strength and blessing. That is the meaning of the state of Israel."[51] In this way, he interprets Jacob's wrestling with the angel.

Another aspect of biblical thinking which Kaplan explains is the tendency to project ideals backward in time rather than forward as we might today. The Garden of Eden story is easily seen in this light, but Kaplan also applies the principle to the actions of the patriarchs. The ideal of the Jewish people was obedience to God's will. No matter how difficult life was, Jews believed it was incumbent upon them to maintain their trust in God. It was natural for the Jews, according to Kaplan, to see the progenitor of the race as fulfilling the ideal toward which they were working. Thus, in Abraham, "the task for which Israel lived met with fulfillment."[52] He was tested and tried as the Jewish people were tested, but Abraham remained obedient and faithful; his descendants did not always do as well.

Once the ideal is projected back to the patriarchs, it becomes part of the justification for Israel's selection. It is obvious that Israelite leaders perceived the masses as constantly falling short of the ideal. Why then was Israel selected? Israel was chosen because the ideal had already been fulfilled in Abraham. The *brit* (covenant) is God's promise to Abraham and his descendants that they would prosper and possess the land; they, in turn, were to obey God's will. This was the way the relationship between God and Israel was supposed to function. They projected the ideal relationship back into the past and then used the story of the patriarch as a guide for interpreting the events of their own time. In Kaplan's words,

Whatever befell Israel was interpreted consciously or subconsciously in terms of the experiences of the ancestors, experiences of trial, questioning, moving toward the prescribed goal and deviating from it, frustration, defeat, rescue, and fulfillment. No matter how far Israel would go astray or how near their great expectations bordered on extinction, the law of history or, in the language of the Torah, the covenant God made with the Patriarchs would bring Israel back into their destined course.[53]

Another dilemma in biblical interpretation is that certain matters were problems to Jews in biblical times but not to us, and vice versa. For example, Kaplan maintains that in biblical times Jews were not troubled about God having an image. It was only in later times that the mental conception one forms of God became an object of concern.[54] To us the fact of death is a given, and life after death is highly problematic. To the biblical mind, it was the opposite; hence, it was necessary to explain the phenomenon of death (one of the functions of the Eden story). Regarding Eve's curse in Genesis 3:16, Kaplan explains, "To the ancient mind the pangs of childbirth appeared unnatural and could be accounted for only on the ground of some primeval curse. The same is true of woman's willing subjection to man." [55]

I have noted previously the propensity to reification in the Bible. Kaplan suggests a number of ways to understand the attitude that is logically prior to the objectifications we find in the text (*logically prior*—not *chronologically*—because the process of objectification was not a conscious matter where ancient thinkers were aware of what they were doing). The attitudes implied in the objectifications and reifications are clearly discernable. One of the ways, according to Kaplan, that would allow us to discern what underlay the ancient projections and reifications is to turn key noun forms into adjectival forms. We can then search for the quality or qualities that have been objectified in a particular entity. Thus, for example, we might talk about that which is *divine* in the world rather than God. Kaplan supplies us with a particular interpretation of that which is divine and of that which is Torah-like and Israel-like.

Kaplan's translations are bound up with his views on God and salvation. In addition to turning the noun into an adjective, it is important to articulate the meaning of the adjective in terms of some recognizable experience.

Divine is therefore whatever possesses the quality of furthering man's perfection or salvation. Torah-like is whatever possesses the quality of rendering the Jewish people aware of its function to further the process of man's perfection or salvation. Israel-like is the people that identifies itself with that process. [56]

Statements about God, Israel, or the Torah should thus not be taken as describing particular entities but rather the extent to which any element of experience is divine, Torah-like, or Israel-like. Applying this mode of interpretation to the Psalms, we see that the verse that reads "The teaching of the Lord is perfect, restoring the soul" would be translated by Kaplan into "that which furthers salvation must be for us the will of God." [57]

Here is probably the clearest statement of Kaplan's openness and universalism. According to this mode of interpretation, salvation and the means to attain it may be found almost anywhere. Note that Kaplan's interpretation of Israel dissolves the covenant. Kaplan expresses this point explicitly in the commentary we are using. He

states, "The teaching that Israel is God's chosen people should mean
that God's chosen people is any people that is consciously dedicated
to the purpose of furthering the perfection or salvation of man."[58]

The technique of reversing theological statements is an old liberal ploy. Many examples are found in John Dewey's *A Common
Faith*. The practice goes back to the nineteenth century and may
have been used first by Ludwig Feuerbach.[59]

Kaplan's earliest concerns regarding the Bible centered around the
problem of miracles. Indeed, by "supernaturalism" he usually means
suspension of the natural order by some outside agency.[60] Kaplan is
not predisposed to accept the suspension of the natural order as
recorded in the Hebrew Scriptures. Commenting on the crossing of
the Red Sea, Kaplan points out that in the song Moses sang after the
crossing (Ex. 15:1–18) the event seems to have a rather natural
tone. Pharoah and his chariots were drowned in the sea by a sudden
storm, which is described in colorful metaphors by the poet. This
poem, which is older than the prose portion that accompanies it,
was taken by a rather literal writer who turned the poetic images
into facts. (The poet had written, "The floods stood straight like a
wall" [Ex. 15:8].) To the poet, the God of Israel can influence
natural phenomena so as to aid his people ("I will sing to the Lord,
for He has triumphed gloriously; horse and driver He has hurled into
the sea" [Ex. 15:1]). To the prose writer, "the God of Israel is the
creator of the world who can remake and unmake it at will."[61]

According to Kaplan, the plagues associated with the exodus
were perceived by the ancient Israelites as evidence of a struggle
between God (Yahveh) and Pharoah, who represented the sun god.
Yahveh had to prove himself as much to the Israelites as to Pharoah. Yahveh is seen here as the great warrior. In commenting on
these events, Kaplan makes no attempt to deal with the historical
reality behind the legendary exaggerations. For Kaplan, the ancient
Israelite belief in these miracles was an indication of "the great
intuitive awareness that they owed to that power [Yahveh] their
capacity to throw off the yoke of the nation that oppressed them."[62]
Then follows a sentence in the manuscript that Kaplan crossed out
but which ought to be restored, for it is the final stage in the

demythologizing process. He wrote, "It means that the mental and social energies in man which give rise to various human societies such as tribes, cities, nations, or the United Nations are the most divine manifestations of the power that makes for man's salvation."[63]

There is no evidence that Kaplan ever wrestled with the historicity of the legends of Genesis or the narrative of Exodus. It may be that the distinction drawn by Ahad Ha-Am between historical truth (that which people believe) and archaeological truth (that which scientific analysis supports) solved the problem of historicity for Kaplan at an early date. Ahad Ha-Am believed that even if archaeological evidence should contradict what people believe about Moses, he would nonetheless continue to be an important historical personage. The force of his image has a generative power all its own.[64]

Kaplan accepted the Pentateuch as a composite document and believed that the Torah was edited rather late. His early verse-by-verse commentary contains many allusions to the different sources behind the text.[65] However, he was not particularly interested in unraveling the whole sequence and rarely spent time indicating which verses came from which sources. In his commentary from the late forties, there is a statement worth noting even though it is only a cryptic remark jotted on the side of a page. It reads, "J = Divinity in Israel, values of people-hood, law. E = Divinity in nature, values of creativity."[66] The problem with this analysis is that Kaplan probably had in mind chapter 1 of Genesis as reflecting E. According to E. A. Speiser, however, most critics agree that chapter 1 is from P (priestly source) rather than from E (Elohist source).[67] E has no part in telling the story of the primeval age. He enters when the narrative is well into the Abraham legends.[68] While P seems to have some elements Kaplan is pointing to, it also relates to genealogy and other matters that militate against Kaplan's neat analysis. Speiser does point out that J tends to be more earthbound than E, E being "led to interpose angels or dreams, or both, the Deity being regarded, it would seem, as too remote for personal intervention."[69] We could retain Kaplan's analysis without tying it to a documentary framework by focussing on his statement "that God reveals himself in a two-fold capacity."[70]

I now turn to a general summary of Kaplan's interpretation of the major themes and events of the Torah. The message of the Torah may be summarized as follows: Israel has been selected to live according to God's will, which is the rule of law and justice. Those who live by force and aggression will perish. The belief that right must triumph over might is established for the Hebrews by seeing these principles actually operative in their protohistory. Man suffers because of his pride and arrogance. The Torah comes into the world in order to offer man the opportunity to reclaim himself. Man can recover his original state of perfection, and movement toward this goal is initiated by God through the Torah and Israel.

For Kaplan, the story of creation is not a scientific explanation or even a metaphysical statement but is rather soterical in nature —it points toward man's salvation. (*Soter* comes from the Greek word meaning "to save.") We learn from Genesis that the world was created in line with God's purpose—the fulfillment of man both individually and collectively. To say that God created the world is to make a statement about the nature of the world and the way in which it will function if we obey God's will, which is the rule of law and justice. Sin and evil come, therefore, from man's arrogance and lust for power. Man's fall is due to his "spirit of self-sufficiency, of willfulness, disobedience, and arrogance, which in classical literature is designated as hubris."[71] The rebelliousness of mankind against God is prefigured in Adam, just as the obedience of Israel to God's will is prefigured in Abraham: "To presume to be a god means to lust for power and to recognize no law higher than one's own will."[72] The sin of Noah's generation was its cold, calculating, destructive intent and not necessarily evil behavior.[73]

The sin of rebellion against God takes the form of aggression and violence. This is the case not only with the generation of Noah but also with those who attempt to build the tower of Babel. The primary point, according to Kaplan, is that "the chief menace to the world comes from the unification of the forces of evil."[74] Kaplan saw the division of mankind into many languages and many nations to be a positive occurrence, for "is not the disregard of differences a form of imperialism which is bound to bring about the dictatorship of a dominant clique which comes to tyrannize over and exploit the multitudes whom it has rendered helpless?"[75]

Abraham, of all the patriarchs, is the clearest symbol of obedience to God. God's command to Abraham to sacrifice Isaac is the supreme test of trust in God and obedience to him. In our age, when everyone is supposed to "do his own thing," the notion of obedience is not in vogue. Yet, it is clear to Kaplan that in Genesis obedience is a prime virtue. Kaplan "translates" the notion of obedience in the following way:

For the ancients obedience to the will of God was the prime virtue. Adam lacked it, Abraham had it. In our own day, this virtue must mean the power to conform to that innermost nature of reality, the basic law of life, obedience to which brings salvation to man and defiance of which leads to disaster.[76]

In commenting on the patriarchs, Kaplan differentiated between the picture of them presented by the rabbis and the picture that emerged from a careful reading of the text. For the rabbis, Abraham is the founder of a religion. Thus, in the Midrash we have the story of Abraham's rejection of his father's idolatry. For the Torah, however, he is the founder of a people. In the former, the focus is on Abraham; in the latter, it is on God. In Kaplan's words,

The Torah's main purpose is to tell the wondrous way in which Yahveh raised up a people unto Himself, using Abraham as His chief instrument. Abraham's virtue on the other hand, consists in willingly lending himself as Yahveh's instrument for that purpose, by obeying His command and displaying faith, in the face of obstacles and postponements. God does not merely intervene in the affairs of the Patriarchs. He is not a deus ex machina. He is the prime mover of the events in their lives, and occupies, as it were, the center of the stage.[77]

For Kaplan, the legends about the patriarchs rise out of the fact that they were perceived as symbolizing the people of Israel. In all Kaplan's detailed remarks on the patriarchal legends, this interpretation is emphasized. Thus, for example, the extraordinary births of both Isaac and Jacob are a reflection of Israelite belief in the unique status of the children of Israel. That uniqueness is concretized by projecting it back onto the patriarchs in the form of the special conditions of their birth.[78]

Another central theme in the early narratives is the relation of the patriarchs to the Land of Israel. These legends reflect the importance of the land to the Jewish people in terms of fulfilling their ultimate destiny. Thus, the Torah emerges as the charter of the Jews to its land, and these legends show that Israel cannot remain rootless and still fulfill its destiny. The Zionist thrust of this interpretation is clear; but, as we know, Kaplan is a man of two civilizations. It is natural for him, therefore, to emphasize the notion of rootedness not only with reference to Eretz Yisrael but also with reference to the lands in the Diaspora where the Jews happen to be living. Kaplan's point here is that the patriarchal legends teach us the value of rootedness and arise out of this value as a goal and ideal of the Jewish people.[79]

Kaplan believed that the version we have of the exodus story comes from the period of the early monarchy. Both the Pentateuch and the prophetic literature reflect the deep impression made on generations of Israelites by these accounts. Regarding the actual historical happenings, Kaplan, surprisingly, does not adopt an evolutionary view of Israelite monotheism but believes, like Yehezkel Kaufmann, that Mosaic religion as it emerged during the exodus was completely novel. In Kaplan's words, "nor did it [Israelite religion] emerge from a long evolutionary process in which long-held beliefs and practices were shed, leaving behind a permanent residue associated with some god or gods. The religion of Israel came like a bolt out of the blue."[80]

The deliverance from Egypt frequently is used as a reason for performing rituals and acting morally. Kaplan sees this process as analogous to Americans conducting (being exhorted to conduct) their public affairs in the spirit of the Declaration of Independence. Americans do frequently recall the Declaration of Independence, but certainly it is not as much a part of American consciousness as the exodus was for traditional Jews, who recalled it everyday in their prayers and blessings.

The exodus from Egypt is the central event of Israelite history. The ancient Hebrews experienced godhood not only in relation to such qualities of life as truth or beauty but as manifested primarily in human association. Yahveh is expressed in the Israelite capacity to act together and to throw off their oppressors.[81] The great power of Yahveh is shown through the plagues and the miracle of the Red Sea.

Coming to the central events at Sinai, Kaplan pointed out that there are only a handful of references to the Sinai theophany in the prophets. This may indicate that the association of the giving of the law with Sinai is rather late. Even though its exact nature is unknown, Kaplan did not doubt that the Israelites experienced a theophany at Sinai. This theophany may not have been originally associated with the law, however. The event does become historical because it "derives from historical connections and sets off fresh historical connections."[82] Kaplan understood the Sinai event as a kind of shock, analogous to experiences in an individual's personal life that lead to a greater awareness. Although he does not discuss in detail the nature of the shock, he says that "miracles reflect the awareness of God's power as a result of crisis in the outer life of the people. Theophany reflects the awareness of God's will as a result of crisis in the inner life of the people."[83]

The covenant itself is demythologized by Kaplan as that which God requires from the Israelites and which is necessary for them to function as a people and to fulfill their destiny. In his words, "They [the laws of the Torah] constitute the behavior which is to Israel what natural law is to any physical or animate being, the distinctive fact that gives Israel its character and helps to maintain it in life."[84]

In conclusion, Kaplan's interpretation of the Hebrew Scriptures may be described as functional. He sought to translate archaic notions into contemporary terms and to bring the attitudes behind ancient mythifications into the present, so that the *Weltanschauung* that flows from these attitudes may again be operative. One might almost say that in his longing for wholeness behind the myths, Kaplan was a rebel against modernity. He was seeking to reconstruct a world in which values are not separated from facts and from hard knowledge.

Notes

1. For Kaplan's views on the Bible, see Mordecai M. Kaplan, *Judaism as a Civilization* (New York: Reconstructionist Press, 1934), index under "Bible." See also idem, *The Future of the American Jew* (New York: Macmillan, 1948), chap. 23, "A New Educational Approach to the Bible"; and idem, *A New Approach to the Problem of Judaism* (New York: Society for the Advancement of Judaism, 1924) sec. 2, "The Meaning of Torah."

2. Kaplan alternated in his homiletics course between an examination of some general religious problems and an examination of the Bible. In his journal he lists the following topics:

   1916–1917—Detailed Examination of Genesis
   1917–1918—The Psychological and Sociological Aspect of the God Concept
   1919–1920—The Problem of Reinterpretation: Scripture and Rabbinic Writing
   1920–1921—Detailed Interpretation of Genesis (*Kaplan Journal*, vol. 2, December 1923, 198)

3. Among Kaplan's papers is a typed outline of the lectures he gave in both of these courses. There is also an abundance of other unpublished material. In his journal, he frequently summarized his sermons and public lectures. There are also two biblical commentaries in typescript; neither is dated nor has a title. The first, which I shall call "The Early Commentary," was composed between 1910 and 1930. Both the quality of the paper and the typing indicate this early period. The second I shall call "The Torah and Salvation: A Modern Reinterpretation of the Bible" (Kaplan approved both these titles) runs to about 250 pages and was composed in the late forties and early fifties. Although in general I shall confine my remarks to the period before 1934, I intend to draw upon the latter commentary in presenting Kaplan's analysis of the Bible.

4. Eugene Kohn, "Mordecai Kaplan as Exegete," in *Mordecai M. Kaplan: An Evaluation*, ed. Ira Eisenstein and Eugene Kohn (New York: Jewish Reconstructionist Foundation, 1952).

5. Ibid., 154.

6. Mordecai M. Kaplan, interview with author, July 1972.

7. Mordecai M. Kaplan, "The Way I Have Come," in *Mordecai M. Kaplan*, ed. Ira Eisenstein and Eugene Kohn, 289.

8. See, for example Harry M. Orlinsky, "Prolegomenon," in Arnold B. Ehrlich, *Mikra Kiphshuto—The Bible According to Its Literal Meaning* (New York: Ktav, 1966). Volume 1 originally appeared in 1899 and dealt with the Pentateuch. Volumes 2 and 3 were published in 1900 and 1901 respectively and dealt with the Prophets and Hagiographa.

9. Ibid., ix.

10. See Ehrlich, *Mikra*, vol. 1, xxxvi.
11. Harry M. Orlinsky, "Jewish Biblical Scholarship in America," *Jewish Quarterly Review* 45, no. 4 (April 1955): 386.
12. Ben Zion Halper, "Arnold B. Ehrlich, Biblical Commentator" (in Hebrew) *Miklat* 2 (1920): 424.
13. Ibid., 422.
14. Ehrlich, *Mikra*, vol. 1, xxxvii.
15. See, for example, his comment on the word *na'aseh* in Genesis 1:26. *Mikra*, vol. 1, 3
16. See his comment on Genesis 12:3, in Ehrlich, *Mikra*, vol. 1, 32.
17. See his comment on Exodus 32:1, in ibid., 198.
18. Orlinsky, "Prolegomenon," xxviii.
19. See his comment on Genesis 12:3, in Ehrlich, *Mikra*, vol. 1, 32.
20. See "Literary Suggestions," in *All the Writings of Ahad Ha-Am* (Jerusalem: Jewish Publishing House, 1953), 288. See also Kaufman Kohler, *Jewish Theology Systematically and Historically Considered* (New York: Macmillan, 1918), 46–47.
21. Harry M. Orlinsky, "Jewish Biblical Scholarship in America," *Jewish Quarterly Review* 45 (April 1955): 382.
22. Alexander Kohut, quoted in Moshe Davis, *The Emergence of Conservative Judaism: The Historical School in Nineteenth-Century America* (Philadelphia: Jewish Publication Society, 1963), 296.
23. Sabato Morais to Kaufman Kohler, quoted in Davis, *Emergence of Conservative Judaism*, 294.
24. Cyrus Adler, "The Standpoint of the Seminary" (1923), quoted in Mordecai Waxman, *Tradition and Change—The Development of Conservative Judaism* (New York: Burning Bush, 1958), 179.
25. Solomon Schechter, "Higher Criticism—Higher Anti-Semitism," in *Seminary Addresses* (Cincinnati: Ark Publishing, 1915), 37.
26. Solomon Schechter, "Zionism—A Statement," in *Seminary Addresses*, 94.
27. Solomon Schechter, "The Study of the Bible," in *Studies in Judaism*, 2d ser. (Philadelphia: Jewish Publication Society, 1908), 39–40.
28. Ibid.
29. Mordecai Kaplan, interview with the author, July 1972; also confirmed in an interview with Louis Finkelstein, April 1973. See also Mordecai M. Kaplan, *Judaism as a Civilization* (New York: Macmillan, 1934), 163, for a statement on Schechter and biblical criticism.
30. Louis Ginzberg, "Law Codes," in *Jewish Encyclopedia*, vol. 8 (New York: Funk and Wagnalls, 1906), 636.
31. Harry H. Mayer, "What Price Conservatism? Louis Ginzberg and the Hebrew Union College," *American Jewish Archives*, vol. 10, 145ff.
32. Louis Ginzberg, "Bible Interpretation: The Jewish Attitude," *United Synagogue Recorder*, 2, no. 3 (July 1922): 2.
33. Mordecai M. Kaplan, *The Supremacy of the Torah* (New York:

Students' Annual of the Jewish Theological Seminary of America, 1914),
183. The same point was made to the Seminary alumni in 1912. See
Mordecai Kaplan, "Paper Read to Meeting of Alumni" (Tannersville,
N.Y., July 1912), passim, Kaplan private papers. Also found in the notes
for a course entitled "Interpretation of the Bible," which Kaplan gave
at Columbia Teachers College in 1915–16. (Kaplan, private papers). See
also Mordecai Kaplan, *A New Approach to the Problem of Judaism*
(1924; reprint, New York: Society for the Advancement of Judaism,
1973), 28, as well as *Society for the Advancement of Judaism* 8 no. 24
(February 1929): 17. Kaplan also alluded to his acceptance of biblical
criticism in his series of articles in the *Menorah Journal* in 1915, 1916,
and 1917. He makes the point also in *Kaplan Journal*, vol. 1, December
1913, 25; and ibid., March 1915, 132.

34. Kaplan, *Supremacy of Torah*, 186.
35. "Heresy in Our Ranks," *Hebrew Standard*, 76, no. 26 (December
    1920): 8.
36. "Official and Personal Heresy" *Hebrew Standard* 77, no. 1 (January
    1921): 8.
37. H. Hirsh, "Kaplanism and What It Means," *Idische Licht* 1, no. 15
    (June 1923).
38. See the article on the meeting of Agudas Ha-Rabbanim, *Jewish
    Morning Journal*, 12 January 1921, 1, entitled "The Agudas Ha-Rab-
    banim Protest against the Half-orthodox."
39. For example, in Kaplan's papers there is a letter from one N. B. Ezra,
    dated 5 November 1926. Apparently, he was the editor of a traditional
    monthly journal in Shanghai. A review of Kaplan's *A New Approach
    to the Problem of Judaism* (1924) appeared in the journal, and Ezra
    requested more of Kaplan's writings, which he said "filled a very impor-
    tant need." Another letter from Abraham Van Son, a Dutch Jew, dated
    1 February 1929, asks why Kaplan is called an "Epicurus," "since in
    Holland the rabbis do not consider higher criticism to be a threat."
    Letters are in the Kaplan Archives at the Reconstructionist Rabbinical
    College.
40. Kaplan's journal is filled with examples of the sense of isolation that
    he felt at this time.
41. Kaplan, "Paper Read to Meeting of Alumni," 7.
42. Ibid., 8.
43. Kaplan's theory of the secondary meaning is close to Schechter's notion
    of *Klal Yisrael* and its importance in being the locus of authority. See
    Schechter, "Study of the Bible," 31–54.
44. Kaplan, *Paper Read to Alumni*, 14.
45. Ibid., 17.
46. See the stinging criticism by Steven Katz, "Mordecai M. Kaplan: A
    Philosophic Demurer," *Sh'ma: A Journal of Jewish Responsibility* 4, no.
    80 (November 1974): 157.

47. See note 3.
48. This sixty-page work is in manuscript form. It was begun in 1929 and was never finished. The other works mentioned here are in typescript.
49. Kaplan, "Torah and Salvation," 74.
50. Kaplan, "Early Commentary," 29.
51. Kaplan, "Torah and Salvation," Sidra Vayishlah. Much of the manuscript lacks pagination. It is divided according to the weekly reading, or *sidra*. Pages and *sidrot* will be given where they occur.
52. Ibid.
53. Ibid., 63.
54. Kaplan, "Early Commentary," 31. Here Kaplan is commenting on the word-image in Genesis 1:26.
55. Ibid., 9.
56. Kaplan, "Torah and Salvation," 30.
57. Ibid., 3. Professor Avraham Holtz of the Jewish Theological Seminary also reported Kaplan using this interpretation in class.
58. Ibid., 31.
59. John Dewey, *A Common Faith* (1934; reprint, New Haven: Yale University Press, 1974). See, for example, "It is a claim of religions that they effect a generic and enduring change in attitude. I should like to turn the statement around and say that whenever this change takes place there is a definitely religious attitude" (17). This book was originally published in 1934, the same year as Kaplan's *Judaism as a Civilization*.
60. See Mordecai M. Kaplan, *Judaism without Supernaturalism* (New York: Reconstructionist Press, 1958), 21–24.
61. Kaplan, "Torah and Salvation," Sidra Beshalah. The quotations here are taken from *The Torah: A New Translation* (Philadelphia: Jewish Publication Society, 1962).
62. Kaplan, "Torah and Salvation," Sidra Bo.
63. Ibid.
64. A personal anecdote may be relevant here. In 1972, I took my son Joshua to see Kaplan. Joshua was at that time about six years old. We had been discussing the exodus and I told him that the story of the plagues was only an exaggeration and that they did not really occur. "Why then," he asked me, "did Pharoah let the children of Israel go?" I could not answer his question. While we were visiting Rabbi Kaplan I encouraged Joshua to pose his question again. Rabbi Kaplan, who was ninety-one at the time, gave a more radical answer than I would have considered. He told Joshua that Moses never asked Pharoah to let the children of Israel go in the first place. The story of the meetings between Moses and Pharoah and, of course, the plagues were fiction. What probably happened, he explained, is that the Israelites just fled. Being slaves it would have made little sense for them, in the course of a rebellion, to ask permission to leave. Ahad Ha-Am's comment on

historical truth is contained in his essay entitled "Moses." See Leon Simon, ed. *Essays, Letters, Memoirs: Ahad Ha-Am* (Oxford: East and West Library, 1946), 102–16.

65. Kaplan "Early Commentary." For example, see 21 (comments on Gen. 4:23–24) and 23 (comments on Gen. 5:22).
66. Kaplan, "Torah and Salvation," 2.
67. E. A. Speiser, ed., *Genesis* (Garden City, N.Y.: Doubleday, 1964), 8.
68. Ibid., xxxiii.
69. Ibid., xxix.
70. Kaplan, "Torah and Salvation," 2.
71. Ibid., 11.
72. Ibid., 12.
73. Ibid., 20.
74. Ibid., 67.
75. Ibid., 68.
76. Ibid., Sidra Vayera.
77. Ibid., 76.
78. Ibid., n.p. Many portions of the manuscript have neither page designations nor *sidra* designations.
79. Ibid.
80. Ibid., Sidra Shemot.
81. Ibid.
82. Martin Buber, *Moses* (London: Horwitz, 1946), 16, 17, as cited in Kaplan, "Torah and Salvation," Sidra Yitro.
83. Kaplan, "Torah and Salvation," Sidra Yitro.
84. Ibid., Sidra Mishpatim.

CHAPTER 15

Kaplan as Liturgist

Ira Eisenstein

Mordecai Kaplan's experiments with liturgy grew directly out of his involvement, as a practicing rabbi, with public worship and the conduct of religious services. Well before he established the Society for the Advancement of Judaism, he had begun to struggle with reconciling ancient texts with his passion for intellectual honesty. He repeatedly insisted: we must say what we mean and mean what we say. When he formulated the "Thirteen Wants" (later called the "Criteria of Jewish Loyalty"), he included as number 7 that "we want the synagogue to enable us to worship God in sincerity and truth."[1] In his early years, he increasingly became aware of the discrepancy between what he believed and what his congregation —and he himself—was called upon to recite.

In the Jewish Center, he was not able to introduce revisions of the liturgy. When the Society for the Advancement of Judaism was organized in 1922, however, Kaplan set out to make the changes he deemed necessary. Indeed, the SAJ had been created so that he might have a free pulpit, and a free pulpit included the right to conduct services in the manner the rabbi thought appropriate to a self-consciously innovative congregation.

One of the first steps in the elimination of what were to him traditional formulations unacceptable to the modern mind was the abolition of Kol Nidrei. In this he was following in the footsteps of early German Reform Judaism, which had taken that step almost a

319

century before. At the conference in Brunswick in 1844, the first of the Reform rabbinical conferences, the delegates had voted to abolish the Kol Nidrei recitation because, as a formula declaring future vows absolved, it had served as a pretext by government authorities to deny the worth of Jewish oaths.[2] Kaplan replaced the Kol Nidrei with Psalm 130, which began with "mi-ma'amakim keratikha" (out of the depths I call to you, O Lord).

As might have been expected, the members of the SAJ, although they acquiesced in the change, were unhappy because many missed the familiar words. How Kaplan was persuaded to reinstate the Kol Nidrei, with additional words, is the subject of a correspondence between him and my grandfather, Judah David Eisenstein, that recently came into my possession.

My grandfather was disturbed in the fall of 1930 by my having accepted the position of executive director of the SAJ. He was particularly exercised over Kaplan's abolition of the Kol Nidrei. In his objections, he remarked that Kaplan did not understand its true meaning. I suggested that he write Kaplan explaining his position. He did and Kaplan responded. As a result of the exchange, Kaplan formulated a revised version of the text that was pasted into the SAJ *Mahzor*. When the Reconstructionist Foundation published its High Holiday prayer book in 1948, this was the version of the Kol Nidrei that was used.

The following are excerpts from the letters between Kaplan and Judah David Eisenstein on this matter.[3] On 1 October 1930, Kaplan wrote Eisenstein:

My reason for opposing the recital of [the Kol Nidrei] is because it is regarded as a prayer. . . . There is no reason why our people should be permitted to expend the little spirituality and devoutness in their dried-up souls upon a juridical formula, absolutely irrelevant to their lives, which is totally meaningless because there is no occasion for the majority of worshippers to need such absolution. Instead of having them recite an outworn formula, we should direct their minds to the wealth of native psalmody, e.g., Psalm 130.

Eisenstein responded on 5 October 1930:

My dear Rabbi Kaplan: Many thanks for your letter. . . . Kol Nidre is an introductory to the Yom Kippur service and is essential to the Day of Atonement, which is a day of good will when every person must forgive the ill-will of his neighbor if he repents and asks forgiveness. As we cannot ask God to pardon our sins until we wipe out all ill-feeling toward others, good will is the keynote of Yom Kippur. . . . For this reason the Kol Nidre was instituted as a prologue before our prayers on Yom Kippur in order to absolve all vows and oaths foolishly and in anger hastily annunciated [sic], [vows that would act] to break up a relationship with a friend, even to separate a son from a father, as was the case mentioned in the Mishnah [when a tanna] vowed not to eat at the table of his son at the wedding of his daughter. [A]nd [there are] many other examples of personal affliction which tend to create discord and hatred in the family and society, as mentioned in Masseket Nedarim. All such vows and oaths are made null and void by a simple process invented by our Talmudic Rabbis, in order to make the road clear for forgiveness and good will to all for the coming year.

Kaplan answered Eisenstein on 12 October 1930:

Dear Mr. Eisenstein: Please accept my thanks for the letter of October 5th. . . . I find the defense you make for Kol Nidre more plausible than any I have thus far come across. . . . There can be no doubt that if this conception of Kol Nidre were summed up in a rubric prefacing the text, there never would have been the slightest reason for objecting to its recital. . . . The way I can account for my failure to identify good will as the function of Kol Nidre is that I live in an environment which, though Jewish in character, is completely lacking in anything that is even reminiscent of the traditional Jewish spirit. . . . I am very grateful to you for having given me what seems to have been the actual purpose of Kol Nidre. I do not want to act precipitately in this matter, but to give it further study. If after several weeks I find myself holding my present opinion, I shall not hesitate to retract my former objections to the recital of Kol Nidre.

The following is the "rubric," as Kaplan called it, which he composed for the Kol Nidrei, according to the High Holiday prayer book he published in 1948:

The Day of Atonement and repentance atone for transgressions of man in his relation to God, but for transgressions between man and man there is no expiation in the Day of Atonement, until the wrongful act has been rectified (Mishnah Yoma viii).

The foregoing doctrine has contributed toward rendering the days preceding Yom Kippur a season of general reconciliation and good will. The Jew considered it his duty to rectify on those days all wrongful acts he had committed against his neighbors. He also resolved to destroy all sentiments of rancor and enmity he harbored against those who had wronged him. As an expression of that resolve, he performed the Rite of Kol Nidre. By this Rite, he asked and received absolution of all vows, by which he had intended to commit himself to the severance of friendly relations with any of his fellowmen. This meaning of Kol Nidre should no longer be left to inference, but should be expressly stated, as in the following version.

Kaplan's clarifying phrases, which made explicit this interpretation of the Kol Nidrei, are inserted in the traditional text as emphasized below:

All vows, bonds, devotions, promises, obligations, penalties, and oaths wherewith we have vowed, sworn, devoted, and bound ourselves, to take effect from this Day of Atonement unto the next Day of Atonement (may it come unto us for good), *so as to estrange ourselves from those who have offended us, or to give pain to those who have angered us*—they shall be absolved, released, annulled, made void, and of none effect.

To drive the lesson home, Kaplan strengthens the conclusion of the traditional formulation in the following manner:

These our vows, *and these only*, shall not be vows; these our bonds, *and these only*, shall not be bonds; these our oaths, *and these only*, shall not be oaths, *to the end that we might have given pain to those who have angered us*.

Kaplan inserted the equivalent Aramaic terms in the original Aramaic text for the sake of consistency.

Not as well publicized, but equally important, were the changes made elsewhere in the liturgy of the SAJ long before a published text was prepared. As is well known, for example, Kaplan modified the *berakhah* over the Torah, "asher bahar banu mikol ha-amim" (who has chosen us from all the peoples), to "asher kerevanu la-avodato" (who has drawn us to his service). The *Alenu* was also modified in this spirit. Instead of "shelo asanu ke-goyey ha-aratzot" (who did not make us like the peoples of the earth), Kaplan inserted "shenatan lanu Torat emet (who gave us a Torah of truth). The last verse of *Eyn Kelohynu* in the Ashkenazi ritual ("Ata hu she-hiktiru avoteynu lefanekha et ketoret ha-samim" [you are he before whom our fathers burned the perfumed incense]) was revised according to the Sefardi version to read "Ata takum terahem Zion" (you shall arise to have mercy on Zion).

Members of the SAJ were not always quite sure which substitutions had been introduced. Attending services while still a student,

I recall becoming aware that unfamiliar words were being recited but could not grasp the overall direction of the innovations. Indeed, only with the publication of Kaplan's *New Haggadah* in 1941 did his liturgical philosophy become fully clear. (It should also be noted that those of us who collaborated with him on the major Reconstructionist liturgical works did not always share his predilections.)

The new Haggadah was the first liturgical work Kaplan undertook. He initiated it because, as rabbi of a congregation, he considered himself responsible for providing his congregants with texts for worship that met his standards of spiritual excellence and intellectual consistency. When the idea of an SAJ congregational *seder* was first suggested in 1939, he proposed that three of us—he, Rabbi Eugene Kohn, and I—work together to prepare an experimental Haggadah. For two years we used a mimeographed text and learned much; finally, in 1941, the printed version was published by Behrman House. (I was responsible for editing the English text.)

This *New Haggadah* is based on several basic principles or guidelines as to what was included, what was eliminated, what was modified, and what was added. The aim of the Haggadah itself was rethought: instead of its being primarily a symbolic reenactment of the ancient Passover sacrifice, it became a dramatic affirmation of freedom in the present and for all time. Kaplan approached each text according to the following criteria: If it presented no problems —ethical, philosophical, or aesthetic—it was to be left alone. If there was a problem, the text was to be retained only if it could be reinterpreted. If it did not lend itself to reinterpretation, it was to be revised or at least supplemented with an "interpretative version" that in effect rewrote the passage. If the text was totally unacceptable, it was to be eliminated. When something was lacking, new readings and prayers were to be composed to fulfill the need.

All these criteria were put into action in the *New Haggadah*. At the beginning, an invocation was added. In the *kiddush*, the phrase "ki vanu vaharta" (because you have chosen us) is replaced by "ki otanu keravta la-avodatekha" (because you have drawn us near to your service), an instance where the elimination of a traditional text and the substitution of another was considered necessary. (Kaplan would not compromise on the need to eliminate the doctrine of the chosen people and considered every alternative formulation either a misinterpretation of the essential and unacceptable meaning of chosenness or plain dishonest; thus, in the *havdalah* service he omitted the phrase "bein yisrael la-amim" because it compared God's separation of the people of Israel from the nations of the world to the separation of light from darkness.)

Throughout the text of the *New Haggadah*, supplementary readings are inserted expatiating on the nature of tyranny and the true meaning of freedom. A daring innovation was the use of midrashic material dealing with Moses and his role as leader of the Israelites at their liberation. The ancient rabbinic authorities had underemphasized Moses in the celebration of the *seder* to the extent that he is not even mentioned by name in the traditional Haggadah. Kaplan believed that there was no longer any danger of idolizing Moses and that, on the contrary, if the message of the exodus was to be relevant, it must contain a portrayal of the great leader of this struggle for freedom. Hence, several passages of the Midrash were chosen that illustrated those aspects of Moses' ethical character that qualified him for the historical part that he played.

In the traditional Haggadah text, the long-range impact of the emancipation of the Israelites was not stressed. Kaplan felt that much more should be made of the injunction to "remember that you were slaves in the land of Egypt," so often recalled in the ethical mandates of the Torah. As a result, he included passages from the *Humash*, which underscored the influence of the historical experience of slavery in the subsequent formulation of commandments of the Torah.

Since the Haggadah was designed for the edification of the young, Kaplan believed that the recitation of the ten plagues, which appeared to him to be gloating over the disasters that befell the Egyptians, should be dropped. He was well aware of the midrash in which the angels are silenced by God when they were about to exult in the destruction of the Egyptians, but Kaplan did not feel that this homily justified the enumeration of the plagues in the presence of children. Similarly, he rejected the recital of the passage "Shefokh hamatekha al ha-goyim asher lo yeda'ukha" (pour out your wrath on the nations that do not know you). Even though in 1941 the Nazis were waging a murderous war against the Jewish people and the United States, he insisted on eliminating this call for vengeance, on the grounds that one should not fall to the level of those who hate you.

When Kaplan, Eugene Kohn, Milton Steinberg, and I began working on the *Shabbat* prayer book, we had considerable experience behind us in reforming that liturgy. For three years, an experimental, mimeographed text had been in use at the SAJ in loose-leaf binders. (I had the boring job of vocalizing the Hebrew.) It was not easy to generate feelings of devotion and piety when handling such a makeshift notebook, but the congregants felt they were participants in a creative endeavor and were most cooperative. The first printed edition finally appeared in 1945.

The four of us were in agreement about the basic approach. We concurred in Kaplan's contention that as far as possible all repetitions were to be eliminated in order to shorten the service. Kaplan expressed the hope that eventually one-fourth of the service should be prayer and three-fourths study. We never achieved that goal at the SAJ, but did aim to make briefer the davening and to draw out the learning and inspiration that took place.

In the introductory section of the *Shaharit* service, we suggested that the worshipper choose to recite "one or more" of certain psalms, and we added as alternative readings a selection of later Hebrew poems by such writers as Solomon ibn Gabirol. One of our most daring innovations occurred in the second paragraph of the *Shema*, "Ve-haya im shamo'a . . ." (Deut. 11:13–21), which asserts that God will withhold the rain if Israel disobeys divine law. Kaplan was determined that no text should be included in the new Sabbath prayer book that ran counter to scientifically established fact. Because rain was caused by changes in atmospheric conditions and bore no connection to the people's religious behavior, this paragraph was thoroughly outmoded. Since society is affected by group behavior, however, another passage on this theme should be substituted. We inserted Deuteronomy 28:1–6, which begins with similar words to the passage excised.

In the opening benediction of the *Amidah*, which refers to the patriarchs and prays that God "will bring a redeemer to their children's children after them," the word "redeemer" (*go'el*) was changed to "redemption" (*ge'ullah*). The Reform prayer book had already made this emendation, which sets aside the idea of a personal messiah. In our case, the change was based also on our conviction that the redemption of the world would be the consequence of the future godliness of mankind. The second paragraph of the *Amidah* affirms the resurrection of the dead, a doctrine that Kaplan insisted had no validity. In its place he proposed the formulation "zokher yetsurav lehayyim be-rahamim" ([God] who in love rememberest thy children unto life).

In the benedictions before the reading of the Torah, the notion of chosen people was eliminated and the phrase "asher kerevanu la-avodato" was substituted. The prayer before *Rosh Hodesh* was rewritten because Kaplan felt that a prayer for the new moon should include more than the hope for health and prosperity only. Lines were added asking for "love of Torah and the practice of piety, uprightness and intelligence, reason and knowledge."

Kaplan proposed that, when the Torah scroll was returned to the ark, two verses in *U-venuho yomar* be omitted: "Let thy priests be clothed with righteousness" and "For the sake of David thy servant turn not away the face of thy anointed." The rationale for these omissions was that the institution of the priesthood and the idea of the personal messiah were both obsolete. Against the sanctity of the ancient priesthood, Kaplan insisted that all Jews were now on an equal religious footing. (He also abolished the practice of having the *kohanim* arise to bless the congregation and the custom of offering the first *aliyot* to the Torah to someone who claimed to be a *kohen* or a *levi*.) The phrase "David thy servant" was a reference to the expected messiah; for the same reason it was dropped, Kaplan eliminated from the benedictions after the *Haftarah* the paragraph that began with *Samehenu*, "Gladden us, O Lord our God with Elijah the prophet, thy servant, and with the kingdom of the house of David, thy anointed."

Revising the *Musaf* service for *Shabbat* presented several problems. First, the *Musaf* contained a duplication of the formal structure of the *Shaharit Amidah*, and we had determined to avoid repetitions. Second, it included the *Tikanta Shabbat*, the prayer calling for the restoration of the Temple sacrifices brought on the *Shabbat*, as well as those ordained for the other days of the year. Kaplan, of course, rejected the hope for the rebuilding of the Temple and reinstituting the sacrificial cult. In substitution of the *Ami-*

dah, Kaplan proposed the *Magen Avot* prayer recited on Friday night. He did retain the *Kedushah* passages on God's holiness. In place of the messianic hope for a new sacrificial system according to the biblical mode, he composed a reading that, after recalling the sacrifices the ancient Israelites had brought, called on the worshippers to render their equivalent in the form of ethical actions. It should be mentioned that the radical revision of the *Musaf Amidah* was not approved unanimously by the editorial committee. In particular, Milton Steinberg felt that his congregation would disapprove of this change to such an extent that he might have difficulty in convincing them to adopt the new prayer book. Finally, he went along with Kaplan's proposal; but in the copies he later used at the Park Avenue Synagogue in New York City, there were pasted those passages omitted from the Reconstructionist version.

Kaplan had always insisted that the content of the service must be varied, maintaining that repetition, week after week, of exactly the same prayers result in bored worshippers and, eventually, their alienation from the synagogue. Furthermore, he was convinced that no matter how noble in places the traditional wording, it did not suffice to satisfy all the spiritual yearnings of modern worshippers. A note of relevance and contemporaneity had to be added to the service in the idiom of their own day. As a result, virtually half of Kaplan's *Shabbat* prayer book consisted of a supplement containing readings and prayers drawn from a wide variety of sources.

Kaplan had begun already to experiment with the idea of an anthology of additional prayers and recitations in 1924, shortly after the SAJ was organized. He prepared a volume of 104 pages, entitled "Supplementary Readings and Meditations," that was issued by the Society. In 1934 the United Synagogue of America published Kaplan's "Supplementary Prayers and Readings for the High Holidays," consisting entirely of original passages. For the *Shabbat* prayer book, Kaplan contributed numerous prayers and readings of his own. Perhaps the most outstanding, the one most often reprinted, was entitled "God, the Life of Nature." It reads in part:

> God is in the oneness
> that spans the fathomless deeps of space
> and the measureless eons of time,
> binding them together in act

as we do in thought.
He is the sameness
in the elemental substance of stars and planets
of this our earthly abode
and of all that it holds.
He is the unity
of all that is,
the uniformity of all that moves,
the rhythm of all things
and the nature of their interaction. . . .
God is the mystery of life,
enkindling inert matter
with inner drive and purpose. . . .
God is in the faith
by which we overcome
the fear of loneliness, of helplessness,
of failure and of death.
God is in the hope
which, like a shaft of light,
cleaves the dark abysms
of sin, of suffering, and of despair.
God is in the love
which creates, protects, forgives.
His is the spirit
which broods upon the chaos men have wrought,
disturbing its static wrongs
and stirring into life the formless beginnings
of the new and better world.

Kaplan also wrote, jointly with me, a series of poetical interpretations of psalms that attempted to put into contemporary language the essential message of each psalm. The following, "Prayer for Integrity" (on Psalm 12), is an example:

O Lord, why has truth-speaking become forgotten?
Why is deceit ingrained in the human spirit?
Where is the firmness of the spoken word?
Where is the sanctity of pledge and promise?
With honeyed praise and sweetened flattery,
Men seek advantages, in their fevered race
For social prominence or moneyed gain.
They furtively resort to sneering whispers,
As though, O Lord,
Thou art not nigh to hear.
Make whole our hearts, O God;

Thy name is truth, for only Truth can be
The bond that binds the hearts of men.

Apropos of his concern for beauty of expression, Kaplan sometimes eliminated a phrase in a prayer, not because it expressed an
objectionable thought, but because it interrupted the flow of language. For example, in the *Shaharit* of *Shabbat*, he omitted the
phrase "Or hadash al Tsiyyon ta'ir" (a new light will shine on Zion)
as an irrelevant digression, despite his strong commitment to Zionism.

Yet another radical liturgical procedure Kaplan sometimes used
was to make substitutions in the readings from the Torah. Thus, he
replaced for the afternoon service of Yom Kippur Leviticus 18 by
Leviticus 19. Although the new selection could be considered more
edifying in itself, it must be admitted that the main reason for the
change was that Kaplan was quite prudish and did not find appropriate the enumeration from the *bimah* of forbidden sexual relations in the traditional selection. In this regard, at the SAJ Kaplan
also dropped the usual *Haftarah* to the *sidra Hayye Sarah* in which
David is described as having a virgin brought to his bed to warm
him; each year Kaplan replaced this reading with a chapter from
one of the prophetic books.

The principles Kaplan set down for editing a worship text were
more easily articulated than implemented with complete consistency. Scrutiny of the various prayer books he edited with his colleagues inevitably raises the question, Why did Kaplan find it possible to accept some ancient formulations and not others?

In this regard, critics have often asked why Kaplan did not resort
merely to "reconstruction by reinterpretation." Certainly, he did
resort to this easier method when he felt that reinterpretation was
feasible and legitimate. In the *Shabbat* prayer book and in the other
liturgical works, "interpretative versions" sometimes obviated the
necessity of revising or eliminating the original text. But there were
numerous instances where Kaplan did not find this device adequate.
Can the instances where he thoroughly demurred from the traditional text be subsumed under a general principle? A reasonable
thesis, which accounts for most, although not all, of the seeming
inconsistencies on this matter, would be that Kaplan drew a line at
affirming as true, or even seeming to affirm as true, what he be-

lieved with certainty to be untrue, such as statements about the historicity of miracles as operations of nature that involved suspension of natural law.

In this regard, Kaplan sedulously avoided including any statement in the prayer book that might sound like a Jewish credo. Thus, the first edition of the *Shabbat* prayer book contained a lengthy introduction that set forth the philosophy of the editors (actually, the philosophy of Kaplan, although we three other editors concurred). The explicit list of crucial items omitted from the prayers included the doctrine of the chosen people, the doctrine of the personal messiah, the doctrine of the restoration of the sacrificial cult, and the doctrine of retribution. We have seen earlier that prayers referring to these items of belief were subject to revision across the board. Contrariwise, prayers and readings that helped the reader experience the reality of God and a oneness with the Jewish people—past and present—were retained and often were given new prominence.

Kaplan was especially concerned with the cultivation of a spirit of holiness, and any text that aroused that spirit was cherished. The traditional categories of issues *bein adam la-Makom* (between man and God) and issues *bein adam la-havero* (between man and his fellow) may be relevant here. Whatever concerned the relationship between humans and God, even when it required interpretation or reinterpretation, was retained by Kaplan. Whatever touched upon relations between human beings was scrupulously examined for affirmations unethical by modern standards; where these were found, they were elided as unacceptable on principle. Among the latter, Kaplan included the divine status of the Jewish people in contradistinction to all the other nations of the world.

Although a man of intense feelings and deep-seated emotions, Kaplan was never frivolous. His colleagues recognized that he never strove for change for its own sake. They could not always fathom the exact memories and associations that moved him to take a firm position on one matter and a lenient one on another. But they knew he was never influenced by "what the Gentiles might say"—not even by what other Jews might say. One can only hope that those who follow such a courageous pioneer will apply this approach with equally fine judgment reinforced by a deep perception of reality, as was Kaplan's.

Notes

1. Mordecai M. Kaplan, *Judaism in Transition* (1936) (New York: Covici Friede, 1936) 238.
2. W. Gunther Plaut, ed., *The Rise of Reform Judaism* (New York: World Union for Progressive Judaism, 1953), 234.
3. The letters between Kaplan and Judah David Eisenstein quoted here are contained in the author's private collection.

Liturgical Works by Mordecai M. Kaplan

Supplementary Readings and Meditations. New York: Society for the Advancement of Judaism, 1924.

Supplementary Prayers and Readings for the High Holidays. New York: United Synagogue of America, 1934.

The New Haggadah for the Pesah Seder. Edited by Mordecai M. Kaplan, Eugene Kohn, and Ira Eisenstein for the Jewish Reconstructionist Foundation. New York: Behrman's Jewish Book House, 1941. Rev. eds., 1942, 1978.

Sabbath Prayer Book, with a Supplement Containing Prayers, Readings, and Hymns and with a New Translation. Edited by Mordecai M. Kaplan and Eugene Kohn, assisted by Ira Eisenstein and Milton Steinberg. New York: Jewish Reconstructionist Foundation, 1945.

High Holiday Prayer Book, with Supplementary Prayers and Readings and with a New English Translation. 2 vols. Edited by Mordecai M. Kaplan, Eugene Kohn, and Ira Eisenstein. New York: Jewish Reconstructionist Foundation, 1948. Vol. 1, *Prayers for Rosh Hashanah.* vol. 2, *Prayers for Yom Kippur.*

Festival Prayer Book, with Supplementary Prayers and Readings and with a New English Translation. Edited by Mordecai M. Kaplan, Jack J. Cohen, and Ludwig Nadelmann. New York: Jewish Reconstructionist Foundation, 1958.

Daily Prayer Book, with a Supplement containing Prayers, Readings and Hymns and with a New Translation. Edited by Mordecai M. Kaplan, Eugene Kohn, Ira Eisenstein, Jack J. Cohen, and Ludwig Nadelmann. New York: The Reconstructionist Press, 1963.

Seven original prayers or readings by Kaplan may be found in the following: *High Holiday Prayer Book.* Edited by Morris Silverman. Hartford: Prayer Book Press, 1951.

PART FIVE

The Ideologist

CHAPTER 16

Kaplan and the Role of Women in Judaism

Carole S. Kessner

Mordecai M. Kaplan was one of the earliest advocates in America for the equality of women in Jewish law and in Jewish life. This is no longer news—nor is the fact that the first *Shabbat* morning bat mitzvah ceremony in the United States was that of Kaplan's own daughter, the eldest of his four daughters. This particular event has become so celebrated as to have become a legend in Judith Kaplan Eisenstein's own time. Mordecai Kaplan's vanguard ideas with respect to women's equality in Jewish law are either attributed to his having had four daughters and no sons or, more seriously explained as the necessary consequence of his rational philosophy of Judaism. There is some truth in both of these explanations; but Kaplan's summary statement in his chapter "The Status of Women in Jewish Law," in *The Future of the American Jew*,[1] ought not be dismissed. This chapter, which calls for the full equality of women in Jewish law and in Jewish life, is surely the culmination of an interplay of many factors, including his own family life as child and as husband and father; conditions in America during his early rabbinic years; his wide-ranging secular studies; and, finally, his grand effort to reconstruct Judaism.

Kaplan was born in Svenziany, Lithuania, on July 11, 1881; there he spent the first seven years of his life. In the setting of this small

village, and within the context of his family of four, he absorbed
powerful formative impressions from the two women closest to him
—his mother and his sister. Kaplan's mother, Anna, was an exceptionally strong woman. Like so many other eastern European women
who attended to the economics of daily life while their husbands
concentrated on the spiritual realm, Anna Kaplan supported her
rabbi husband by running a small grocery. She was, as her grand-
daughter Judith has put it, "like a character in Chaim Grade's
Rabbis' Wives."[2] This childhood experience of the role of women in
Jewish life perhaps lay behind one of the contradictions of Kaplan's
life. He was to espouse the cause of feminism and the equality of
women in all walks of life and was to admire women of intellect
and ambition,[3] yet he was to shape his own married life from the
pattern of his parents. Thus, he recorded in his diary on 2 July 1922
the following appreciation of his wife, Lena:

To say that I am fortunate in having Lena for a wife is but to express feebly
my gratitude to God for having made it possible for me to fulfill myself to
an extent that would never have been possible to me with a woman of
another type. If she had done nothing else but display the patience she does
. . . she would have done enough to earn my lifelong devotion.[4]

What is curious and revealing about this diary entry is that Kaplan
returned to it and revised it eight years later; he dated the revision,
Wednesday, 8 October 1930. He crossed out "made it possible for me
to fulfill myself" and amended it to the less self-centered wording
that she "enabled me to achieve things and to develop spiritually."
He also added a reference to "my mother, God bless her."

Anna Kaplan's hold over her son was, as we see here, long lasting. She was exceedingly intelligent but was also controlling and
ambitious for him. She pushed him to excel—yet ultimately she
disapproved of him because of his heterodox views. An illustration
of Anna's long-term interference in her son's life and of their stormy
relationship is revealed in a diary entry of 22 September 1922—
during the first year of the establishment of the Society for the
Advancement of Judaism. Kaplan noted that his mother-in-law had
approached him to report that he had been criticized by family
members and some congregants for "shouting on Yom Kippur Eve"
about decorum and that he was "driving away customers with his

rough treatment." Then, comparing his gentler mother-in-law to his own mother, he wrote:

As a rule my mother-in-law, who has a good deal of common sense, never discusses with me matters pertaining to my work. She knows that I am very touchy on that point, and am ready to explode at the least provocation. My own mother knows the same too about me, and most of the time observes the same rule of avoiding inflammable conversation, but she often forgets the rule, and there is a scene.[5]

Anna Kaplan's own capacity for intellectual achievement was exhibited in her ability to absorb languages quickly. Although she and her two children spent less than a year in Paris in transit from Lithuania to America while her husband, Israel, went to New York City to join Rabbi Jacob Joseph's rabbinical court, she managed to learn to speak French quite well. Even though she was a grown woman with children when she arrived in America in July of 1889, she learned not only to speak but also to read and write English fluently—an accomplishment not easily achieved by adult immigrants, male or female.

Kaplan's sister Shprintse (renamed Sophie once in America) provided yet another female model for her brother, who was four years younger. While still in Lithuania, Israel Kaplan recognized his daughter's native ability and decided to teach her to read Hebrew and to study Jewish texts. Not surprisingly, this caused scandal in the village, but Rabbi Kaplan did not yield to community pressure and continued to educate his daughter. From this the young Mordecai Kaplan learned two lessons: first, that women certainly had the capacity to study and second, that one must maintain the strength of one's convictions in the face of community opposition. And the two points were linked together.

Although Anna Kaplan's ambition for her son had been communicated positively to him in his childhood, he would be forced to view it later from the less positive perspective of his sister Sophie. Sophie's intellectual ability was without question. In different circumstances she could have achieved much more—had she been the eldest of a family of daughters, had she been born in America, had her mother been less of a factor in her married life perhaps she, too, might have found self-fulfillment. But such was not the case. After some years in the United States, she married a rabbi, a classmate of her brother Mordecai. But her husband, Phineas Israeli, was not cut out to be a strong public figure, and he is recalled by the family as sweet and mild, though something of a failure. Sophie, herself, is characterized by her niece Judith in words of admiration and of regret: "Sophie should have been something more. She was educated in things Jewish; she knew French, and as an old lady she would read the Bible in both Hebrew and French."[6]

How much of Sophie's arrested development and her husband's lack of success was due to the overbearing influence of Anna Kaplan is difficult to assess with certainty; but her constant comparison of her favored son with her unprepossessing son-in-law, her imperious control of her daughter with whom she lived most of the time, and her interference in the upbringing of her daughter's children could scarcely have been a small factor in the lives of Sophie and Phineas Israeli. All this was patently clear to Mordecai Kaplan, who in a diary entry of October 1922 wrote wryly about a "sin" he committed in order to pacify his mother and spare his sister.

I am in the habit of writing regularly every Friday to my mother who is now with my sister at Woonsocket. Last Friday I forgot to write. When I reminded myself, it was already Sabbath. Knowing that mother would be very much worried and help to make Sophie's life miserable if she were not to receive her usual Saturday morning letter from me, I went into the bathroom after supper and wrote a letter to her.[7]

The primary relationships with mother and sister undoubtedly were formidable psychological factors with respect to Mordecai Kaplan's attitudes toward women—conscious and less than conscious. But family relationships alone cannot account for his later radical opinions. These early experiences were a base for the next level—Kaplan's conscious endorsement of women's rights. Quite as important to the development of his theories about women (as distinct from his emotional attitudes) was that his early adult years in America were coincident with what is commonly referred to as the Progressive Era—roughly the years between 1900 and 1917, during the administrations of Roosevelt, Taft, and Wilson. This was an age characterized by Woodrow Wilson in 1913 as "nothing short of a new social age, a new era of human relationships, a new stage-setting for the drama of human life."[8] How could a young man with so strong a rational, pragmatic bent as Kaplan fail to be influenced by the dynamic events of these years? It is of importance to remember that Mordecai Kaplan's education in the first part of this century was not restricted to rabbinic training and Jewish texts. He received his bachelor's degree from City College in 1900 and a master's degree from Columbia University in 1902, where his studies concentrated on the comparative disciplines of anthropology and sociology—the new social sciences. His academic studies eventuated in a series of articles in the *Menorah Journal* in 1915 and 1916 that expressed his deep conviction that the best way to study religion in general and Judaism in particular is by applying the techniques of the secular disciplines of the social sciences.

In 1903 Kaplan had accepted a position as rabbi of the most affluent eastern European Orthodox congregation in New York, Kehilath Jeshurun. But he grew increasingly unhappy in his role as leader of a community of Orthodox *nouveaux riches,* for his own religious and social ideas were growing more and more unorthodox. Fortunately, by 1909 Solomon Schechter rescued him by offering him a position at the newly formed Teacher's Institute of the Jewish Theological Seminary, and in 1910 he began his long and controversial career teaching at the Rabbinical School of the Seminary. During the next several years, he widened his experience further by serving the New York *kehillah,* by lecturing at the Ninety-second Street YMHA, by speaking before a wide variety of groups in and beyond New York City—in sum, extending his range of experiences and acquaintances—and inevitably, drawing comparisons between Jewish life and American life.

What, then, were some of the burning issues igniting the fires of political and social reform—issues that were the targets of muckraker exposés? A good many of these revelations related in one way or another to women. Though today we do not think of the years between 1910 and 1920 as a decade of sexual revolution, the facts are that such issues as women's suffrage, changing sexual mores, increasing prostitution, venereal disease, and white slave traffic were front-page news. The so-called Protestant ethic, which had prevailed in the United States (not only in terms of work but also in terms of sexual attitudes) from the early colonial times to the beginning of the twentieth century, was by 1910 undergoing a radical transformation. In part, this was due to the massive wave of immigration from European countries where somewhat different sexual standards were common. The open activity of the prostitutes on Allen Street on the Lower East Side of New York City was notorious. The conditions are described graphically and powerfully in Michael Gold's reminiscence of life among the immigrants in these early years of the twentieth century:

The East Side of New York was then the city's red light district. . . . There were hundreds of prostitutes on my street. . . . The girls winked and jeered, made lascivious gestures at passing males. They pulled at coat-tails and cajoled men with fake honeyed words. They called their wares like push-cart peddlers. At five years I knew what it was they sold. . . .

Earth's trees, grass, flowers could not grow on my street; but the rose of syphilis bloomed by night and by day.[9]

About the year 1910 there grew widespread perturbation concerning the prevalence of prostitution and the concomitant spread of venereal disease. Houses of prostitution existed openly not only on Allen Street in New York but in every city. (In New Orleans, a guidebook to such establishments was printed annually.) The United States Immigration Commission's investigation of the so-called white slave traffic uncovered that not only were women being recruited from the hinterlands of America, but they were being imported from Europe as well. This investigation led to the passage of the well known Mann Act. By 1914, forty-five states had passed laws against pimps and madams profiting from prostitution; in about thirty cities, the red-light districts were closed.[10]

Agitation for social reform was the hallmark of the era. Some of the efforts, such as the Mann Act, advanced women's rights. Other responses, however, such as the New York vice squad's attempt to suppress Theodore Dreiser's outspoken novel *Sister Carrie* (1900), were atavistic attempts to impose a dying Victorian morality. Most of the reformists were motivated by fear of venereal disease, not fear of God, for social control through the Protestant ethic was a thing of the past. Religious dread of damnation had long since lost its power, and Hester Prynne was soon replaced by Theda Bara in the American imagination. Whereas it generally is assumed that morals did not ease until after World War I, as a result of the exposure of American troops to European mores and, in the case of women, because of the wartime experience of nurses and Red Cross workers, the historical truth is that the tango—symbol of the risqué —was banned by women's clubs as early as 1914. One Reverend Henry Van Dyke complained that jazz, the most popular dance music of the teens, was "a sensual teasing of the strings of sexual passion." Not to be overlooked also was the change in women's fashions. The short skirt did not make its entrance until after World War I, but the obligatory protective corset made its exit before the war, symbolizing the removal of strait-laced inhibition in favor of a new moral freedom for women.[11]

Furthermore, the weakening of religious sanctions was not unrelated to the rise of the new psychology and psychoanalysis. Havelock Ellis's pseudoscientific *Studies in the Psychology of Sex* appeared in America in 1910. Freud and Jung were already lecturing in the United States, and by 1916 New York City could boast of five hundred practicing psychoanalysts. Indeed, for many, psychoanalysis became their new religion.[12]

In these years of changing sexual attitudes, Kaplan—who was something of a prude—did not speak directly to the subject of the new mores, nor did he address the specific issues at great length. But by the time he published *Judaism as a Civilization* (1934), his thinking on the subject of sexual morality was fully worked out. That he was quite aware of and concerned about the issues of prostitution and white slavery (albeit from the Jewish angle), we learn from a note on the Jewish family in chapter 28. Kaplan commented:

In 1931 there were at least 10,000 cases of Jewish women in eastern Europe whose husbands had abandoned them, had journeyed to other countries, and had re-married. These women are compelled to abide all their life in a thraldom from which the Jewish community does nothing to free them. The existence of such a condition contributes largely to the spread of prostitution and white slavery.[13]

Since Kaplan here put the issues into the Jewish context of the *agunah*, he also characteristically lost no chance to snipe at Orthodox rigidity. The last sentence of the paragraph reads, "The facts disclosed at a recent conference in London to deal with the problem of white slavery among Jews reveal the tragic effects of the unwillingness of the Orthodox authorities to deal with the situation in an enlightened manner."[14]

This chapter on the Jewish family presents Kaplan's now fully formed ideas about the role of sexuality in Jewish life and its containment within the Jewish family. In a historical observation about ancient Jewish and early Christian interpretations regarding the central message of the Hebrew prophets, Kaplan claimed that the earliest interpreters "selected denunciations of sexual morality as the keynote . . . whereas modern interpreters regard the call to righteousness as the hallmark of prophecy." The prophets, he continued, were speaking of idolatry, but since their words continued to be regarded as divinely inspired, they could not lose their force once polytheism was replaced by monotheism. Instead, the sin of idolatry became translated as the sin of licentiousness; thus, the rabbis and church fathers became exponents of chastity. For the Christians the highest form of chastity was celibacy; for the Jews, chastity meant lawful sexuality—a distinction that led Kaplan to his idealization of the Jewish family because it is the social instrument through which the ideal of chastity is actualized. Thus, he concluded, *"Christianity evolved the institution of monasticism as a means of exalting the ideal of chastity. Judaism exalted the family, and made it the end to be served by chastity. . . . Chastity is best furthered when it is treated not as an end in itself, but as a means of conserving the family."*[15]

Kaplan was to enlarge upon the relationship of sexuality to the institution of the family in later writings. An article written in 1949 stated that the two areas most prone to moral evil are "sex hunger" and ambition. Hindu and medieval Western civilization, Kaplan claimed, have regarded the physical hungers as man's chief stumbling block, but "Judaism, on the other hand, may be said to have been the first civilization to insist that the field of human relations is the area most in need of being brought within the dimension of moral law. The tendency of the strong and the clever to exploit the weak and the simple is, in the estimate of Judaism, the source of man's undoing."[16] While pointing out that "there can be no question that the Jews possessed a more wholesome sex morality and a more adequate appreciation of the family institution than other peoples,"[17] he admitted that Judaism was full of sexual taboos and rules; but these were intended to contain the sexual drive from running riot. Moreover, they do so for the social health of the community. "Only to the extent, however, that human relations are implicated in these physical hungers do those hungers become subject to moral law."[18]

It is not surprising, then, that Kaplan did not rely on Freudian psychology. Though he characterized Freud as having great "intellectual caliber," Kaplan only addressed himself to Freud's attack on religion in *The Future of an Illusion* and did not comment on his theories of sexuality.[19] More congenial to Kaplan was the work of psychologist Harry Stack Sullivan, who dealt almost exclusively with interpersonal relations. For all Mordecai Kaplan's words on self-fulfillment and self-dignity, these, he asserted, were best achieved within the context of the group, which made Sullivan's approach the more attractive.

In the passages just cited we see that Kaplan linked sexual exploitation to exploitation in general—he said that the *original sin* of Adam was the sin "which is the source of all sins, and which may well be held responsible for the whole gamut of preventable human ills." This sin "is the abuse of human freedom by the attempt of men to make their own interests and passions the sole determinants of their behavior."[20] Kaplan was not alone in noting the relationship between sexual and economic exploitation—a point never so clear as in the early years of this century in America. The conditions are, once more, concretely described by his contemporary Michael Gold:

The Jews had fled from the European pogroms; with prayer, thanksgiving, and solemn faith from a new Egypt into a new Promised Land. They found awaiting them the sweatshops, the bawdy house, and Tammany Hall.[21]

As Kaplan and Gold observed, the houses of prostitution were one depot for immigrant women, and the sweatshops were the other —most especially the New York City garment and textile factories that Kaplan knew firsthand. Not only was he confronted daily by the fact of the sweatshops as he walked through the Lower East Side to the Teacher's Institute, which was located in the center of the neighborhood; not only had his congregation numbered many wealthy garment manufacturers; but his own wife's family was in the garment industry and one brother-in-law owned a silk mill in Paterson, New Jersey. In 1916, during the period when Kaplan was in the midst of grave doubts about his own career, he took a trip with his brother-in-law to look at the mill. In a diary entry, dated 29 August 1916, he wrote:

Today I went with my brother-in-law Edward Rubin to take a look at his silk mill in Paterson. The Hyde of materialistic ambition is not completely doomed in me. It asserted itself last Friday night when I had a talk with him. I dreamed once again of turning to the practical affairs of life, and when he suggested that I go to take a look at the mill, I gladly consented to do so. When I rode with him and his son Milton on the train this morning I had them both explain to me the business situation as it concerned him, and the details involved in the manufacture of silk. At one moment it appeared to me as an enchanting Romance, at the other as a sordid aimless pursuit. This latter conviction gained on me when Milton took me to Paterson while his father remained in New York. From my conversation with him it was borne in upon me that Ed gets very little out of life that is worthwhile. He is not even laying the foundation of future happiness. He is squandering all his energies in money-getting without the prospect of ever enjoying what he will have amassed. When I came to the mill I was sorely disappointed. I had expected to see a sanitary, well managed factory. What I saw impressed me as noisy, unsafe, and unsanitary, with disorder and waste quite rampant. As I returned my heart was very much saddened at the hard pitiless grind of the average well-to-do Jewish businessman, whose life is ill-organized, empty, and futile. In addition they have as wives women who have not the least conception of their husbands' toil, whose greatest problem is that of getting upstairs girls and nurses, and who grow stout and neurasthenic for want of anything worthwhile to occupy their minds with.[22]

In this excerpt Kaplan not only expressed astonishment at the poor conditions at the factory and empathy and sorrow for the futility of his brother-in-law's life, but analyzed the cause of the "neurasthenic" condition of the wives. No Freudian, Kaplan attributed their physical lassitude to mental stultification. This passage immediately follows an account of a meeting he had had with a young woman named Haynalka Langer, who "is a graduate of the Teacher's Institute and has become one of the chief workers in the Bureau of Education. Her interest at present," he recorded, "is centered on Jewish homemaking. I intend to have her begin that work with the women of the W. S. Center as soon after the holidays as possible. She is a personable young lady of about twenty-five, a college graduate and an excellent teacher. . . . She possesses a gift for details and executive ability."[23] The linking of two contrasting accounts of women's lives was probably not a matter of chronology alone. In addition, Kaplan's description of the "neurasthenic" wives also must have been prompted by the blatant contrast between these wealthy but indolent women and the plight of the women who worked in the plant itself—a contrast that for years had been the subject of newspaper accounts and about which Kaplan had spoken out on from the pulpit.

The years between 1903 and 1917 saw the growth of the first unions composed largely of women. The natural place for women-dominated unions to originate, Eleanor Flexnor explains in her history of the women's movement, was "in the garment trades where a large proportion of the labor force was female, working under sweatshop conditions which were a strong incentive to organization."[24] Indeed, the first significant strike, not only in the history of the ILGWU, but in the organization of working women, was that of the shirtwaist makers of New York City and Philadelphia in 1909–10. This strike was prompted by resentment of the intolerable conditions of the two largest shops, Leiserson and Company and the Triangle Waist Company—the factory that only two years later would have one the most infamous fires in the history of labor. This was the strike that was to catapult into fame a teen-aged Jewish girl, Clara Lemlich, who electrified the crowd with her call to action.

These were the very years when the women's suffrage movement finally came of age. Closely related to the agitation within the garment industry was the establishment of a functioning headquarters in New York City in 1910 for the Women's Suffrage movement. Until then, the National American Women's Suffrage Association had maintained a "headquarters" in Warren, Ohio, where the treasurer lived. But now, with a gift from Mrs. O. H. P. Belmont and with the impetus of the New York women garment workers, a national center was established in New York City. The alliance between wealthy women, such as Mrs. Belmont, and working women, such as Rose Schneiderman, the eloquent leader of the cap makers' union, in common cause became patently visible in the annual spring parades for women's suffrage in New York City. A newspaper account of 15 April 1912 reports in words of inspiration:

Women who usually see Fifth Avenue through the polished windows of their limousines and touring cars, strode steadily side by side with pale-faced, thin-bodied girls from the sweltering sweatshops of the East Side. Mrs. O. H. P. Belmont walked but a few steps ahead of Rebecca Goldstein who runs a sewing machine in a shirt-waist shop.[25]

Mrs. Belmont and women like her must have stood out in bold relief against the "neurasthenic" women of Kaplan's acquaintance. So would women such as Rose Schneiderman, whose oratorical gifts became legendary. One of her most powerful speeches, given on March 20, 1912, was in response to a statement by a New York senator that women would lose their femininity if they were given the vote. She responded sharply:

We have women working in the foundries, stripped to the waist, if you please, because of the heat. Yet the Senator says nothing about the women losing their charm. They have got to retain their charm and delicacy, and work in the foundries. Of course you know that the reason they are employed in foundries is that they are cheaper and work longer hours than men. Women in the laundries, for instance, stand for thirteen or fourteen hours in terrible steam and heat with their hands in hot starch. Surely these women won't lose any more of their beauty and charm by putting a ballot in a ballot box once a year than they are likely to lose standing in foundries or laundries all year round. There is no harder contest than the contest for bread, let me tell you that.[26]

Though women's suffrage in the first two decades of this century was a prominent issue, it had not yet produced a federal amendment affirming the right to vote regardless of gender. True, Theodore Roosevelt's Progressive party made women's suffrage a plank in its 1912 presidential platform, but at this time Taft and Wilson did not support it. But by the summer of 1916 women's suffrage had been ratified by twelve states, and the National Women's party in these states refused to endorse Wilson. Wilson had considered the issue while still governor of New Jersey; and, as Eleanor Flexnor explains, he "passed through successive phases in which he pleaded that he could no nothing unless his party acted, since he was solely its representative and spokesman," that he could do nothing until Congress did something, and that he could not "invade the province of a Congressional Committee to hasten its action" because the issue was entirely a state issue.[27]

Nevertheless, Wilson ultimately supported women's suffrage. On

October 9, 1915, just before the New Jersey referendum, he stated publicly that he would go to his home in Princeton to cast his affirmative vote. By 1916 it was clear that he would support a federal amendment.

Although Kaplan has left us no written record of his support for women's suffrage, there is no doubt that he unequivocally endorsed it. His daughter Judith vividly remembers that in the year 1916, when she was only seven years old, she stopped at the home of her mother's sister and brother-in-law. She recalls her uncle, who was normally a gentle person, vigorously announcing that he intended to vote for Taft; he certainly did not want Wilson to be president because then women would get the vote! That this episode made a long-lasting impression on so young a child is undoubtedly the effect of having heard the opposite from her own father. In a recent remembrance of her own childhood, Judith Eisenstein writes, "By the time I was eleven the Women's Suffrage amendment had been passed. A conscious feminism in our household began to have some echoes in the environment, but only beyond our family."[28]

More directly to the point is Kaplan's own diary entry of 3 September 1916. Though it bears only inferentially on the specific issue of suffrage, his words encapsulate his frame of mind at that time and are a poignant portent of the task that, by now, he knew was before him—a task that he knew would not be an easy one, and one that was to occupy him for the rest of his life:

Yesterday I walked to Elberon [New Jersey] to hear President Wilson deliver his speech of acceptance of the nomination for re-election. I experienced some of that awe which was meant to be voiced in the blessing *sheheheyanu*. I could not help thinking of the contrast between the Jewish people moribund and spiritless, and the American people in the prime vigor of youth. How happy the lot of those that lead the one, how wretched the lot of those doomed to stand by the deathbed of the other.[29]

Most likely, such a painful contrast as this, when applied to the future of the American Jewish woman, would lead to Kaplan's observation that "already during the first decades of the era of Jewish emancipation the Jewish woman became aware that she was accorded a more dignified status outside Jewish life. This explains why many talented Jewish women not only began to lose interest in Jewish life, but actually turned against it. . . . If we do not want our talented women to follow their example, we must find in Judaism a place for their powers. This cannot come about unless all taint of inferiority will be removed from the status of the Jewish woman."[30]

Between 1915 and 1922, when Kaplan served as rabbi of the new Jewish Center on the Upper West Side of New York City, he expressed his ideas and expounded his theories in the *Menorah Journal* and discussed them with a group of his rabbinical colleagues whom he had organized into the Society for Jewish Renascence.[31] But it was not until the Jewish Center split over his radical positions that Kaplan and his supporters formed the Society for the Advancement of Judaism, where he hoped to put theory into practice. Three of the most immediate innovations that he proposed had to do with the status of women in the synagogue. The first proposal was to institute mixed seating; the second was to institute the bat mitzvah ceremony; and the third was the decision to call the women's organization the Women's Division rather than the Sisterhood.[32]

Today it is difficult to grasp how startling was Kaplan's suggestion that there should be mixed seating at the SAJ—particularly when we have just noted that the Society was formed by supporters of Kaplan's heterodoxy. In a diary entry of 27 April 1922, however, only months after the establishment of the SAJ, Kaplan revealed that he is in the "throes of a moral conflict" over an offer from Dr. Stephen Wise to join the faculty that he was organizing for the Jewish Institute of Religion. Kaplan admitted that if the offer had come before he had organized the SAJ, he would have "grasped the opportunity with both hands." But now he believed that the Society would break up if he accepted Wise's offer. Though he had made it clear to them that he was "through with Orthodoxy," accepting Wise's offer would "shock them into a clear realization of how far removed I am from what is probably their notion of me, for Wise is to most of them the last word in Jewish heterodoxy." Kaplan then went on to complain of his unhappiness at the slowness with which the Society has been progressing toward the goal he has in mind— "the goal of a dynamic socialized Judaism." He admitted that he has succeeded surreptitiously in making a change in the ritual for petition of return of the sacrificial service; but he ascribed this to the fact that because he had not announced or explained the change, most were unaware of what he has done. The majority of the worshippers, he wrote, have other things on their mind when the cantor chants the *Amidah*.

Mixed seating, however, was quite another story. "When it came . . . to another more visible change," he explained, "there was protest and the protestors have had their way. I wanted that men and women should not be divided off as is done in the Orthodox synagogues. I believe that there is no reasonable excuse for continuing the custom of separating the sexes during prayer now that men and women sit promiscuously at all other functions social and educational." At this point Kaplan gave in to the "organizers" who were afraid that mixed seating might identify them as "reformed Jews."[33] By May of 1922, however, Kaplan succeeded in convincing the trustees to allow mixed seating at the upcoming High Holidays. Nonetheless, he was skeptical about their motivation and wondered whether their capitulation was due to "their own realization that it is absurd to maintain a custom that is so out of keeping with the attitude assumed towards women today, and that is so much a hindrance to active participation in the prayer on the part of every member of the family," or whether it was because another well-known rabbi who was always regarded as Orthodox had taken a pulpit in a neighborhood synagogue that had abolished separate seating.[34]

When the High Holidays arrived, Kaplan was pleased to observe that "as a result of the wives sitting with their husbands and children, I succeeded in doing away with continual conversation and disinterest in the service." One is tempted to conclude from this that the importance to Kaplan of mixed seating is as much due to his desire for decorum as it is to his commitment of equality for women. But the issue was still not entirely settled. In an amusing postscript, Kaplan noted that his own brother-in-law, Moe, came to Kaplan's mother-in-law to complain that he had lost his temper during the Kol Nidrei service and had scolded the congregation for their "lackadaisical spirit." His mother-in-law, whom Kaplan had praised earlier for her good sense, now approached him with Moe's criticism—and, sounding like a latter day Glueckel of Hameln, with her own complaint. Kaplan recorded the encounter:

I acted like a model son-in-law, listened to all that she had to say—and she had a good deal to say about her wisdom and foresight in getting all her nine children—God bless them—to be good Jews and marrying them all off successfully. I ought to give heed to her advice and not permit men and women to sit together at the S.A.J. house during services, and to control my temper in the pulpit. I was non-committal on the former, and on the latter I promised her that next Yom Kippur I would demonstrate to her how even tempered I can be.

I had to make up, of course, for my good behavior during the interview with her by indulging in an extra fit of the blues over the fact that my hands are tied by a number of *women of both sexes* [italics added].[35]

The issue of mixed seating finally was resolved at a meeting of the Board of Trustees of the SAJ on October 8, 1922. The question of having the family-pew system came up again, and Kaplan wrote that he made it clear that "if it were at all practicable to have it I certainly will insist on it."

If the question of mixed seating caused such a commotion, the introduction of bat mitzvah appears to have occurred with little congregational opposition. Of the now-celebrated first bat mitzvah at the SAJ, Kaplan made only the following cursory entry: "Last Sabbath (March 19) I inaugurated the ceremony of the bat mitzvah at the S.A.J. Meeting House (41 W. 86th Street)—about which more details later. My daughter Judith was the first one to have her bat mitzvah celebrated there."

There are, however, no further questions recorded, although Judith Kaplan Eisenstein herself recalls with amusement that the night before the event both of her grandmothers sat in her bedroom rocking back and forth, wringing their hands. Her grandmother Kaplan, she vividly recalls, said, "*Machateniste*, tell your son-in-law not to do it." "*Machateniste*," replied the other, "tell your son not to do it." There was indeed a greater to-do, at least within the family, than her father records in his diary.[36]

Judith herself has written that about this time when she had joined a Hebrew-speaking club in the Central Jewish Institute on Eighty-fifth Street, she found the first group of girls who had "feminist" interests like her own and who planned to work when they grew up. "Most" she writes, "would have to work. They would be expected to contribute to support their families. Being exceptionally bright and aggressively feminist, they planned to go through college and to fulfill themselves—and not settle for helping in the store, or getting secretarial jobs. . . . These same girls formed a silent claque at the Sabbath Service at the new Society for the Advancement of Judaism when I became a bat mitzvah. . . . They were all there to rejoice in this innovation, representing the rights of women to participate actively in anything where they had been denied before."[37]

Innovation it was, despite Kaplan's matter-of-fact record of the event. And though he never gave the further details that he promises in his diary entry, one may assume that there indeed was controversy—not only because the bat mitzvah took place on a *Shabbat* morning, but also because it was conducted with exactly the same ritual required for the bar mitzvah ceremony. This alone distinguished the event from any other female initiation ceremony that might have been in practice at the time, such as the Reform movement's confirmation ritual. That Kaplan's intention to apply all the requirements of the bar mitzvah to the bat mitzvah was deliberate is substantiated in his account of a bat mitzvah celebration he witnessed in a synagogue in Rome only a few months later.

In the summer of 1922, Mordecai and Lena Kaplan took a trip abroad where they spent a few days in Rome. On *Shabbat* morning they attended services, at which, Kaplan notes, there were one hundred men in the auditorium and the women sat in the gallery. The services were dull and mechanical and did not in the least interest the worshippers. But he "was very pleased to see that they had the custom of taking cognizance of a girl's becoming bat mitzvah."

They call it entering *minyan* at the age of twelve. The ceremony consists of having the father called up to the Torah on the Sabbath that the girl becomes bas mitzvah. She accompanies him to the *bima* and when he is through with his part, she recites the benediction of *she-heheyanu*. Before *Musaph*, the Rabbi addresses her on the significance of her entering *minyan*. On the Sabbath I was at the synagogue there were three girls and one boy who entered *minyan*. The assistant Rabbi who was supposed to address them, read something to them out of a book in a very mechanical fashion. The fathers of the girls acted as if they were very infrequent visitors at the synagogue.[38]

Since this Italian-style bat mitzvah occurred only four months after that of Kaplan's daughter Judith, we should not be surprised by his mixed response to it. No doubt he responded to this event with the double reaction of rabbi and of father, both being roles he assumed with great seriousness—and in his role as father he could act with overmuch seriousness. He himself expected, at least of his first-born, somewhat more than might be expected by another father. Judith Eisenstein recalls the educational content of her tender years:

> By the time I was nine I had had Hebrew lessons. . . . I had had two years of music in the children's centers of the Institute of Musical Art. . . . I had two years of private French lessons with a French woman who never uttered a word in English. I was in the sixth year in public school, having skipped a number of grades, thus never learning to do long division, nor to knit and sew. . . . I had a first-hand acquaintance with some of the music of the greatest composers . . . and had a large repertoire of synagogue and early Zionist songs. . . . All of this made me very different from practically anyone I knew.[39]

Judith Kaplan's father, it appears, had such great expectations for his eldest daughter that, Henry Higgins–like, he made her his personal crucible for testing his ideas about education and women —as later, the SAJ would be the laboratory for his communal experimentation. And as he proved to be the demanding educator of his congregation, so was he in his home—with small recollection, however, of what it was to be a child. No wonder that he was so profoundly hurt when his adolescent daughter rebelled. Kaplan records a touching and revealing family story that occurred shortly after Judith's bat mitzvah. It is a long entry—but one of interest here because it reveals his authoritarianism but also his fatherly hypersensitivity.

> This has been one of the unhappiest weeks of my life. It began with Lena showing me what my Judith thinks of me whenever I find it necessary to insist upon her realizing that she is after all my child and that she still owes me a certain degree of filial obedience. God knows I do my utmost to develop in her a sense of self-reliance, but until I can be certain that she has the necessary reasonableness and self-control to make self-reliance safe, I deem it my duty to exercise guardianship. She is only thirteen at present. Yet when upon a single occasion I crossed her will, she became so overwrought that she charged me in her diary with being a despot. There are a number of irrelevant charges she brings against me in what she says there —which fact leads me to believe that *I am bound to be disappointed if I look forward to having in her an intellectual companion.* She does not

seem to have the love for me that my other little ones have. If I do not engage her in conversation she is apt to ignore me for weeks as though I did not exist. There are probably explanations for all this coldness, the explanations we may find in the books on adolescence. Nevertheless, the experience of it hurts me to the core. [Italics added.][40]

Three days later on December 10, Kaplan's mood changed radically. "The cloud that overhung my mind during the previous week is almost dissipated. Here are the gratifying experiences that have brought back the sunshine to me." In the rest of this entry he described how during *Shabbat* he took advantage of Judith's mention of her diary to encourage her to show it to him. He wanted her to understand his motive in having crossed her will, "the day when she indited those bitter charges" against him in her diary. When his daughter finally produced the diary, there were some pages torn out. But, he said, of her own accord she admitted that she had removed some pages because they had some things in it that she did not care to retain in her diary. "Later on," he wrote, "when Lena tried to find out why she had torn out these pages, she asked Lena not to press for the reason, because she was far too ashamed to think of what she had written to want to talk about it. As soon as I realized that Judith's ill will against me was only momentary and superficial, and that all traces of it were completely obliterated, I was myself again."[41]

Although Mordecai Kaplan was to write extensively on the subject of education, this passage reveals something of his deficit in the area of child psychology. And in this deeply felt expression of a wounded ego, perhaps the most compelling confession is his lament that he despairs of ever having this thirteen-year-old child become his "intellectual companion." Implicit in this passing remark is the point that Judith's future husband, Ira Eisenstein, later would make —that there were many anomalies in Mordecai Kaplan's life and thought. Though he early espoused the cause of feminism in his theory and practice, he chose a wife that, no intellectual, would serve his personal needs; and what he did not expect or want from his wife, he yearned for from his daughter. Though he educated his daughter according to modern ideas about the equality of men and women, he was old-fashioned with regard to the relationship of parents to children. Finally, his total commitment to the primacy of the group left shortcomings in his ability to understand and respond to the needs of the individual—this, despite his many words on the subject of the "self." Nonetheless, his daughter Judith's dual legacy is happily summed up in her own words: "I have had the best of two worlds, and have enjoyed a freedom given to few of my acquaintances, male and female."[42] The legacy Kaplan bequeathed to Jewish women in general is summarized in the paragraph that introduces his chapter on "The Status of the Woman in Jewish Law," in *The Future of the American Jew*.

Few aspects of Jewish thought and life illustrate so strikingly the need of reconstructing Jewish law as the traditional status of the Jewish woman. In Jewish tradition, her status is unquestionably that of inferiority to the man. If the Jewish woman is to contribute her share to the regeneration of Jewish life, and if in turn Jewish life is to bring out the powers for good that are in her, this status must be changed. She must attain in Jewish law and practice a position of religious, civic, and juridical equality with the man, and this attainment must come about through her own efforts and initiative. Whatever liberal-minded men may do in her behalf is bound to remain but a futile and meaningless gesture. The Jewish woman must demand the equality due her as a right to which she is fully entitled. That right is conceded to her in other civilizations where she is treated as a full-fledged person. There is no reason why the Jewish civilization should persist in treating her in this day and age as though she were an inferior type of human being.[43]

Notes

1. Mordecai M. Kaplan, *The Future of the American Jew* (New York: Macmillan, 1948), 402–12.
2. Judith Kaplan Eisenstein, interview with author, July 1987.
3. Kaplan's admiration for women of intellect is illustrated in a diary entry of 4 October 1922 when he responds to a report from Max Kadushin that his High Holiday services had impressed a young woman named Evelyn Garfiel: "For a sophisticated person like her to have been inspired by those services is to me very encouraging. Miss Garfiel is a highly intelligent young woman, about twenty-three and of excellent scholastic attainments—she has just completed her doctor's thesis—and is preparing herself to do personnel work under the auspices of the S.A.J. with the League of Jewish Youth."
4. *Kaplan Diaries*, vols. 1 and 2, Jewish Theological Seminary. Vol. 2, 2 July 1922.

5. Ibid., 22 September 1922.
6. Judith Eisenstein, interview July 1987.
7. Ibid., 20 October 1922.
8. Quoted in Samuel Eliot Morison, *The Oxford History of the American People* (New York: Oxford University Press, 1965), 812.
9. Michael Gold, *Jews without Money* (New York: Horace Liveright, 1930), 6–7.
10. Morison, *History of the American People*, 905.
11. Ibid., 906.
12. Ibid., 907.
13. Mordecai M. Kaplan, *Judaism as a Civilization* (New York: Macmillan, 1934), 548.
14. Ibid.
15. Ibid., 421.
16. Mordecai M. Kaplan, "A Philosophy of Jewish Ethics," in *The Jews: Their History, Culture and Religion*, ed. L. Finkelstein (New York: Harper and Brothers, 1949), 41.
17. Kaplan, *Future of the American Jew*, 408.
18. Kaplan, "Philosophy of Jewish Ethics," 41.
19. Kaplan, *Judaism as a Civilization*, 309.
20. Kaplan, *Future of the American Jew*, 5, 274.
21. Gold, *Jews without Money*, 6.
22. *Kaplan Diaries*, vol. 1, 29 August 1916.
23. Ibid.
24. Eleanor Flexnor, *Century of Struggle: The Woman's Rights Movement in the United States* (Cambridge: Harvard University Press, 1975), 249.
25. Ibid., 267.
26. Ibid.
27. Ibid., 288.
28. Judith K. Eisenstein, memoir, 4.
29. *Kaplan Diaries*, vol. 1, 3 September 1916. Words that appear in Hebrew script in the original diary entries are transliterated in this essay.
30. Kaplan, *Judaism as a Civilization*, 409.
31. Kaplan's spelling of "Renascence" is probably a result of his great admiration for Matthew Arnold, who uses this spelling in his essay "Hebraism and Hellenism." Arnold gives the following explanation: "I have ventured to give to the foreign word *Renaissance*—destined to become of more common use amongst us as the movement which it denotes, comes, as it will, increasingly to interest us—an English form." Kaplan certainly knew this essay.
32. Eisenstein, memoir, 13.
33. *Kaplan Diaries*, vol. 2, 27 April 1922.
34. Ibid., 25 May 1922.
35. Ibid., 3 October 1922.
36. Judith K. Eisenstein, interview with author.

37. Eisenstein, memoir, 4–5.
38. *Kaplan Diaries*, vol. 2, 22 August 1922.
39. Eisenstein, memoir, 2–3.
40. *Kaplan Diaries*, vol. 2, 7 December 1922.
41. Ibid., 10 December 1922.
42. Eisenstein, memoir, 1.
43. Kaplan, *Future of the American Jew*, 402.

CHAPTER 17

Kaplan's Influence on
Jewish Social Work

Harriet A. Feiner

As with his other work, Mordecai Kaplan expressed his ideas on
•social work in the context of an integrated view of the American
Jewish life of his era. Although his teaching, writing, and lecturing
related to Jewish social work comprise only a small part of his
contribution to Jewish thought, his influence extended at least from
1925, when he began to teach at the Training School for Jewish
Social Work in New York—later known as the Graduate School for
Jewish Social Work—to 1964, when he last spoke to the annual
meeting of the National Conference of Jewish Communal Service.
During those years, he addressed varied contemporary social welfare issues; however, his major message for the Jewish social work
community involved his conviction that a vital organized democratic Jewish community was essential for healthy Jewish life in the
United States.

When Jews came to the United States, they brought with them a
long tradition of providing for the needs of their own poor, sick, and
aged members through a well-organized community structure. In
the United States, they also established institutions to take care of
the needy. However, the structured community context of Old World
Jewry was absent. Nevertheless, as early as 1895, Jews organized
local federations of agencies, initially to raise philanthropic funds

and later to plan for community needs as well. These federations became models for the community chests organized in the nonsectarian community. By 1938, there were seventy local Jewish federations that had joined together in 1935 to form the National Council of Jewish Federations and Welfare Funds.[1] The federations were a mechanism for providing for that part of the Jewish population that had difficulty in adjusting to the United States or in meeting the needs of Jews in general.

Those who arrived earlier were particularly interested in the economic adjustment and Americanization of later immigrants. In addition, hospitals were founded, partly to provide health care for the Jewish poor, but also to provide hospital connections for Jewish physicians. The 1925 budget of the New York Federation provided more than three times as much money for medical care and medical social services as for community centers.[2] By and large, federations spent only a small part of their budgets on Jewish educational or cultural activities. Until the massive unemployment of the 1930s, Jewish philanthropic agencies met the needs of Jewish people because the government took negligible responsibility for the subsistence of those who could not provide for themselves. Philanthropy was still a private matter.

In 1899, the National Conference of Jewish Social Service was organized by lay and professional leaders of federation agencies.[3] In time, this organization became the professional organization of Jewish social workers, paralleling a similar organization of social workers in the general community. One of the major purposes of the conference was the establishment of standards for professional social work practice in Jewish agencies. This Jewish concern for professional standards emerged as the social work profession itself was emerging. The first school of social work in the United States was founded in 1898 by the New York Charity Organization Society.[4] Thus, it can be said the professional Jewish social work was born in the United States at the same time that professional social work was born.

Jewish social work was defined as social work with Jewish clients in agencies under Jewish auspices supported by Jewish contributions. From the beginning, tension existed between those who believed that, though social workers needed to understand the cultural heritage of their clients, the methods of social work were universal and those who believed that Jewish social work required not only knowledge of the client's culture but a commitment to furthering the interests of the Jewish community. The latter group defined social work in broader terms to include cultural, recreational, educational, and organizational aspects. This tension became more acute after the 1930s, when economic conditions made it impossible for private philanthropy, including Jewish agencies, to meet the overwhelming need brought on by economic upheaval. Government began to assume ever-increasing responsibility, partly through public agencies and partly through grants to private agencies. (At present, almost no agencies can resist the seduction of public funds. But these funds do not come without concomitant obligations to serve regardless of ethnic or religious identification and to provide designated kinds of services.)

As early as 1933, articles that address the nature and direction of Jewish social work can be found in the *Jewish Social Service Quarterly*.[5] Samuel Kohs, who also serviced on the faculty of the Graduate School for Jewish Social Work, said that there were Jewish social workers who fallaciously believed, among other things, "that Jewish life has no content, that Jewish culture has no significance, that Jewish social work has nothing to do with either of these, and therefore has nothing to contribute to American or any other civilization."[6] This is only one of ten fallacies that he listed. As a corrective, he proposed that "the development, advancement, enrichment, and the productiveness of Jewish small community life should be a primary obligation of all Jewish social workers."[7]

Kohs's thinking was clearly influenced by his colleague, Mordecai Kaplan, whose broad view of social work encompassed the organization of a structured community, educational and cultural activities, as well as economic relief and assistance with emotional and interpersonal problems. Though Kaplan frequently deplored the Jewish illiteracy of both the professional and lay leadership of federations, he still hoped that the National Council of Jewish Federations and Welfare Funds could evolve into an organic, functioning, democratic Jewish community.

The 1923 National Conference of Jewish Social Service established the Training School for Jewish Social Work, which opened in

1925. The purpose of the school was to professionalize social work practice in Jewish agencies by educating a corps of social workers trained in up-to-date professional methods and techniques as well as in Jewish history, culture, and problems. The conference discussion that led to the decision to proceed with plans for a school showed a split between those who wished the school to provide a full curriculum, including both Jewish and social work content, and those who recommended that the school provide only the Jewish content with social work courses taken at an already established school of social work. The latter was the majority and carried the day. The minority group accused the majority of having inadequate Jewish commitment and of being assimilationist.[8] However, when the school opened, both Salo Baron and Kaplan were on the faculty —hardly assimilationist teachers. It is likely that both factions were strongly committed to Jewish life and that the differences between them reflected disagreement on the possibility of living in two civilizations. Nevertheless, there were those in the Jewish community "who charged the Graduate School for Jewish Social Work with evidencing assimilationist tendencies." A letter written by Kaplan in 1933 answered the charges when, in reference to the students, he stated:

I doubt, however, whether they could have said anything about the school which should have led you to conclude that its spirit is assimilationist. . . . You are probably aware that the purpose of the Council for the Advancement of American Jewish Life is not to further assimilation. . . . I ask you in the name of reason, can you or anybody conceive that as President of that Council I would have presented Dr. Karpf's paper if it showed assimilationist leanings?[9]

During the entire duration of the school, from 1925 to 1940, students did take some of their work at the New York School of Social Work, now part of Columbia University; however, examination of the 1934 curriculum demonstrates that the school had moved from a one-year to a two-year degree program and that social work courses as well as Jewish content were offered.[10] S. C. Kohs, Maurice Karpf (director of the Graduate School for Jewish Social Work), Salo Baron, and Kaplan, all committed Jews, taught there. Salo Baron confirmed that the faculty was committed to Jewish life and to Jewish content in social work. He indicated, however, that some of the students during the depression years believed that the wealthy board members of the school—people like Felix Warburg or Louis Kirstein of Filene's—were subsidizing the school to prevent the revolution that students felt was necessary in order to correct the devastating economic situation.[11]

Kaplan taught courses entitled "Social and Religious Institutions of the Jew" and "Problems of Jewish Adjustment to American Life." In the preface to *Judaism as a Civilization*, he indicated that this teaching forced him "to correlate the meaning of Judaism with some of the problems of inner conflict with which Jewish social workers are called upon to deal."[12] He hoped that the Graduate School of Jewish Social Work would provide the Jewish community with more knowledgeable leaders and thereby further some of his programs for Jewish life in the United States. When asked about Kaplan's influence, Abraham Cohen, who attended the school from 1933 to 1935, wrote:

The highlights of the Jewish part of the program were the first year with Salo Baron and the second with Kaplan. I have so often said they were *the* academic experience of my life. The year we had with Kaplan was also the year his magnum opus, *Judaism as a Civilization*, was published and of course we used it a lot. . . . He was a wonderful, stimulating teacher—his knowledge and understanding in so many fields, his insistence on straight, honest thinking (no bluffing or pretending allowed), a good sense of humor, etc.[13]

Graenum Berger, who attended the school in 1930, also has clear recollections of Kaplan's teaching. He recalls Kaplan's insistence that his program for the Jewish community must be understood as a whole, not just piecemeal. Two major issues were at stake: first, the development of an overall, organic, democratically organized Jewish community that would include and meet the needs of all Jews; second, the development of the local Jewish community centers as institutions that would serve all Jews and provide opportunities for extensive Jewish experience and education. Berger confirmed Kaplan's influence on his own activities in the Staten Island Jewish Community Center.[14] Both Cohen and Berger devoted their lives to leadership in the Jewish community, the former in Israel and the latter in the United States. It seems fair to say that Kaplan influenced the thinking and Jewish identification of a significant proportion of the social work students whom he taught, particularly those who went on to work in Jewish community centers and federations. It is likely, however, that the more politically and economically radical students were not interested in Kaplan or Jewish content.

In 1930, the directors of the Wieboldt Foundation, concerned with fundamental principles of philanthropy, published a volume entitled *Intelligent Philanthropy*. Included were chapters written from a Catholic, Protestant, and Jewish viewpoint. Kaplan's piece, "Jewish Philanthropy: Traditional and Modern," reflected his total approach to Jewish religion and community. His ideas on philanthropy were set in the context of religious naturalism, humanism, and evolving civilization. At the outset, he clarified his premises about the evolution of Jewish religion so that there would be no question about the basis of his religious interpretations. Utilizing the model he developed for analyzing other issues confronting modern Jews, he examined the Jewish tradition of philanthropy and evaluated its relevance to the needs and conditions of contemporary life. When it was possible to do so, he developed a synthesis of what already existed; when impossible, he analyzed the source and reasons for the changes he believed were necessary. In his discussion of traditional approaches to philanthropy, he noted the following:

1. the biblical assumption that responsibility for the maintenance of the poor belonged to the same category as maintenance of the priests and Levites, implying that the poor have the right to community support as an entitlement rather than as charity;
2. public administration of charity funds, with assessment according to means, was the most remarkable product to emerge from Jewish self-government;
3. the duty of charity was rooted in communal responsibility rather than individual benevolence;
4. the prophets, who made strong connections between poverty and social unrighteousness, taught that poverty was not the fault of the individual but of the social order;
5. the rabbinic sages emphasized *gemilut hasadim*, the principle that giving must be with loving kindness, that is, in a manner that does not provoke shame.

The excellent set of principles is not yet the basis for modern social welfare planning. Despite the merits of these principles, Kaplan believed that the traditional approach was inadequate because its underlying principle was theological—that it was based on the belief that God requires the poor to be cared for. He believed that a transvaluation from a theocentric to a humanistic rationale was needed.

The chief end of ethical conduct is human well-being. In the case of philanthropy, no other end is tolerated but that of so improving the condition of the poor and the helpless that they become more capable of helping themselves.[15]

He carried his argument beyond mere humanism, by asserting that the meaningful nature of reality was the final rational justification for philanthropy.

Moreover, the Jewish religion refuses to abdicate because it regards the humanistic approach by itself inadequate. . . . But with the increasing tendency to push our demand for a rationale for all human activities to the utmost boundaries of reality, we cannot possibly remain content with making even human welfare the ultimate reason for giving of ourselves and of our means and energy to those with whom fate has dealt unkindly. We must feel convinced or accept on faith that service has its justification in the very nature of reality. Unless the universe be accepted as a meaningful totality in which our actions somehow count, no humanistic scheme of social improvement can ever arouse much enthusiasm or call forth much sacrifice.[16]

He proposed two additional principles to guide philanthropic efforts: First, "the rightness or wrongness of an action is to be determined by the consequences which flow from it for the welfare of the race." Second, "a maximum of human individuality plus a maximum of human cooperation" must be sought.[17] Thus, Kaplan honored traditional principles but provided a new rationale based on religious naturalism, thereby combining tradition and modernity in his Jewish approach to social work.

Just as Kaplan evaluated Jewish tradition in the light of modernism, so he evaluated contemporary issues in the light of the Jewish tradition. In considering the question of government versus private responsibility for philanthropy, Kaplan stated, "The experience of the Jewish People would help to reinforce the conception of the state as in duty bound to exercise the function of taking care of the poor."[18] He left open the question of whether the state should meet its obligation directly or by assisting the voluntary sector. His discussion of the tension between the good of the community and the needs of the poor person reflected both the complexity of his thinking and his refusal to accept stereotypical solutions. His confidence that professional social work practice, based on research in the social and behavioral sciences, would yield effective solutions to the problems of society was an example of his underlying faith that science would provide answers where theology could not. This essay was probably the nearest he ever came to a formula to establish the relationship between all relevant aspects of the needed synthesis.

The book in which the article on philanthropy appeared was not widely read or studied, and this thought-provoking effort, which clearly illustrated the integrated approach that Kaplan used to examine diverse issues, did not receive the attention it deserved. It had little impact on either the Jewish or the professional social work community. The importance of the work lies in its early use of the model that Kaplan developed more fully four years later in *Judaism as a Civilization*.

Certain basic themes recur in the addresses that Kaplan gave to the National Conference of Jewish Social Service in 1935 and in 1964, and in the articles that he wrote in Jewish social work journals. These concerns are framed in the light of the central problems of the specific time. It is evident that Kaplan hoped that his conception of an organic Jewish community could evolve by bringing local Jewish federations and welfare funds into a national organization.[19] The major focus of his work in Jewish social work journals was to advocate the development of an organized, inclusive, democratic Jewish community based on the principle of *"kol Yisrael arevim zeh bazeh* (all Jews are responsible for one another)."[20] In Kaplan's words,

This condition makes it imperative that we channel all the constructive forces which operate in Jewish life into a planned and concentrated effort to create the sort of Jewish community that will command the loyalty of every Jew because it has made itself indispensable to him.[21]

He presented detailed programs for achieving such a community, while leaving open the possibility that a democratic process might achieve the goal in a different way. The goal itself, however, was clear. He believed that the basic need of the Jew for status, self-respect, and cosmic orientation could be met only through an organized Jewish community which fostered its own historical, national, and spiritual values to a maximum degree compatible with his life as an American.[22] Thus, the community would enrich itself as well as America and the lives of other minority groups.[23] He explained, "Jews cannot serve the cause of genuine democracy better than by surviving as a group, and rendering the group activities creative of cultural, ethical, and spiritual values."[24]

In 1935 the world was in the throes of a major economic upheaval. For Jews in the United States, this meant severely curtailed economic opportunity. This was additional evidence to Kaplan that the Jewish community needed to be reorganized so that it could respond to the economic needs of its members. In his view, "To feed a people sermons when they need bread is to indulge in that mockery of the poor which our Scriptures tell us is tantamount to blasphemy."[25] He believed that the Jewish community had to assist its members to achieve "cultural differentiation and economic assimilation,"[26] though he observed that at that time, the reverse was more likely to be the case.

Kaplan's conviction that all Jews were responsible for one another led him to insist that Jews who had achieved some economic security through business or the professions continued to be responsible to Jewish laborers whose economic interests were different from their own. He strongly believed in the necessity for cooperation and deplored the personal and institutional individualism that pervaded American society and affected the Jewish community: "the criterion of what is socially just [is based on] the principle that in every human relationship there should be a synthesis of the maximum cooperation with the maximum personal liberty."[27] Yet Kaplan never used the principle of mutual responsibility among Jews as a rationalization for avoiding responsibility for the welfare of humanity in general. The Jewish community was obliged to cooperate with others in taking action to alleviate need in the entire community. Nevertheless, he emphasized that Jewish needs could only be met in the context of an organized community that functioned on the basis of cooperative values:

The creation of such an all-comprehensive Jewish organism is what is needed to establish the principle of Jewish collectivism in the place of the present personal and institutional individualism.[28]

In 1940–41, during the Hitler era, when writing "The Implications of the World Situation for Jewish Cultural Life in America," Kaplan reiterated his conviction that the survival of the Jewish people could best be ensured by the establishment of a real community. Only in this way could Jews be helped to understand the meaning of being Jewish in the face of such intense hostility. While recognizing the dehumanizing character of Nazism, Kaplan maintained his belief in the potential of humanistic religion:

If we assume, as we must, in order to be able to live at all that there is a spiritual urge in man that will compel him to remain human, we cannot but conclude that the masses will ultimately cast off that leadership and achieve their justifiable aims by methods that will not destroy their humanity.[29]

Obviously, Kaplan's program for the development of an organic, democratic Jewish community was not implemented. Fragmentation and competition are still the hallmarks of Jewish life in the United States, except in times of major threat to Israel. The development of federations and welfare funds with the ability to raise significant sums of money has done little to unify the community. Competition for funding continues within the federations. Nevertheless, some of Kaplan's ideas have trickled down. Yeshiva University established the Wurzweiler School of Social Work for the purpose of educating social workers for service to the Jewish community. Although the school is under Orthodox auspices, it sees itself as a Jewish school, not an Orthodox one. The curriculum is intended to provide students with an understanding of the totality of American Jewish life—its sociology, its diversity, and its value structure—as well as offer professional social work education. Although the founders do not believe that Kaplan had any direct influence on the school's philosophy,[30] their program does reflect Kaplan's thinking and shows how his ideas were absorbed into the public domain.

The Jewish center movement, with its emphasis on programming for Jewish living, also owes a debt to Kaplan. During the past decade, Jewish federations have become increasingly attuned to the need to develop programs that address issues of Jewish survival in agencies under their auspices. There has been increased funding for Jewish education, for Jewish family-life education, and for other programs that include Jewish content or respond to specifically Jewish needs. Nevertheless, it is difficult to assess how much of this is a response to conditions in Jewish life and how much is owed to Kaplan's influence. Clearly, Kaplan's analysis of Jewish life demonstrated the necessity for providing opportunities for Jewish living in order to ensure meaningful Jewish continuity. It is likely, therefore, that the recent developments reflect a confluence of Kaplan's thinking and the pressures on Jewish life in America.

Rereading Kaplan's articles in the social work literature, I was struck by the continuing relevance of his analysis, his method, and his program. How would social work function in an organic Jewish community? Currently the term *Jewish social work* is frequently used, but it has no clear meaning. Is Jewish social work any social service provided by an agency under Jewish auspices? Must both the client and the auspices be Jewish? Must the social worker be Jewish? Must the social worker be a knowledgeable Jew? Is the content of a service provided by a Jewish agency different from the service provided by a nonsectarian agency? Does an agency under Jewish auspices have an obligation to consider issues related to group survival when addressing the needs of an individual or family? Is an agency Jewish by virtue of its auspices whether its clients are Jewish or not? When an agency under Jewish auspices accepts government funds, how is the service it provides affected? Questions proliferate, and answers remain ambiguous. Lack of clarity is a function of the absence of a real community. Most Jews do not feel any real connection to the service providers. Only the large contributor has any impact on the allocation of funds. The communal purpose of the services provided is not clear. The temptation to accept public funds is overwhelming, and those funds are available only for certain kinds of services that must be offered to all applicants on a nondiscriminatory basis. Under these conditions, Jewish social work does not really exist. There is only professional social work, with its own knowledge base and its own value system that is sometimes provided to Jewish clients in agencies under Jewish sponsorship.

Were there to be an organic Jewish community of which all or even most Jews felt a part, there would take place a natural process of interaction between professional principles of helping and Jewish communal life. Each would contribute to the other and enrich the other. In such a community, Jewish tradition could be brought to bear on contemporary concerns—biomedical decision-making, family disorganization, alienation, and anomie, to name just a few. Were there to be an organic Jewish community, new needs might be addressed more quickly and effectively—for example, the need for quality day-care programs. Such programs, in turn, could enrich the Jewish lives of young families. If the Jewish community regularly met such needs, perhaps Jewish survival would be less threatened by high rates of intermarriage and low birth rates.

An organic Jewish community could provide the kind of mutual social system that would function as a bulwark against isolation and individualism. Perhaps alienation among young Jews would then be more limited. One hopes that it is not yet too late to implement Kaplan's urgent program.

Notes

1. M. J. Karpf, *Jewish Community Organization in the United States* (New York: Bloch, 1938), 103–4, 107, 120.
2. *Records of the Graduate School for Jewish Social Work*, Archives of the Yeshiva University Main Library, Box 486-2.
3. Karpf, *Jewish Community Organization*, 118.
4. W. I. Trattner, *From Poor Law to Welfare State* (New York: Free Press, Macmillan, 1974), 199.
5. S. C. Kohs, "Current Fallacies Regarding Jewish Social Work: Is It Drifting toward Extinction?" *Jewish Social Service Quarterly* 9, no. 3 (June 1933): 296–304. See also G. W. Rabinoff, "Where Is Jewish Social Work Going?" *Jewish Social Service Quarterly* 9, no. 2 (March 1933): 252–55.
6. Kohs, "Current Fallacies," 297.
7. Ibid., 298.
8. *Proceedings of the National Conference of Jewish Social Service, 1923* (New York: National Conference of Jewish Social Service, 1924), 50–59, 411–27.

9. Mordecai Kaplan to Rabbi Morris Silverman, *Records of the Graduate School for Jewish Social Work*, box 347, November 10, 1933, Archives, Yeshiva University Main Library.
10. Ibid., box 230.
11. S. Baron, telephone conversation with author, 17 December 1987.
12. M. M. Kaplan, *Judaism as a Civilization: Toward a Reconstruction of American Jewish Life* (1934; reprint, New York: Schocken, 1967) xiii.
13. A. Cohen, letter to author, 4 April 1987.
14. G. Berger, interview with author, 23 April 1987.
15. M. M. Kaplan, "Jewish Philanthropy: Traditional and Modern," in *Intelligent Philanthropy*, ed. Ellsworth Faire, Ferris Laune, and Arthur J. Todd (Chicago: University of Chicago Press, 1930), 77–78.
16. Ibid., 79.
17. Ibid., 85.
18. Ibid., 82.
19. Kaplan, *Judaism as a Civilization*, 59, 298; and idem, "Welfare Conference Proceedings," *Jewish Social Service Quarterly* 11, no. 4 (June 1935): 321, 324.
20. Kaplan, "Conference Proceedings," 321. Cf. Talmud, Shevu'ot 39a.
21. Ibid., 322.
22. M. M. Kaplan, "The Organization of American Jewry," *Jewish Social Service Quarterly* 12, no. 1 (September 1935): 50.
23. Ibid., 62.
24. M. M. Kaplan, "The Implications of the World Situation for Jewish Cultural Life in America," *Jewish Social Service Quarterly* 17, no. 1 (September 1940):36.
25. Kaplan, "Welfare Conference Proceedings," 322.
26. Kaplan, "Organization of American Jewry," 50.
27. Kaplan, "Implications of the World Situation," 41.
28. Kaplan, "Organization of American Jewry," 2.
29. Kaplan, "Implications of the World Situation," 34.
30. M. Teicher, telephone conversation with the author, 17 August 1987.

CHAPTER 18

Kaplan and Jewish Education: Reflections on His Influence*

William Cutter

Mordecai Kaplan and Reconstructionism are virtually interchangeable in most treatments of American Judaism. No transformation in the Reconstructionist movement since Kaplan's retirement and death has deflected thinkers from identifying its basic position with his. Jewish history has rarely seen a religious tendency attached to one person to quite this degree except, perhaps, Hasidism's reverence for the life and lore of the Baal Shem Tov. There is yet another similiarity between the two movements in that the ideologies of both Reconstructionism and Hasidism developed out of viewing the Jewish tradition and its paradigms explicitly through the prism of the social reality of the Jewish people.

The social reality that produced Kaplan was an interplay of three perspectives, according to Charles Liebman's prodigious essay "Reconstructionism in American Jewish Life": the Jewish tradition, American philosophical thought, and the American Jewish experience.[1] Jewish educators have fretted about how these three perspectives have affected Jewish education ever since Kaplan's ideas first became a recognized fixture of American Jewish discourse in the 1930s. (The "fretting" may not always have been fully explicit, but

---

*A first draft of this paper was written with Dr. Isa Aron, a good friend and colleague. I want to express my thanks to her.

serious issues are often latent in discussions of other topics.) Not the least of Kaplan's historical roles was that he kept asking educators, What are the ends toward which they direct their efforts?

Liebman's analysis is more troublesome than others because contrasting the norms of the Jewish tradition with the pragmatic consciousness Kaplan encouraged can create a dissonance that plagues educators. They are less bothered by interpretations, such as that of Jonathan Woocher, in which communal pragmatism and a modernist ideology are seen as interacting without great concern for imperatives derived from the Jewish tradition.[2] Applying the norms of the tradition forces a confrontation between simple communal loyalty and the conviction that a main subject of Jewish education ought to be standards and values. To make matters even more complicated, Kaplan's Reconstructionism sharply criticized traditional norms—norms of synagogue worship and in the field of education. One Jewish norm that Kaplan sustained, of course, was the idea of community. In Reconstructionism, this idea was to be embodied in the basic Jewish corporate body—the *kehillah*.

Kaplan's place in American Jewish life has been reassessed periodically as to his impact, timeliness, and realism. His influence was vast, even though the movement that springs from him is rather small and the number of those who fully grasp the implications of his position even smaller. Liebman's study, which provided a sociological basis for understanding Reconstructionism in the broad context of American religious life, concluded that Kaplan's Reconstructionism was the only Jewish religious development the origins of which are purely American and in which the leading personalities view Judaism from the perspective of a specifically American Jewish experience.[3] Woocher agrees that the link between Reconstructionism and American civil religion is especially comfortable and organic.[4] Arnold Eisen's description of Kaplan's proposal that "vocation" should be substituted for the unacceptable concept of "chosenness" seems to lend support to that generalization.[5] Eisen confirms the extent of Kaplan's influence (*influence* is not the same as *agreement*, a point to which I shall return later in this essay) with his ironic comment that it was Kaplan's sharp opposition to chosenness that led so many Jewish thinkers to expend so much effort defending the idea. Liebman's stimulating essay, Woocher's acute observations on the natural connection between Kaplanism and American civil religion, and Eisen's valuable analysis of the relationship of theology to politics agree on Kaplan's importance and facilitate the removal of writing on Kaplan from the realm of hagiography. These three works are crucial for the current essay, even though other books, especially Jeffrey Schein and Jacob Staub's *Creative Jewish Education*,[6] have contributed to my understanding of Kaplan as an educational theorist.

Kaplan wrote on so many aspects of Jewish life and had such a diverse following that Jewish intellectuals do not usually associate his name with education per se. (Unfortunately, American Jewish intellectuals seldom engage in serious discourse on Jewish education.) We can rectify an imbalance and stimulate reconsideration of Kaplan's place in this field by examining his writings on education and by reviewing the secondary literature on his career as educator. What is the extent and depth of Kaplan's impact, amidst the many other influences that have affected American Jewish life since the time when Kaplan was most active?

Although educators of the 1980s can hardly feel triumphal, the last two decades have certainly thickened the texture of American Jewish education and enlivened it immensely. Since Israel Chipkin wrote on Kaplan's contribution to Jewish education,[7] more attention has been devoted to Jewish education than Kaplan's contemporaries would ever have thought possible. This flurry of activity has obscured the links between Kaplan's thinking and what followed because the more time that intervenes between conception and execution, the more difficult it is to determine primary causation. Chipkin was thoroughly aware of the conception of Kaplan's ideas, but he did not anticipate (nor could he have anticipated) what was to happen to Jewish education afterwards.[8]

A reconsideration of Kaplan's influence on education must begin with the question, How can one distinguish the effect of a thinker upon a society's schools from that person's effect on society as a whole? That is, in what ways is it possible for an intellectual's general views to shape educational policy? As applied to Kaplan, was his influence exerted directly on educationalists through his writings on this subject? Was it exerted through face-to-face relationships with friends and students involved in education and educational management? Or, was it an indirect outgrowth of his social theories that others transplanted to the field of pedagogy? Was it the *kehillah* in practice or the *kehillah* in theory that has had the greatest influence?[9] Education is a problematic area for intellectual historians. Cultural commentators all too easily can oversimplify the assessment of "influence," especially out of frustration with the status quo. Thus, in recent years there have been smoothly written accounts of the supposed overwhelming responsibility of Rousseau, Nietzsche, John Dewey, Robert Hutchins, and even Horace Kallen for the successes or failures of American education.[10] Unfortunately for such blanket judgments, educational policy involves a maze of factors and many discrete, pragmatic steps: lesson planning, curriculum development, instructional methods, institutional implementation, follow-through procedures, and so forth. The impact of a theorist on these factors and steps can be felt immediately or only decades after the publication of his "influential" work. Kaplan may be less frequently mentioned in the context of specific educational projects and movements than in the context of the overall religious orientation of American Jewry, yet he administered education programs and dealt directly with significant numbers of students who absorbed his ideas firsthand.[11]

It is difficult enough to evaluate the influence exerted by a thinker when the changes he is purported to have effected are still in midstream. Moreover, there is a large and growing literature on the impact of "great people and great deeds" that may lead to new frameworks for linking cause and effect in cultural matters. In various ways, these studies point out that, besides direct and measureable lines of influence, attention must be paid to new forms of interpretation, attribution, and exegesis that allow us to distinguish between perceived and real impact and between direct and dialectical connections.[12] Many of Kaplan's followers are still living, writing, and talking to us. How can we assess the range of vectors connecting them to such a practical and programmatic thinker as Kaplan, considering the intervening forces that may have intruded? How can we determine the proximate, the indirect, and the formal influences? Should not Kaplan, for example, be given some credit for communal developments that have enlarged the budgets of the nondenominational bureaus of Jewish education in many American cities, a development of which he would certainly approve? Was the New York Bureau the paradigm for bureaus throughout the United States? Or were there other forces bringing them to the fore?

Richard Libowitz cites some of the specific institutional developments within American Jewish education that he feels are a legacy of Mordecai Kaplan:

Eventually many of the programs and ideals espoused by Kaplan were accepted by American Jewry, often without realization of their origins. The concept of the synagogue center remains Kaplan's most widely accepted idea; if it has not proven to be the Jews' Club, it has led to Men's Clubs and Sisterhoods, cultural and athletic programs, and benches and tables of the storefront *shtibels* and Orthodox *shuls* in which Kaplan was raised. The bat mitzvah has been adopted by almost all non-Orthodox congregations.[13]

To this list can been added *havurot* (camps) and Israel programs; even social service projects within schools are possible indications of Kaplan's influence in the non-Orthodox educational activities of American Jewry. Certainly, most of the features of a *kehillah*, of which Kaplan spoke in *Judaism as a Civilization*, have found one expression or another even in today's communities. But how can we be certain that the educators who affirm Kaplan's influence on them were not attributing to him the effect of extraneous factors?

Jeffrey Schein and Jacob Staub, in their book *Creative Jewish Education*, argue for a "congruity" between contemporary attitudes to Jewish education and Reconstructionism, as if congruity automatically demonstrated influence. In a chapter of that book, Etan Levine confuses the problem further when he comments that "Reconstructionist thought recognizes that all education is a process of transformation, a program for becoming."[14] One does not have to be a historical revisionist to argue that the kind of influence postulated here may be ascription rather than fact.

While remaining skeptical, we must appreciate the ripple effects of Kaplan's thought. (Perceived influence is a fact, too.) Scholars are rightly skeptical about the influence of founders on the functioning of their institutions and the relationship that may obtain between canonical text and events in the real world. Much of what

Kaplan wrote has become canonical, especially among his followers who have been reluctant to use the very sociological tools that enabled Kaplan to understand the broad spectra of people's behavior. What is being written about Kaplan's importance for education deals too little with a dialectic of influence that would show how Kaplan's ideas affected events, how events affected Kaplan's discussion of them, and how later discussions filtered to us through the actions of his followers. What would Kaplan have said about American Jewish spirituality of the 1980s? (I refer to a growing concern with spirituality taken by some as inherent in the current situation, a development that Schein and Staub imply will impel Reconstructionism to move forward.) [15] In Jonathan Woocher's view, Kaplan did not anticipate the current emotional climate of American Jewry, a shortcoming he attributes to Kaplan's unwillingness to deal with the tragic dimension of people's lives.[16] One might ask, Would Kaplan have been "Copernican" enough to place the learner's growth, rather than the survival of the people, at the center of the educator's attention? Can a *kehillah* ever place the learner in the center at the expense of the centrality of the *kehillah* itself? Kaplan found a way out of this possible contradiction by viewing the *kehillah* as a means for instruction and organization as well as an object of study—a model for the child's sense of society. More than any other Jewish thinker, Kaplan took ideas that were already in place in American life and activated them within the context of American Jewry. This attributes to Kaplan no little authority, but it requires a loyal adherent and an objective researcher alike to explicate the intricate weave of American intellectual currents that contributed to Kaplan's thinking, especially in educational matters.

Focusing on Reconstructionism as a religious movement, we may lose awareness of the day-to-day effect of Kaplan as a leader. Founders of religions do not usually run schools. Kaplan's thought has attracted a degree of attention that is not usually given to people whose thinking is primarily educational and institutional, as indicated by the recent appearance of an entire volume devoted to Reconstructionist education. In my opinion, he has to be viewed from a more comprehensive perspective. It is not sufficient to limit analysis to the relationship of Kaplan to Dewey or Kaplan's views of *havurot*. Reconstructionism had a stunning effect on American

Jewish life long before its emergence as a separate movement. Especially important in this regard is the lively group that formed around
Kaplan as a result of his early efforts to create synagogue communities and through his role as principal of the Teacher's Institute of
the Jewish Theological Seminary. Personal anecdotes abound, relating his conversations with Eugene Kohn, Leo Honor, Samuel Berkson,
Meir Ben-Horin, Milton Steinberg, and Samuel Dinin. In these anecdotes it is clear that the group of educators with which he was
identified were, in effect, a hothouse for the nurturing of ideas that
captured the imaginations of a larger public of Jewish educators
between 1920 and 1950. A full account must treat the realm of
influence in its practical as well as its theoretical dimensions. Kaplan's influence was effectuated as much by his being part of a
circle of educators who carried out his *program*, as by his published
essays on the subject.

Liebman's analysis, cited earlier, represents the beginning of a consideration of the crucial American dimension of Kaplan's thought.
Kaplan's ideas were remarkably congruent with a period of American history during which there occurred the climax of the enormous
wave of Jewish immigration from eastern Europe, the development
of Palestine into Israel, the Holocaust, the decline of heavy industry
in the northeastern United States, and the expansion of American
economic centers westward. For each of these developments, one
can find a specific tangent in his thought. Kaplan's position was
especially suitable to the dominant American spirit of optimism
and pragmatism, and to the chaotic manner in which ideologies
and social movements seem to have emerged in America at that
time.[17] Besides being quintessentially American, Kaplan absorbed a
variety of Jewish expressions, incorporating some of them into his
system as "sanctions," rejecting others as "bunkum." The influences on him seem rather obvious: Dewey, Kallen, and Kilpatrick
for their educational pragmatism; Durkheim and Mead for their
sense of communal polity; Ahad Ha-Am and Dubnow for having
laid out the goals of Jewish cultural nationalism; Josiah Royce for
the metaphysical grounding of his idealism and concern with universal loyalties; even Spinoza for unlinking theology and polity.
    Kaplan not only viewed Judaism from an American perspective

but, on the basis of what he understood to be the drift of the 1930s and 1940s, he created a perspective according to which Jews could contribute to the texture of American religion in return for the hospitable climate America provided. He did this out of a deep affection for the American atmosphere, despite his despair at the widespread failure of people to understand his synthesis.[18]

Some philosophical methodologists have had difficulty in explaining why Kaplan, not a particularly complicated thinker nor a philosopher in the technical sense, deserves to be called "the most creative Jewish thinker to concern himself with a program for American Judaism."[19] The post-1950s era in Jewish life, with its influx of highly trained academics, made demands for precision in our intellectual labels that was missing earlier; thus Israel Chipkin, in a collection of essays on Kaplan written in the 1950s, casually used the terms *philosopher*, which younger scholars, like Isa Aron and Michael Rosenak, reject.[20] Making a sharp distinction between educational philosophy and educational ideology, Aron identifies Kaplan as an ideologue rather than a philosopher.[21] Liebman insists that Kaplan was unique in that his creativity included "concerning himself with a program," for it was his active involvement in the daily routine of institutions that helped his theoretical views gain special prominence. He was concerned with arranging programs, funding them, and sharing aspirations with the laity and young professional leaders of the time. His thinking, and the activities spawned by his thinking, captured an American Jewish frame of mind attracted to behavioral pluralism, thus permitting the American Jew to adhere to Jewish practice in a random manner that could be subsumed under the broad heading of "American-Jewish." This approach was especially suited to educational developments in America. If we view the Kaplanian notion of sancta in the context of education, we can understand why deeds were inevitably ascribed such a priority in American Jewish life. Elsewhere I have attempted to point up the importance of acts as part of the Jewish *narrative*, in the sense in which this term is now used in literary criticism and theology.[22]

The eclectic quality of Reconstructionism and its encouragement of Jewish behavior as crucial to the Jewish ethos constitute the mainstream of American Jewish educational attitudes today. The connection between Kaplan's ideas and our current educational activities is increasingly apparent (as *Creative Jewish Education* ingeniously calls to our attention), a connection underscored by an evaluation of the curricula of the Conservative and Reform movements. Jewish peoplehood is the irreducible element in most liberal Jewish curricula, and peoplehood underpins the textbooks produced recently by the commercial publishing houses. Even if all these efforts are not directly attributable to Reconstructionism's founder, they are surely related to his efforts.

Kaplan was the most influential spokesman for pluralism in Jewish professional life, and he envisioned the educator as one of the most important channels for affirming that pluralism. Like a good curriculum that inculcates the sancta of the people, a good professional model permits the emergence of the many kinds of Jewish professionalism needed to support the elaborate programs unfolding in schools, camps, centers, study groups, and art teams. Kaplan's insistence on the development of a professionalized Jewish education to increase the options for Jewish careers is consistent with this pluralistic message. (I believe that most writers on Jewish education have overlooked this link.) But the nexus between professionalism and ideology in Kaplan's thought, crucial as it is, is secondary to his conception of the nation as a mansion with rooms for different groups within it.

An examination of the Menorah Curriculum of the Conservative movement and the Melton Program, as well as of the Schuster Curriculum of the Reform movement, is telling in this regard. These materials reflect an assumption that it is possible for American Jews to live comfortably within two civilizations and that the American and the Jewish civilizational aspects can both be perpetuated. Educators from the major non-Orthodox denominations in America have formulated paradigms and programs that imply an easy fusion of these two elements. Sometimes that has been a diachronic synthesis—that is, a sequence of programs for school, youth, and camping. Less frequently this has been synchronic synthesis, expressing an explicit articulation of both components in the hyphenate Jewish-American. The key word here is *explicit*, for what has not yet happened is a focused and aggressive acknowledgment of the problems involved in maintaining tradition, while accepting change or merging the sometimes clashing civilizational agendas. A casual acceptance of this goal, while not directly influenced by Kaplan, is consistent with Kaplan's rather easygoing use of the words *American* and *Jewish*. In other words, some of our educational theories have taken the synthesis too much for granted and are untroubled by complexities lurking under the surface.

There are ample pressures on American Jewish life to prompt a reassessment of what is now the pragmatic cornerstone of American Jewish education. Among the new issues are an ambivalence toward *aliyah*, an increased pressure to incorporate the latest technology, the as-yet unfulfilled promise of Judaic studies on American college campuses, and the so-called ethical decline in our culture. (Jewish culture certainly has shared in the decline of American high culture.) Immigration patterns have decisively changed. Not only are the descendants of eastern European immigrants fully at home here now, but new sources feed the American melting pot, with complicated results. Finally, Kaplan failed to anticipate changes in the emotional climate of American Jewry, a fact that has not yet been adequately noted by educators. Kaplan did not adequately deal with the turmoil and uncertainty in the lives of his Jews. Notwithstanding an awareness of the effects of the Holocaust on Jews in the late 1940s, Kaplan's thought did not seek to offer many answers to the Jew who sought existential fulfillment in Hasidic customs and the homiletics of such men as Soloveitchik and Steinsaltz.

Jewish life has changed, but Jewish educational theory does not reflect these changes. Asked why they teach what they teach, Jewish educators usually refer to the importance of maintaining the Jewish tradition and the principle of *kelal Yisrael*. The survival of the Jewish community is the *telos* of Jewish education far more than are the private religious needs of individuals and the values of the tradition. *Mitzvot* are not taught as commandments; they are good deeds and folkways. Otherwise, there would be a greater struggle over the propriety of this or that observance, as in the Orthodox community. The hermeneutic liberalism prevalent within interpretative circles neatly dovetails with pragmatism and even opportunism, since one person's reading of the tradition is treated as seriously as another's—as long as the intent is to nurture Jewish survival. Rarely is there serious discussion about the meaning of prayers, of the experience of praying, or of particular religious acts. Of course, Kaplan thought seriously about the meaning of prayer, but the absence of educational self-consciousness in such matters is a negative fallout from the way educators have read the slogan "Judaism is a civilization." In their article on the spiritualization of Reconstructionism, Schein and Staub caution against such a misreading. Their effort to fill this vacuum is itself a manifestation of his influence.

There are several notable areas in which Kaplan's hopes have definitely fallen short of reality. The failure of part-time Jewish education, discontent about our relation with Israel, and the lack of richness in American Jewish culture—all leave one dubious about Kaplan's most optimistic description of the Jewish future. Jewish defense activities remain more popular than the development of cultural models. Kaplan never established a clear link between his Judaism and the ways to teach it. Reconstructionist thought lacked, until this generation, any sense of the manner in which its pedagogy might concretize the ideology of the movement. Theories of instruction, priorities of genre and subjects, and the relationship of institutions to values were left by Kaplan to his students and followers to work out in detail. One would do well to examine the theoretical writing of contemporary Jewish educational leaders in America to understand how these problems have become manifest.[23] The intellectual climate since the 1960s (the years during which Kaplan's physical strength was on the wane) yielded new epistemologies in a debate that, I believe, would have fascinated him. I am speaking of the rising interest in hermeneutics, the legitimation of educational philosophy as a form of discourse, and new developments in computer and communications technology. The real sadness in the lives of individuals would have been a challenge to a young, vigorous Kaplan, whose writings addressed communal shock rather than personal trauma.

I have referred to the way in which intervening social and intellectual forces obscure the influence of an idea upon an event, as well as of the relationship of events to the future of ideas. As Allan Bloom writes, "what might be contained in what."[24] A development in American life that is less obscured by problems of intellectual texture is Kaplan's influence on higher Jewish education.

Soon after the Second World War, Kaplan made several speeches on Jewish education to audiences of wealthy American Jews and students at the Jewish Theological Seminary which indicated that he was quite aware that the Jews in the United States were reeling from the blows of Hitler's attempted genocide. He spoke of the turmoil and stress of the time, evoking in his audience the special opportunity to realize the vocation he saw for them. He differentiated between the courageous and the faint of heart, encouraging his listeners to support those for whom each strenuous task contained the possibility of a creative solution.[25] By implication, at least, Kaplan was referring to aspects of his own life. (His biographers recount Kaplan's struggle to achieve recognition, his despair of the low ethical level of American life, and his dislike of *halakhists* who formulated an unrealistic framework for the perpetuation of Judaism in this country.) In addresses of this period, he indicated that these challenges had special meaning in relation to professional leadership and Jewish vocation. At no other time in American Jewish history would such a select audience be as aware of its destiny and special obligation to foster Jewish continuity and formulate concrete plans for the Jewish future. No other community in modern Jewish history combined a potential strength of optimism and professionalism with such superficiality and confusion as to purpose. Avoiding recourse to the undifferentiated population of American Jews to which educational rhetoric too often appeals, Kaplan described the specific forms of leadership needed to carry out educational projects requisite for American Jewry's future. Even if he did find support among intellectuals, who applauded his labeling as "bunkum" some of the notions that had been accepted in religious discourse, it was a far more difficult matter to assemble a group of young, native-born Jewish Americans who combined a critical religious frame of mind with a commitment to the future of Jewish civilization—two poles of Jewish life that usually existed in fragile connection (and which, contrary to Kaplan's hope, have subsequently gone their own separate ways).

It is symbolic of Kaplan's place in American Jewish life that he was assigned to work in California in the late 1940s, for in California so much of American cultural innovation takes place. It was during his stay in California that Kaplan envisioned a "University of Judaism," which would epitomize a higher Jewish education combining professional and popular Jewish learning. In California Kaplan spoke frequently of his five-part program for higher Jewish education, which added to the existing programs of the Jewish Theological Seminary a pluralistic professional training and a wide-reaching and high-level connection with the arts and adult Jewish education.

The failure to produce a serious non-Orthodox Jewish intellectual culture is not a failure of Kaplan's grasp of the issues. Kaplan's notions grew naturally out of the intellectual soil of his surroundings. In many ways the construction of some of our contemporary American Jewish institutions enable us to speak of an effective Kaplanism. Where he rowed against the stream, he resembles other disappointed thinkers and writers whose visions were premature or were unable to reshape the institutions for which they were intended. Kaplan's vision, like that of other founders, failed to foretell what was going to happen next to his society. A new generation of teachers will have to adapt the ideology to a new social reality. This process will give continuity and strength to the model of civilization they share with Kaplan.

Notes

1. Charles Liebman, "Reconstructionism in American Jewish Life," *American Jewish Year Book, 1970* (Philadelphia: Jewish Publication Society, 1970):3–101.
2. Jonathan S. Woocher, *Sacred Survival* (Bloomington: Indiana University Press, 1986), 174–79.
3. Liebman, "Reconstructionism," 3. See also Marc Lee Raphael, *Profiles in American Judaism* (San Francisco: Harper and Row, 1984).
4. Woocher, *Sacred Survial*, 177.
5. Arnold Eisen, *The Chosen People in America* (Bloomington: Indiana University Press, 1983), 94.
6. Jeffrey Schein and Jacob Staub, eds., *Creative Jewish Education* (Chappaqua, NY: Rossel, 1985.) This book, which deals with Kaplan in a more sentimental fashion than did the works of Liebman, Eisen, and Woocher, takes on special meaning and makes greater sense against the background of these three presentations.
7. Israel S. Chipkin, "Jewish Education," in *Mordecai M. Kaplan: An*

Evaluation, ed. Ira Eisenstein and Eugene Cohen (New York: Jewish Reconstructionist Foundation, 1952), 85–118.

8. Kaplan's most important writings on education are the following: Chap. 31 of *Judaism as a Civilization* (1934; reprint, New York: Schocken, 1967) (as well as many other places in this opus); "Hitpathuto shel ha-talahlih ha-hinukhi" (Lecture delivered at the Hebrew University, 1938); "From Strength to Strength" (Address delivered at the Jewish Theological Seminary, 4 February 1945); "The Impact of Dr. Benderly's Personality," *Jewish Education* 20, no. 3 (Summer 1949); and "The Problem of Jewish Education in the Diaspora," in *The Religion of Ethical Nationhood* (New York: Macmillan, 1970). See also Emanuel S. Goldsmith and Mel Scult, editors, *Dynamic Judaism: The Essential Writings of Mordecai M. Kaplan* (New York: Schocken Books and the Reconstructionist Press, 1985), 199–212. Of the secondary literature, I found one of the most imaginative assessments in Gordon Tucker, "Professor Mordecai Kaplan's Torah in a Post-Copernican Age," *Proceedings of the Rabbinical Assembly, 1986*. Building on Kaplan's use of "Copernican" as a major shift in thinking, Tucker goes on to distinguish among different systems of perceiving reality. While Tucker does not deal with the execution of Kaplan's views as such, he points to suggestive new directions to which his thought could give rise.

9. Arthur A. Goren, *New York Jews and the Quest for Community* (New York: Columbia University Press, 1970), especially pp. 245–52.

10. On Rousseau and Dewey, see E. D. Hirsch, *Cultural Literacy: What Every American Needs to Know* (Boston: Houghton Mifflin, 1987). On Nietzsche, see Allan Bloom, *The Closing of the American Mind* (New York: Simon & Schuster, 1987).

11. The personal aspect of Kaplan's influence was brought home to me in a lengthy interview with Dr. Samuel Dinin, Kaplan's friend and protégé. An entire chapter remains to be written on Kaplan's relationships with Benderly, Honor, Dinin, Chipkin, Gamoran, Ben-Horin, and other Jewish educationalists. The true measure of his influence may indeed become clear through anecdotes rather than published materials.

12. Leo Braudy, *The Frenzy of Renown* (New York: Oxford University Press, 1986); James Burns, *Leadership* (New York: Harper Colophon, 1978); Harold Bloom, *The Anxiety of Influence* (New Haven: Yale University Press, 1983) are examples of the wide range of recent approaches to this concept.

13. Richard Libowitz, *Mordecai M. Kaplan and the Development of Reconstructionism* (New York: Mellen Press, 1983).

14. Etan Levine, "Educational Implications of Reconstructionism," in *Creative Jewish Education*, ed. Jeffrey Schein and Jacob Staub, 115ff.

15. "Introduction," *Creative Jewish Education*, ed. Jeffrey Schein and Jacob Staub, 1–10.

16. Woocher, *Sacred Survival*, 178.

17. I am indebted to my colleague David Ellenson for this notion; I am
    always in his debt when understanding of an intellectual climate of
    opinion is at stake.
18. Liebman, "Reconstructionism," especially p. 31 and pp. 56–57.
19. Ibid., 3.
20. Michael Rosenak, *Commandments and Concerns: Jewish Religious Ed-
    ucation in a Secular Society* (Philadelphia: Jewish Publication Society,
    1987). On Rosenak's distinctions between philosophy of education and
    other kinds of ideology, pp. 15–26.
21. Isa Aron, "To Create a Liberal Philosophy of Jewish Education," *Reli-
    gious Education* (Fall 1986): 547.
22. William Cutter and Alan Henkin, "Particularism and Universalism:
    Where Ends and Means Collide," *Journal of Reform Judaism* (Spring
    1979).
23. See, for example, Seymour Fox, "Prolegomenon to a Philosophy of
    Jewish Education," in *In Many Directions, A Single Aim* (in Hebrew)
    (Jerusalem: Hebrew University, 1969).
24. Bloom, in this instance, cautions that Wittgenstein helped to import
    dangerous ideas of Nietzsche to an unaware intellectual public.
25. See Mordecai M. Kaplan, "From Strength to Strength," in *A Proposal
    for a University of Judaism* (New York: Jewish Theological Seminary of
    America, 1945); and idem, *Higher Jewish Education and the Future of
    the American Jew* (Los Angeles: University of Judaism Press, 1963).

CHAPTER 19

The Quest for Economic Justice: Kaplan's Response to the Challenge of Communism, 1929–1940*

Rebecca Trachtenberg Alpert

One implication of Mordecai Kaplan's important idea that it is possible to live simultaneously in two civilizations was that Judaism and secular culture were compatible. One can remain Jewish and at the same time learn from various phenomena in American culture. In fact, certain American trends can enhance Jewish life. It is well known that Kaplan himself was interested in biblical scholarship, sociology, religious naturalism, and pragmatism and that he found creative ways to incorporate his studies into a theory of Jewish life and practice. Less attention has been given to another important influence on Kaplan—that of Marxist ideology and the Communist experiment in Russia.

Kaplan was deeply challenged by Marxism for several reasons. First, many Jews chose to leave Jewish life, expressing their social concerns through their involvements in Communism or socialism.[1] That so many Jews did not perceive Jewish life as meaningful was of utmost importance to Kaplan, and he sought to persuade them of

*I am grateful to Mel Scult, Richard Libowitz, and Mordechai Liebling for their help in formulating ideas for this chapter and to Jacob Staub and Christie Balka for their thoughtful comments on an earlier draft.

the compatibility of Judaism and Communism. Second, Kaplan found much to recommend in the Marxist critique of capitalism. He himself was opposed to the inequities of the capitalist system and saw in Marxism a blueprint for a just economic order. Kaplan certainly can be included among the many Jewish intellectuals of his era who were drawn to the ideas of the Left.[2] Third, Kaplan knew that Marxism presented a challenge to Judaism. He fought against the Marxist critique of religion and nationalism, while at the same time used this criticism to call the Jewish community to account on issues of economic justice and the need to reshape the Jewish religion.

Ultimately, the greatest challenge of Marxism for Kaplan was personal. He had chosen as his life's work the reconstruction of Jewish life in America. Kaplan frequently questioned the value of his work in relation to the larger questions of economic justice.

These matters first appeared in his diary at the time of World War One and the Russian Revolution, when Kaplan was struggling with his role as rabbi of the (Orthodox) Jewish Center. In 1919 he lamented in his diary that every time he preached on a vital economic or political question, he "was accused of being a Bolshevik. Not that I am ashamed of being classed with the Bolsheviki. I would rather be classed with them than the bourgeois profiteers."[3]

It was clear to him that he was working for the "self-satisfied bourgeois class,"[4] and this caused him great discomfort. He was sure that the Russian Revolution was a precursor to a worldwide destruction of the capitalist system and assumed that his congregants at the Jewish Center would be swept away by "bullets and bayonets."[5] At one point he questioned his work with these people, which he saw as a stumbling block to becoming "an active participant in the Social Revolution."[6] George Bernard Shaw had commented that under our system clergymen are captains of private ships. Kaplan took comfort that he responded to the challenge like the prophets: "What ships," he asked himself, "have greater need for chaplains?"[7]

Kaplan would struggle with these questions for many years, continuing to ask himself what validity there was to his work as a rabbi and with Jewish tradition in the midst of the political and economic turmoil of his day. These early ruminations foreshadowed a coming to terms with questions related to economic justice during the

Depression. It was during the Depression that many Jews looked to Communism as an alternative to capitalism, and Kaplan would be called upon publicly to articulate his understanding of the Communist challenge and his ideas about economic justice.

Published during the depression years, Kaplan's first two major works, *Judaism as a Civilization* (1934) and *The Meaning of God in Modern Jewish Religion* (1937), included sharp critiques of the capitalist economic system. In *Judaism as a Civilization*, Kaplan concentrated on the ways in which capitalism interfered with the development of Jewish life. First, it created a situation where accumulation was a basic life goal, a good in itself. This goal was all absorbing, involving most of people's energy and weakening the resources for spiritual pursuits.[8] Furthermore, the only people who could afford to be involved in building Jewish institutions were the wealthy, who have "escaped from the more relentless phases of the economic struggle."[9] The result was that the synagogue served only one class of Jews and could not fulfill its function of serving the entire Jewish people. Indeed, the capitalist system, and therefore the synagogue, divided them by class.

Kaplan continued his criticism of the economic order in *The Meaning of God in Modern Jewish Religion*, in which he attacked the injustices of capitalism. He was critical of the ever-growing concentration of wealth in the hands of the few while the workers grew more helpless; of unemployment that causes loss of self-respect; of the stimulation of artificial wants; of the emphasis on selfish motivation; and the bitter struggle involved in competitive profit seeking—all of which "deprives the vast multitudes of that minimum of security which is indispensable to happiness."[10] His diary entries express his bitterness about the competitive nature of the capitalist enterprise and the economic insecurity it engendered. He was outraged by poverty and by the injustice of a system that allowed so many to do without the satisfaction of basic human needs and produced such vast differences between rich and poor.[11]

His attitude was summed up in a diary entry in which he discussed the response of a professor of economics to some questionable practice a student engaged in to make money to continue in school. To the student's suggestion that "one has to live," the professor answered, "nobody *has* to live." To Kaplan, this was an outrage. Society was to be held responsible for enabling all those who have been given life to maintain life decently. According to Kaplan, this professor was a modern Cain who exclaimed, "Am I my brother's keeper?" clearly implying that he was not.[12]

Kaplan insisted that there could be no justice without economic justice; that human beings who were without food, clothing, and shelter could not appreciate other freedoms. He was convinced that the economic order represented by the capitalist system had not created a society in which justice prevailed. Furthermore, it was the business of religion to "denounce and combat the social wrongs, the greed and monopolistic graft that are responsible for this situation."[13] It grieved Kaplan that Judaism in America did not take that role.

Although Kaplan's critique of capitalism was similar in many respects to other critiques presented by writers on the Left, he did not see Communism or socialism as a panacea to correct the inadequacies of the capitalist system. He had many problems with Marxism, which he outlined in *Judaism in Transition* (1936), in a 1935 article in the *Reconstructionist* magazine, and at length in his diary during the 1930s.

Kaplan had four major objections to Communist ideology: First, he strongly objected to the idea that religion was merely "the opiate of the masses." Kaplan agreed that religion, in general, and Judaism, in particular, did function to support the status quo throughout much of history. This was particularly true of the rabbinic and medieval era when other-worldly salvation was the main goal of life.[14] But it was not true of reconstructed religion nor of the prophetic tradition, neither of which Marx understood. The prophets invoked religion to "sanction their rebellion against the status quo."[15] And reconstructed religion has essentially the same goals as Communism—to mobilize human beings, through their own powers, to combat social evils.[16]

Second, Marxist philosophy rested on economic determinism that failed to see the significance of the spiritual dimension of reality. It was patently an "oversimplification to interpret the whole of history in light of man's efforts to wrest a living from nature."[17]

Marxism failed to take into account the importance of ethics, seeing all ideas only as the by-products of the class struggle, not as sources of social change. In the diaries, Kaplan developed a lengthy explanation of the error of omitting the quest for salvation as an intrinsic goal of human life. To his mind, all philosophies by definition were quests for salvation, the search for life abundant. This was no less true of Communism, which had as its ultimate value the classless society.[18] In failing to recognize this, Marxism omitted what Kaplan understood as life's most vital force. He could not accept a theory that did not take salvation seriously.

Third, Marx's critiques of nationalism and especially Zionism were repugnant to Kaplan. Claiming that nations are the cause of war, he said, was like claiming that families are the cause of feuds.[19] He predicted that even the Soviet Union would not be able to create a culture devoid of Russian nationalism because inevitably it must rely on the Russian language and historic traditions.[20] More importantly, he defended the Zionist endeavor against charges of imperialism. He asserted that the Zionists' objectives were not aggressive, that their wealth was created by their own endeavors, and that "they have done nothing to curtail the full national-cultural development of the Arab people in Palestine."[21] Nonetheless, he suggested that Zionists do need to be vigilant against developing a capitalist industrialism in Palestine and that the Jewish people must build "on foundations of social justice and cooperation, not private competition and profit seeking."[22]

Finally, Kaplan had a serious problem with "bloody revolution." At that time he was a pacifist and did not approve of the use of violence, even for justifiable ends.[23] He expected that change in the economic order would, in fact, necessitate a revolution, but he wanted it to be a peaceful one. Kaplan hoped religion would play an important role in making peaceful change possible. He disagreed with Marx's views as he understood them—that might makes right, that violent revolution was an inevitable feature of history, and that the middle class was powerless and unable to affect the outcome. Kaplan's Enlightenment optimism led him to assume that the messianic age could be brought about through peaceful human efforts. He believed that thinking people could be the instruments of change, but he was not sure that they would follow through on this responsibility. He mused in his diary: "Will the middle classes be awakened and realize their moral degradation? If not, then the prophecy of Marxism will be fulfilled."[24]

Kaplan envisaged that violent revolution might indeed take place if the necessary reconstruction of society did not. Society could be reconstructed through educational processes that would help people understand how social forces work, and through political action in the form of a new political party that would not be an instrument of big business.[25] Without a "decided effort to collectivize and socialize the economic system, we are heading for universal ruin."[26]

By 1940 he was confident in his judgment concerning violent revolution. He attributed the "present debacle of Communism" to its attempt to create radical upheaval, which he saw as contrary to "second nature." He was still convinced that although private ownership is "second nature," that society should not sanction private possession and control to the extent that it does now. These present conditions could only be reversed by "dissolving gradually the forces of second nature, not by violence against present owners."[27]

Despite discomfort with crucial aspects of Marxist ideology, Kaplan saw in its analyses significant criticisms of Jewish life and the social order. He used the Marxist critique of religion as an opiate to make a similar critique himself, a critique calling for the reconstruction of Judaism to incorporate a this-worldly concept of salvation. And he used Marxist criticisms of Zionism to illustrate his own program for Jewish nationalism.

Kaplan saw the goals of Marxism and prophetic Judaism as parallel. Both looked to a new society on earth, one calling it a classless society, the other the kingdom of God. Both saw the inescapability of a new social order, derived from different premises than that of present society. Both concluded that not everyone will be able to live under the new premises.[28]

With that in mind, Kaplan wrestled with the question of whether someone could be a good Jew and a good Communist. He was emphatically opposed to the Communist assumption that Judaism should be put aside until the class struggle is over. Neither battle is more urgent than the other; both need to be pursued at the same time. In *Judaism in Transition*, he concluded that "there is inherently no reason why a Jew may not take an active part in Jewish communal life and at the same time participate . . . in Communist propaganda."[29] In his diary he remarked that there was enough in both systems to make "being a Jew compatible with that in Communism which is of permanent value."[30] Kaplan pondered the dilemma that identifying with Communism might destroy the Jewish people. Yet, if the Jews did not commit themselves as a people to working on solutions for the general problems of humanity,[31] they ran the risk of isolating themselves from the rest of the world.

Of course, Kaplan was aware of the dangers of identifying with Communism and was careful to qualify his views in his published writings. Some of his ambivalence and bitterness is clear in this 1940 diary entry:

Nazism [is] a world revolution directed against the hypothetical capitalist democracy. Unfortunately, we Jews have been manuevered into the position of having to defend this kind of democracy, because the moment we begin drawing distinctions between genuine and counterfeit democracy we are accused of being Communists. But the fact is that, viewed objectively from the standpoint of the masses of mankind, democracy has meant little more than freedom to starve.[32]

The question of the extent to which a rabbi could or should devote himself to the cause of economic justice deeply troubled Kaplan in his roles as magazine editor, pulpit rabbi, and teacher of rabbis. Many editorials appeared in the *Reconstructionist* magazine in the late 1930s that took a positive stand on a variety of issues related to the Communist movement. In 1935 the magazine praised the Communist magazine, *New Masses*, for exposing anti-Semitism. The editorial suggested that the Communists were the only ones who really understood the social and economic roots of anti-Semitism.[33] The following year an editorial suggested that Communist anti-Zionism was amenable to change through education.[34] The magazine supported the Biro-Bidjan project, a short-lived attempt to encourage Russian Jews to resettle in an autonomous Siberian region of the USSR.[35] Editorials frequently opposed efforts to disassociate Jews from the Communist party[36] and spoke out in favor of Communist efforts in support of religious values.[37] Between 1935 and 1937, the magazine published eight articles on the subject of Communism and its relationship to Judaism, Zionism, and religion in general. As an editor, Kaplan clearly maintained a lively interest in the subject.

As a practicing rabbi, Kaplan was also a protagonist in the various debates about Communism. He developed a reputation for such, running a seminar on economic justice for the Rabbinical Assembly in 1933 and speaking on Marxism and Judaism several times from 1933 to 1935, including a series of lectures under the joint auspices of the Orthodox, Conservative, and Reform rabbinical organizations. Eventually, he tired of speaking on this theme and refused a request to speak in Boston, asking instead if he could address a subject he "happened to be interested in at the time . . . the evolution of Jewish religion."[38]

At the Society for the Advancement of Judaism (where Kaplan served as rabbi), he presented a series of lectures on Marxism and Judaism in 1933 and delivered a variety of sermons on economic justice and the prophets, on the role of economics in Jewish life, and on socialism, capitalism, and related matters. Occasionally, Kaplan would comment in his diaries about the effects of working with upper-class Jews at the SAJ. Kaplan thought the idea of class struggle was both simplistic and destructive but was reminded on occasion that he and his congregation were also from different classes. He conjectured that he had problems at the SAJ because his congregants sensed that he was not in sympathy with the economic status quo. He mentioned some criticism in the congregation of his magazine editorials as "anti-capitalistic and therefore criminal."[39]

Kaplan himself was by no means a political activist and for the most part confined himself to editorial writing and speech making. At one point in 1935, he did threaten to resign from the editorial board of *Opinion* magazine in protest over the forced resignation of its editor. James Wise was accused by advertisers of going too far to the left in support of what they called "Communist propaganda." Kaplan told Wise that he was interested in *Opinion* because of its Communist leanings, as it "represented the diversity of choices possible in Jewish life."[40] In a similar vein, the *Reconstructionist* editorial board offered aid to Eli Jaffe of Oklahoma, a Communist who was given a $5,000 fine and ten years in prison in 1940. They offered to help him through the Civil Liberties League rather than through the International Labor Defense, which was known to be a

Communist organization, so as to avoid accusations of Communist sympathies.[41]

Most of Kaplan's experiences involving Communism were in his role as professor at the Jewish Theological Seminary, at the Teacher's Institute, and at the Graduate School for Jewish Social Work. His political concerns took shape primarily through his role as teacher. Students in the 1930s were drawn to socialist and Communist causes. Some declared their membership openly, and many struggled with leaving Judaism for more radical pursuits. According to Ira Eisenstein, Kaplan had an enormous influence over many students, keeping them connected to the Jewish cause. Kaplan saw his work as a teacher as his most important role, and, his contacts with these future rabbis and teachers enabled him to exert a significant influence on Jewish life in the next generation.[42]

Kaplan himself was frequently under suspicion of being a radical. He recorded in his diary in 1935 a conversation between himself and Maurice Karpf of the Graduate School for Jewish Social Work. Karpf had discussed with Cyrus Adler, the president of the Jewish Theological Seminary, a "Communist uprising" among some students, and Adler questioned him on Kaplan's role. Karpf reported that he told Adler that Kaplan exerted a "wholesome influence."[43] Kaplan was pleased, because he wanted it to be clear that his primary concern was for the future of the Jewish people. Yet, it is also obvious that he had deep political concerns and liked playing the role of the radical at the Seminary.

Kaplan did recommend to his rabbinical students that they use sermons, particularly on the holidays, as a means to "interpret the present crisis of world affairs as a demonstration in the negative form of the inevitability of God's laws of justice."[44] The majority of students thought that the crisis called for "nothing less specific than the advocacy of a program like that being carried out at the present time in Russia."[45] Kaplan agreed that talks from the pulpit must be concrete but implored his students not to teach violence. He argued that sermons, forums, and study circles were an important antidote to "bloody revolution" and that such talks presented "organized religion's opportunity to redeem itself from the charge of being a tool of capitalism."[46]

In the winter of 1933, Kaplan offered a course at the Seminary on ethical aspects of economic issues. His preparation for the course convinced him that economic justice was the underpinning of all ethical endeavor. The students studied Hobson's *Economics and Ethics* and dealt with the relationship of economics to spiritual matters; with attempts to reconstruct the current social order; with the morality of rent, interest, and profit; and with the most feasible means of achieving a just society. For Kaplan, teaching this class was a watershed. It is noteworthy that he was able to discuss these crucial issues in the context of study at the Jewish Theological Seminary, where he could influence a large number of rabbinical students.[47]

In March 1934, Kaplan ruminated again about dilemmas facing young people doing Jewish work. He saw them as "victims of inner conflict as a result of its irrelevance as compared with the more realistic approach to life's problems, offered by Communism."[48] He was constantly confronted with students at all three institutions where he taught who were Communist sympathizers. His ambivalence is apparent in the following statement:

God knows I feel very much as the students do . . . [but] I doubt whether I could give myself body and soul to a movement which has me repudiate the entire past and the past of my people.[49]

Following along in that vein, Kaplan concluded that he often judged himself and Judaism too harshly. Rabbis were not successors to the prophets; they were not failures if they did not devote themselves exclusively to the causes of social justice. Their function was to keep alive the culture of the Jewish people.[50]

Kaplan went on to write that the rabbi must preach a religion based on the Marxist principle "from each according to his ability, to each according to his needs." Then he need not find fault with himself for "not giving up the rabbinate and joining the Communist organization." He came back again to his proposition of 1919: the rabbi had to be the "gadfly and conscience of the people who thrive on the capitalist economy."[51]

Kaplan's involvement with student Communists lasted until he left for Palestine in 1937. In 1935 he led an honors group at the Teacher's Institute who chose as their topic "Judaism versus Communism" and saw this setting as a safe place to discuss the issue.[52]

At one point he wrote that Abraham Halkin and Hillel Bavli, two Teacher's Institute professors, attended a session and were impressed that Kaplan was more moderate in his views than they had been led to believe.[53] There is no doubt that Kaplan was a controversial figure at the Seminary and that his involvement in this issue raised concern amongst other faculty members. Nonetheless, Kaplan did not shrink from helping students with their ideological dilemmas, arguing with them that the Jewish issues ought not be put aside to fight the battles against the economic system.[54]

It was Kaplan who was called in by Cyrus Adler to address the problems caused when a group known as the Jewish Teachers Association (JTA), made up primarily of Teacher's Institute graduates, chose to march in the 1936 May Day parade. They were accused by a rival teachers' organization of disloyalty to the Jewish people. Other Jewish groups had decided not to march as a reaction to anti-Semitism in the Communist party. Kaplan responded that the parade was sponsored not only by the Communist party but also by Sidney Goldstein of the Jewish Institute of Religion and Harry Ward of the Union Theological Seminary, who called on religious workers to join the parade. Representatives of the JTA apologized, claiming that they were ignorant of the fact that other Jewish organizations were boycotting the parade because of Communist anti-Zionist propaganda, and that they wholeheartedly reaffirmed their support of Zionism.[55] In his diary, Kaplan treated this as a battle between rival teachers' groups and did not view it as a significant political event. Nonetheless, it is clear that, when necessary, Kaplan did support unpopular causes when he believed that an injustice was being done.

Kaplan was deeply torn by the call of social ideology. He was perplexed by the extent to which he found himself at the mercy of the capitalist system. Feeling trapped and powerless left him depressed.[56] In his diary, he often confided his thoughts of joining the Communist party, moving to Russia, and starting over again. He would fantasize about serving as a shop chairman, teaching English, and applying to representatives of the Russian government in the United States to tell them of his plans. Then he would have second thoughts: "They would undoubtedly tell me I am too old to

begin life anew," he wrote in 1931.[57] The following year he suggested that even the theories of Communism scared him but then
went on to say:

At times I despair of any improvement ever being achieved through reason.
Then I feel like breaking loose from everything and everybody and joining
a Communist unit and die fighting for a better world. This is probably one
of my suppressed wishes.[58]

When depressed, Kaplan felt keenly the futility of his endeavors
and saw the Communist revolution as an antidote to the petty day-
to-day problems he encountered. He wavered, at times despairing of
the Communist experiment, at times holding it up as the only hope
for humanity. He experienced conflict over Communist analyses of
Zionism and religion in view of his ultimate desire to effect a
synthesis between them.[59]

Perhaps Kaplan's most revealing comment about this issue was
recorded in the diary in 1934, when he wrote of his split personality:

I shall call one Mordecai (the old Adam) and the other Menahem (the
regenerate me). Mordecai is a liberal bourgeois, Menahem is an out and
out Communist. Who am I in this business?[60]

After two years spent in Palestine and after the signing of the
Nazi-Soviet Pact, Kaplan was finally convinced that Communism
was not the answer. The pact "put an end to the last shred of hope
that at least in Russia the foundations of a new and better world
were being laid." He admitted that although he expressed publicly
his dislike of Communism, he nevertheless had retained a hope in
his heart that "something good might ultimately come out of
Russia."[61]

In 1934 Kaplan considered for his next project formulating a system
of religious communism.[62] Had he carried out the project, it might
have been a constructive resolution to the conflicts Kaplan experienced. Much of his published writing on this subject was a tentative
step in this direction and serves as an example of the creative ways
in which Kaplan sought to reconstruct Judaism.

His goal was to create Jewish communal organizations that would
be concerned with the economic welfare of the Jewish masses and
that would "take up the cudgels for social justice."[63] Kaplan's vi-

sion was to replace economic determinism with ethical determinism[64] and to use the Jewish religion as a goad to give all who live within its framework a sense of life's creative possibilities. He wanted to bring issues of economic justice into the curriculum of religious schools and adult study, and actually did so.[65] He called for the courageous and intelligent reconstruction of economic institutions involving a transfer of power and wealth. He demanded a change in the social order "so that it shall conform to the ethical command for human equality,"[66] and asserted that "human rights, without a secure economic foundation, are merely the right to starve."[67] In conclusion, he suggested that

the Jewish protagonists of social idealism should realize that the Jewish religion came into being as a result of the first attempt to conceive of God as the defender of the weak against the strong, and that it can therefore continue to serve as the inspiration in the present struggle. There would then come about a rapprochement between these streams of social energy. . . . Every such rapprochement brings mankind nearer to its goal.[68]

Kaplan envisioned a form of communism that would take its Jewish ethical roots seriously, because he believed that the economic order needed to be changed in keeping with the ideals of the human spirit. It was his aim to heal the split between Communism and Judaism and in so doing provide a new ideology for those Jews who could no longer find meaning in their tradition. As in other areas, Kaplan made a noble effort at synthesis, suggesting what might be possible in terms of Jewish reconstruction and healthy cross-fertilization with the ideas of the times.

Notes

1. *Kaplan Diary*, vol. 1, 2 July 1916, 219. Kaplan lamented in his diary that religion failed to move people who seemed to find meaning more "in this or that movement to improve social, economic or industrial conditions." The original of the Kaplan Diary is at the Jewish Theological Seminary.
2. For discussions of the relationship of the Jews and the Left, see Arthur Liebman, "The Ties that Bind: The Jewish Support for the Left in the United States," *American Jewish Historical Quarterly* 66, no. 2 (December 1976): 285–321. For a more personalized account, see Melech

Epstein, *The Jews and Communism, 1919–1941* (New York: Trade Union Sponsoring Committee, 1959). For an overall contemporary view of the period, see Maurice Isserman, *Which Side Were You On?* (Middletown, Conn.: Wesleyan University Press, 1982).

3. *Kaplan Diary*, vol. 1, 28 July 1919, 371.
4. Ibid., 26 December 1918, 361.
5. Ibid., 11 November 1918, 357.
6. Ibid., 7 January 1919, 365.
7. Ibid.
8. Mordecai M. Kaplan, *Judaism as a Civilization* (New York: Macmillan, 1934), 30.
9. Ibid., 32.
10. Mordecai M. Kaplan, *The Meaning of God in Modern Jewish Religion* (New York: Reconstructionist Press, 1962). See the chapters entitled "God as the Power that Makes for Social Regeneration" and "God as the Power that Makes for Cooperation," esp. 124–28 and 232–33.
11. See *Kaplan diary*, vol. 5, 21 December 1929, 299; ibid., 1 January 1930, 312; vol. 6, 6 September 1930, 66; ibid., 8 October 1930, 80; ibid., 21 August 1931, 205; vol. 7, 25 March 1933, 105–7. Kaplan's distaste for competition is a dominant theme in his writings. It is a primary motivating factor in his arguments against the chosen people doctrine, which he sees as fostering competitive attitudes among peoples. At one point in his diary, Kaplan suggested that what was needed was a capacity—socialism—a movement to abolish all distinctions that make people feel inadequate. See *Kaplan Diary*, vol. 5, 19 January 1930, 330.
12. *Kaplan Diary*, vol. 6, 14 August 1931, 197–98.
13. Ibid., 3 June 1931, 141.
14. Mordecai M. Kaplan, *Judaism in Transition* (New York: Covici-Friede, 1936) 106. Kaplan justified their response as better than falling into despair and viewing the world as irredeemable.
15. Ibid., 102.
16. Mordecai M. Kaplan, "Marxism and the Jewish Religion," *Reconstructionist* 1, no. 5 (March 1935): 13.
17. Kaplan, *Judaism in Transition*, 104. It is ironic that Kaplan's arguments against Marx (a lack of appreciation of the spiritual dimension) frequently have been used to substantiate a criticism of Reconstructionism.
18. *Kaplan Diary*, vol. 10, 30 November 1940, 46.
19. Kaplan, *Judaism in Transition*, 108.
20. Ibid.
21. Ibid., 110.
22. Ibid.
23. See *Kaplan Diary*, vol. 5, 2 January 1930, 334; vol. 6, 27 March 1932, 303; vol. 7, 3 October 1934, 336; ibid., 10 February 1935, 385; ibid., 10

March 1935, 406. His abhorrence of violence was a major theme in the diaries.

24. *Kaplan Diary*, vol. 7, 17 March 1933, 100–101.

25. Ibid., 25 March 1933, 108.

26. Ibid., 109. Kaplan made these comments in 1933 when the economic situation was the most bleak. Nonetheless, a 1941 diary entry echoes the same sentiment. In it he calls on democracy to "come forth with a definite scheme . . . of social order" (ibid., vol. 10, 26 September 1941, 256–57).

27. Ibid., 30 October 1940, 6.

28. Ibid., vol. 7, 24 March 1933, 102.

29. Kaplan, *Judaism in Transition*, 112.

30. *Kaplan Diary*, vol. 7, 6 May 1934, 249.

31. Ibid., vol. 8, 8 September 1935, 46; and 12 September 1935, 52.

32. Ibid., vol. 9, 30 May 1940, 239.

33. *Reconstructionist* 1, no. 1 (January 1953): 6. In 1935 the Communist party in America began an attempt to win Jewish support by changing their policies on Jewish issues. Clearly, they convinced the editorial board of *Reconstructionist* magazine. Others remained skeptical.

34. *Reconstructionist* 2, no. 2 (March 1936): 3.

35. *Reconstructionist* 1, no. 1 (January 1935): 10; ibid., 1, no. 18 (January 1936): 3; ibid., 2, no. 12 (October 1936): 6. When Biro-Bidjan was closed in 1937, there was an editorial expressing disappointment. It concluded, "The *Reconstructionist* is not given to Red-baiting. It will continue to look with sympathetic interest and with hope, if not with blind faith, to the economic and social developments in Russia" *(Reconstructionist* 3, no. 17 [December 1937]: 3).

36. Ibid., 1, no. 16 (December 1935): 4; ibid., 2, no. 11 (October 1936): 6.

37. Ibid., 2, no. 12 (December 1936): 7.

38. *Kaplan Diary*, vol. 7, 20 February 1935, 391.

39. Ibid., vol. 9, 3 January 1940, 140.

40. Ibid., vol. 7, 20 February 1935, 394.

41. Ibid., vol. 10, 10 December 1941, 343.

42. Ira Eisenstein, telephone conversation, with the author, 21 August 1986.

43. *Kaplan Diary*, vol. 8, 21 April 1935, 75.

44. Ibid., vol. 6, 1 September 1931, 210.

45. Ibid.

46. Ibid., 211.

47. Ibid., vol. 7, 75, 87, 89, 111. (Various entries made while teaching this course from January to April 1933.)

48. Ibid., 4 March 1934, 231.

49. Ibid.

50. Ibid., 232.

51. Ibid., 233.
52. Ibid., vol. 8, 27 October 1935, 65.
53. Ibid., 13 February 1936, 99.
54. Ibid., 100. Kaplan got into an argument with a Teacher's Institute student who asserted that the Communists did not care about beliefs and that Kaplan could, in fact, be accepted into the Communist party even if he taught and practiced the Jewish religion. Kaplan allowed him to pursue the matter, but left the session feeling that there was no meeting ground between Jews who were primarily concerned with anti-Semitism and radical Jews who were primarily concerned with Communism.
55. Mordecai Kaplan to Cyrus Adler, 20 May 1936.
56. *Kaplan Diary*, vol. 6, 2 July 1931, 181.
57. Ibid.
58. *Kaplan Diary*, vol. 7, 18 December 1932, 67.
59. Ibid., 20 February 1935, 394.
60. Ibid., 25 July 1934, 295.
61. Ibid., vol. 9, 23 August 1939, 53.
62. Ibid., vol. 7, 8 May 1934, 25.
63. Kaplan, *Judaism as a Civilization*, 34.
64. *Kaplan Diary*, vol. 7, 6 March 1933, 87.
65. Ibid., vol. 6, 14 August 1931, 194–96.
66. Kaplan, *Meaning of God*, 223.
67. Ibid.
68. Kaplan, "Marxism and Jewish Religion," 15.

CHAPTER 20

Reflections on Kaplan's Zionism

Jack J. Cohen

In the spring of 1961, I informed Mordecai M. Kaplan that I would be leaving for Jerusalem during the coming winter to become director of the B'nai B'rith Hillel Foundations in Israel. Kaplan pleaded with me to reconsider my decision, arguing that my contribution to Jewish life should be made in the United States. Only when I pointed out to him that I believed my *aliyah* to be a logical outgrowth of *his* philosophy did he desist from efforts to dissuade me and, however reluctantly, gave me his blessing.

Two decades later, after Kaplan had been living several years in Jerusalem, I was responsible to a great extent for his return to New York City, when his frailty and illness had become too heavy a psychological and physical burden for his wife, Rivkah, to bear. His children wanted him near them so as to ensure proper care for him and remove some of the load from Kaplan's wife. He finally acceded to their request, as mediated by Moshe Davis and myself, and returned to the United States.

These incidents dramatically symbolize the tension that marked Kaplan's ideological and emotional attitudes to the Land of Israel and the American diaspora. Both elements were indispensable to his philosophy of Judaism and to his Jewish feelings. He sought to maintain a balance between the rational need for a land to ensure the creative continuity of the Jewish people—an understanding that followed upon his mystical awareness that only Eretz Yisrael could be that land—and a conviction that the future of the Jewish people demanded a strong Diaspora. Without a vital center in Eretz Yisrael where Judaism could be the primary civilization of the Jews, the Diaspora would lack an essential source of inspiration and purpose. Kaplan loved the Jewish community of the United States, but he equally loved the *yishuv*. He related to both of them as a devoted offspring for whom the loss of either parent would be irreparable.

With this in mind and aware that we are dealing with an ideology of unending tension, I should like to explore the contributions of Mordecai Kaplan to Zionist thought. This ideology, properly assessed, can inject a measure of much-needed realism into the debates on Jewish identity and polity that currently threaten to rend the Jewish people asunder.

As long as a people lives, it must undergo periodic metamorphoses as it adjusts to ongoing change in its environment. Kaplan's pragmatic approach is more readily applicable to this process than are other visions of Jewish survival. Kaplan's Zionism was no abstraction; it paid careful attention to the uncertainties attendant upon the complex human search for fulfillment. This characteristic of Kaplan's intellectual honesty is an essential feature of his pragmatism, and it accounts for his occasional vacillation. A modicum of hesitancy, after all, as to which of several paths is most likely to make possible maximum growth for a people is necessary in the intellectual maturation of all but "true (i.e., blind) believers." Humility is a safety valve that prevents decent persons from foisting their convictions arbitrarily upon others. This spirit of openness animated Kaplan's Zionist career, as it did his whole life's enterprise. In some such flexibility might be mere vacuousness and lack of conviction; but for Kaplan self-criticism, awareness of changing circumstances, ambivalence in implementing his views, and constant search for partners in dialogue went hand-in-hand with an ardently held approach to life. What were the components of that approach as they underpin his views on Zionism?

First, Kaplan was nothing if not a realist. One might choose to surrender to facts, do battle with them, try to maneuver around them, but one had to reckon with their force. For Kaplan, the salient facts with which Jewish survivalists had to deal were the distancing of most Jews from supernatural religion, the manner in which modern nationalism undermined minority cultures, and the appeal of democratic values to most Jews in the free world. For Kaplan, these facts necessitated a rethinking of the concept of Jewish identity and the formation of a new program for a Jewish polity. If Jews were to live creatively as a distinctive people, they would have to learn how to develop their own nationalism on the basis of a naturalistic (or "transnaturalist") conception of existence and shape a spiritually oriented, voluntary, "transterritorial" polity with its democratic center in Eretz Yisrael. Zionism, he wrote, "proposes a radical solution to the problem of the future of the Jewish people with its social and religious heritage in a world where the climate of thought is modern naturalism and modern nationalism the dominant social pattern."[1] To navigate in these as yet badly charted waters, the Jewish people must be adventurous enough to try out new ideas and new structures through the Zionist movement. Kaplan's formula is one of the first to respond to the full extent of the challenge.

In a late formulation of his position, Kaplan argued that "group religion cannot raise the ethical standard of men and nations unless it is rooted in the realities of physical and human nature." He also held that "group religion founded on reality is buttressed not upon what man means to God—but on what God means to man. Only the transposition of Judaism into the key of naturalism can secure a creative future for the Jewish people."[2] Furthermore, Kaplan stressed throughout his career the importance of democracy for the modern Jewish mind. In Kaplan's opinion, without that democratic mindset, the reclamation of Eretz Yisrael and the self-government and self-education of Jews in the State of Israel would have been impossible.[3]

Kaplan believed that many, perhaps most, Jews paid only lip service to naturalism and democracy. While they proved by their departures from the traditional Jewish life style that they no longer considered supernaturalism to be a firm grounding for Judaism, they were far from integrating their new orientation satisfactorily. Nor did they implement democratic thought in Jewish corporate life to the extent that circumstances demanded. Perhaps this inconsistency can be attributed mainly to the inability of many persons to see reality wholly and organically.

After his sharp sense of reality, a second crucial component of Kaplan's Zionism was his recognition of the inherent tension between democracy and the theologies of historical revelation. Democracy has thus far been humankind's most reliable political guarantor of freedom; the theologies of revelation, which purport to transmit God's will and truth to chosen individuals and groups, often oppose, in theory if not in practice, the pluralism of thought and conduct that is the very stuff in which a free and creative society is nurtured. Kaplan responded to this tension by searching for ways to ensure Jewish unity in diversity. He saw no contradiction between this endeavor and his relentless attack on fundamentalist traditionalism—an attack that stemmed from a concern that democratic tolerance might lead many to underestimate the threat that various forms of supernaturalism represent to democratic freedoms. He hoped that, in the process of establishing a homeland in Eretz Yisrael, the Jewish people would gain experience in orchestrating the vast differences between traditionalists and modernists, so that the former would learn how to agree to negotiations and concessions for the common good. Kaplan was given to grave doubts about the success of this task, however, because he never lost sight of the danger that religious extremism could pose for the stability of a Jewish society in Eretz Yisrael and for *kelal Yisrael*—the unity of the Jewish people everywhere.

Kaplan never sought a Jewish unity that would be purchased at the price of abandoning beliefs, of coercion by the majority, or of shallow compromise. His concept of unity was based on the assumption—or at least the hope—that the we-feeling of the Jewish people would prove to be sufficiently strong to induce Jews to debate their differences democratically within the community in accordance with accepted rules of the game. His optimism was based on the experience of the Zionist movement thus far. He observed:

Democracy as an orientation to life in which primacy is accorded to the purpose of combatting all forms of exploitation and oppression and of furthering freedom and equality in all human relations among individuals and groups has operated not only in the evolution of the aim to acquire a

Jewish national home in Eretz Yisrael; it has operated, also in the measures which have been taken to prepare for the achievement of that aim.[4]

Thus, the Zionist movement provided a social structure in pre-State days that was motivated by the goal of unifying the people and supportive of unity in diversity, or that at least tolerated it. To anti-Zionists, the rules of the democratic game were too forbidding to enable them to participate in the pursuit of Jewish unity. Even now, after the establishment of the State of Israel, they refuse to countenance any unity that is not founded on their particular conceptions of uniformity. To them, compromise is abandonment of principle, and they view Zionists as either hypocrites or heretics. "The Jewish people is one," therefore, is an objective, not yet a fact.

In the last years of his life, Kaplan became aware that, in the context of the State, the cause of Jewish unity had become a double-edged sword. In the name of unity, Israel's democratic structure was manipulated by Orthodox religious parties to secure legislation that was opposed by the majority of Israel's Jewish citizens and by most of world Jewry. In some regards, the programs of the religious parties violated generally accepted standards of human rights. Although the political structure of the State of Israel had been erected on secular, democratic rather than *halakhic* foundations, strict constructionists of the *halakhic* system argued that the unity of the Jewish people would be sundered unless *halakhic* rulings in matters of personal status became the law of the land. Relentless pressure by the Orthodox, including the moderate wing represented by the National Religious party, convinced Kaplan that if the *halakhically* oriented parties had their way, non-Orthodox Jews would be forced to violate principles of freedom. Otherwise, the Orthodox prophecy of a split Jewry could come to pass. In either case, the cause of creative unity would be subverted.

Kaplan's insistence that the transformation of Judaism from a supernatural and *halakhic* civilization to a naturalistic and democratic one rested on his conviction that only through such a universe of discourse would it be possible to sustain a voluntary and united Jewish people. Kaplan was not alone in his fear that the Jewish people might disintegrate, but he was one of the first to assess accurately the damaging effect on the Jewish state of a supernatural theology wedded to the *halakhic* conception of polity. Kaplan might be faulted for holding too sanguine a view of the appeal of his analysis to all rational Jews; he certainly underestimated the extent to which secular Zionists—particularly the founding fathers of the State of Israel and their heirs—had become impervious to theoretical concerns about the role of religion in Jewish life, in general, and in the Jewish polity, in particular. These secularists were too overwhelmed by the problems of creating a viable economy and societal base for the homeland-in-the-making before 1948 to pay close attention to such seemingly abstract considerations. Once they were involved in affairs of state after 1948, they were preoccupied with the need to integrate waves of immigrants with widely different cultural backgrounds. There was no room in their agenda for theoretical considerations of the kind that Kaplan proposed.

A third element of Kaplan's Zionism was the conviction that the primary motivation for Zionism should come from the internal conditions and needs of the Jewish people, rather than viewing it as a countermeasure to anti-Semitism. Kaplan's thoughts on Zionism have been described by one young Israeli, Ehud Ben-Zvi, as a major feature of American Zionism:

It is a Zionism which grew out of the background of developing Jewish communities. It is a Zionism which emerged out of interaction between the Jews and their environment, out of their identification with America and its values, as these were understood by them. This is a Zionism of freedom, which found its inspiration in the inner resources of Judaism and not in the persecution of the Jews.[5]

Ben-Zvi correctly perceives that Kaplan's Zionism evolved from his conception of Judaism as the religious civilization of a Jewish people trying to survive in a free world. However, what exactly is the relationship of Kaplan's position to the mainstream of Zionist theory?

It makes a considerable difference whether we envisage Judaism as the product of the national life of the Jewish people or conceive of it as a separate entity, of which the Jewish people happens to be the bearer. An example of the latter position is enunciated by Simhah Bunem Urbach, who writes:

The Greek people created philosophy; it is the people of philosophy, in contrast to the Jewish people that is the bearer of religion and faith and is the people of prophets. . . . The point of departure of all philosophical speculation and of all scientific research is doubt—systematic, methodical, consistent doubt, concentrated and intentional.[6]

Urbach concludes that because Judaism has its source in divine revelation—supernatural and superhuman——to place the Torah on the level of human wisdom is to deprive it of its true status.

Many scholars have enunciated ways to avoid the necessity to read the Bible merely as a human document, thus maintaining the Bible's spiritual authority and setting it apart from human authorship alone. At best, these readings involve the acknowledgment that, although the Bible was divinely inspired, such inspiration was mediated by human beings. The various permutations of this effort have resulted in tortured interpretations of such concepts as revelation, covenant, *halakhah*, Torah, and chosenness. Kaplan, too, tried this path of temporization but abandoned it when he concluded that the Bible, like every other expression of Jewish creativity, had to be judged with the same tools of consciousness and conscience with which every manifestation of the human mind must be evaluated.

In Kaplan's view, an evolving civilization cannot simply apply a set of traditional formulas to the challenges that face a living society. The study of Torah texts will not solve all the problems of the Jewish group and the Jewish individual, because the teachings of those texts are themselves part of the problem. Moreover, there are situations that could not have been anticipated by Toraitic authors, and new insights are needed that are unavailable to persons incapable of opening their minds to all warranted sources of knowledge and wisdom. While Kaplan acknowledged that man cannot be the measure, man is the *measurer*. This is true of the individual as well as his collectivities. Kaplan tried to convince his fellow Jews to reconstruct their polity to ensure that the Jewish people would become self-perpetuating, self-educating, and self-governing.[7]

Placing the people at the core of his phenomenology of Judaism opened Kaplan to the charge of sociolatry. He was accused of sociologizing Judaism and of offering a shallow theology that deprived God of his ineffable and mystical qualities and made God into a figment of the human imagination—devoid of power and will and incapable of being addressed. Clearly, Kaplan's critics overlooked the main thrust of his humanism. When he appealed for a Jewish nationalism that would foster a humane and humanizing way of life, he was putting forward the claim that the natural right to survive must not be construed as an end in itself. Life is meaningless without the moral and spiritual purpose to energize it. Kaplan maintained that, without religion, Zionism would produce only another power-ridden society. Without the check upon moral and spiritual arrogance that only an intellectually honest theology calls forth, the Jewish religion would also give rise to a coercive and chauvinistic state.

Although Kaplan's Zionism was conceived under the conditions of American freedom, he was nonetheless sympathetic to those Zionists who highlighted the threat of anti-Semitism as a major reason for resettlement in Eretz Yisrael. He acknowledged the catalytic force of anti-Semitism in the growth of the Zionist movement and in the rise of the State of Israel. But even as he welcomed the challenge, he feared the dangers of freedom to Jewish survival. In his view, Zionism would have to be oriented in two directions.

The first direction was that of rebuilding Eretz Yisrael, which required a proper assessment of the role of a land in the evolution of a vibrant civilization. A full explication of Kaplan's position on the land requires a detailed comparison with the views of Ahad Ha-Am, A. D. Gordon, Abraham Isaac Kook, Franz Rosenzweig, and others. However, within the limited context of this essay, mention must be made at least of Kaplan's views on the blessing and the danger of territory. Whereas Rosenzweig, for example, saw landlessness as a spiritual blessing, Kaplan wanted the Jewish people to have a soil of its own in order to reestablish a natural basis for its civilization. Yet Rosenzweig was right to fear the dangers of sinking roots in the earth. Long before 1948, Kaplan observed that the real test for Zionism would come when the Jewish people would have to use its collective power for the enhancement of the natural resources of Eretz Yisrael and the construction of a humane society.

The second direction of Zionism would be transterritorial. The Zionists would eventually have to strengthen the Jewish periphery as well, requiring that a new kind of voluntary association—founded on common spiritual, ethical, and cultural interests—would have to be devised and given structural actuality. For the foreseeable future, Jews would continue to live where they would feel free and accepted. No amount of moral pressure from the center would induce them to chose to live as part of the majority in a Jewish state, unless they were impelled to do so by their own conscience and will. Given these two vectors, Kaplan felt that the Zionist movement would have to take on duties specific to the *yishuv* in Eretz Yisrael and specific to the Diaspora as well.

As a democracy, the State of Israel would have to nourish its pluralistic constituency and, in the course of time, produce a new Israeli nation—with the Jews as its most influential element but one that includes Arabs, Druse, and even other ethnic and religious groups. Jews in Israel would live in two civilizations as they do elsewhere, with the decisive difference that in Israel their culture would be the dominant factor in the common society.

Furthermore, in place of an aggressive negation of the Diaspora, the Jewish community of Israel would have to play a major role in strengthening the unity of world Jewry and in stimulating free diaspora Jewries to greater creativity, whether this would lead to increased *aliyah* or not.

Diaspora Zionists would have to foster a Jewish education that would hold up for examination the two life styles available for sincere, serious Jews. Given a fair opportunity to choose to settle in Israel and being shown the particular salience of this option at this juncture in Jewish history, Kaplan believed that many Jews would opt for *aliyah*. He was never under the illusion that it was either desirable or possible to engineer the life style of men and women according to a preconceived blueprint. Models supply alternatives for choice, but people choose according to their inclinations, felt needs, and wants. Therefore, it was the responsibility of Jewish educators to provide each Jew, young and old, with a clear picture of the values and drawbacks of membership in Jewish minority communities in the Diaspora in contrast to the majority Jewish community in Israel. Then, each individual could decide for himself or herself.

Kaplan's reasoned, balanced approach was not likely to arouse a mass movement of return. But it is a formidable critique of the distortions that inevitably trouble a movement when it becomes massive and driven by forces uncontrolled by reason. Kaplan's Zionism deserves to be reexamined because his position, totally unacceptable for decades in Eretz Yisrael and partly unacceptable in the Diaspora, can now shed light on the mistakes Zionists made and point the way to their correction.

Both Diaspora and Eretz-Yisrael Zionists were incapable of grasping Kaplan's thesis that Zionism "must reconstitute and unify the Jewish people and redefine its status vis-à-vis the rest of the world."[8] The Jews of Israel have given only lip service to Kaplan's insight "that their future is bound up with the future of world Jewry." They have, of course, looked to the Diaspora for political and financial support but have never fully fathomed what is implicit in the slogan that the Jewish people is one. By affirming the Diaspora, Kaplan virtually assured his not being heard in Israel before 1948 or until now. By affirming the Diaspora on more than pragmatic grounds, he touched the central nerve of the whole Zionist system.

Kaplan could have rested his case on the common-sense premise that most Jews who are integrated as equal citizens in an open society are unlikely candidates for *aliyah*. He could have argued that such Jews, despite their refusal to become Israelis, nonetheless affirm their Jewishness; therefore, they must be given at least a share in the development of the State. However, Kaplan affirmed the Diaspora for a more important reason. Zionism was meant not only to establish a secure Jewish homeland but to supply an essential instrument for the revival of Jewish life wherever possible. The instrumentality of a creative Jewish community in Israel was to provide the focus for a new type of transterritorial people. This idea is still anathema to Zionist leaders in Israel, who refuse even to raise the possibility that there can be any value to the Jewishness of the Diaspora. In their opinion, it is only a matter of time before Jews outside of Israel will drown through assimilation.

Although there is no sign that Israelis are looking into Kaplan's Zionist thought, they have begun to ponder the disturbing phenomenon of *yeridah*, as well as the growing gap between Israeli and Diaspora Jewries, and the ever-clearer fact that majority status alone provides neither security nor a clear solution to the spiritual problems of Jewish existence. To those Israelis whose thinking penetrates below the surface, it has become obvious that the success or failure of the Zionist enterprise in the long run will be dependent on whether the minorities in Israel, without having to relinquish their ancestral cultures and commitments to their respective peoples, will come to feel they can experience a measure of fulfillment living in a Jewish civilization. To accomplish this, it will be necessary for Israelis to acquire a more profound understanding than they now possess of Jewish minority existence under freedom.

This brings us to Diaspora resistance, more specifically to American Zionist resistance to Kaplan's thesis. His support of political Zionism placed him in the mainstream of American Zionism, but he parted company with those leaders and activists who behaved as if involvement in the Zionist movement was sufficient to guarantee the future of American Jewry. For many decades, his efforts to articulate a unifying religious ideology for Zionism were ignored by the Reform and Conservative movements, in their rejecting his plea that they join the World Zionist Organization. The Orthodox were involved in the organized Zionist movement, but they had no intention of fashioning a new religious ideology to deal realistically with the fact of pluralism. The religious non-Orthodox had too constricted an ideology to enable them to deal pragmatically with the integration of nationalism and religion in their programs. To the extent that they faced the problem (and some did), they too avoided active interaction with those who held different views. Kaplan's motivations played little perceptible role in their recent decisions to join the World Zionist Organization. In fact, the alignment of vested interests forced the hand of the non-Orthodox denominations; it was political considerations, rather than Kaplanian spiritual nationalism or peoplehood, that motivated their entrance into the Zionist movement.

Yet Kaplan has won that battle. Reform and Conservative participation in the organized Zionist movement inevitably forced consideration of the implications of religious pluralism for Jewish peoplehood and for the status of religion in Diaspora Jewery and the State of Israel. It is unlikely that this relatively new demographic base for the Zionist movement will induce its leadership to reexamine Kaplan's analysis, unless some authority (currently not on the scene) discovers his ideas and forces the movement to do so. But even without Kaplan's vision, the conditions of freedom, voluntarism, and pluralism will eventually evoke the full scope of the issues that disturbed him decades ago.

The relationship between Jews and Arabs was constantly on Kaplan's mind, even though he published very little on the subject. His concern for it, however, is evident in his journals, where he indicates his conviction that the success of the Zionist effort would rest upon its resolution. Kaplan followed the tradition of Ahad Ha-Am and A. D. Gordon in urging Zionists to give more and fairer attention to the Arab presence. He criticized discrimination against Arab workers and called upon the *yishuv* to treat the Arabs as partners in the revivification of the land. "Jews should have realized," he wrote in 1939, "that they have to live with the Arabs, and should not have written in the statutes of the Jewish National Fund the prohibition of Arab labor. No effort or ingenuity should have been spared in devising ways or means of effecting a modus vivendi that would have been satisfactory to all who have an interest in the land."[9]

One-half of Israel's Jews today either ignore the presence of Arab citizens or look upon them with animosity. The other half realizes the need to come to terms with the Arabs but are confused about how to achieve conciliation with them. Some observers believe that the antipathy toward Arabs is a post-State phenomenon. No doubt the current intensity of enmity exceeds the feelings of pre-State days, but it cannot be denied that the Zionist movement never completely lived up to the high standards of intergroup relations often enunciated by its leaders. Therefore, it is easy to understand why Kaplan's Zionism should have made hardly a ripple in the stream of Zionist history. He was merely a minor link in a noble but ineffectual tradition that included Ahad Ha-Am, A. D. Gordon, Judah Magnes, Martin Buber, and others whose warnings were considered unrealistic even by liberal, democratic-minded Zionists who set the tone during the struggle for the State and have continued to articulate social policy in the same vein since its establishment. The full implications of a hard-headed, democratic liberalism are not yet realized by those who profess it.

To be sure, Kaplan did not grasp the complexity of the struggle of two peoples for the same land. His employment of the biblical roots of Jewish history to justify the Jewish claim to Eretz Yisrael remains common to most Zionists—those who believe in the divinity of the Bible and secularists alike. This appeal to the distant past convinces no Palestinian Arab, who also loves the land but is unprepared by experience and culture to assess the fine distinctions—theological, moral, and historical—that embellish the biblically based argument. The aggressive and violent Arab response to Jewish settlement bespeaks an inability to consider any reasonable compromise, an intransigence which, in turn, has elicited a counter-resistance that beclouds the rational objectives of the Zionist movement.

In the struggle for territory or power, ownership of a land usually has been the result of conquest. But nations should not take pride in having conquered a national soil. Rather, they must accept the responsibility that their sovereignty be morally defensible. Israel must continue to strive for just and peaceful relations among its Jewish and Arab citizens and with Arabs elsewhere. Although Kaplan has little to say regarding these particular issues, the thrust of his philosophy would lead us to suppose that he would be most critical of any policy that would require the Jewish majority to rule over a resentful Arab population.

If Kaplan can teach us something about how to turn the heart of the Arabs, he can teach the Zionist movement much about avoiding ideas that distort the character of free men and women and exacerbate problems so that they last for generations. It is time to pay serious attention to Kaplan's total system, within which the Zionist movement for Jewish national liberation takes on a profoundly moral and spiritual coloration. Only in Kaplan's broad, contextual thinking can a movement like Zionism retain the positive values of a faith in the life-giving power of Eretz Yisrael and in the ability of Jews to construct there a "people in the image of God."

Lest we mistakenly label Kaplan as an ivory-tower thinker, I will conclude with his view that, after all, ideals are not the main motivating factors in history. In criticizing Ahad Ha-Am for putting his faith in the small number of talented idealists who would emigrate to Eretz Yisrael voluntarily, Kaplan wrote, "The driving forces of necessity, plus a degree of preparedness for utilizing them for higher ends, make history. This is the truth in political Zionism."[10]

Zionism is still driven by necessity. Let us hope that it will transform that drive and energy into universally worthy purposes.

Notes

1. Mordecai M. Kaplan, *The Greater Judaism in the Making* (New York: Reconstructionist Press, 1960), 391.
2. Mordecai M. Kaplan, *The Religion of Ethical Nationhood* (New York: Macmillan, 1970), 1–2.
3. See, for example, Mordecai M. Kaplan, *The Future of the American Jew* (New York: Macmillan, 1948), 359–71.
4. Ibid., 361.
5. Ehud Ben Zvi, "The Zionist Doctrine of Rabbi Mordecai M. Kaplan" (unpublished paper, 1985), 1 [in Hebrew].
6. Simhah Bunem Urbach, *Pillars of Jewish Thought* (Jerusalem: World Zionist Organization, Department for Torah Education and Culture, 1953), 1:13–14 [in Hebrew].
7. Cf. Kaplan and Arthur A. Cohen, *If Not Now, When? Toward a Reconstruction of the Jewish People* (New York: Schocken Books, 1973), 120.
8. Kaplan, *Religion of Ethical Nationhood*, 119.
9. Mordecai M. Kaplan, "Palestine Jewry: Its Achievements and Shortcomings," *Reconstructionist* 5, no. 11 (September 1939).
10. Ibid.

Complete Bibliography of the Writings of Mordecai M. Kaplan

This bibliography is based on the version prepared by Gerson D. Cohen and published in the *Mordecai M. Kaplan Jubilee Volume, on the Occasion of His Seventieth Birthday* (New York: Jewish Theological Seminary of America, 1953). Roberta Newman located additional items published before 1953 or republished in new editions and Kaplan's articles, reviews, and books published between 1953 and 1987.

1909

Judaism and Nationality.
   The Maccabaean, vol. XVII, no. 2 (Aug. 1909), pp. 59–64.

1910

Report of Committee on Jewish Education.
   Report of the Executive Committee presented at the First Annual Convention of the Jewish Community (Kehillah) (New York, Feb. 26 and 27, 1910), pp. 25–36.
   [Reprinted in *American Hebrew*, vol. LXXXVI, no. 18 (March 4, 1910), pp. 458–59, and in *Jewish Education*, vol. XX, no. 3 (Summer, 1949), pp. 113–16 (in *Jewish Education*: "by Mordecai M. Kaplan and Bernard Cronson").]

1914

The Supremacy of the Torah.
   Students' Annual, Jewish Theological Seminary of America (New York, 1914), pp. 180–92.

1915

What Judaism Is Not.
  The Menorah Journal, vol. I, no. 4 (Oct. 1915), pp. 208–16.
What Is Judaism?
  The Menorah Journal, vol. I, no. 5 (Dec. 1915), pp. 309–18.

1916

The Function of the Religious School.
  The Jewish Teacher, vol. I (Jan. 1916), pp. 5–13.
How May Judaism Be Saved?
  The Menorah Journal, vol. II, no. 1 (Feb. 1916), pp. 34–44.
Judaism and Christianity.
  The Menorah Journal, vol. II, no. 2 (April 1916), pp. 105–15.
The Future of Judaism.
  The Menorah Journal, vol. II, no. 3 (June 1916), pp. 160–72.
The Jewish Center.
  Photographs and Maxims Published for the Family Gathering of the Jewish Centre, November 12, 1916 (New York), 19 + 5 pp.

1918

Where Does Jewry Really Stand Today?
  The Menorah Journal, vol. IV, no. 1 (Feb. 1918), pp. 33–43.
The Jewish Center.
  The American Hebrew, vol. CII, no. 20 (March 22, 1918), pp. 529–31.
The Place of the Jewish Center in American Jewish Life.
  Jewish Center Day: Dedication Exercises and Festivities (New York, The Jewish Center, March 24, 1918), pp. 7–19.
Affiliation with the Synagogue.
  The Jewish Communal Register of New York City 1917–1918 (New York, Kehillah (Jewish Community), 1918), pp. 117–22.
Judaism as a Living Civilization, *American Jewish Chronicle*, 4, 24 (April 19, 1918), 676–79

1919

Commencement Address.
  Commencement Addresses June 8, 1919, by Sol M. Stroock, Esq., Professor Louis Ginzberg, Professor Mordecai M. Kaplan (New York, The Jewish Theological Seminary of America, 1919), pp. 24–37.

1920

A Program for the Reconstruction of Judaism.
  The Menorah Journal, vol. VI, no. 4 (Aug. 1920), pp. 181–96.

The Society of the Jewish Renascence.
The Maccabaean, vol. XXXIV, no. 4 (Nov. 1920), pp. 110–13.
[Reprinted by *Zionist Publications* (New York, Zionist Organization of America, 1920, 15 pp.).]

1923

The Toothbrush and "Schmad."
S. A. J. Review, vol. I, no. 2 (June 8, 1923), pp. 1–2.
Judaism—What Is It?
S. A. J. Review, vol. I, no. 3 (June 15, 1923), pp. 1–2.
Impressions of German Jewry.
S. A. J. Review, vol. I, no. 8 (Aug. 3, 1923), pp. 1–3.
If They Were Only Reindeer.
S. A. J. Review, vol. I, no. 9 (Aug. 10, 1923), pp. 2–4.
Wanderers.
S. A. J. Review, vol. I, no. 10 (Aug. 17, 1923), pp. 1–2.
The Society for the Advancement of Judaism.
(New York, The Society for the Advancement of Judaism, [1923]), 25 pp.

1924

Parlor Idealism.
S. A. J. Review, vol. III, no. 2 (May 23, 1924), pp. 2–6.
Filial Reverence.
S. A. J. Review, vol. III, no. 3 (May 30, 1924), pp. 2–5.
The Dangerous Age.
S. A. J. Review, vol. III, no. 5 (June 13, 1924), pp. 2–7.
The Remaking of Human Nature.
S. A. J. Review, vol. IV, no. 2 (Oct. 3, 1924), pp. 2–10.
"The Survival of the Fittest" in Jewish Life.
S. A. J. Review, vol. IV, no. 3 (Oct. 10, 1924), pp. 2–11.
Back to Nature.
S. A. J. Review, vol. IV, no. 4 (Oct. 17, 1924), pp. 2–6.
Sentimentalism.
S. A. J. Review, vol. IV, no. 5 (Oct. 24, 1924), pp. 2–9.
Midrash Aggada Paraphrased and Interpreted.
S. A. J. Review,
    vol. IV, no. 8 (Nov. 14, 1924), pp. 3–5;
    vol. IV, no. 9 (Nov. 21, 1924), pp. 2–5;
    vol. IV, no. 11 (Dec. 5, 1924), pp. 5–8;
    vol. IV, no. 12 (Dec. 12, 1924), pp. 2–6;
    vol. IV, no. 13 (Dec. 19, 1924), pp. 6–9;
    vol. IV, no. 14 (Dec. 26, 1924), pp. 2–7.
Angels, Men, and Asses.

S. A. J. Review, vol. IV, no. 10 (Nov. 28, 1924), pp. 2–4.
The Jewish Conception of Loyalty.
S. A. J. Review, vol. IV, no. 11 (Dec. 5, 1924), pp. 2–4.
Get the Americans to Understand America.
The Jewish Tribune (Dec. 5, 1924), pp. 7–8.
[Excerpts under title: "Bigotry Is Treason to Basic Covenant of America" in *S. A. J. Review*, vol. IV, no. 13 (Dec. 19, 1924), pp. 2–4.]
A New Approach to the Problem of Judaism.
(New York, Society for the Advancement of Judaism, 1924), iv + 70 pp.
[Reprinted under title: *A New Approach to Jewish Life* (Bridgeport: Hartmore House, 1973).]
Supplementary Readings and Meditations.
(New York, Society for the Advancement of Judaism, 1924), vi + 104 pp.

1925

Midrash Aggadah Paraphrased and Interpreted.
   S. A. J. Review,
       vol. IV, no. 15 (Jan. 2, 1925), pp. 2–6;
       vol. IV, no. 16 (Jan. 9, 1925), pp. 2–5;
       vol. IV, no. 17 (Jan. 16, 1925), pp. 2–7;
       vol. IV, no. 18 (Jan. 23, 1925), pp. 2–6;
       vol. IV, no. 19 (Jan. 30, 1925), pp. 2–6;
       vol. IV, no. 20 (Feb. 6, 1925), pp. 2–6;
       vol. IV, no. 21 (Feb. 13, 1925), pp. 3–8;
       vol. IV, no. 22 (Feb. 20, 1925), pp. 2–6;
       vol. IV, no. 23 (Feb. 27, 1925), pp. 2–7.
Judaism Articulate—The University a Living Definition.
   The New Palestine, vol. VII, no. 13 (March 27, 1925), p. 286.
   [Reprinted under title: "The Hebrew University and the Jewish Rena-
   scence" in *S. A. J. Review*, vol. IV, no. 27 (March 27, 1925), pp. 4–7.]
Now My Joy Is Complete.
   The New Palestine, vol. VIII, no. 14 (April 8, 1925), pp. 469–70.
   [Reprinted in *S. A. J. Review*, vol. IV, no. 30 (April 14, 1925), pp. 2–7.]
The Sense of Responsibility.
   S. A. J. Review, vol. V, no. 2 (Sept. 25, 1925), pp. 2–10.
Rabbinic Comments on "Shir Hashirim."
   S. A. J. Review, vol. V, no. 3 (Oct. 2, 1925), pp. 10–11.
An Anthology of Rabbinic Lore.
   S. A. J. Review,
       vol. V, no. 11 (Nov. 27, 1925), pp. 2–6;
       vol. V, no. 12 (Dec. 4, 1925), pp. 2–6;
       vol. V, no. 14 (Dec. 18, 1925), pp. 2–8.
The "Thirteen Principles" of the S. A. J.

[Program of] Dinner and Dance Dedication at the S. A. J. House,
December 13, 1925.

1926

An Anthology of Rabbinic Lore.
    S. A. J. Review,
        vol. V, no. 21 (Feb. 5, 1926), pp. 2–8;
        vol. V, no. 22 (Feb. 12, 1926), pp. 2–7;
        vol. VI, no. 1 (Sept. 7, 1926), pp. 7–11.
The Philosophy of the Jewish Center.
    S. A. J. Review, vol. V, no. 38 (June 4, 1926), pp. 10–11.
Isaiah 6:1–11.
    Journal of Biblical Literature, vol. XLV, nos. 3–4 (1926), pp. 251–59.
The Desire to Be Let Alone.
    S. A. J. Review, vol. V, no. 39 (June 11, 1926), pp. 6–13.
Religion as Social Righteousness.
    S. A. J. Review, vol. V, no. 40 (June 18, 1926), pp. 6–13.
Self Criticism.
    S. A. J. Review, vol. VI, no. 2 (Sept. 17, 1926), pp. 5–13.
Moral Growth.
    S. A. J. Review, vol. VI, no. 3 (Sept. 22, 1926), pp. 3–11.
Gratitude.
    S. A. J. Review, vol. VI, no. 4 (Sept. 29, 1926), pp. 5–10.
Public Worship.
    S. A. J. Review, vol. VI, no. 5 (Oct. 8, 1926), pp. 5–11.
The City Righteous.
    S. A. J. Review, vol. VI, no. 6 (Oct. 15, 1926), pp. 5–11.
They Who Never Grow Weary.
    S. A. J. Review, vol. VI, no. 8 (Oct. 29, 1926), pp. 5–11.
Justifying God.
    S. A. J. Review, vol. VI, no. 9 (Nov. 5, 1926), pp. 5–13.
The Divine Drama.
    S. A. J. Review, vol. VI, no. 10 (Nov. 12, 1926), pp. 4–11.
Wherein Religion and the Law Fail Us.
    S. A. J. Review, vol. VI, no. 11 (Nov. 19, 1926), pp. 4–9.
Parents and Children.
    S. A. J. Review, vol. VI, no. 12 (Nov. 26, 1926), pp. 5–11.
Hanukkah and the S. A. J.
    S. A. J. Review, vol. VI, no. 13 (Dec. 3, 1926), pp. 4–12.
The Scientific Approach to Religion.
    S. A. J. Review, vol. VI, no. 14 (Dec. 10, 1926), pp. 4–14.
The Prophet Who Inaugurated the Spiritual Revolution.
    S. A. J. Review, vol. VI, no. 16 (Dec. 24, 1926), pp. 4–12.

What the Zionist Organization of America Needs.
  S. A. J. Review, vol. VI, no. 17 (Dec. 31, 1926), pp. 4–10.

1927

The Unity of Israel.
  S. A. J. Review, vol. VI, no. 19 (Jan. 14, 1927), pp. 5–11.
Jewish Survival.
  S. A. J. Review, vol. VI, no. 21 (Jan. 28, 1927), pp. 5–11.
Jewish Art.
  S. A. J. Review, vol. VI, no. 23 (Feb. 11, 1927), pp. 6–11.
Abraham Lincoln—Apostle of Democracy.
  S. A. J. Review, vol. VI, no. 24 (Feb. 18, 1927), pp. 4–12.
The Religion of Renascent Israel.
  S. A. J. Review, vol. VI, no. 26 (March 4, 1927), pp. 4–11.
Sabbath Observance and Recreation.
  S. A. J. Review,
    vol. VI, no. 27 (March 11, 1927), pp. 5–11;
    vol. VI, no. 28 (March 18, 1927), pp. 7–13.
An Antidote to Jewish Antisemitism.
  S. A. J. Review, vol. VI, no. 29 (March 25, 1927), pp. 5–12.
Paradox—As Witness of the Spiritual.
  S. A. J. Review, vol. VI, no. 30 (April 1, 1927), pp. 5–11.
God in Nature and in History.
  S. A. J. Review, vol. VI, no. 32 (April 15, 1927), pp. 5–12.
Freedom: A Spiritual Ideal.
  S. A. J. Review, vol. VI, no. 33 (April 21, 1927), pp. 4–13.
Life—The Song of Songs.
  S. A. J. Review, vol. VI, no. 34 (April 29, 1927), pp. 5–13.
Toward a Reconstruction of Judaism.
  The Menorah Journal, vol. XIII, no. 2 (April 1927), pp. 113–30.
  [Reprinted in Menorah Pamphlets, no. 4 (New York, The Menorah Press, 1927), 40 pp.]
Religious Experience.
  S. A. J. Review, vol. VI, no. 35 (May 6, 1927), pp. 5–11.
The Relation of Religion to Social Life.
  S. A. J. Review,
    vol. VI, no. 36 (May 13, 1927), pp. 5–12;
    vol. VI, no. 37 (May 20, 1927), pp. 6–11.
The History of Judaism as Reflected in Its Literature.
  S. A. J. Review,
    vol. VII, no. 1 (Sept. 16, 1927), pp. 6–14;
    vol. VII, no. 2 (Sept. 23, 1927), pp. 6–13;
    vol. VII, no. 3 (Sept. 30, 1927), pp. 5–13;

    vol. VII, no. 4 (Oct. 7, 1927), pp. 6–13;
    vol. VII, no. 7 (Oct. 28, 1927), pp. 5–14;
    vol. VII, no. 8 (Nov. 4, 1927), pp. 6–12;
    vol. VII, no. 9 (Nov. 11, 1927), pp. 6–12;
    vol. VII, no. 10 (Nov. 18, 1927), pp. 8–18;
    vol. VII, no. 11 (Nov. 25, 1927), pp. 6–15;
    vol. VII, no. 12 (Dec. 2, 1927), pp. 6–14;
    vol. VII, no. 13 (Dec. 9, 1927), pp. 5–12;
    vol. VII, no. 14 (Dec. 16, 1927), pp. 6–15;
    vol. VII, no. 15 (Dec. 23, 1927), pp. 6–13;
    vol. VII, no. 16 (Dec. 30, 1927), pp. 5–16.
The Shamelessness of the Orthodox Union.
    S. A. J. Review, vol. VII, no. 10 (Nov. 18, 1927), pp. 2–3.
Preface to Second Edition.
    Kitab al Kahazari by Judah Hallevi, translated by Hartwig Hirschfeld
    (New York, Bernard G. Richards Co., 1927).

1928

The History of Judaism as Reflected in Its Literature.
    S. A. J. Review,
        vol. VII, no. 17 (Jan. 6, 1928), pp. 6–12;
        vol. VII, no. 18 (Jan. 13, 1928), pp. 6–14;
        vol. VII, no. 19 (Jan. 20, 1928), pp. 6–15;
        vol. VII, no. 20 (Jan. 27, 1928), pp. 6–16;
        vol. VII, no. 21 (Feb. 3, 1928), pp. 9–15;
        vol. VII, no. 22 (Feb. 10, 1928), pp. 6–12.
When Mixed Marriage Became High Treason.
    S. A. J. Review, vol. VII, no. 23 (Feb. 17, 1928), pp. 10–15.
The Place of Adult Education in Jewish Life.
    S. A. J. Review,
        vol. VII, no. 24 (Feb. 24, 1928), pp. 8–15;
        vol. VII, no. 25 (March 3, 1928), pp. 11–19.
Judaism's First Champion.
    S. A. J. Review, vol. VII, no. 26 (March 9, 1928), pp. 4–10.
When the Days of Miracles Were Over.
    S. A. J. Review, vol. VII, no. 27 (March 16, 1928), pp. 10–18.
Judaism as an Unconscious Evolution.
    S. A. J. Review, vol. VII, no. 29 (March 30, 1928), pp. 9–16.
Emancipation or Redemption—Which?
    S. A. J. Review, vol. VII, no. 30 (April 4, 1928), pp. 4–8.
The Rise of Sects in Judaism.
    S. A. J. Review, vol. VII, no. 31 (April 13, 1928), pp. 10–16.
Intimations of Other-Worldliness.

S. A. J. Review, vol. VII, no. 31 (April 20, 1928), pp. 11–22.
Judaism's First Encounter with Scepticism.
    S. A. J. Review, vol. VII, no. 35 (May 11, 1928), pp. 4–15.
A Survival of Primitive Judaism.
    S. A. J. Review,
        vol. VII, no. 36 (May 18, 1928), pp. 11–17;
        vol. VII, no. 37 (May 24, 1928), pp. 12–22.
The Sovereignty of God—An Interpretation.
    S. A. J. Review, vol. VIII, no. 1 (Sept. 14, 1928), pp. 4–10.
The Law of Group Survival as Applied to the Jews.
    S. A. J. Review, vol. VIII, no. 2 (Sept. 21, 1928), pp. 4–11.
Revaluation of Jewish Values.
    S. A. J. Review, vol. VIII, no. 3 (Sept. 28, 1928), pp. 4–12.
The God Idea in the Problem of Revaluation.
    S. A. J. Review, vol. VIII, no. 5 (Oct. 12, 1928), pp. 8–18.
Aspirations and Handicaps of the Zionist Organization.
    S. A. J. Review, vol. VIII, no. 6 (Oct. 19, 1928), pp. 10–17.
The Relation of Religion to Nationalism.
    S. A. J. Review, vol. VIII, no. 7 (Oct. 26, 1928), pp. 13–22.
The Beginnings of Humanist Culture among Jews.
    S. A. J. Review,
        vol. VIII, no. 9 (Nov. 9, 1928), pp. 5–11;
        vol. VIII, no. 10 (Nov. 16, 1928), pp. 4–12.
Judaism as a Civilization: Religion's Place in It.
    The Menorah Journal, vol. XV, no. 6 (Dec. 1928), pp. 501–14.
Moral Courage.
    S. A. J. Review, vol. VIII, no. 14 (Dec. 14, 1928), pp. 4–8.
Judaism as a Civilization.
    *Proceedings of the Rabbinical Assembly of the Jewish Theological
    Seminary of America*, vol. II (1928), pp. 115–30.

1929

An Anthology of Rabbinic Lore.
    S. A. J. Review,
        vol. VIII, no. 19 (Jan. 18, 1929), pp. 19–20;
        vol. VIII, no. 20 (Jan. 25, 1929), pp. 19–20;
        vol. VIII, no. 21 (Feb. 1, 1929), pp. 17–19;
        vol. VIII, no. 22 (Feb. 8, 1929), pp. 17–19.
A Reply.
    S. A. J. Review, vol. VIII, no. 21 (Feb. 1, 1929), pp. 10–15.
    [To Simon Greenberg: "Olam Habba and Self-Realization," *ibid.*,
    pp. 4–9.]
Why It Is Hard to Be a Jew.

S. A. J. Review,
   vol. VIII, no. 22 (Feb. 8, 1929), pp. 4–12;
   vol. VIII, no. 23 (Feb. 15, 1929), pp. 11–19;
   vol. VIII, no. 24 (Feb. 22, 1929), pp. 7–19.
Judaism's Adjustment to the Environment.
I. The Adjustment of Orthodoxy.
   S. A. J. Review, vol. VIII, no. 25 (March 1, 1929), pp. 10–24.
II. Critique of the Adjustment of Orthodoxy.
   Ibid., no. 26 (March 8, 1929), pp. 11–19.
III. The Adjustment of Reform.
   Ibid., no. 27 (March 15, 1929), pp. 4–17.
IV. Critique of the Adjustment of Reform.
   Ibid., no. 28 (March 22, 1929), pp. 12–24.
Judaism as a Civilization.
   S. A. J. Review,
   vol. VIII, no. 29 (March 29, 1929), pp. 13–22;
   vol. VIII, no. 30 (April 5, 1929), pp. 11–22.
The Relation of Religion to Civilization.
   S. A. J. Review, vol. VIII, no. 31 (April 12, 1929), pp. 8–23.
The Stages of the Jewish Civilization.
   S. A. J. Review,
   vol. VIII, no. 32 (April 19, 1929), pp. 4–15;
   vol. VIII, no. 33 (April 24, 1929), pp. 4–15.
The Revaluation of the Concept "Torah."
   S. A. J. Review, vol. VIII, no. 34 (May 3, 1929), pp. 9–19.
The Revaluation of the Concept "Israel."
   S. A. J. Review, vol. VIII, no. 35 (May 10, 1929), pp. 11–20.
The Nationhood of Israel.
   S. A. J. Review, vol. VIII, no. 36 (May 17, 1929), pp. 13–24.
A Reply.
   S. A. J. Review, vol. VIII, no. 36 (May 17, 1929), pp. 12–13.
   [To Simon Greenberg: "The Problem of Revaluation," ibid., pp. 4–12.]
Nationhood, the Call of the Spirit.
   S. A. J. Review, vol. VIII, no. 37 (May 24, 1929), pp. 12–20.

1930

Jewish Philanthropy: Traditional and Modern.
   Intelligent Philanthropy, edited by Ellsworth Faris, Farris Laune, and
   Arthur J. Todd (Chicago, University of Chicago Press, 1930), pp. 52–89.
The Significance of Ruth.
   [Introduction to] The Story of Ruth Graphically Told, by Z. Raban (New
   York, American-Palestine Art Publishing Co., 1930).

1931

Electra versus Job.
  Opinion, vol. I, no. 3 (Dec. 21, 1931), pp. 6–8.

1932

The Jewish Method in Homiletics.
  The Homiletic Review, vol. CIII, no. 2 (Feb. 1932), pp. 111–16.
Aims of Jewish Education in America.
  Opinion,
      vol. II, no. 2 (June 13, 1932), pp. 5–8;
      vol. II, no. 3 (June 20, 1932), pp. 9–11.
Open Letter to Federations and Congregations from the Rabbinical Assembly
  of the Jewish Theological Seminary.
  Jewish Education, vol. IV, no. 3 (Oct. 1932), p. 129.
What the American Jewish Woman Can Do for Adult Jewish Education.
  Jewish Education, vol. IV, no. 3 (Oct.-Dec. 1932), pp. 139–47.
Dynamic Religion.
  Opinion, vol. III, no. 2 (Dec. 1932), pp. 17–18.
An Open Letter.
  Ibid., p. 31.
The Place of Dogma in Judaism.
  *Proceedings of the Rabbinical Assembly of the Jewish Theological
  Seminary of America*, vol. IV (New York, 1932), pp. 280–300.
The Relation of the Synagogue to Jewish Communal Life.
  Yearbook: Central Conference of American Rabbis, vol. XLII (Cincinnati,
  1932), pp. 236–56.

1933

Philo and the Midrash.
  Jewish Quarterly Review, vol. XXIII, no. 3 (Jan. 1933), pp. 285–91.
  [Review of Edmund Stein: *Philo und der Midrasch*, Giessen, 1931.]
Joseph Bragin—Educator.
  Jewish Education, vol. V, no. 1 (Jan.-March 1933), pp. 18–20.
On Creeds and Wants: A Study in the Evolution of Judaism.
  The Menorah Journal, vol. XXI, no. 1 (Spring 1933), pp. 33–52.
The Rabbinic Training for Our Day.
  Jewish Education, vol. V, no. 2 (April-June 1933), pp. 67–78.

1934

A Challenge to Jewish Federations.
  Opinion, vol. V, no. 2 (Dec. 1934), pp. 8–13.

Judaism and Intercultural Contacts.
 Modern Trends in World Religions, edited by A. Eustace Haydon (Chicago, University of Chicago Press, 1934), pp. 179–88.
Judaism and Modern Scientific Thinking.
 Ibid., pp. 15–24.
Judaism as a Civilization—Toward a Reconstruction of American-Jewish Life.
 (New York, The Macmillan Company, 1934), xiv + 601 pp.
 [Reprinted in 1957 (New York, The Reconstructionist Press); 1967 (New York, Schocken); 1981 (New York, Jewish Publication Society and Reconstructionist Press).]
Supplementary Prayers and Readings for the High Holidays (New York, United Synagogue of America, 1934), v + 68 pp.

1935

Is a Religious Training Essential to Character?
 The Reconstructionist, vol. I, no. 1 (Jan. 11, 1935), pp. 11–18.
Marxism and the Jewish Religion.
 The Reconstructionist, vol. I, no. 5 (March 8, 1935), pp. 6–15.
Toward a Jewish Community.
 Opinion, vol. V, no. 5 (March 1935), pp. 6–10.
How Maimonides Reconstructed Judaism.
 The Reconstructionist, vol. I, no. 11 (April 5, 1935), pp. 7–15.
The Meaning of Rosh Ha-Shanah for Our Day.
 The Reconstructionist, vol. I, no. 11 (Oct. 4, 1935), pp. 6–11.
The Pilgrimage Festivals.
 The Reconstructionist, vol. I, no. 12 (Oct. 18, 1935), pp. 7–13.
The Organization of American Jewry.
 Jewish Education, vol. VII, no. 3 (Oct.-Dec. 1935), pp. 131–54, also appears in the *Jewish Social Service Quarterly*, vol. XII, no. 1 (September 1935); 50–73.
A Note on the God Idea in Judaism.
 The Reconstructionist, vol. I, no. 14 (Nov. 15, 1935), pp. 13–16.
God Our Redeemer: A Piyyut for the Geulah Prayer.
 The Reconstructionist, vol. I, no. 16 (Dec. 13, 1935), pp. 7–8.

1936

Revelation of God in Nature: A Piyyut for the First Benediction of the Evening Prayer.
 The Reconstructionist, vol. I, no. 18 (Jan. 10, 1936), pp. 11–13.
In Reply to Rabbi Agushewitz.
 Ibid., pp. 9–11.

[To Jacob B. Agushewitz: "The Problem of the Hitler-Proselyte," *ibid.*, pp. 6–9.]
The Status of the Jewish Woman.
    The Reconstructionist, vol. II, no. 1 (Feb. 21, 1936), pp. 7–14.
Freedom as a Spiritual Ideal.
    The Reconstructionist, vol. II, no. 4 (April 3, 1936), p. 15.
Why Humanism Is Not Enough.
    The Reconstructionist, vol. II, no. 7 (May 15, 1936), pp. 12–16.
Reply to Letter.
    The Reconstructionist, vol. II, no. 9 (July 12, 1936), p. 16.
    [On definition of "otherworldliness" in medieval Judaism.]
Incompatible Notions about God.
    The Reconstructionist, vol. II, no. 16 (Dec. 11, 1936), pp. 7–9.
The Jewish Reconstructionist Papers,
    edited by Mordecai M. Kaplan (New York, Behrman's Jewish Book House, 1936), xiii + 269 pp.
Judaism in Transition.
    (New York, Covici-Friede, 1936), xii + (13) + 312 pp.
Mesillat Yesharim: The Path of the Upright, by Moses Hayyim Luzzatto: a critical edition provided with a translation and notes by Mordecai M. Kaplan.
    (Philadelphia, The Jewish Publication Society of America [The Schiff Library of Jewish Classics], 1936).
    [Reprinted in 1948 and 1966 (New York, Jewish Publication Society).]
    Hebrew title page: Mesilat Yesharim le-Rabi Moshe Hayim Luzzato. Hotza'h Hadashah 'im shinuyey Nuseḥa'ot u-Marey Mekomot veTirgum veHe'arot BeSafat Anglit. 2 + xxxvii + 230 + 230 pp.

1937

Is Jewish Unity Possible?
    The Menorah Journal, vol. XXV, no. 1 (Jan.-March, 1937), pp. 128–31.
The Resurrection of the Jewish Spirit.
    The Reconstructionist, vol. II, no. 7 (May 14, 1937), pp. 14–16.
Gisha Ḥadasha leḤinukh.
    Ha-Aretz, Dec. 9, 1937, pp. 3–4.
Hitpathuto Shel HaTahalikh HaHinukhi, Hartsa-at Petihah (The evolution of the educative process, an inaugural lecture). (Yerushalayim, Hevrah Hotsa'at Sefarim al Yad HaUniversitah Ha-Ivrit, 5698 [1937]), 22 pp.
The Meaning of God in Modern Jewish Religion.
    (New York, Behrman's Jewish House, 1937), xii + (2) + 368 pp.
    [Reprinted in 1947 (New York, Jewish Publication Society).]

1938

HaHinukh Bemisgeret Ha-medini'ut.
    Ha-Aretz,

March 22, 1938, p. 5;
March 22, 1938 (Tosefet Erev), p. 5;
March 23, 1938 (Tosefet Erev), p. 5.
A Message from Doctor Kaplan.
The Reconstructionist, vol. IV, no. 12 (Oct. 21, 1938), pp. 5–8.
Di Tsukunft fun der Yidishe Religye Oder di Religye-Kulturistishe Oyffasung
fun Yidntum (New York, The Society for the Advancement of Judaism,
1938), 292 pp.
'Erkey HaYahadut veHithadshutam Kegilui HaHiyuniyut She-ba-emunah
HaYisra-eylit. . . . Tirgum Me-anglit Avraham Regelson Behishtatfut
HaMehaber (Yerushalayim, Hotsa'at Reuvayn Mas, 1938) 359 'Am.
[Translation of The Meaning of God in Modern Jewish Religion.)]

1939

HaMahzor HaRishon.
Hed ha-Hinukh, vol. XIII, no. 4 (2d Shevat, 5699), pp. 61–63.
Signon Hayim he-Haser: Shitat Hinukh.
Ha-Aretz, April 3, 1939, pp. 5–6.
Palestine Jewry: Its Achievements and Shortcomings.
The Reconstructionist, vol. V, no. 11 (Sept. 29, 1939), pp. 7–16.
Ha-Idi'ologi'ah Ha-Demokratit Mahi?
Bitzaron, vol. I, no. 1 (Oct. 1939), pp. 20–32.
The Sun Riseth and the Sun Goeth Down.
The Reconstructionist, vol. V, no. 14 (Nov. 10, 1939), pp. 7–8.
Jewish Education for Democracy.
The Reconstructionist, vol. V, no. 15 (Nov. 24, 1939), pp. 11–16.
Derushah: Ahad-Ha-Amiyut Mehudeshet.
Hadoar, vol. XX, no. 7 (Dec. 22, 1939), p. 99.
Message to the Rabbinical Assembly at the Annual Convention, May 2,
1933.
Proceedings of the Rabbinical Assembly of America, vol. VI (New York,
1939), pp. 177–202.
The Teacher's Institute and Its Affiliated Departments.
The Jewish Theological Seminary of America, Semi-Centennial Volume,
edited by Cyrus Adler (New York, The Jewish Theological Seminary of
America, 1939), pp. 121–43.
What Jewish Education Can Do to Advance Democracy.
Education for Democracy. The Proceedings of the Congress On Education
for Democracy held at Teachers College, Columbia University, August
15, 16, 17, 1939 (New York, Teachers College, Columbia University,
1939), pp. 210–20.

1940

Needed: A Spirit of Inquiry in Jewish Religion.
The Reconstructionist, vol. V, no. 19 (Jan. 19, 1940), pp. 6–11.

The Meaning of Reconstructionism.
The Reconstructionist, vol. VI, no. 1 (Feb. 16, 1940), pp. 8–19.
[Reprinted as *Reconstructionist Pamphlet no. 1* (New York, 1940), 23 pp.]
Judaism A la Spengler.
The Reconstructionist, vol. VI, no. 5 (April 12, 1940), pp. 11–13.
[Review of Harry Infeld: *Israel in the Decline of the West.*]
Passover, the Festival of Freedom.
Hadassah News Letter, vol. XX, no. 6 (April 1940), pp. 8–10.
The Belief in God and How to Teach It.
Jewish Education, vol. XII, no. 2 (Sept. 1940), pp. 102–13.
The Implications of the World Situation for Jewish Cultural Life in America.
The Jewish Social Service Quarterly, vol. X, no. 1 (Sept. 1940), 31–42.
The American Rabbi in the Modern World.
The Reconstructionist,
vol. VI, no. 12 (Oct. 16, 1940), pp. 5–11;
vol. VI, no. 13 (Nov. 1, 1940), pp. 9–16.
Don't Be Your Own Enemy!
The National Jewish Monthly, vol. LV, no. 2 (Oct. 1940), pp. 42, 63–64.
Schechter's Influence on American Judaism.
The Reconstructionist, vol. VI, no. 17 (Dec. 27, 1940), pp. 7–8.
The Reconstructionist Viewpoint.
Reconstructionist Pamphlet, no. 2 (New York, 1940), 8 pp.

1941

Tokhen Ve-Tzurah Ba-Tarbut Ha-Ivrit.
Hadoar, vol. XXI, no. 21 (March 21, 1941), pp. 331–32.
The New Haggadah.
The Reconstructionist, vol. VII, no. 5 (April 18, 1941), pp. 17–18.
Traditional Judaism and Its Interpretation.
Current Religious Thought, vol. I, no. 6 (June 1941), pp. 20–23.
Judaism in Transition.
(New York, Behrman's Jewish Book House, 1941), xviii + 1 + 312 pp.
The New Haggadah for the Pesah Seder,
edited by Mordecai M. Kaplan, Eugene Kohn, and Ira Eisenstein for the Jewish Reconstructionist Foundation (New York, Behrman's Jewish Book House, 1941), xv + 1 + 176 pp.
[Revised editions, 1942 and 1978.]

1942

A Reply.
The Reconstructionist, vol. VII, no. 18 (Jan. 9, 1942), pp. 13–19.

[To Ben Zion Bokser: "A Criticism of the Suggested Guide to Jewish Ritual," *ibid.*, pp. 6–13.]
The Influences that Have Shaped My Life.
  The Reconstructionist, vol. VIII, no. 10 (June 26, 1942), pp. 27–36.
The Jewish Conception of Education.
  Jewish Education, vol. XIV, no. 2 (Sept.-Dec. 1942), pp. 71–76.
What Is Prophetic Religion?
  The Reconstructionist, vol. VIII, no. 13 (Oct. 30, 1942), pp. 10–14.
In Reply to Doctor Gordis.
  The Reconstructionist, vol. VIII, no. 15 (Nov. 27, 1942), pp. 15–21.
  [To Robert Gordis: "Authority in Jewish Law—Toward a Solution," *ibid.*, no. 14 (Nov. 13, 1942); and "Permanence and Change in Jewish Law," *ibid.*, no. 15 (Nov. 27, 1942).]

1943

Religious Foundations of Democracy.
  The Reconstructionist, vol. IX, no. 5 (April 16, 1943), pp. 10–15.
On American Approaches to Jewish Education.
  The Jewish Review, vol. I, no. 1 (May 1943), pp. 5–12.
Survivalists and Euthanasians.
  The Reconstructionist, vol. IX, no. 7 (May 14, 1943), pp. 8–15.
All in the Name of Patriotism.
  The Reconstructionist, vol. IX, no. 9 (June 11, 1943), pp. 21–23.
  [Review of D. C. Holton: *Modern Japan and Shinto Nationalism*, Chicago, 1943.]
What the American Jewish Conference Should Ask For.
  The Reconstructionist, vol. IX, no. 10 (June 25, 1943), pp. 7–13.
Palestinian Educators in Search of Religion.
  The Reconstructionist, vol. IX, no. 11 (Oct. 4, 1943), pp. 18–20.
The Authority of Tradition.
  The Reconstructionist, vol. IX, no. 13 (Oct. 29, 1943), pp. 19–21.
The Basis of Modern Man's Belief in God.
  The Reconstructionist, vol. IX, no. 17 (Dec. 24, 1943), pp. 19–22.

1944

The Quest for Salvation.
  The Reconstructionist, vol. IX, no. 18 (Jan. 7, 1944), pp. 16–18.
God as the Power that Makes for Salvation.
  The Reconstructionist, vol. IX, no. 19 (Jan. 21, 1944), pp. 21–24.
Is Religion Compatible with Naturalism?
  The Reconstructionist, vol. X, no. 2 (March 3, 1944), pp. 20–23.
What Is Man?
  The Reconstructionist, vol. X, no. 9 (June 9, 1944), pp. 9–13.

[Review of Reinhold Neibuhr: *The Nature and Destiny of Man* (2 vols.), 1941–1943.]

Reconstructionism as Both a Challenging and Unifying Influence.
The Reconstructionist, vol. X, no. 11 (Oct. 6, 1944), pp. 16–21.

A Wrong Plea for a Right Case.
The Reconstructionist, vol. X, no. 15 (Dec. 1, 1944), pp. 20–22
[Review of Waldo Frank: *The Jew in Our Day*, 1944.]

Comments on Doctor Gordis' Paper.
Proceedings of the Rabbinical Assembly of America, 1941–1944, vol. VIII, pp. 95–97.
[To Robert Gordis: "Authority in Jewish Law," *ibid.*, pp. 64–94.]

How Man Comes to Know God.
Ibid., pp. 256–71.

The Training of Teaching and Leadership Personnel.
Ibid., pp. 350–55.

The Freedom to Be Jews.
Reconstructionist Pamphlet, no. 7 (New York, The Jewish Reconstructionist Foundation, Inc., 1944), 14 pp.

Jewish Survival and Its Opponents.
Reconstructionist Pamphlet, no. 6 (New York, The Reconstructionist Foundation, Inc., 1944), 16 pp.

La Civilizacion de Israel en la Vida Moderna.
(Buenos Aires, Editorial Israel, 1944), xvi + 286 + 2 pp.
[Translation of *Judaism as a Civilization*, by Rebecca Trabb. Preface to Spanish edition by Mordecai M. Kaplan, pp. xv–xvi.]

La Liberta di essene Ebrei.
(Rome, Circolo Ebraico di Rome, 1944) [In Italian.], 15 pp.

1945

Shall We Retain the Doctrine of Israel as the Chosen People?
The Reconstructionist, vol. XI, no. 1 (Feb. 23, 1945), pp. 20–29.

Reconstructionism—A Method of Living in Two Civilizations.
The Reconstructionist, vol. XI, no. 8 (June 1, 1945), pp. 10–19.

Yidishe Kehile-Lebn in Amerike.
Zukunft, vol. L, no. 6 (June 1945), pp. 369–73.

The Truth about Reconstructionism.
Commentary, vol. I, no. 2 (Dec. 1945), pp. 50–59.

From Strength to Strength.
A Proposal for a University of Judaism (New York, The Jewish Theological Seminary of America, 1945), pp. 1–22.

The Implications of the Herem.
A Challenge to Freedom of Worship; A Statement (New York, The Jewish Reconstructionist Foundation, Inc., 1945), pp. 7–11.

The Jewish Contribution to a World Order.

World Order: Its Intellectual and Cultural Foundations, A Series of Addresses, edited by F. Ernest Johnson. (New York and London, Institute for Religious Studies, distributed by Harper and Brothers, 1945), pp. 137–52.

Sabbath Prayer Book; with a supplement containing prayers, readings, and hymns and with a new translation [edited by Mordecai M. Kaplan and Eugene Kohn].

(New York, The Jewish Reconstructionist Foundation, Inc., 1945), 573 pp.

Seder Tefilot Leshabat 'im Tosefet Tefilot, Amirot Veshirim Ve'im Tirgum Angli Ḥadash.

Added title page: *Sabbath Prayer Book;* with a supplement containing prayers, readings, and hymns and with a new translation [edited by Mordecai M. Kaplan and Eugene Kohn] (New York, The Jewish Reconstructionist Foundation, Inc., 1945), xxx + 573 pp.

1946

The Chosen People Idea: An Anachronism.
The Reconstructionist, vol. XI, no. 17 (Jan. 11, 1946), pp. 13–20.
The Rabbinical Assembly at the Crossroads.
Conservative Judaism, vol. II, no. 3 (April 1946), pp. 1–7.
How to Envisage Jewish Community.
The Reconstructionist,
    vol. XII, no. 6 (May 3, 1946), pp. 9–15;
    vol. XII, no. 7 (May 17, 1946), pp. 17–22.
"Matarat HaḤinukh Hayehudi Be-Amerika", *Yesodot HaḤinukh Hayehudi Be-Amerika, Koveṭz Maamarim Lemalat Sheloshim Veḥamesh Shanim Lebeyt Hamidrash Lamorim Asher al Yad Beyt Hamidrash Lerabanim Shel Amerika.* Ne'erakh Al Yedey Tzvi Sharfstein (New York, Behatzaʿat Beyt Hamidrash Lemorim, 5707) 9–28.
Horaʿat Hatanakh Bizemaneynu.
    ibid., pp. 48–75.
Random Thoughts.
The Reconstructionist,
    vol. XII, no. 11 (Oct. 4, 1946), pp. 21–22;
    vol. XII, no. 12 (Oct. 20, 1946), pp. 20–21;
    vol. XII, no. 13 (Nov. 1, 1946), pp. 19–21;
    vol. XII, no. 14 (Nov. 15, 1946), pp. 16–18;
    vol. XII, no. 15 (Nov. 29, 1946), pp. 19–21;
    vol. XII, no. 16 (Dec. 13, 1946), pp. 18–20;
    vol. XII, no. 17 (Dec. 27, 1946), pp. 24–25.
Comments.
Jewish Frontier, vol. XIII, no. 12 (Dec. 1946), pp. 10–13.
[On Daniel Bell: "A Parable of Alienation," *Jewish Frontier,* Nov. 1946.]

An Exchange of Views on Reconstructionism between Emil Bernard Cohn and Mordecai M Kaplan: Doctor Kaplan's Reply.
   The Reconstructionist, vol. XII, no. 16 (Dec. 13, 1946), pp. 13–15.
A University of Judaism: A Compelling Need.
   Principles behind the proposal for a University where those who wish to serve Jewish life may acquire the necessary knowledge and techniques (New York, United Synagogue of America, 1946), 19 pp.

1947

Random Thoughts.
   The Reconstructionist,
      vol. XII, no. 18 (Jan. 10, 1947), pp. 18–21;
      vol. XII, no. 19 (Jan. 24, 1947), pp. 27–29;
      vol. XII, no. 20 (Feb. 7, 1947), pp. 23–25;
      vol. XIII, no. 1 (Feb. 21, 1947), pp. 18–21;
      vol. XIII, no. 2 (March 7, 1947), pp. 20–22;
      vol. XIII, no. 3 (March 21, 1947), pp. 16–18;
      vol. XIII, no. 4 (April 4, 1947), pp. 21–22;
      vol. XIII, no. 5 (April 18, 1947), pp. 23–24;
      vol. XIII, no. 6 (May 2, 1947), pp. 22–24;
      vol. XIII, no. 7 (May 16, 1947), pp. 23–24;
      vol. XIII, no. 8 (May 30, 1947), p. 24;
      vol. XIII, no. 9 (June 13, 1947), pp. 25–27;
      vol. XIII, no. 10 (June 27, 1947), pp. 32–33;
      vol. XIII, no. 11 (Oct. 3, 1947), pp. 21–22;
      vol. XIII, no. 12 (Oct. 17, 1947), pp. 17–19;
      vol. XIII, no. 13 (Oct. 31, 1947), pp. 22–23;
      vol. XIII, no. 14 (Nov. 11, 1947), pp. 21–22;
      vol. XIII, no. 15 (Nov. 28, 1947), pp. 23–24;
      vol. XIII, no. 16 (Dec. 12, 1947), p. 23.
We Still Think We Are Right: A Reply to a Christian Critic of Reconstructionism.
   The Reconstructionist, vol. XIII, no. 6 (May 2, 1947), pp. 14–19.
Exile or Diaspora, Which?
   The Reconstructionist, vol. XIII, no. 14 (Nov. 14, 1947), pp. 22–23.
   [Review of Yitzhak F. Baer: *Galut*, New York, 1947.]
Democracy and Zionism.
   Foundations of Democracy, a Series of Addresses edited by F. Ernest Johnson (New York and London, Institute for Religious and Social Studies, distributed by Harper and Brothers, 1947), pp. 239–66.
Toward a Philosophy of Cultural Integration.
   Approaches to Group Understanding, Sixth Symposium edited by Lyman Bryson, Louis Finkelstein, and R. M. MacIver (New York, The Conference on Science, Philosophy, and Religion in Their Relation to the

Democratic Way of Life, distributed by Harper and Brothers, 1947), pp. 589–625.

Unity in Diversity in the Conservative Movement.
Toward the clarification and formulation of the philosophy and program of the Conservative Movement (New York, United Synagogue of America, 1947), 18 pp.
[Also appears in *Reconstructionist Judaism* pamphlets, vol. 1.]

1948

The Place of Religion in a Democracy.
The Review of Religion, vol. XII, no. 2 (Jan. 1948), pp. 179–92.
Random Thoughts.
The Reconstructionist,
vol. XIII, no. 18 (Jan. 9, 1948), pp. 22–23;
vol. XIII, no. 19 (Jan. 23, 1948), p. 18;
vol. XIII, no. 20 (Feb. 26, 1948), pp. 25–26;
vol. XIV, no. 1 (Feb. 20, 1948), pp. 19–21;
vol. XIV, no. 2 (March 5, 1948), pp. 22–23;
vol. XIV, no. 3 (March 19, 1948), pp. 21–23;
vol. XIV, no. 4 (April 2, 1948), pp. 22–24;
vol. XIV, no. 5 (April 16, 1948), pp. 25–26;
vol. XIV, no. 6 (April 29, 1948), p. 30;
vol. XIV, no. 7 (May 14, 1948), pp. 28–30;
vol. XIV, no. 8 (May 28, 1948), pp. 31–32;
vol. XIV, no. 9 (June 11, 1948), pp. 30–32;
vol. XIV, no. 10 (June 25, 1948), pp. 24–25;
vol. XIV, no. 11 (Oct. 15, 1948), pp. 29–30;
vol. XIV, no. 12 (Oct. 22, 1948), p. 24;
vol. XIV, no. 13 (Oct. 29, 1948), p. 23;
vol. XIV, no. 14 (Nov. 12, 1948), pp. 21–22;
vol. XIV, no. 15 (Nov. 26, 1948), p. 32;
vol. XIV, no. 16 (Dec. 10, 1948), pp. 22–24;
vol. XIV, no. 17 (Dec. 24, 1948), pp. 30–31.
Address in Symposium: The Future of Torah in America.
Symposia and Addresses of the Inauguration of Dr. Nelson Glueck as the Fourth President of the Hebrew Union College, March 12–15, 1948, at Cincinnati, Ohio, pp. 15–31.
When Will American Judaism Be Born?
The Reconstructionist, vol. XIV, no. 15 (Nov. 26, 1948), pp. 11–19.
The Future of the American Jew.
(New York, The Macmillan Company, 1948), xx + 571 pp.
[Reprinted in 1967 and 1981 (New York, The Reconstructionist Press).]
High Holiday Prayer Book; with supplementary prayers and readings and with a new English translation [edited by Mordecai M. Kaplan, Eugene

Kohn, and Ira Eisenstein] (2 vols., New York, The Jewish Reconstruc-
tionist Foundation, Inc., 1948); vol. I, Prayers for Rosh Hashanah, xii + 360
pp.; vol. II, Prayers for Yom Kippur, xv + 597 pp.
Hebrew title page: Maḥzor Leyamim Nora-im 'im Tefilot Ve-amirot No-
safot Ve-'im Tirgum angli Ḥadash.
Kerakh A: Seder Tefilot Lerosh Hashanah.
Kerakh B: Seder Tefilot Leyom Kipur.
Reconstructionism.
Religion in the Twentieth Century, edited by Vergilius Ferm (New York,
Philosophical Library, 1948), pp. 433–45.

1949

Random Thoughts.
The Reconstructionist,
vol. XIV, no. 18 (Jan. 7, 1949), pp. 22–23;
vol. XIV, no. 19 (Jan. 21, 1949), p. 22;
vol. XIV, no. 20 (Feb. 4, 1949), pp. 25–26;
vol. XV, no. 1 (Feb. 18, 1949), pp. 30–31;
vol. XV, no. 2 (March 4, 1949), p. 30;
vol. XV, no. 3 (March 18, 1949), pp. 21–22;
vol. XV, no. 4 (April 1, 1949), pp. 29–30;
vol. XV, no. 5 (April 17, 1949), pp. 29–30;
vol. XV, no. 6 (April 29, 1949), p. 23;
vol. XV, no. 7 (May 13, 1949), pp. 29–30;
vol. XV, no. 8 (May 27, 1949), pp. 28–30;
vol. XV, no. 9 (June 10, 1949), pp. 22–23;
vol. XV, no. 10 (June 24, 1949), pp. 31–32;
vol. XV, no. 11 (Oct. 7, 1949), pp. 20–21;
vol. XV, no. 12 (Oct. 21, 1949), pp. 22–24;
vol. XV, no. 13 (Nov. 4, 1949), pp. 22–23;
vol. XV, no. 14 (Nov. 18, 1949), pp. 23–24;
vol. XV, no. 15 (Dec. 2, 1949), pp. 22–24;
vol. XV, no. 16 (Dec. 16, 1949), pp. 21–22;
vol. XV, no. 17 (Dec. 30, 1949), pp. 23–24.
The First Step toward Organic Jewish Community.
The Reconstructionist, vol. XV, no. 1 (Feb. 18, 1949), pp. 18–24.
The Impact of Dr. Benderly's Personality.
Jewish Education, vol. XX, no. 3 (Summer 1949), pp. 16–20, 26.
The State of Israel and the Status of the Jew.
The Reconstructionist, vol. XV, no. 10 (June 24, 1949), pp. 10–16.
A Program for Labor Zionists.
Jewish Frontier, vol. XVI, no. 7 (July 1949), pp. 12–16.
[Reprinted in *Jewish Frontiers*, vol. LI, no. 1 (Jan. 1984), pp. 13–16.]

Some Questions Raised by "The Future of the American Jew," A Dialogue
   by Correspondence between Joseph R. Narot and Mordecai M. Kaplan.
   The Reconstructionist,
      vol. XV, no. 14 (Nov. 18, 1949), pp. 14–20;
      vol. XV, no. 15 (Dec. 2, 1949), pp. 17–22.
The Next Step in the Reform Movement.
   Hebrew Union College Quarterly, vol. XXXVII, no. 4 (Dec. 1949),
   pp. 3–6.
The Contribution of Judaism to World Ethics.
   The Jews—Their History, Culture, and Religion, edited by Louis
   Finkelstein (2 vols., New York, Harper & Brothers, 1949), vol. I, pp. 680–
   712.

1950

Random Thoughts.
   The Reconstructionist,
      vol. XV, no. 18 (Jan. 13, 1950), pp. 23–24;
      vol. XV, no. 19 (Jan. 27, 1950), pp. 22–24;
      vol. XV, no. 20 (Feb. 10, 1950), pp. 24–25;
      vol. XVI, no. 1 (Feb. 24, 1950), p. 30;
      vol. XVI, no. 2 (March 10, 1950), pp. 29–30;
      vol. XVI, no. 3 (March 24, 1950), pp. 28–29;
      vol. XVI, no. 4 (April 7, 1950), pp. 27–28;
      vol. XVI, no. 5 (April 21, 1950), pp. 31–32;
      vol. XVI, no. 6 (May 5, 1950), pp. 31–32;
      vol. XVI, no. 7 (May 19, 1950), pp. 31–32;
      vol. XVI, no. 8 (June 2, 1950), pp. 31–32;
      vol. XVI, no. 9 (June 16, 1950), pp. 31–32;
      vol. XVI, no. 10 (June 30, 1950), pp. 29–31.
Milton Steinberg's Contribution to Reconstructionism.
   The Reconstructionist, vol. XVI, no. 7 (May 19, 1950), pp. 9–16.
The Torah as Our Life and the Length of Our Days.
   The Reconstructionist, vol. XVI. no. 7 (May 19, 1950); pp. 9–16.
      vol. XVI, no. 11 (Oct. 6, 1950), pp. 10–15.
Know How to Answer.
   The Reconstructionist,
      vol. XVI, no. 11 (Oct. 6, 1950), pp. 29–31;
      vol. XVI, no. 12 (Oct. 20, 1950), pp. 30–31;
      vol. XVI, no. 13 (Nov. 3, 1950), pp. 31–32;
      vol. XVI, no. 14 (Nov. 17, 1950), pp. 27–30;
      vol. XVI, no. 15 (Dec. 1, 1950), pp. 27–30;
      vol. XVI, no. 16 (Dec. 15, 1950), pp. 29–31;
      vol. XVI, no. 17 (Dec. 29, 1950), pp. 29–31.
Introduction.

The Birth of the Bible, A New Approach by Immanuel Lewy (New York, Bloch Publishing Company, 1950), pp. 5–7.

The Need for Normative Unity in Higher Education.

Goals for American Education—Ninth Symposium edited by Lyman Bryson, Louis Finkelstein, and R. M. MacIver (New York, published by the Conference on Science, Philosophy, and Religion in their relation to the Democratic Way of Life. Distributed by Harper & Brothers, 1950), pp. 293–339.

Toward the Formulation of Guiding Principles for the Conservative Movement.

(New York, The Rabbinical Assembly of America, 1950), 24 pp.

[Published as a supplement to *Conservative Judaism,* vol. VI, no. 4 (May 1950).]

1951

Israel, Diaspora, and National Survival: Unity.

Zukunft, vol. 56 (Jan. 1951), pp. 8–12.

[Symposium in Yiddish.]

Know How to Answer.

The Reconstructionist,

    vol. XVI, no. 18 (Jan. 12, 1951), pp. 29–31;
    vol. XVI, no. 19 (Jan. 26, 1951), pp. 30–31;
    vol. XVI, no. 20 (Feb. 9, 1951), pp. 21–24;
    vol. XVII, no. 1 (Feb. 23, 1951), pp. 27–31;
    vol. XVII, no. 2 (March 9, 1951), pp. 26–29;
    vol. XVII, no. 3 (March 23, 1951), pp. 30–31;
    vol. XVII, no. 4 (April 6, 1951), pp. 29–32;
    vol. XVII, no. 5 (April 20, 1951), pp. 29–31;
    vol. XVII, no. 6 (May 4, 1951), pp. 27–30;
    vol. XVII, no. 7 (May 18, 1951), pp. 28–30;
    vol. XVII, no. 8 (June 1, 1951), pp. 27–29;
    vol. XVII, no. 9 (June 15, 1951), pp. 31–32;
    vol. XVII, no. 10 (June 29, 1951), pp. 29–32;
    vol. XVII, no. 11 (Oct. 5, 1951), pp. 27–29;
    vol. XVII, no. 12 (Oct. 19, 1951), pp. 30–31;
    vol. XVII, no. 13 (Nov. 2, 1951), pp. 29–31;
    vol. XVII, no. 14 (Nov. 16, 1951), pp. 30–32;
    vol. XVII, no. 15 (Nov. 30, 1951), pp. 28–31;
    vol. XVII, no. 16 (Dec. 14, 1951), pp. 29–31;
    vol. XVII, no. 17 (Dec. 28, 1951), pp. 29–31.

The Role of Modern Scholarship in the Evolution of Judaism.

The Reconstructionist, vol. XVII, no. 13 (Nov. 2, 1951), pp. 7–13.

The Faith of America; prayers, readings and songs for the celebration of

American holidays, compiled by Mordecai M. Kaplan, J. Paul Williams, and Eugene Kohn.
  (New York, H. Schumann, 1951), XXX + 328 pp.
A Heart of Wisdom.
  The Reconstructionist, vol. XVII, no. 6 (May 4, 1951), pp. 10–17.
Know How to Answer: A Guide to Reconstructionism.
  (New York, The Jewish Reconstructionist Foundation, Inc., 1951), 135 pp.

1952

Know How to Answer.
  The Reconstructionist,
       vol. XVII, no. 18 (Jan. 11, 1952), pp. 30–32;
       vol. XVII, no. 19 (Jan. 25, 1952), pp. 28–32;
       vol. XVII, no. 20 (Feb. 8, 1952), pp. 22–23;
       vol. XVIII, no. 1 (Feb. 22, 1952), pp. 29–31;
       vol. XVIII, no. 2 (March 7, 1952), pp. 31–32;
       vol. XVIII, no. 3 (March 21, 1952), pp. 30–31;
       vol. XVIII, no. 4 (April 7, 1952), pp. 30–31;
       vol. XVIII, no. 5 (April 18, 1952), pp. 31–32;
       vol. XVIII, no. 6 (May 2, 1952), pp. 30–32;
       vol. XVIII, no. 7 (May 16, 1952), pp. 29–32;
       vol. XVIII, no. 8 (May 29, 1952), pp. 29–30;
       vol. XVIII, no. 10 (June 27, 1952), p. 31;
       vol. XVIII, no. 12 (Oct. 17, 1952), pp. 30–31;
       vol. XVIII, no. 14 (Nov. 14, 1952), pp. 31–21;
       vol. XVIII, no. 16 (Dec. 12, 1952), pp. 30–31;
       vol. XVIII, no. 17 (Dec. 26, 1952), pp. 31–32.
Martin Buber: Theologian, Philosopher and Prophet.
  The Reconstructionist, vol. XVIII, no. 6 (May 2, 1952), pp. 7–10.
The Need for Diaspora Zionism.
  The Reconstructionist, vol. XVIII, no. 9 (June 13, 1952), pp. 22–27.
Martin Buber's *Israel and Palestine.*
  The Reconstructionist, vol. XVIII, no. 14 (Nov. 14, 1952), pp. 28–29.
How to Live Creatively as A Jew.
  Moments of Personal Discovery, edited by R. M. MacIver (New York and London, Published by the Institute for Religious and Social Studies, distributed by Harper and Brothers, 1952), pp. 93–104.
The Way I Have Come.
  Mordecai M. Kaplan: An Evaluation, edited by Ira Eisenstein and Eugene Kohn (New York, Jewish Reconstructionist Foundation, 1952), pp. 283–321.

1953

Know How to Answer.
> *The Reconstructionist,*
>> vol. XVIII, no. 18 (Jan. 9, 1953), pp. 31–32;
>> vol. XVIII, no. 19 (Jan. 23, 1953), pp. 30–33;
>> vol. XVIII, no. 20 (Feb. 6, 1953), pp. 25–26;
>> vol. XIX, no. 1 (Feb. 20, 1953), pp. 28–30;
>> vol. XIX, no. 2 (March 6, 1953), pp. 27–29;
>> vol. XIX, no. 3 (March 20, 1953), pp. 28–30;
>> vol. XIX, no. 4 (April 3, 1953), pp. 28–30;
>> vol. XIX, no. 5 (April 17, 1953), pp. 27–30;
>> vol. XIX, no. 11 (Oct. 9, 1953), pp. 30–31;
>> vol. XIX, no. 12 (Oct. 23, 1953), p. 32;
>> vol. XIX, no. 13 (Nov. 6, 1953), pp. 29–32;
>> vol. XIX, no. 14 (Nov. 20, 1953), pp. 30–31;
>> vol. XIX, no. 15 (Dec. 4, 1953), pp. 28–30;
>> vol. XIX, no. 16 (Dec. 18, 1953), pp. 30–32.

Reviews of *The Existentialist Revolt* by Kurt F. Reinhardt and *Tragedy Is Not Enough* by Karl Jaspers.
> *The Reconstructionist,* vol. XIX, no. 8 (May 29, 1953), pp. 21–23.

What Is Our Human Destiny?
> *Judaism,* vol. 2, no. 3 (July 1953), pp. 195–203.

Has American Jewry Come of Age?
> *The Reconstructionist,* vol. XIX, no. 11 (Oct. 9, 1953), pp. 10–16.

The Metamorphosis of Man.
> *Judaism,* vol. 2, no. 4 (Oct. 1953), pp. 307–15.

1954

Know How to Answer.
> *The Reconstructionist,*
>> vol. XIX, no. 17 (Jan. 1, 1954), pp. 30–32;
>> vol. XIX, no. 18 (Jan. 15, 1954), pp. 30–31;
>> vol. XIX, no. 19 (Jan. 29, 1954), pp. 29–30;
>> vol. XX, no. 1 (Feb. 26, 1954), pp. 29–31;
>> vol. XX, no. 3 (March 26, 1954), pp. 30–32;
>> vol. XX, no. 4 (April 9, 1954), pp. 30–31;
>> vol. XX, no. 8 (June 4, 1954), pp. 28–30;
>> vol. XX, no. 11 (Oct. 1, 1954), pp. 30–32;
>> vol. XX, no. 14 (Nov. 12, 1954), pp. 29–30;
>> vol. XX, no. 16 (Dec. 10, 1954), pp. 29–31;
>> vol. XX, no. 17 (Dec. 24, 1954), pp. 30–31.

"'Interpretations.''
> *The Reconstructionist,*

vol. XX, no. 5 (April 23, 1954), pp. 30–32;
    vol. XX, no. 6 (May 7, 1954), pp. 27–29.
On Receiving a World Brotherhood Award.
    The Reconstructionist, vol. XX, no. 7 (May 21, 1954), pp. 18–19.
Needed: A New Zionism.
    The Reconstructionist, vol. XX, no. 9 (June 18, 1954), pp. 10–17.
The Reconstructionist Viewpoint.
    The Reconstructionist, vol. XX, no. 10 (July 2, 1954), pp. 27–29.
The Meaning of the Tercentenary for Diaspora Judaism.
    The Reconstructionist, vol. XX, no. 12 (Oct. 15, 1954), pp. 10–18.
    [Reprinted in *American Jewry: The Tercentenary and After, 1694–1954*,
    edited by Eugene Kohn (New York, The Reconstruction Press, 1955).]
Can Reconstructionism Guide Us? An Open Letter and Reply.
    The Reconstructionist, vol. XX, no. 13 (Oct. 29, 1954), pp. 22–27.
    [with Max Weiner.]

                                1955

Know How to Answer.
    The Reconstructionist,
        vol. XX, no. 18 (Jan. 7, 1955), pp. 29–30;
        vol. XX, no. 19 (Jan. 21, 1955), pp. 28–30;
        vol. XX, no. 20 (Feb. 4, 1955), p. 26;
        vol. XXI, no. 1 (Feb. 18, 1955), pp. 62–63;
        vol. XXI, no. 3 (March 18, 1955), pp. 29–30;
        vol. XXI, no. 4 (April 1, 1955), pp. 29–31;
        vol. XXI, no. 5 (April 15, 1955), pp. 29–30;
        vol. XXI, no. 6 (April 29, 1955), pp. 29–31;
        vol. XXI, no. 9 (June 10, 1955), pp. 30–31;
        vol. XXI, no. 14 (Nov. 18, 1955), p. 32;
        vol. XXI, no. 15 (Dec. 2, 1955), pp. 30–31;
        vol. XXI, no. 16 (Dec. 16, 1955), pp. 30–31.
Review of *The Seekers* by William Alva Gifford.
    The Reconstructionist, vol. XX, no. 18 (Jan. 7, 1955), pp. 28–29.
Does Reconstructionism Offer an Adequate God Idea?—An Open Letter
    and a Reply.
    The Reconstructionist, vol. XXI, no. 1 (Feb. 18, 1955), pp. 24–31.
    [With Myron M. Fenster.]
The Advantage of Living in Two Civilizations.
    The Reconstructionist, vol. XXI, no. 2 (March 4, 1955), pp. 17–20.
Principles of Reconstructionism.
    The Reconstructionist, vol. XXI, no. 3 (March 18, 1955), p. 22.
Should We Drop Tish'a B'Ab?
    The National Jewish Monthly, vol. 69, no. 11 (July-Aug. 1955), pp. 2–3.

Anti-Maimunism in Modern Dress—A Reply to Baruch Kurzweil's Attack on Ahad Ha-Am.
  Judaism, vol. 4, no. 4 (Fall 1955), pp. 303–12.
Toward a University of Judaism.
  The Reconstructionist, vol. XXI, no. 11 (Oct. 7, 1955), pp. 25–29.
The Christian Dilemma with Regard to the Jews.
  The Reconstructionist,
      vol. XXI, no. 12 (Oct. 21, 1955), pp. 15–19;
      vol. XXI, no. 13 (Nov. 4, 1955), pp. 19–24.
Torah in Our Day.
  The Reconstructionist, vol. XXI, no. 17 (Dec. 30, 1955), pp. 28–29.
The Future of Religious Symbolism—A Jewish View.
  Religious Symbolism, edited by F. Ernest Johnson (New York, Institute for Religious and Social Studies, Jewish Theological Seminary, 1955).
Has American Judaism Come of Age?
  American Jewry: The Tercentenary and After, 1694–1954, edited by Eugene Kohn (New York, The Reconstructionist Press, 1955).
A New Zionism.
  (New York, Theodor Herzl Foundation, 1955), 172 pp.

1956

Can Judaism Survive without Naturalism?
  Jewish Education, vol. XXVII, no. 2 (Winter 1956–57), pp. 10–23.
Torah in Our Day.
  The Reconstructionist,
      vol. XXI, no. 18 (Jan. 13, 1956), pp. 30–32;
      vol. XXI, no. 19 (Jan. 27, 1956), pp. 29–31;
      vol. XXII, no. 1 (Feb. 24, 1956), pp. 27–29;
      vol. XXII, no. 2 (March 9, 1956), pp. 29–31;
      vol. XXII, no. 3 (March 23, 1956), pp. 30–32;
      vol. XXII, no. 6 (May 4, 1956), pp. 28–30.
Reviews of *Happiness through Creative Living* by Preston Bradley and *The Dynamics of Casework and Counseling* by Herbert H. Aptekar.
  The Reconstructionist, vol. XXI, no. 19 (Jan. 27, 1956), pp. 24–25.
An Appeal to the World Zionist Congress.
  The Reconstructionist, vol. XXII, no. 4 (April 6, 1956), pp. 8–12.
The Need for Reconstructionism.
  The Reconstructionist, vol. XXII, no. 7 (May 18, 1956), pp. 15–19.
The Meaning of the Current Religious Upsurge.
  The Reconstructionist, vol. XXII, no. 9 (June 15, 1956), pp. 12–16.
Israel S. Chipkin—a Eulogy.
  Jewish Education, vol. 27, no. 1 (Fall 1956), pp. 5–6.
The Labor Movement and Jewish Secularism.
  Jewish Frontier, vol. XXIII, no. 9 (Oct. 1956), pp. 9–12.

The Religious Use of "Whitemail."
   The Reconstructionist, vol. XXII, no. 13 (Nov. 2, 1956), pp. 17–20.
The Covenant Proposal and Its Implementation.
   The Reconstructionist, vol. XXII, no. 16 (Dec. 14, 1956), pp. 7–13.
Know How to Answer.
   The Reconstructionist, vol. XXII, no. 17 (Dec. 28, 1956), pp. 31–32.
Foreword.
   Judaism under Freedom, edited by Ira Eisenstein (New York, The Reconstructionist Press, 1956).
Questions Jews Ask: Reconstructionist Answers.
   (New York, The Reconstructionist Press, 1956).
   [Revised in 1966.]

1957

Know How to Answer.
   The Reconstructionist,
      vol. XXII, no. 18 (Jan. 11, 1957), pp. 29–31;
      vol. XXIII, no. 1 (Feb. 22, 1957), pp. 29–31;
      vol. XXIII, no. 2 (March 8, 1957), pp. 28–29;
      vol. XXIII, no. 4 (April 5, 1957), pp. 29–32;
      vol. XXIII, no. 5 (April 19, 1957), pp. 28–30;
      vol. XXIII, no. 9 (June 14, 1957), pp. 29–31;
      vol. XXIII, no. 17 (Dec. 27, 1957), p. 24.
The Covenant Proposal Reviewed.
   The Reconstructionist, vol. XXIII, no. 3 (March 22, 1957), pp. 12–18.
Hayim Greenberg: Realist, Humanist, Idealist.
   Jewish Frontier, vol. XXIV, no. 3 (March 1957), pp. 5–7.
Can Jewish Religion Survive without Supernaturalism?
   The Reconstructionist,
      vol. XXIII, no. 6 (May 3, 1957), pp. 15–20;
      vol. XXIII, no. 7 (May 17, 1957), pp. 18–23.
Eulogy—Leo Lazarus Honor.
   Jewish Education, vol. XXVIII, no. 1 (Fall 1957), pp. 5–8.
A Turning Point in Zionism.
   The Reconstructionist,
      vol. XXIII, no. 11 (Oct. 4, 1957), pp. 9–13;
      vol. XXIII, no. 12 (Oct. 20, 1957), pp. 13–19.
The Cornerstone of Our Future Civilization.
   The Reconstructionist, vol. XXIII, no. 14 (Nov. 15, 1957), p. 22.
If Theology Were to Be Our Metier . . .
   Conservative Judaism, vol. 11 (Winter 1957), pp. 20–25.
The Jewish People in Search of an Ideology.
   The Reconstructionist, vol. XXIII, no. 16 (Dec. 13, 1957), pp. 7–13.
Basic Values in Jewish Religion.

(New York, The Reconstructionist Press, 1957.)
[Reprinted from *The Future of the American Jew.*] [See 1948]
Judaism as a Modern Religious Civilization.
Two Generations in Perspective, edited by Harry Schneiderman (New York, Monde Publishers, 1957).
[Reprinted as *Reconstructionist Pamphlet no. 4* (New York, The Reconstructionist Press).]

1958

Know How to Answer.
The Reconstructionist,
vol. XXIII, no. 19 (Jan. 24, 1958), pp. 30–31;
vol. XXIV, no. 2 (March 7, 1958), pp. 31–32;
vol. XXIV, no. 4 (April 4, 1958), p. 30;
vol. XXIV, no. 5 (April 18, 1958), p. 29;
vol. XXIV, no. 6 (May 2, 1958), p. 30.
Reconstructionism as a Method for Jewish Living.
The Reconstructionist, vol. XXIII, no. 20 (Feb. 7, 1958), pp. 7–12.
Random Thoughts.
The Reconstructionist, vol. XXIV, no. 1 (Feb. 21, 1958), p. 30.
America and the World Council of Synagogues.
The Torch, vol. XVII, no. 2 (Spring 1958), pp. 26–27.
What Should Be Zionism's Main Task?
The Reconstructionist, vol. XXIV, no. 3 (March 21, 1958), pp. 18–19.
A Response to Eugene B. Borowitz, "The Idea of God."
The Reconstructionist, vol. XXIV, no. 7 (May 16, 1958), pp. 18–19.
The Revelation of God in the Human Spirit.
The Reconstructionist,
vol. XXIV, no. 8 (May 30, 1958), pp. 7–12;
vol. XXIV, no. 9 (June 13, 1958), pp. 12–15.
Religion and Nationalism.
The Reconstructionist, vol. XXIV, no. 12 (Oct. 17, 1958), pp. 27–28.
Why a Greater Zionism?
The Reconstructionist, vol. XXIV, no. 15 (Nov. 28, 1958), pp. 6–12.
Festival Prayer Book; with supplementary prayers and readings and with a new English translation [edited by Mordecai M. Kaplan, Jack J. Cohen, and Ludwig Nadelmann] (New York, The Jewish Reconstructionist Foundation, Inc., 1958), xviii + 547 pp.
Judaism without Supernaturalism: The Only Alternative to Orthodoxy and Secularism.
(New York, The Reconstructionist Press, 1958), 254 pp.
Toward the Formulation of Guiding Principles for the Conservative Movement and Unity and Diversity in the Conservative Movement.

Tradition and Change (New York, The Burning Bush Press, 1958), pp. 289–312, 211–28.

1959

The Greater Zionism. A reply to C. Bezalel Sherman.
  The Reconstructionist, vol. XXIV, no. 18 (Jan. 9, 1959), pp. 25–29.
Ideology and Jewish Existence.
  Forum, vol. IV (Spring 1959), pp. 102–5.
The Next Step in Zionism.
  Forum, vol. IV (Spring 1959), pp. 29–40.
The Third Approach to Zionism.
  Forum, vol. IV (Spring 1959), pp. 319–21.
On Jewish Survival.
  The Reconstructionist, vol. XXV, no. 5 (April 17, 1959), p. 32.
Religious Imperatives of Jewish Peoplehood.
  The Reconstructionist, vol. XXV, no. 9 (June 15, 1959), pp. 3–9.
Questions Jews Ask.
  The Reconstructionist,
      vol. XXV, no. 11 (Oct. 2, 1959), pp. 30–31;
      vol. XXV, no. 12 (Oct. 16, 1959), pp. 29–30;
      vol. XXV, no. 17 (Dec. 25, 1959), pp. 30–31.
Rabbis and Teachers as Guides to the Perplexed.
  The Reconstructionist, vol. XXV, no. 11 (Oct. 2, 1959), pp. 8–14.
Random Thoughts.
  The Reconstructionist,
      vol. XXV, no. 11 (Oct. 2, 1959), p. 7;
      vol. XXV, no. 13 (Oct. 30, 1959), p. 6;
      vol. XXV, no. 15 (Nov. 27, 1959), p. 7.
Know How to Answer.
  The Reconstructionist, vol. XXV, no. 14 (Nov. 13, 1959), pp. 29–31.
A Founding Father Recounts.
  Alumni Association Bulletin (New York, Jewish Theological Seminary) (Dec. 1959), pp. 5–7.
Zionism and Jewish Religion.
  The Reconstructionist, vol. XXV, no. 16 (Dec. 11, 1959), pp. 8–15.
Zionism and Jewish Religion.
  The Reconstructionist, vol. XXV, no. 16 (Dec. 11, 1959), pp. 8–15. *A New Zionism* 2nd Enlarged Edition (New York: The Herzl Press and the Jewish Reconstructionist Press, 1959), 190 pp.

1960

Questions Jews Ask.
  The Reconstructionist,

vol. XXV, no. 18 (Jan. 8, 1960), pp. 25–27;
vol. XXVI, no. 4 (April 1, 1960), pp. 29–30;
vol. XXVI, no. 6 (April 29, 1960), p. 27;
vol. XXVI, no. 7 (May 13, 1960), p. 30;
vol. XXVI, no. 9 (June 10, 1960), pp. 31–32.
Religion in a New Key.
   The Reconstructionist, vol. XXVI, no. 1 (Feb. 19, 1960), pp. 15–18.
"Jewish Chosenness" by Trude Weiss-Rosmarin. A Reconstructionist Reply, from the Writings of Mordecai M. Kaplan.
   The Reconstructionist, vol. XXVI, no. 5 (April 15, 1960), pp. 17–19.
   [Reprinted from *The Future of the American Jew*.] [See 1948]
The Task of the Modern Rabbi.
   The Reconstructionist, vol. XXVI, no. 5 (April 15, 1960), pp. 27–31.
Where Reform and Reconstructionism Part Company.
   Journal of the Central Conference of American Rabbis (April 1960), pp. 3–10.
Reform and Reconstructionism.
   The Reconstructionist, vol. XXVI, no. 8 (May 27, 1960), pp. 8–14.
Should the United Synagogue of America Join the World Zionist Organization? "Yes," says Mordecai M. Kaplan.
   The Torch, vol. XIX, no. 1 (Winter 1960), pp. 7–13.
The Paradox of Israeli Jewry.
   The Reconstructionist, vol. XXVI, no. 16 (Dec. 16, 1960), pp. 7–11.
The Greater Judaism in the Making: A Study of the Modern Evolution of Judaism.
   (New York, The Reconstructionist Press, 1960), 565 pp.

1961

The Way I Have Come.
   Jewish Spectator, vol. XXVI, no. 6 (June 1961), pp. 9–14.
The Sovereignty of the Moral Law.
   The Reconstructionist, vol. XXVII, no. 11 (Oct. 6, 1961), pp. 6–9.
Escaping Judaism: Sin or Neurosis?
   The Reconstructionist, vol. XXVII, no. 12 (Oct. 20, 1961), pp. 6–12.

1962

Principles of Reconstructionism.
   The Reconstructionist, vol. XXVII, no. 18 (Jan. 12, 1962), p. 32.
The Reconstitution of the Jewish People.
   The Reconstructionist, vol. XXVII, no. 19 (Jan. 26, 1962), pp. 5–14.
Our Religious Vocation.
   The Reconstructionist, vol. XXVII, no. 20 (Feb. 9, 1962), pp. 5–13.
Why the Prophets Have Failed.

Jewish Frontier, vol. XXIX, no. 2 (March 1962), pp. 24–28.
Aims of Reconstructionism.
   The Reconstructionist, vol. XXVIII, no. 9 (June 15, 1962), pp. 23–26.
The Problem of Jewish Education.
   The Reconstructionist, vol. XXVIII, no. 11 (Oct. 5, 1962), pp. 7–16.
The Two Aspects of Religion.
   The Reconstructionist, vol. XVIII, no. 16 (Dec. 14, 1962), pp. 6–13.
The Meaning of God in Modern Jewish Religion.
   (New York, The Reconstructionist Press, 1962).
   [Reprinted in 1975.]

1963

Naturalism, Morality, and Religion.
   The Reconstructionist, vol. XXIX, no. 1 (Feb. 22, 1963), pp. 6–11.
The Unsolved Problem of Evil.
   The Reconstructionist,
      vol. XXIX, no. 7 (May 17, 1963), pp. 6–11;
      vol. XXIX, no. 8 (May 31, 1963), pp. 11–16.
What Is Jewish Education?
   Jewish Information, vol. 4 (Fall 1963), p. 54.
Can Zionism Reconstitute the Jewish People?
   The Reconstructionist, vol. XXIX, no. 11 (Oct. 4, 1963), pp. 7–15.
Wage Peace or . . .
   Jewish Spectator, vol XXVII, no. 8 (Oct. 1963), pp. 9–13.
   [Reprinted from *Proceedings of the Rabbinical Assembly, 1963*, edited by
   J. Harlow (New York, Rabbinical Assembly, 1963), pp. 47–56.]
Applied Research in Contemporary Judaism.
   The Reconstructionist, vol. XXIX, no. 14 (Nov. 15, 1963), pp. 6–11.
*An Agenda for American Jews: A Symposium with Mordecai M. Kaplan
   and Moshe Sharett.*
   Current Jewish Affairs Pamphlet no. 1. (New York, Farband-Labor Zionist
   Order, 1963), 23 pp.
The Daily Prayer Book.
   (New York, Reconstructionist Foundation, 1963).
   [with Jack Cohen, Ira Eisenstein, Eugene Kohn, and Ludwig
   Nadelmann.]
Higher Jewish Education and the Furture of the American Jew.
   Los Angeles, University of Judaism Press, 1963).

1964

The Supremacy of the Torah.
   The Reconstructionist, vol. XXX, no. 7 (May 15, 1964), pp. 7–16.
More Questions Jews Ask.

The Reconstructionist, vol. XXX, no. 9 (June 12, 1964), pp. 30–31.
Jewish Communal Services and the Jewish Future.
   Journal of Jewish Communal Services, vol. XLI, no. 1 (Fall 1964), pp. 5–15.
When Is a Religion Authentic?
   The Reconstructionist,
      vol. XXX, no. 11 (Oct. 2, 1964), pp. 9–18;
      vol. XXX, no. 12 (Oct. 16, 1964), pp. 20–26.
Intermarriage from a Religio-Ethnic Perspective.
   Proceedings of a Conference Sponsored by Commission on Synagogue Relations, edited by Jack J. Zurofsky (New York, Federation of Jewish Philanthropies of New York, 1964), pp. 1–9, 25.
The Purpose and Meaning of Jewish Existence: A People in the Image of God.
   (Philadelphia, Jewish Publication Society of America, 1964), 326 pp.

1965

Lessons of Catholic Ecumenism.
   Jewish Spectator, vol. XXX, no. 1 (Jan. 1965), pp. 8–10.
Reconstructionism Is Ecumenical.
   Jewish Spectator, vol. XXX, no. 2 (Feb. 1965), pp. 12–14.
A God to Match the Universe.
   The Reconstructionist, vol. XXXI, no. 3 (March 19, 1965), pp. 22–27.
Twenty-five Years Ago: "On Agencies and Jewish Values."
   Journal of Jewish Communal Service, vol. 42 (Fall 1965), p. 109.
   [Extract.]
The Sovereignty of God.
   The Reconstructionist, vol. XXXI, no. 11 (Oct. 1, 1965), pp. 7–13.
Yom Kippur.
   The Reconstructionist, vol. XXXI, no. 11 (Oct. 1, 1965), p. 32.
   [Reprinted from *The Purpose and Meaning of Jewish Existence*.] [See 1964]
The Lulav.
   The Reconstructionist, vol. XXXI, no. 12 (Oct. 15, 1965), pp. 31–32.
   [Reprinted from *The Meaning of God in Modern Jewish Religion* (see 1937), pp. 209–10.
Response.
   Jewish Identity, edited by B. Litvin (New York, Feldheim, 1965), pp. 232–35.
Sabbath Prayers.
   (New York, The Reconstructionist Press, 1965), 573 pp.
   [With Eugene Kohn.]

1966

On Teaching the Bible.
  The Reconstructionist, vol. XXXI, no. 18 (Jan. 7, 1966), p. 32.
  [Reprinted from *The Future of the American Jew*.] [See 1948]
The Decalogue in Our Day.
  The Reconstructionist, vol. XXXII, no. 1 (Feb. 18, 1966), pp. 7–11.
Toward Religious Unity: A Symposium.
  Judaism, vol. 15, no. 2 (Spring 1966), pp. 148–63.
What Psychology Can Learn from Religion.
  The Reconstructionist, vol. XXXII, no. 6 (April 29, 1966), pp. 7–11.
Shavuot.
  The Reconstructionist, vol. XXXII, no. 7 (May 13, 1966), p. 32.
  [Reprinted from *The Meaning of God in Modern Jewish Religion*.] [See 1937]
What Religion Can Learn from Psychology.
  The Reconstructionist, vol. XXXII, no. 7 (May 13, 1966), pp. 7–10.
The State of Jewish Belief: A Symposium.
  Commentary, vol. 42, no. 2 (Aug. 1966), pp. 108–10.
Reconstructionism in Brief.
  Jewish Spectator, vol. XXXI, no. 7 (Sept. 1966), pp. 10–13.
Interview with Editorial Board.
  The Reconstructionist, vol. XXXII, no. 11 (Oct. 14, 1966), pp. 15–22.
The Human Person.
  The Reconstructionist, vol. XXXII, no. 13 (Nov. 11, 1966), pp. 7–13.
The Jewish Artist.
  The Reconstructionist, vol. XXXII, no. 16 (Dec. 23, 1966), p. 31.
  [Reprinted from *The Future of the American Jew*.] [See 1948]
No So Random Thoughts.
  Jewish Spectator, vol. 31 (Dec. 1966), p. 30.
  [Excerpt.]
The Aims of Reconstructionism.
  Reconstructionist Pamphlet Series (New York, The Reconstructionist Press, 1966), 12 pp.
Answer.
  The Condition of Jewish Belief: A Symposium Compiled by the Editors of Commentary Magazine (New York, Macmillan, 1966), pp. 117–23.
Between Two Worlds.
  Varieties of Jewish Belief, edited by Ira Eisenstein (New York, The Reconstructionist Press, 1966), pp. 133–46.
Not So Random Thoughts.
  (New York, The Reconstructionist Press, 1966), 296 pp.
Questions Jews Ask: Reconstructionist Answers.
  (New York, The Reconstructionist Press, 1966), 532 pp.
When Is a Religion Authentic?

When Is a Religion Authentic?
   Reconstructionist Pamphlets Series (New York, The Reconstructionist Press, 1966), 16 pp.

1967

"A Knowable God." Reply to Trudy Weiss-Rosmarin.
   Jewish Spectator, vol. 32 (January 1967), pp. 11–12.
Torah in Israel.
   The Reconstructionist, vol. XXXII, no. 17 (Jan. 6, 1967), p. 32.
   [Reprinted from *A New Zionism*.] [See 1955]
The Jewish Social Worker.
   The Reconstructionist, vol. XXXII, no. 18 (Jan. 20, 1967), p. 31.
   [Reprinted from *Journal of Jewish Communal Service* (Fall 1964)]
Comment on "The God We Worship," by Bernard Martin.
   The Reconstructionist, vol. XXXII, no. 19 (Feb. 3, 1967), pp. 18–23.
The Philosophy of a Minority.
   The Reconstructionist, vol. XXXIII, no. 2 (March 17, 1967), p. 32.
   [Reprinted from *The Meaning of God in Modern Jewish Religion*.] [See 1937]
Redemptive and Erotic Love.
   The Reconstructionist, vol. XXXIII, no. 3 (March 31, 1967), p. 32.
   [Reprinted from *The Future of the American Jew*.] [See 1948]
Mordecai M. Kaplan's Idea of God.
   Jewish Spectator, vol. XXXII (April 1967), p. 26.
The Cardinal's Commentary: Comment by Mordecai M. Kaplan.
   Jewish Spectator, vol. XXXII, no. 5 (May 1967), pp. 25–26.
   [Letter to the editor.]
The Functions of a Reconstructionist Synagogue.
   The Reconstructionist, vol. XXXIII, no. 10 (July 7, 1967), pp. 25–27.
Issues of Faith.
   Dimension, vol. 1 (Winter 1967), pp. 14–18.
   [A symposium.]
The Evolution of the Idea of God in Jewish Religion.
   The Seventy-fifth Anniversary Volume of the Jewish Quarterly Review, edited by Abraham B. Neuman and Solomon Zeitlin (Philadelphia, Jewish Quarterly Review, 1967), pp. 332–46.
Greater Judaism in the Making.
   (New York, The Reconstructionist Press, 1967), 565 pp.
Interdependence of Religion and Science.
   Shiv'im: Essays and Studies in Honor of Ira Eisenstein, edited by Ronald A. Brauner (New York and Philadelphia, Reconstructionist Rabbinical College and Ktav, 1967), pp. 15–20.
Buber's Evaluation of Philosophic Thought and Religious Tradition.
   The Philosophy of Martin Buber, edited by Paul Arthur Schilpp and

Maurice Friedman. Vol. 12 of *The Library of Living Philosophers* (La Salle, Ill., Open Court Press, 1967), pp. 248–72.
A Program for Labor Zionists.
Jewish Frontier Anthology, 1945–1967 (New York, Jewish Frontier Association, 1967), pp. 495–504.

1968

Jewish Religion as Wisdom.
   The Reconstructionist,
      vol. XXXIII, no. 18 (Jan. 12, 1968), pp. 7–15;
      vol. XXXIII, no. 19 (Jan. 26, 1968), pp. 16–23.
Israel, the Jewish People, and the World: A Symposium.
   The Reconstructionist, vol. XXXIII, no. 20 (Feb. 9, 1968), pp. 16–20.
Anti-Semitism: A Force for Conservation.
   The Reconstructionist, vol. XXXIV, no. 2 (March 8, 1968), p. 31.
   [Reprinted from *Judaism as a Civilization.*] [See 1934]
Jewish Ecumenism and Jewish Revival: A Symposium.
   The Reconstructionist, vol. XXXIV, no. 9 (June 14, 1968), pp. 7–12.
Spiritual Leaders for Our Day.
   The Reconstructionist, vol. XXXIV, no. 13 (Nov. 8, 1968), pp. 7–10.

1969

To Educate Spiritual Leaders for Jewish Life.
   The Reconstructionist, vol. XXXIV, no. 20 (Feb. 14, 1969), pp. 7–9.
The Capacity for Social Forethought.
   The Reconstructionist, vol. XXXV, no. 8 (July 25, 1969), pp. 27–31.
The Religious Creed of Nationalism: After Sixty Years.
   The Reconstructionist, vol. XXXV, no. 13 (Dec. 12, 1969), pp. 7–13.

1970

Why a Reconstructionist Rabbinical College?
   The Reconstructionist, vol. XXXV, no. 14 (Jan. 2, 1970), pp. 7–9.
Wage Peace or Else.
   The Reconstructionist, vol. XXXV, no. 15 (Jan. 23, 1970), pp. 7–10.
A Conversation with Mordecai M. Kaplan.
   Jewish Spectator, vol. XXXV (March 1970), pp. 7–9.
Letter on Halacha.
   Dimensions, vol. 4 (Summer 1970), p. 50.
"Religious Inquiry," by Henry N. Wieman.
   Judaism, vol. 19, no. 3 (Summer 1970), pp. 369–73.
A Program for the Reconstruction of Judaism.
   The Reconstructionist, vol. XXXVI, no. 10 (Oct. 23, 1970), pp. 7–20.

Reply to "But Rabbi Kaplan: The Evolution Isn't Over," by Marc A. Triebwasser.
  The Reconstructionist, vol. XXXVI, no. 12 (Dec. 4, 1970), pp. 13–14.
The Meaning of God for the Contemporary Jew.
  Tradition and Contemporary Experience, edited by Alfred Jospe (New York, Schocken Books 1970), pp. 62–76.
The Religion of Ethical Nationhood: Judaism's Contribution to World Peace.
  (New York, Macmillan, 1970), x + 205 pp.

1971

In Tribute to Alexander M. Dushkin.
  Jewish Education, vol. 41, nos. 1 and 2 (Summer-Fall 1971), pp. 43–44.

1972

Needed: A Jewish Ecumenical Universe of Discourse.
  Jewish Heritage, vol. 14, no. 1 (Spring 1972), pp. 36–39.
The Sabbath Eve Seder: An Indispensible Innovation.
  The Reconstructionist, vol. XXXVIII, no. 2 (March 17, 1972), pp. 17–20.
A Seder Every Week.
  Jewish Digest, vol. 17 (Summer 1972), pp. 20–22.
The Question: Is Our Schizophrenia Historically Important?
  [A symposium.] *Response*, vol. 6 (Fall 1972), pp. 54–62.
What is Jewish Consciousness?
  The Reconstructionist, vol. XXXVIII, no. 6 (Sept. 22, 1972), pp. 7–11.
S.A.J. Jubilee—1922–1972.
  The Reconstructionist, vol. XXXVIII, no. 9 (Dec. 1972), pp. 25–29.

1973

God, Jews, and Israel: A Response.
  Journal of the Central Conference of American Rabbis (Spring 1973), pp. 93–101.
Jewish Homecoming: Commencement Address.
  The Reconstructionist, vol. XXXIX, no. 6 (Sept. 1973), pp. 7–13.
If Not Now, When? Toward a Reconstruction of the Jewish People: Conversations between Mordecai M. Kaplan and Arthur A. Cohen.
  (New York, Schocken Books, 1973), 134 pp.
The Meaning of God in Modern Jewish Religion.
  Understanding Jewish Theology, edited by Jacob Neusner (New York, KTAV and the Anti-Defamation League of B'nai B'rith, 1973), pp. 196–203.
A New Approach to Jewish Life.

(Bridgeport, Conn., Hartmore House and the Jewish Reconstructionist Foundation, 1973), 88 pp.
[Originally *A New Approach to the Problem of Judaism*, 1924.]

1975

Our God as Our Collective Conscience.
The Reconstructionist, vol. XLI, no. 1 (Feb. 1975), pp. 13–16.
Some Basic Definitions.
The Jewish Spectator, vol. 40, no. 2 (Summer 1975), pp. 24–25.

1976

Interivew with S. J. Jacobs.
Jewish Spectator, vol. 41 (Winter 1976), pp. 25–28.

1977

The Interdependence of Science and Religion.
The Reconstructionist, vol. XLIII, no. 1 (Feb. 1977), pp. 7–11.
The Pragmatic Theology of the Hebrew Bible.
The Reconstructionist, vol. XLIII, no. 6 (Sept. 1977), pp. 7–12.

1978

Message from Mordecai M. Kaplan.
The Reconstructionist, vol. 44 (Oct. 1978), p. 31.
[Letter.]

1979

Mordecai M. Kaplan Remembers 1909.
The Bulletin of the Alumni Association of the Seminary College, Teacher's Institute, and Graduate School of the Jewish Theological Seminary of America (May 1979), pp. 1, 12.
Not So Random Thoughts.
The Reconstructionist, vol. 45 (June 1979), p. 13.

1981

Future of the American Jew.
(New York, The Reconstructionist Press, 1981), 571 pp.
[Reprint.]

1984

A Program for Labor Zionists.
Jewish Frontier, vol. 51 (Jan. 1984), pp. 13–16.
[Reprinted from July 1949.]
Kaplan on the Meaning of Salvation.
Jewish Digest, vol. 29 (March-April 1984), p. 43.
[Excerpt from *The Meaning of God in Modern Jewish Religion*.] [See 1937]
Early Kaplan Diary.
The Reconstructionist, vol. 49 (Fall 1984), p. 30.
Not So Random Kaplan.
The Reconstructionist, vol. 49 (Fall 1984), p. 30.
[Diary excerpt.]

1985

Dynamic Judaism: The Essential Writings of Mordecai M. Kaplan, edited by Emanuel S. Goldsmith and Mel Scult (New York, Schocken Books and The Reconstructionist Press, 1985), 263 pp.

1987

Mordecai Kaplan on Spiritual Leadership.
The Reconstructionist, vol. LII, no. 5 (March-April 1987), pp. 18–19.
Religion and Solitude.
The Reconstructionist, vol. LIII, no. 2 (Oct.-Nov. 1987), p. 2.

Undated

How to Live Creatively as a Jew.
Moments of Personal Discovery (Institute for Religious and Social Studies, Religion and Civilization Series), pp. 93ff.
The Organic Jewish Community.
Reconstructionist Pamphlet (New York, The Reconstructionist Press).
[with Daniel J. Elazar.]
Passover.
(New York, Women's League of the United Synagogue of America), 15 pp.
The Reconstructionist Viewpoint.
What Is Conservative Judaism? edited by Theodore Friedman (New York, Jewish Theological Seminary), pp. 82–108.

Index